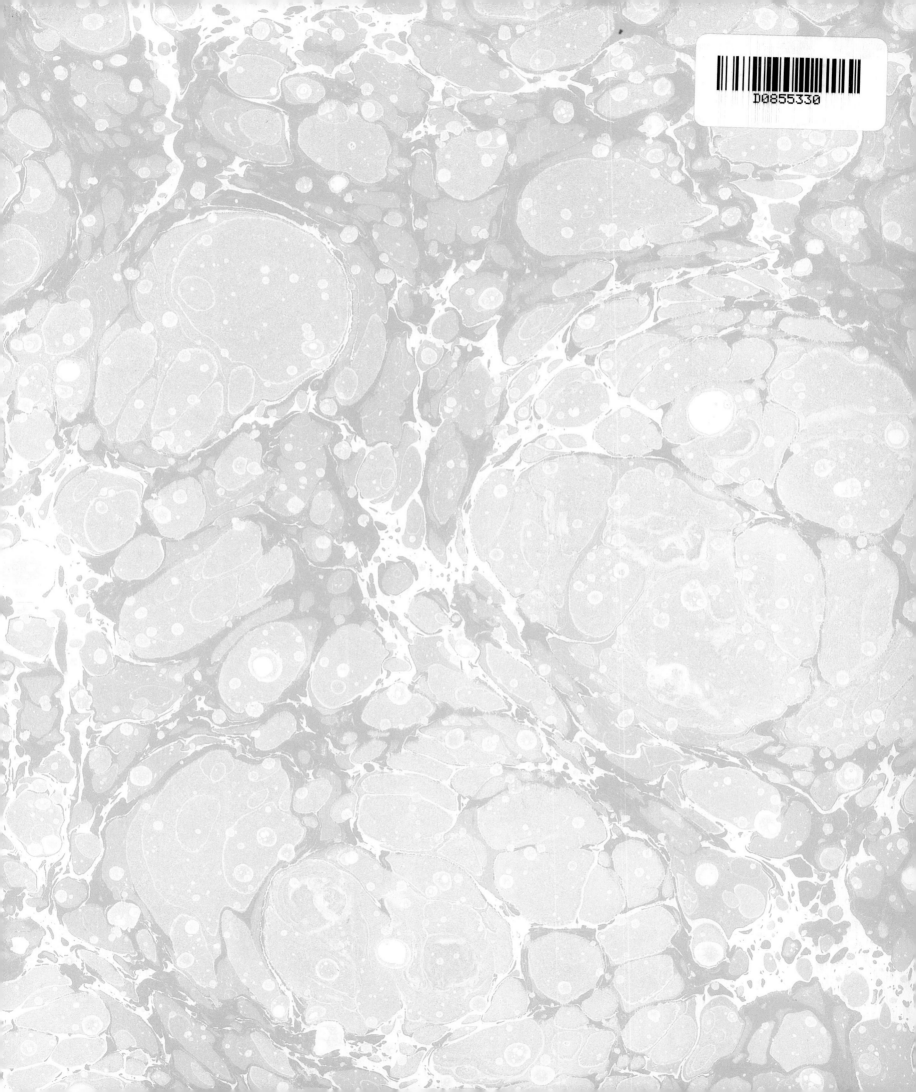

REMARKABLE
DIARIES

REMARKABLE DIARIES

THE WORLD'S GREATEST DIARIES, JOURNALS, NOTEBOOKS, AND LETTERS

Foreword

Professor Kate Williams

Contributors

R.G. Grant, Andrew Humphreys, Esther Ripley,
and Iain Zaczek

DK LONDON

Senior Editor Angela Wilkes
Senior Art Editor Gadi Farfour
Assistant Editor Daniel Byrne
Designer Daksheeta Pattni
US Editor Jennette ElNaggar
Picture Researcher Sarah Smithies
Managing Editor Gareth Jones
Senior Managing Art Editor Lee Griffiths
Senior Production Editor Andy Hilliard
Senior Production Controller Rachel Ng
Jacket Design Development Manager Sophia M.T.T.
Associate Publishing Director Liz Wheeler
Art Director Karen Self
Publishing Director Jonathan Metcalf

DK DELHI

Senior Editor Janashree Singha
Editors Rishi Bryan, Tanya Singhal
Senior Art Editor Chhaya Sajwan
Project Art Editor Sourabh Challariya
Art Editor Shipra Jain
Assistant Art Editor Ankita Das
Managing Editor Soma B. Chowdhury
Senior Managing Art Editor Arunesh Talapatra
Senior DTP Designers Neeraj Bhatia, Vishal Bhatia
DTP Designers Nityanand Kumar, Mohammad Rizwan
Production Manager Pankaj Sharma
Pre-production Manager Balwant Singh
Jacket Designers Suhita Dharamjit, Priyanka Bansal

First American Edition, 2020
Published in the United States by DK Publishing
1450 Broadway, Suite 801, New York, NY 10018

Copyright © 2020 Dorling Kindersley Limited
DK, a Division of Penguin Random House LLC
21 22 23 24 10 9 8 7 6 5 4 3 2
005–316695–Sep/2020

A catalog record for this book
is available from the Library of Congress.
ISBN 978-0-7440-2043-4

DK books are available at special discounts when purchased
in bulk for sales promotions, premiums, fund-raising, or
educational use. For details, contact: DK Publishing Special
Markets, 1450 Broadway, Suite 801, New York, NY 10018
SpecialSales@dk.com

Printed and bound in China

For the curious
www.dk.com

Contents

CHAPTER 1
BEFORE 1500

CHAPTER 4
1800–1860

CHAPTER 5
1860–1900

FOREWORD

Professor Kate Williams is an author, historian, and broadcaster. She has written five history books, including *England's Mistress* and *Rival Queens*, and four historical novels. She is a regular on television and radio, presenting her own shows, including *The Stuarts*, *Inside Versailles*, and *Restoration Home*, and discussing history, politics, and culture on shows from *Newsnight* to *The Great British Bake Off*. CNN's royal historian, she is Professor of History at the University of Reading, UK, and gives lectures around the world.

CONTRIBUTORS

R. G. Grant has written extensively in the fields of history, biography, and culture. He contributed to *1001 Books You Must Read Before You Die* (2006), *501 Great Writers* (2008), and *Writers: Their Lives And Works* (2018).

Andrew Humphreys is a journalist, author, and travel writer, who has written or cowritten more than 35 books. His journalism often involves travel with a historical slant, and he is the author of two books on the golden age of travel in Egypt.

Esther Ripley is a writer and editor who began her career in journalism and was a managing editor at DK. She studied literature with psychology and writes on a range of cultural subjects.

Iain Zaczek studied at Oxford University, UK, and at the Courtauld Institute, London. He has written more than 30 books on various aspects of literature, history, and art.

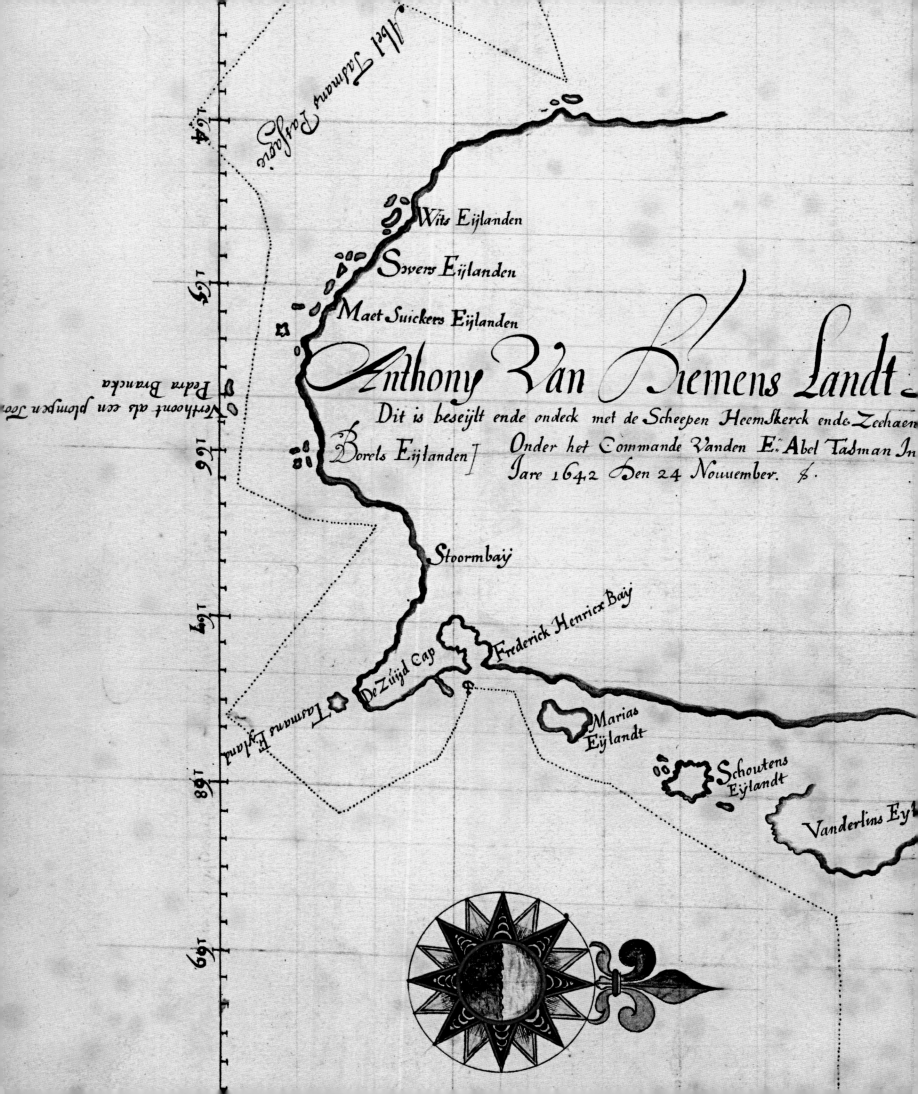

Abel Tasmans Passage

Wits Eijlanden

Swers Eijlanden

Maet Suickers Eijlanden

Anthony Van Diemens Landt

Dit is beseijlt ende ondeck met de Scheepen Heemskerck ende Zeehaen

Borels Eijlanden] Onder het Commande Vanden E: Abel Tasman In

Jare 1642 den 24 Nouuember. ⸹

Pedro Branda

Verhoont als een plompen Toom

Stoormbaij

Frederick Henricx Baij

De Zuijd Cap

'T Tasmans Eijland

Marias Eijlandt

Schoutens Eijlandt

Vanderlins Ey'

Foreword

On June 12, 1942, Anne Frank, a young German Jewish girl living in Amsterdam, received a present—an autograph book with a lock. It was her 13th birthday and she had chosen the diary from a local shop. The Frank family had left Frankfurt in 1933 after Adolf Hitler came to power. Anne's father, Otto, had then forged a career in Amsterdam, but Germany invaded the Netherlands in 1940. When Anne started her diary, there were already severe restrictions on Jewish inhabitants of Amsterdam, but her early entries revel in birthday parties and ping-pong clubs. "I hope I will be able to confide everything to you," Anne wrote. But within weeks, the family had to go into hiding in a secret annex in her father's office, where she wrote her diary until the family was found by the Nazis two years later. Her words became for many the best-known and most powerful diary in history, an unforgettable voice of one of the six million who died in the Holocaust.

"Memory … is the diary that we all carry about with us," said Oscar Wilde. But so many of us never record our memories, or we start diaries in January and never finish them. This book compiles the diaries of those who did continue to write and found it a great solace. Politicians and rulers, such as the Kangxi Emperor and Queen Victoria, often keep diaries, but some of the greatest diarists were ordinary people who became witnesses to extraordinary events. Dr. Michihiko Hachiya, a physician and director of the Hiroshima Communications Hospital, was enjoying a peaceful sunny morning when a nuclear bomb was dropped on his city, destroying it. Eighteenth-century American mother, Elizabeth Sandwith Drinker wrote about everyday life but also about the struggles of being a Quaker during the American War of Independence, when her family's religious pacifism was often seen as suspect.

Some of the diaries showcased here were written on papyrus, others on vellum. Some were typed. Many are not diaries as we might know them but notebooks, or the sketches and jottings of a genius such as Leonardo da Vinci: 6,000 observations on everything from physics to architecture, complete with astonishing drawings and inventions for flying machines. Some reveal the beginnings of a scientific system, as with Carl Linnaeus. Some were written to be read widely; others were private. Many were hidden, censored, or cut. Diaries can be dangerous—they bear witness, tell the truth.

Some mark great heroism and bravery, such as the notebooks of Marie Curie, still so radioactive after she recorded her groundbreaking experiments that they have to be stored in a lead-lined box. Others provide fascinating insights into great creative minds: the brilliance of Vincent van Gogh, the creativity of Frida Kahlo, the innovative ideas of Antoni Gaudí, the intense vision of Charlotte Brontë and Leo Tolstoy, or the acid observations of Lady Murasaki. All show us people's instinct to document their lives, no matter how painful. Captain Robert Falcon Scott kept a diary of his doomed expedition to the Antarctic in 1912: "It's a pity, but I do not think I can write more," he wrote on the last day of his journal, as he lay dying. When his frozen body was found seven months later, his diary was next to him. There are the many diaries that we now find disturbing: those of explorers once honored as adventurers, who seized land from native peoples and killed them when they tried to defend themselves, or those of European travelers who exploited local resources and young people. For while most of these diaries represent humanity at its most generous, some do not.

"Keep a diary and someday it will keep you," said Mae West in 1937. How grateful we are that our ancestors did not always think this. Diaries are among our greatest historical treasures—they bring a place, a person, the world to life. They are invaluable for the historian, the literature student, the sociologist, and the scientist. Through times of great change, upheaval, or suffering, people keep writing, to save themselves, to know that they are still present, not alone. At its best, as Anne Frank proved, the diary reveals the triumph of the human spirit.

PROFESSOR KATE WILLIAMS

Introduction

The diary is the most democratic form of writing. In the hands of professional authors, it has become a well-established literary genre, but it is open to anyone with basic literacy to record their daily life. Justifying his own voluminous diary, the 19th-century British clergyman Francis Kilvert wrote that it seemed "a pity that even such a humble and uneventful life as mine should pass away without some such record." Keeping a diary means taking a stand against the passing of time, which sweeps all passing thoughts, emotions, events, and experiences into oblivion. It also opposes dishonesty—the frank opinions and feelings jotted down in the heat of the moment providing evidence against later false memories or the reinvention of the past to which everyone is prone.

A diary is both a private document and a literary experiment. There is no clear-cut distinction between purely personal musings and diaries written with an eye to possible future publication. Journals are written to be read, if only by their authors, in the years to come. They have often been written in code or kept locked to protect them from prying eyes—intimate self-analysis and frank confessions are common features. But there are also many diarists who avoid such personal matters altogether and fill their pages with more objective topics—gossip and anecdotes, observations about other people or places they have visited, ideas, and reflections. Most readers would probably agree with French author Maurice Blanchot: "the truth of the journal does not lie in the interesting and literary remarks to be found in it, but in the insignificant details that tie it to everyday reality."

People have often started to keep a diary in response to major events, such as a political upheaval or the outbreak of a war. Some diarists, whether bystanders at a royal court or soldiers fighting in the trenches, are very conscious of their responsibility as eyewitnesses producing the first draft of history. The travel journal is another distinctive genre—notes and sketches made on trips to exotic lands that are often revised at a later date to form the basis of a book. There is little difference between these and memoirs, which are also often based on daily notes that have been reworked by their author at a later date.

Many writers have used letters alongside or instead of diaries to record the minutiae of their everyday lives and to explore their personal musings. Letters, notebooks, memoirs, journals, and diaries form a distinctive strand of "personal writing"—immediate, spontaneous, and open

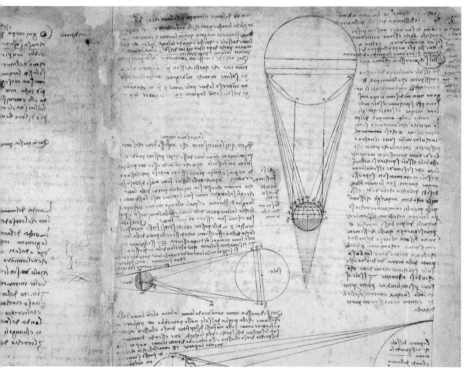

▲ **INVENTIVE NOTEBOOKS** The multitalented Renaissance genius Leonardo da Vinci filled the pages of his notebooks with the daily workings of his fertile mind, using diagrams, sketches, and explanatory notes.

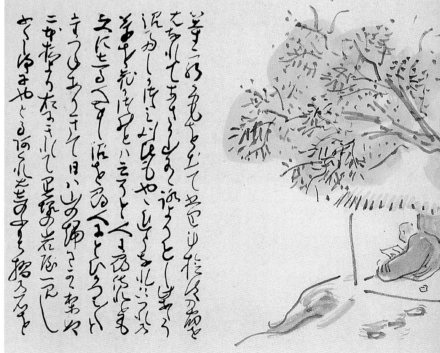

▲ **BASHŌ'S JOURNEY** In his celebrated travel diary, *The Narrow Road to the Deep North*, the 17th-century Japanese poet Matsuo Bashō described the experience of a pilgrimage on foot to the Ise shrine.

> ## "I never travel without my diary. One should always have something sensational to read in the train."
>
> **OSCAR WILDE, *THE IMPORTANCE OF BEING EARNEST***

of form—that admits both the trivial and the serious, replicating the jumble of unfiltered experience characteristic of life.

Nothing conveys the immediacy of such writing as well as the original manuscripts of diaries and letters. There is something moving about seeing the actual marks made by a diarist as he or she traced the characters on the page. Nor is this restricted to words, for many visually gifted diarists, whether artists or not, have recorded their observations, thoughts, and experiences in the form of images—from sketches of nature to scientific diagrams and quick caricatures.

This book covers a wide range of personal writing, from scientific notebooks and travel journals to the classic diary—a chronological record of everyday life and the

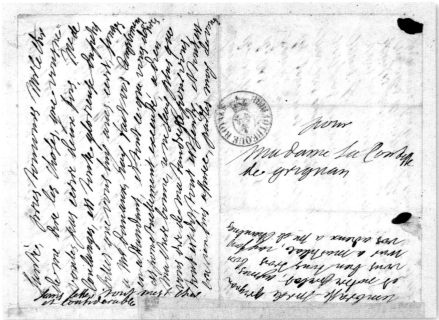

▲ **MOTHER'S LETTERS** The many letters written by the 18th-century French aristocrat Madame de Sévigné to her daughter provide a diary-like account of her thoughts and feelings as well as the life of the society around her.

thoughts it provokes. Some of the authors were famous writers or celebrated individuals with lives in the public eye, whereas others were completely unknown but for the faint yet evocative trace that they have left behind in their journals. All of them produced work, however diverse, that has the freshness of immediacy, giving us an intimate insight into their lives and thoughts.

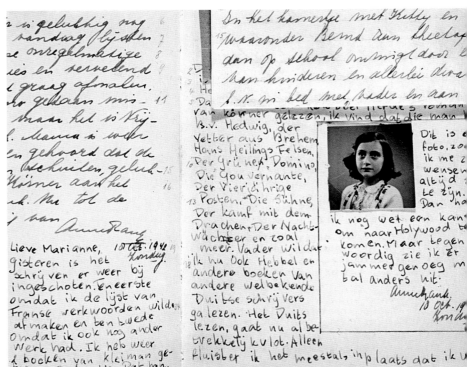

▲ **DIARY OF ANXIETY** From 1910 to 1923, Czech author Franz Kafka kept diaries recording his thoughts and dreams, expressing his anguished sense of isolation and his alienation from the world. All of this later fed into his novels.

▲ **HOLOCAUST VICTIMS** The diary of the young Dutch Jewish girl Anne Frank tells of her life in hiding from the Germans during World War II. She was eventually captured and died tragically in captivity.

se exta duplicata : quibus portendi milies & ducenties
habiturum. Et habebat simodo ut coepit aliena testa
menta qd est improbissimum genus fallis ipsis quoʒ
sunt ulla dictauerit, VALE.

C. PLINII CECILII SECVNDI ORATORIS EPI
STOLARVM LIBER TERTIVS INCIPIT.
PLINIVS CALVISIO SVO
SALVTEM . Nescio an ullū
iocundius tempus exegerim q̄ quo
nuper apud Spurinam fui adeo qd̄
ut neminem magis in senectute si
modo senescere datum est emulari
uelim . Nihil est enim ullo uitæ genere distinctius.
Me autem ut certus sideʒ cursus ita uita hominū dispo
sita delectat senuin præsertim . Nam iuuenes adhuc
confusa quædam & quasi turbata non indecent . Seni
bus placida omnia & ordinata conuenunt : quibus
industria seruatur pis ambitio est. Hanc regulam Spu
rina constantissime seruat. Quin et parua hæc si non
quotidie fiant ordine quodam & uelut orbe circuagit.

1

BEFORE 1500

People in the ancient world did not keep diaries, but some personal documents have survived that bring those distant ages vividly to life. The first travel journals appeared during the 10th century CE, written by Muslim and East Asian voyagers. With the "pillow books" of Japanese court ladies writing at the end of 900 CE, the diary first emerged as a literary genre. In Europe, medieval accounts of religious revelation, such as *The Book of Margery Kempe*, initiated a tradition of inward reflection on personal experience. During the intellectual ferment of the early Renaissance, ordinary citizens, such as the Florentine apothecary Luca Landucci, jotted down their lively eyewitness accounts of troubled times, and the illustrated notebooks of Leonardo da Vinci recorded the daily thoughts and ideas of his fertile and creative mind.

Two vertical columns describe
the activities of each day

Only worn fragments of the
papyrus roll have survived

In the Age of the Pharaohs

C.2562BCE ▪ INK ON PAPYRUS ▪ EGYPTIAN

MERER: ANCIENT EGYPTIAN OFFICIAL

About 4,500 years ago, an official of the Egyptian state involved in the building of the Great Pyramid at Giza wrote down a daily record of his working life. In 2013, this journal was discovered by a team of Egyptologists led by Pierre Tallet and Gregory Marouard, who were exploring the site of an Ancient Egyptian port at Wadi al-Jarf on the Red Sea. Along with other documents from the same site, these are the oldest papyri with writing that have ever been found.

The author of this journal is named Merer and accorded the title of "inspector." Nothing is known of him except what can be gleaned from the journal itself. Merer was in charge of 200 workers transporting stone for the Great Pyramid, referred to in the journal as "Akhet-Khufu." Limestone blocks for the external facing of the pyramid, then approaching completion, were quarried at Tura, on the east bank of the Nile. Merer's task was to organize the transportation of these blocks by boat along the Nile River and purpose-built canals to the Giza construction site. The journal describes Merer and his men engaged in constant activity, making two or three round trips between Tura and Giza every 10 days. Merer reported to the pharaoh's half brother and chief-of-works Prince Ankhhaf at an administrative center named as "Ro-She Khufu."

The journal covers the period from July to November in the 26th year of the reign of Pharaoh Khufu, possibly 2562BCE. When it ends, Merer disappears from history. The discovery of the journal at the port at Wadi al-Jarf suggests he may have been responsible for importing scarce metal ores and turquoise from across the Red Sea. Opening a small but clear window upon such a distant past, the document has been described as the most important Egyptian find of the 21st century.

◀ **DELICATE PAPYRUS** Now exhibited in the Egyptian Museum in Cairo, Merer's journal was inscribed with a reed pen in ink on papyrus. These worn, fragile fragments have survived for more than four millennia. The document is written in a mix of hieratic script, the everyday form of Ancient Egyptian handwriting, and the hieroglyphics typically used for inscriptions on monuments.

> 66 **Day 21**: [Inspector] Merer spends the day with his [phyle] loading a transport ship-*imu* at Tura North, sets sail from Tura in the afternoon.
> **Day 22**: Spends the night at Ro-She Khufu. In the morning, sets sail from Ro-She Khufu; sails toward Akhet-Khufu; spends the night at the Chapels of [Akhet] Khufu.
> **Day 23**: The director of Hesi spends the day with his naval section in Ro-She Khufu. 99
>
> **MERER'S JOURNAL, PAPYRUS B, SECTION B IV**

In context

◀ **WONDROUS TOMB** The Great Pyramid, built at Giza, to the west of the Nile River, was one of the Seven Wonders of the Ancient World. The largest of three pyramids at the site, it originally rose to a height of 480ft (146m). Probably intended as a monumental tomb for Pharaoh Khufu, the structure has lost the limestone casing that would once have given it a smooth outer surface.

▶ **PHARAOH KHUFU** Often known by his Greek name, Cheops, Khufu was an Egyptian pharaoh of the Fourth Dynasty. Reigning around 2589–2560BCE, he is traditionally believed to have commissioned the Great Pyramid at Giza. This small ivory statuette is the only representation of him thought to have survived from his lifetime.

Letters from Imperial Rome

97–100CE ▪ MANUSCRIPT COPY ON PARCHMENT ▪ 10 BOOKS ▪ ROMAN

PLINY THE YOUNGER: SENATOR AND WRITER

Living from 61 to 113CE, Gaius Plinius Caecilius Secundus, known as Pliny the Younger, was the adopted son of a famed writer and naturalist, Pliny the Elder (23–79CE). As a member of the cultured elite in the golden age of the Roman Empire, the younger Pliny was a friend of prominent figures such as the historian Tacitus and the biographer Suetonius. He rose to be an imperial adviser and administrator and was eventually appointed governor of the province of Bithynia-Pontus on the Black Sea coast.

Around 97CE, he began writing a series of letters, the *Epistulae*. Although addressed to friends, they were couched in a formal, rhetorical style that was intended for the eyes of a wider public. Nine books composed of his letters were published between 100 and 109CE. As a provincial governor, Pliny also corresponded with Emperor Trajan. These official letters, which were probably not meant for publication, appeared posthumously as the tenth book of the *Epistulae*. Pliny had, in effect, invented an open literary form that allowed him to cover a range of topics—criticizing the ill-treatment of enslaved people, lauding the virtues of education, describing country gardens, commenting on senatorial debates and law cases, and drawing moral lessons from the behavior of his friends. His two most famous letters, addressed to Tacitus, recount his memories of the eruption of Vesuvius, which he witnessed as an 18-year-old and in which his adoptive father met his death. Once dismissed as fanciful, his account of the volcanic disaster, viewed from Misenum on the other side of the Bay of Naples, is now considered scrupulously accurate. His letters to Trajan contain the earliest view of Christian practices written by an outsider. Taken together, the *Epistulae* convey a more intimate and detailed view of life in the higher echelons of Roman society than any other Latin texts.

> ▶ **HISTORIC SURVIVAL** The oldest surviving fragment of Pliny's letters consists of six leaves of parchment from a manuscript copy made in Italy around 500CE. The rest of this manuscript, used as the basis for the first complete printed edition of the letters published in Venice in 1508, has been lost. This page shows the first letter of Book Three, which opens: "C. Pliny to his Calusius, greeting...."

In context

◀ **VESUVIUS ERUPTS** This painting by Angelika Kauffmann of Pliny the Younger and his mother at Misenum shows the eruption of Mount Vesuvius in 79CE, which destroyed the Roman coastal towns of Pompeii and Herculaneum. Thousands were killed, among them Pliny the Elder. The younger Pliny's eyewitness account includes a description of a volcanic tsunami.

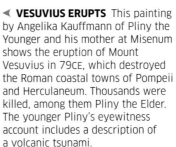

▲ **PERSECUTION OF CHRISTIANS** The newly founded religion of Christianity, described by Pliny as "depraved excessive superstition," faced persecution in the Roman Empire because its adherents refused to pay lip service to the state-approved Roman gods. In this Roman mosaic, a Christian martyr is being tortured by Romans and wild animals in an amphitheater.

> ❝ On the other side [of the bay] the black, fearsome cloud of fiery vapor burst into long, twisting, zigzag flames and gaped asunder, the flames resembling lightning flashes.... Then the ashes began to fall, but not thickly: I looked back, and a dense blackness was rolling up behind us, which spread itself over the ground and followed like a torrent ... the blackness of night overtook us, not that of a moonless or cloudy night, but the blackness of pent-up places which never see the light. You could hear the wailing of women, the screams of little children.... ❞

LETTER TO TACITUS, BOOK 6, DESCRIBING THE ERUPTION OF VESUVIUS

Travels in China

838–847CE ▪ INK ON MANUSCRIPT ▪ FOUR VOLUMES ▪ JAPANESE

ENNIN: SCHOLAR-MONK

Ennin, a Buddhist monk, was part of a diplomatic mission sent from Japan to the Tang court of China in 838CE. Selected to study and collect the texts of the Tendai doctrine of Buddhism, Ennin remained in China for more than nine years, during which he meditated with Buddhist masters and learned the tenets and rituals of different schools of Buddhism. From 840CE, he lived in Chang'an, the Chinese Tang capital, but in 847CE he was sent back to Japan as a result of the anti-Buddhist policies adopted by the new Tang emperor, Wuzong.

On returning to his homeland, Ennin completed a day-by-day account of his time in China, which he called *Record of a Pilgrimage to China in Search of the Law*. Not only was it the first Japanese travelogue, but it was also the first document about China written by a foreigner. Ennin begins the diary by recalling the dangers of the sea voyage from Japan to China in a time when sailors did not use a compass—he was literally washed ashore in China. He observes everyday life there as he travels on foot and by boat along the Great Canal of China. Noting local customs and traditions, Ennin comments on everything, from the varied landscapes he travels through to the state of the economy. Above all, he writes about monastic life and how Buddhism is practiced in China. Ennin depicts it as an inclusive religion; he meets female pilgrims and describes an impressive festival where the monasteries prepared and opened their baths to the public. Although Ennin doesn't reveal many of his personal thoughts, his diary is treasured today as a fascinating insight into the late Tang Dynasty.

Back in Japan, Ennin became the chief abbot of the Enryakuji monastery on Mount Hiei, near Kyoto, and head of the Tendai sect of Buddhism in Japan. He was given the posthumous title "Great teacher of compassionate awareness" and became an important spiritual figure in Japanese history.

In context

▲ **SITE OF BUDDHIST PILGRIMAGE** Ennin spent time at Mount Wutai, one of the four mountains sacred to Chinese Buddhists and the site of numerous temples. Wutai came to prominence in the 5th century CE, when it became associated with the enlightened monk Manjushri. By the time Ennin visited, it was attracting scholars and pilgrims not only from all over China but also from other Asian countries.

▼ **THE TANG TORMENTOR** Ennin was in China during the reign of the Tang emperor Wuzong, who launched the Great Anti-Buddhist Persecution of 842–846CE. A Taoist, Wuzong regarded Buddhism as a foreign religion harmful to Chinese society. He ordered Buddhist buildings to be destroyed and monks to be defrocked. Visiting monks were forced into laity and expelled.

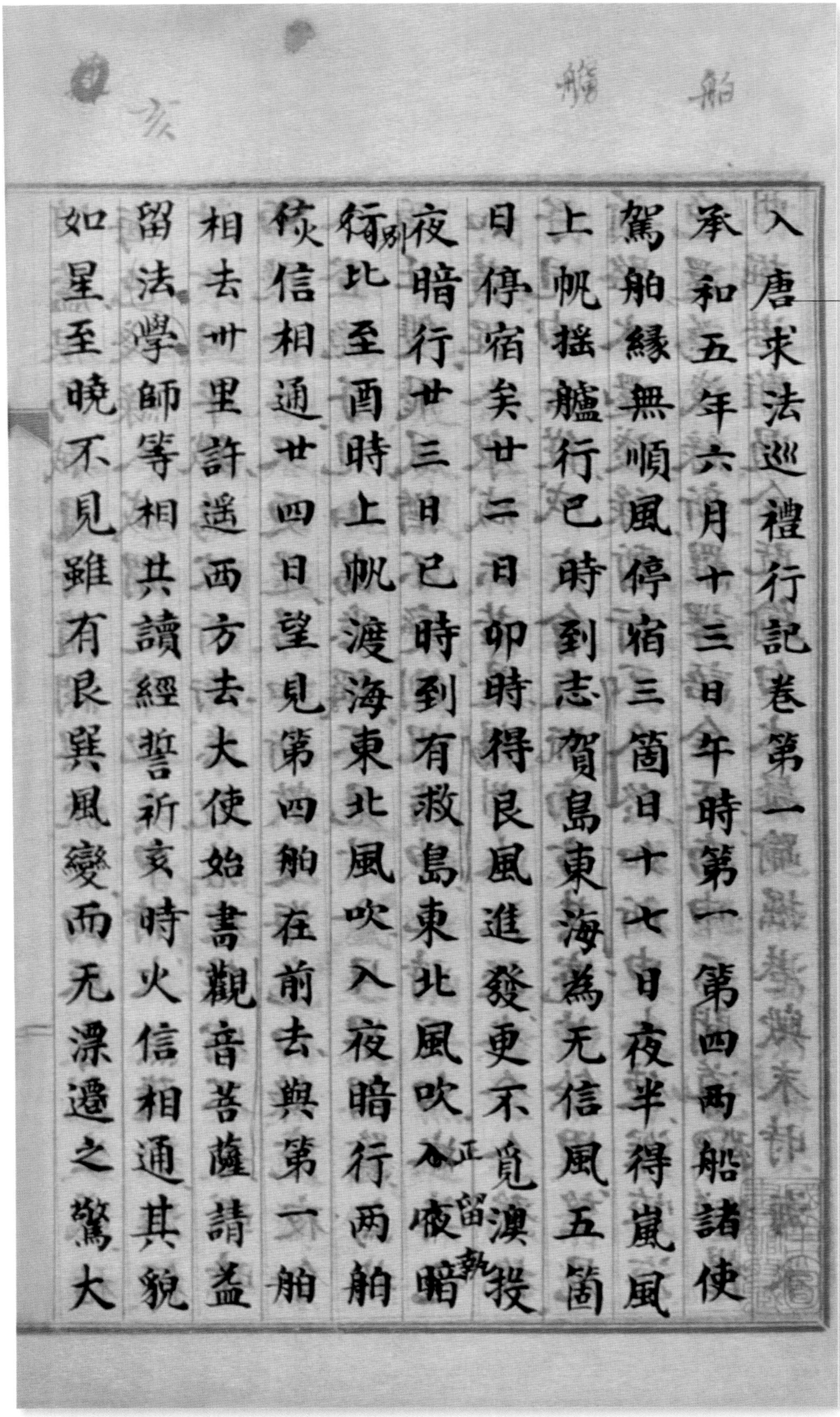

入唐求法巡禮行記卷第一

承和五年六月十三日今年時第一第四兩船諸使
駕舶縁無順風停宿三箇日十七日夜半得嵐風
上帆搖艫行巳時到志賀島東海為无信風五箇
日停宿矣廿二日卯時得良風進發更不覓澳投
夜暗行廿三日巳時到有救島東北風吹入夜暗
行北至酉時上帆渡海東北風吹正留執暗
俟信相通世四日望見第四舶在前去與第一舶
相去卅里許遙西方去大使始書觀音菩薩請盖
留法學師等相共讀經誓新亥時火信相通其貌
如星至曉不見雖有艮風變而无漂遷之驚大

Two complete copies of Ennin's diary have survived. The earliest was transcribed by a monk named Kenin in 1291

> 6th MOON, 28th DAY: We reached Yang-chou and saw the monks and nuns of the city being sent back to their places of origin with their heads wrapped up. The monasteries are to be destroyed, and their money, estates, and bells are being confiscated by the government. Recently a document came on Imperial command saying that the bronze and iron Buddhas of the land were all to be smashed....

ENNIN'S DIARY

◄ **WRITING IN A FOREIGN TONGUE** Just as a contemporary European scholar would write about their faith in Latin, Ennin composed most of his diary in classical Chinese, which is read from top to bottom. With a total of 70,000 Chinese characters, Ennin's diary roughly equates to the length of 100,000 English words. The text was compiled into four folio manuscripts known as *maki*, meaning "scrolls."

A Tale of Court Life

c.1008–1010 ▪ INK ON VELLUM ▪ JAPANESE

MURASAKI SHIKIBU: WRITER

In the early 11th century, Murasaki Shikibu (c.973–c.1020) wrote *The Tale of Genji,* thought to be the world's first novel. Murasaki was a lady-in-waiting at the Imperial court during the Heian period, when the capital was Heian-kyo, now known as Kyoto. Japanese culture—from literature and poetry to painting—was flourishing at this time. Empresses surrounded themselves with ladies-in-waiting who were adept at writing pieces that honored them. Murasaki wrote for the Empress Shoshi, one of two rival empresses at the court. She included scenes of court life both in her novel and her private writings, which were later published as *The Diary of Lady Murasaki.*

The diary is not a day-by-day account of Murasaki's life but a series of sketches, only some of which are dated. It opens with the words, "As autumn advances, the Tsuchimikado mansion looks unutterably beautiful." Much of the diary describes the time during the Empress Shoshi's pregnancy and the subsequent birth of a male heir to the throne. Murasaki describes the intricacies of court rituals and the attire of her fellow ladies-in-waiting in great detail, with occasional touches of self-deprecating humor: "My dress … was in the very latest fashion, and it would perhaps have been better if a younger lady had worn it."

Although the diary was written more than a thousand years ago, Murasaki's candor makes it seem quite modern, especially when she is describing her own feelings, such as her loneliness after her husband's death. Able to be both subtle and damning, Murasaki also shares shrewd observations of the empress's all-powerful father, the Lord Prime Minister Fujiwara no Michinaga (see bottom right), who, she reveals, was often drunk and abusive and something of a sexual predator.

▲ **ILLUSTRATED *EMAKI*** An *emaki* is a scroll of sheets of paper or silk joined horizontally and rolled around a dowel. In the 13th century, artisans produced an *emaki* of Murasaki's diary, in which the text is illustrated by paintings. These are executed in a style known as *fukinuki yatai* (literally meaning "blown-off roof"), in which they are depicted from above, as if looking down into a room.

This scene shows the Empress Shoshi with her newborn son. The figure to the bottom right might be Murasaki

◀ **THE TALE OF GENJI** Murasaki's *The Tale of Genji* is a lengthy romance about the heir to the throne, Shining Genji, and his amorous exploits with countless women. It contains vivid depictions of aristocratic life in Heian Japan and the nobility's political machinations. This 15th-century painting illustrates a chapter called "The Picture Contest."

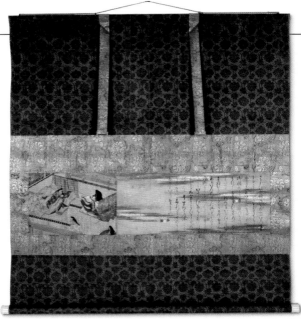

◄ **EXTANT SCROLL** Only four segments of the *emaki* of *The Diary of Lady Shikibu* have survived, from an original that may have consisted of 10 to 12 scrolls. Between them they contain 24 scenes that represent only around 15 percent of the diary. These pieces are owned by three Japanese organizations, including the Tokyo National Museum, which holds this mounted segment.

> " I can see the garden from my room beside the entrance to the gallery. The air is misty, the dew is still on the leaves. The Lord Prime Minister is walking there…. He breaks off a stalk of omenaishi … which is in full bloom by the south end of the bridge. He peeps in over my screen! His noble appearance embarrasses us, and I am ashamed of my morning [not yet made-up] face. He says, 'Your poem on this! If you delay so much the fun is gone!' "

THE DIARY OF LADY MURASAKI

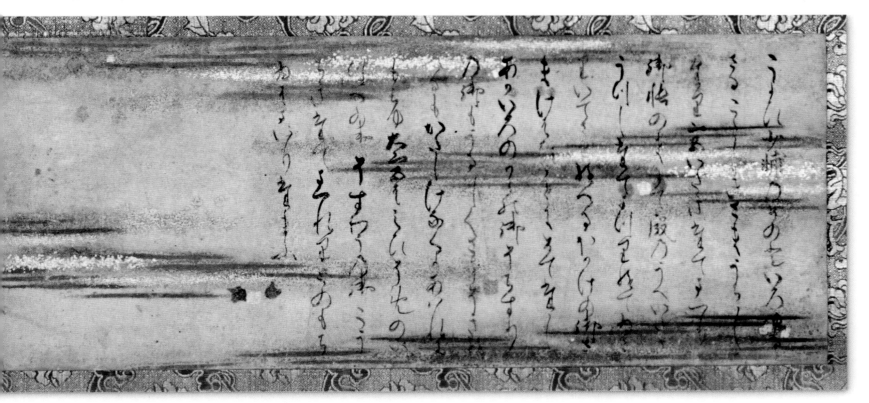

FUJIWARA NO MICHINAGA'S DIARY

Michinaga is a recurrent character in Murasaki's diary. A member of the powerful Fujiwara family, he became one of the most influential people at the Japanese Imperial court in the late 10th and early 11th centuries by marrying four of his daughters to emperors. Michinaga kept a diary, known as the *Mido Kanpakuki*, chronicling the political, economic, and social events of his time. Although only 14 of the original 36 volumes have survived, it is thought to be the world's oldest diary in the author's handwriting. Michinaga lived during a time when Japanese court culture was at its peak, and his pride in his achievements can be gauged from a poem that he wrote in 1018, which reads: "This world, I think / Is indeed my world. / Like the full moon I shine, / Uncovered by any cloud."

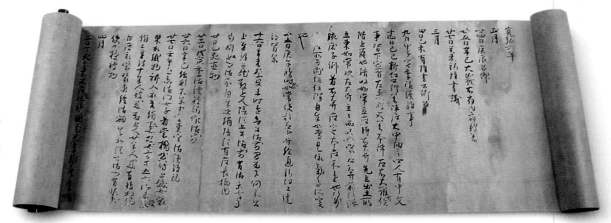

▲ **Scroll of** the *Mido Kanpakuki*, Fujiwara no Michinaga's diary

A Godly Life

C.1438 ▪ PEN AND INK ON PAPER ▪ 124 PAGES ▪ ENGLISH

MARGERY KEMPE: CHRISTIAN MYSTIC

The medieval visionary Margery Kempe (c.1373–1438) produced a fascinating day-to-day account of her religious and personal life. Written in Middle English, the common language spoken at the time, *The Book of Margery Kempe* is the earliest known autobiography in English.

Margery Kempe lived in Lynn, a well-to-do town in East Anglia. She owned a horse mill at one time, ran a brewery, had 14 children, and later went on her travels. The book covers her life from her first pregnancy until her mid-60s. At its heart is the religious crisis that Margery experienced after the birth of her first child, when she had visions of devils, who encouraged her to reject Christ and abandon her family, and then a vision of Christ asking why she had forsaken him. These visions were followed by "conversations" with Christ, God, and the Virgin Mary, which cemented Margery's religious faith and set her on her path as a mystic. Margery subsequently agreed with her husband that their marriage should be chaste so that she could devote herself to God.

In the book, Margery describes the intensity of her religious experiences (when moved, she was prone to weeping and wailing) and talks about her lengthy pilgrimages. She also recounts her difficulties when she was accused of practices forbidden by the Catholic Church at the time, such as wearing white, a color reserved for nuns.

Margery could not read or write, so she dictated her story to a number of scribes. The manuscript was complete by 1438 and was probably kept safe by monks, but it then went missing. In 1934, it was rediscovered in a country house and has since been translated into modern English and published. It is now prized as a unique, firsthand account of the life of a woman in the 15th century.

▶ **THE BOOK OF MARGERY KEMPE** This neatly written manuscript, bound in parchment-covered boards, is a copy of the original book and the only manuscript that has survived. It was owned by the Carthusian monastery of Mount Grace in Yorkshire and probably passed into private hands when Mount Grace was closed in 1539. It is now kept at the British Library in London.

In context

◀ **JULIAN OF NORWICH** Margery met Julian of Norwich, who was an anchoress (a female hermit walled up in a small room so that she could devote herself to a life of prayer). Julian confirmed that Margery's visions were signs that the Holy Spirit was within her and approved her claims that she had conversations with God.

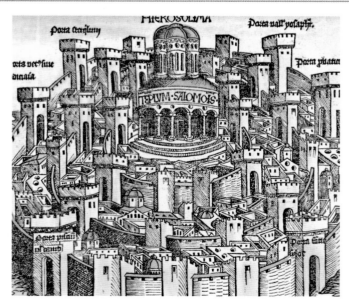

◀ **PILGRIMAGES** The book describes Margery's travels to shrines and holy places in England and abroad. Her longest trip was to the Holy Land, with visits to Assisi and Rome on the way back. Such long journeys were very unusual in the Middle Ages, especially for a woman, and entailed great hardship—both because of poor roads and the danger of attack or robbery.

72

Margery is referred to in the third person, as "she" or "the said creature"

This part of the book recalls an occasion when Margery wept uncontrollably on seeing an image of the Virgin Mary

Some of the annotations and punctuation in red ink may have been added by monks at Mount Grace Priory

New paragraphs are signaled by large red initial letters

◀ **HERESY** Margery was tried for several offenses that broke church laws. These included preaching (forbidden to women) and speaking directly to God. She was also suspected of being a Lollard, one of a group of people who were highly critical of some of the beliefs and practices of the Catholic Church. Lollards faced punishment and were sometimes put to death, but Margery was not found guilty.

> When she came into the churchyard of St Stephen's [where a priest she knew had been buried], she cried, she roared, she wept, she fell down to the ground, so fervently did the fire of love burn in her heart. She had such holy thoughts and such holy memories that she could not control her weeping nor her crying. And therefore people were astonished at her, supposing that she had wept because of some fleshly or earthly affection and said to her, "What is wrong with you, woman? Why are you behaving like this? We knew him as well as you." Then there were some priests in the same place who knew her way of behaving, and they … made her welcome with much kindness.

THE BOOK OF MARGERY KEMPE

▲ **EYEWITNESS ACCOUNT** On August 17, 1497, Luca Landucci describes a political execution. The Florentine government had sentenced five prisoners to death for plotting against it with one of the Medicis: "They were put to death the same night, and I could not refrain from weeping when I saw that young Lorenzo carried past ... on a bier, shortly before dawn," writes Landucci.

Here, Landucci lists the names of the men who have been sentenced to death

A Citizen's View

1450–1516 ■ PEN AND INK ON PAPER ■ 90 PAGES ■ FLORENTINE

LUCA LANDUCCI: APOTHECARY

In the 15th century, Florence was one of the largest, richest, and most cultured cities in Europe. It was the heart of the Italian Renaissance, and wealthy Florentines, particularly the Medici family, became patrons of the arts, commissioning work from great painters, sculptors, and architects. Observing all of this from his shop in central Florence was Luca Landucci (1436–1516), an apothecary, who kept a remarkable diary.

Landucci's diary begins in 1450, when he was just 14 years old, but the manner in which the entries whisk through the early years suggests that he began writing it many years later. Around 1578, his entries become more detailed and frequent, but by no means daily. Landucci may have been a humble shopkeeper, but he lived through momentous times and chronicled the history of the city as it unfurled. Much of what he wrote about were things he had seen himself, some of them quite extraordinary. He records the opening of Ghirlandaio's great frescoes in the Santa Maria Novella, the assassination attempt on Lorenzo de' Medici, and the rise of the fundamentalist monk Savonarola, including the "bonfire of the vanities," where his supporters collected and burned thousands of "vain things."

> ❝ The marble giant [Michelangelo's *David*] was taken out of the Opera [Office of Works of the Duomo] … and they had to break down the wall above the door so that it could come through. During the night stones were thrown at the giant to injure it, therefore it was necessary to keep watch over it. It went very slowly, being bound in an erect position, and suspended so that it did not touch the ground with its feet… It was moved along by more than 40 men…. The said giant had been made by Michelangelo Buonarroti. ❞
>
> **THE DIARY OF LUCA LANDUCCI, MAY 14, 1504**

The diary records natural phenomena, such as floods and eclipses, and also provides an eyewitness account of daily events. Landucci describes the works of artists, but he also attends hangings and dissections. A cross after the entry for March 19, 1516, marks his death, but the entries continue until 1542, perhaps written by his son. A landmark among early diaries, this diary of an ordinary citizen provides a compelling insight into everyday life in Renaissance Florence.

In context

▲ **PHARMACY** Landucci trained as a bookkeeper and apprenticed with an apothecary before setting up his own business. The son of an accountant, he had a natural talent for recording things and keeping stock, all of which helped him create his rich inventory of life in Florence.

▲ **THE BURNING OF SAVONAROLA** The Dominican friar Girolamo Savonarola railed against the immorality of the Medicis and those who coveted riches. He amassed a following but went too far when he criticized the pope. He was tried as a heretic and burned at the stake on May 23, 1498, an event described in lurid detail by Landucci.

Notebooks of a Genius

1478–1519 ▪ PEN AND INK ON PAPER ▪ 6,000 PAGES ▪ ITALIAN

LEONARDO DA VINCI: ARTIST AND SCIENTIST

One of the greatest painters of all time, Leonardo da Vinci (1452–1519) was a multitalented genius of the Italian Renaissance. He left behind more than 6,000 pages of notes, which he probably made on loose sheets of paper that were later folded together and bound to make notebooks known as codices. These contained his observations, discoveries, and ideas in a vast array of fields ranging from physics, architecture, and engineering to anatomy and botany. Packed with detailed scientific descriptions, diagrams, and stunning pen-and-ink drawings, the notebooks are unique because Leonardo was not just a phenomenal artist but also an innovative scientist and a painstaking observer. Each sheet of paper is tightly covered with an elaborate hodgepodge of text and images, ideas, and inventions. In the 15th century, most scientists relied on the opinions of ancient writers, but Leonardo preferred the evidence of his own eyes.

Leonardo began to jot down his thoughts and observations from about 1478, and kept his notebooks until the end of his life. During this time, he was working as an artist, architect, and military and naval engineer for a series of rich and powerful patrons—the Duke of Milan, the Medici family in Florence, and François I of France. Some of the entries in the notebooks, such as city plans for Milan or diagrams for sculptures and elaborate devices, are closely linked to the interests of his patrons. Others are whimsical studies that helped Leonardo perfect his paintings or develop an idea.

There is some evidence that Leonardo was preparing the notebooks for publication toward the end of his life. After his death, a pupil gathered his notes together, but some of the material, including many of the pages on painting, was later lost. No one took much notice of what had survived. The notebooks were not taken up by other scientists because Leonardo had trained as an artist and had not had a scientific education. By the 20th century, the notebooks had been scattered around the world, ending up in collections in Europe and the US. They have also been published and translated, and readers today still marvel at the enormous range of Leonardo's writings and how advanced his thinking was.

> "Many will think that they can with reason blame me, alleging that my proofs are contrary to the authority of certain men held in great reverence by their inexperienced judgements, not considering that my works are the issue of simple and plain experience which is the true mistress. These rules enable you to know the true from the false, and this induces men to look only for the things that are possible and with due moderation—and they forbid you to use a cloak of ignorance, which will bring about that you attain to no result and in despair abandon yourself to melancholy ... Experience has been the mistress of all who have written well; so as mistress I will cite her in all cases."

LEONARDO DA VINCI'S NOTEBOOKS

> ## "Painting cannot be taught to those not endowed by nature, like mathematics...
> **LEONARDO DA VINCI'S NOTEBOOKS**

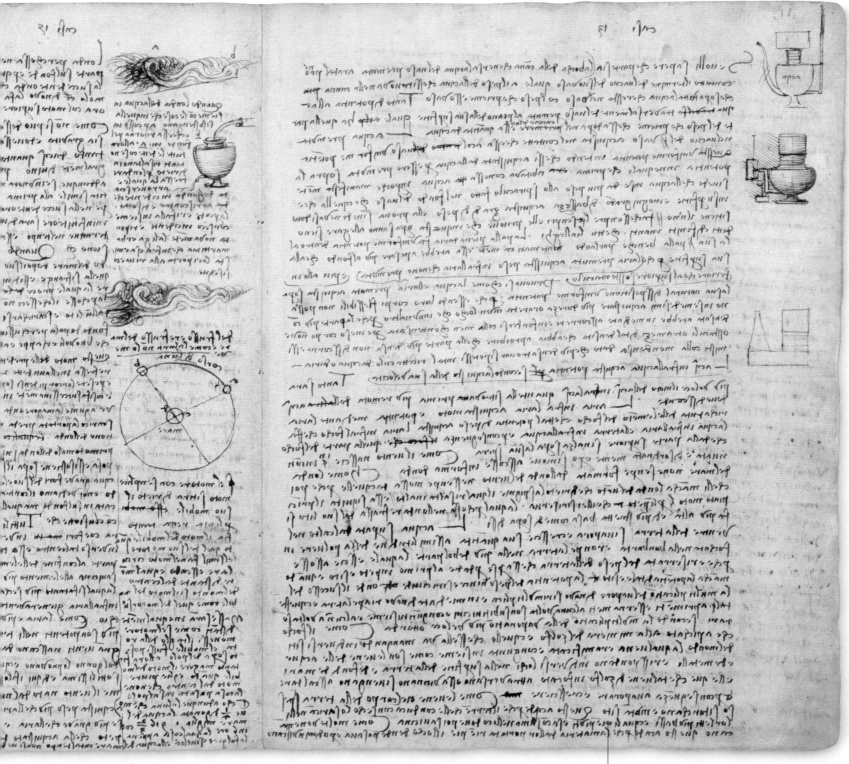

▲ **ON WATER** Much of one volume, the *Codex Leicester*, records Leonardo's study of water. He describes how water flows around obstacles, the origin and development of rivers, the erosion caused by water and the action of floods, storms, and tides, alongside other topics. The illustrations in the center show waves hitting a shore–Leonardo wrote that it was impossible to understand this with the current theories of gravitation.

Leonardo used mirror writing, so his text reads from right to left. He may have done this to stop others from reading what he had written or because he was left-handed and it was easier for him to write this way

In detail

Leonardo was interested in a huge number of subjects. During the Renaissance, people believed that it was possible for one person to excel in every field of knowledge, and Leonardo came close to achieving this. He jotted down notes and diagrams on subjects as diverse as geometry, mathematics, geology, flight, music, and military engineering. He also made major advances in the study of water, astronomy, and anatomy. Some of his work—such as the plans for cities or fortifications, or his designs of crossbows or water fountains—would have been useful to his wealthy patrons.

Among the other inventions were contraptions such as a helicopter, a flying machine with flapping wings, and a parachute—ideas so far ahead of their time that they were still challenging inventors 400 years later. The notebooks reveal not just the scope of Leonardo's knowledge and his questing scientific mind but also personal details: a list of his clothes, for example, shows his liking for pink tights. The extent of his private research also helps explain why, although he was a great artist, he produced relatively few paintings and took years to finish some of them.

> " The **eye** ... called the **window of the soul,** is the chief means whereby the **understanding** may most fully ... appreciate the **infinite works of nature.** "

LEONARDO DA VINCI'S NOTEBOOKS

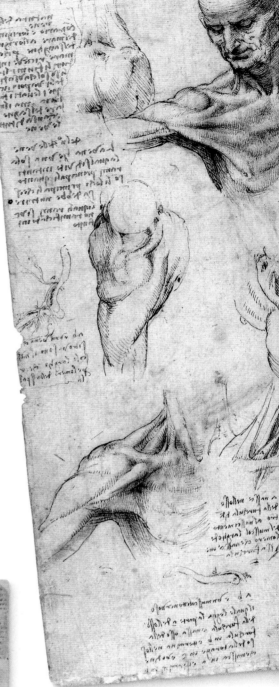

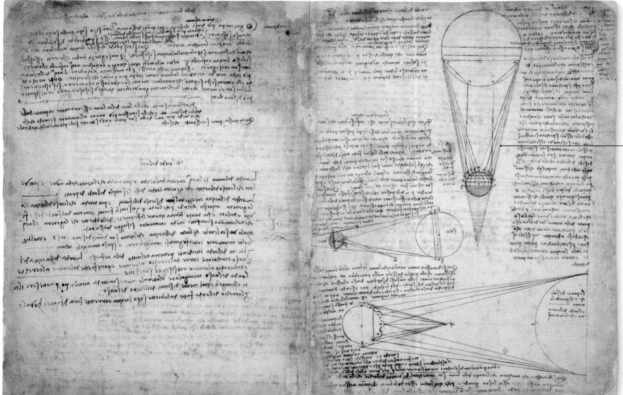

This diagram shows how Leonardo thought that light from the sun fell on the Earth

◄ **THEORIES ABOUT LIGHT** The *Codex Leicester* contains Leonardo's notes on water and the moon. Leonardo thought that the moon was covered with water and deduced that light from the sun was reflected from the water's rippled surface in different directions, softening the moon's glow. We now know that this theory is false, but Leonardo's reasoning was rigorous, and he backed it up with drawings of the light's rays bouncing off the heavenly bodies.

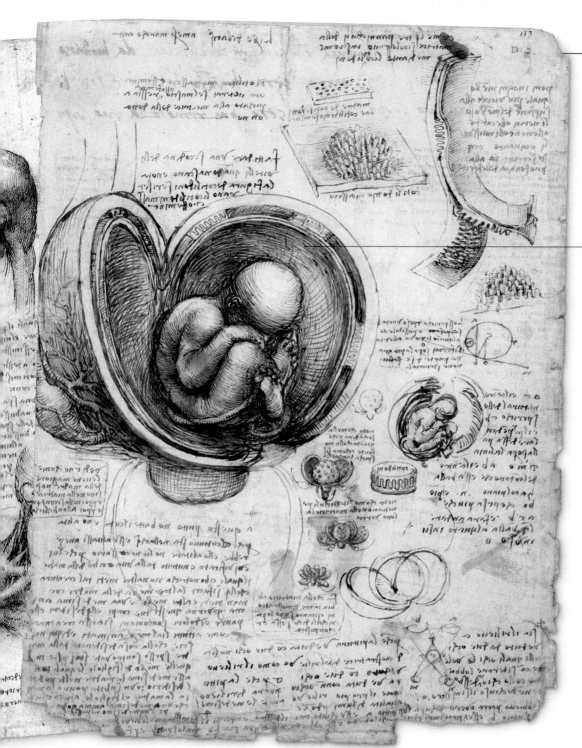

◄ **THE HUMAN BODY** Leonardo believed that in order to draw the human body, he had to understand anatomy. He learned how to dissect corpses, and his notebooks contain meticulous drawings of bones, muscles, sinews, nerves, and blood vessels. He also studied how muscles and bones move and how a fetus grows in the womb.

Here, Leonardo has imagined a womb cut open to reveal the fetus curled up inside

LEONARDO'S **PAINTINGS**

Only about 15 of Leonardo's paintings have survived, and they are considered outstanding works of art, prized for their great realism, for the artist's superb handling of paint, and for his sensitivity to human expressions and gestures. Many of the paintings are of biblical subjects or portraits and depict people like the Virgin Mary or Jesus's disciples in a way that suggests their characters and emotions.

The research in Leonardo's notebooks fed into his painting. His understanding of anatomy helped him make his portrayals lifelike, and his studies of plants and buildings provided reference for the backgrounds of many of his works. His scientific skills also helped him devise new paint mixes, which he tried out in some of his paintings.

▲ *Litta Madonna,* Leonardo da Vinci, 1480–1490

◄ **WAR MACHINE** Leonardo made many drawings of weapons and war machines. One of his patrons, Ludovico Sforza, Duke of Milan, was especially interested in his talents as a military inventor and engineer. This design for the Duke of Milan depicts a war chariot with rotating scythe blades that are driven by the motion of the vehicle's wheels.

Directory: Before 1500

▼ THE MEDITATIONS OF MARCUS AURELIUS

ROMAN (C.170CE)

Born into a prominent Roman family as Marcus Annius Verus in 121CE, the author of the celebrated *Meditations* took the name Marcus Aurelius on becoming Roman Emperor in 161CE. He is known as the last of the Five Good Emperors, providing principled leadership to an empire ravaged by plague and menaced by the incursions of barbarian tribes.

It was chiefly while leading his army on campaigns against Rome's enemies on the frontier with the Danube River that Marcus Aurelius jotted down the intimate notes that were later gathered into the 12 books of his *Meditations*. Writing in Koine Greek, the language commonly used in the Roman Empire, he expressed a personal worldview based on the philosophy of the Ancient Greek Stoics. In epigrammatic style, he urges himself never to forget the brevity and cosmic insignificance of human life and the need to "check desire and extinguish appetite" and pursue a high standard of personal conduct.

The emperor's private reflections were rediscovered almost a thousand years after his death and were recognized as providing a unique insight into the ancient world.

THE RISALA OF AHMAD IBN FADLAN

ARABIAN (921–922CE)

In 921CE, Caliph al-Muqtadir, ruler of the Muslim Abbasid Empire, sent an embassy to the Bulgars who lived on the Volga River. Ahmad ibn Fadlan, an expert in Islamic law and theology, traveled with the expedition, which journeyed from the Abbasid capital, Baghdad, across Central Asia into what is now Russia. The *Risala* (meaning "message" in Arabic) is his personal account of the marvels that he witnessed on a trip that covered 2,500 miles (4,000 km). His

narrative is best known for its graphic account of the customs of the Rus, Scandinavian Vikings who ran the trade route along the Volga. Ahmad was astounded by their physical strength, their tattoos, and their poor personal hygiene. His lurid account of a Viking ship funeral is justly famous. Only fragments of the *Risala* were known until a complete text was discovered in 1923.

THE PILLOW BOOK OF SEI SHŌNAGON

JAPANESE (C.993–C.1002CE)

Born into a family of scholars and poets, Sei Shōnagon (c.966–c.1017CE) served as a lady-in-waiting to the Empress Teishi at the Japanese imperial court in Kyoto during the Heian era. For her own pleasure, she kept a journal of her daily life at court, recording her thoughts, feelings, and observations. Written in the Japanese hiragana symbols, rather than the Chinese characters used at the time

by male Japanese authors, *The Pillow Book* offers a charming mix of gossip, anecdotes of court life, reminiscences, personal reflections, sensitive descriptions of nature, and idiosyncratic lists–of "Unsuitable Things," "Elegant Things," "Things That Irritate Me," and "Things That Make Me Fondly Recall the Past." Shōnagon wrote of "never intending these notes to be seen," but even in her lifetime, her journal was read and admired in court circles. Spontaneous and sophisticated, it has since come to be regarded as one of the finest Japanese literary works of its era.

THE SAFARNAMA OF NASIR KHUSRAW

PERSIAN (1046–1052)

The renowned Persian philosopher and poet Nasir Khusraw was born in Khorasan, eastern Iran, in 1004CE. He worked as a government official until about the age of 40 when, by his own account, a vision in a dream impelled

him to travel in search of spiritual enlightenment. He traveled for seven years, making the pilgrimage to Mecca but also visiting a wide area of the Muslim world–from central Asia to Syria, Jerusalem, the Arabian Desert, and Cairo.

During his travels, he kept a journal recording the political and social state of each country, the buildings of its cities, and his conversations with local people, from shopkeepers to scholars. When he returned to Khorasan, he used his notes as the basis for the *Safarnama* (Book of Travel), which is both an exemplary work of Persian literature and an invaluable source of information for historians. Having embraced the Ismaili branch of Shia Islam, in old age, Khusraw was driven from Khorasan by Sunni Muslims and died in exile in 1088.

THE DIARY OF IBN AL-BANNĀ

IRAQI (1068–1069)

One of the earliest known diaries in the Muslim world was written by Ibn al-Bannā (1005–1079), a prominent scholar and teacher who lived in Baghdad, the capital of the Abbasid caliphate. A fragment of the journal in Ibn al-Bannā's own handwriting, which has survived and is preserved in a library in Damascus, Syria, covers 14 lunar months of the Islamic years 460–461, equivalent to the period from August 1068 to September 1069 in the Christian calendar.

Ibn al-Bannā's diary mainly offers personal observations on events in the political and academic life of Baghdad, along with accounts of miracles and wonders of which he had heard. It includes interpretations of more than 20 dreams, experienced either by Ibn al-Bannā himself or by members of his family or friends. There are also obituaries of prominent figures of the day who died while he was keeping the diary. Ibn al-Bannā may have kept the diary as a source of material for a scholarly chronicle of his times that he planned to write.

Folio from the Codex Vaticanus, which contains the earliest copy of the *Meditations*

THE REVELATIONS OF JULIAN OF NORWICH

ENGLISH (c.1373)

The Revelations of Divine Love were written by a Christian anchoress (a type of hermit) who lived in a cell beside the church of St. Julian in the English city of Norwich, and who is hence known as Julian of Norwich. Born around 1343, the anchoress fell gravely ill at the age of 30 and was being administered the last rites when she experienced the first of 16 "shewings" of the Passion of Christ, vivid religious visions that effected a miraculous cure.

Immediately after her recovery, Julian wrote a short account of the visions "showed by the goodness of God to a devout woman." Some 30 years later, she completed a much longer form of the text, elaborating on her mystical experience. Both versions of her *Revelations* were written in English, the common spoken language of the day rather than the learned language of Latin, and have survived thanks to manuscript copies made in the century following Julian's death in 1416. The short text was rediscovered only in 1911. Admired as devotional writing, the *Revelations* are of historic importance as the first English book written by a woman.

THE DIARIES OF GREGORIO DATI

FLORENTINE (c.1385–1427)

Gregorio Dati (1362–1435) was a silk merchant who lived in the city-state of Florence in the early Renaissance. He kept diaries primarily as a record of his business transactions. Married four times and the father of 26 children, he writes about his family affairs in the same tone that he uses for his business, emphasizing the size of dowry that he received for each marriage, which he used as capital for commercial ventures and to pay off his debts.

One of Dati's diaries, the *Libro Segreto* (Secret Book), gives more insight into his personal psychology, recording the self-denying resolutions that he made—to remain chaste on Fridays, for example—as he struggled

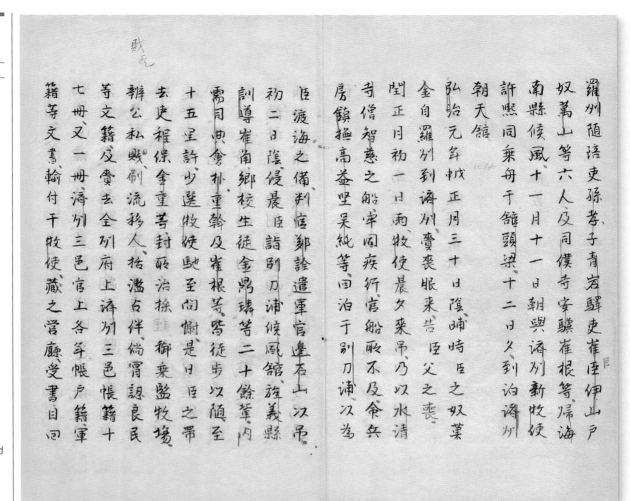

A copy of Choe Bu's travel diary, kept at Havard Library

to reconcile Christian morality with self-interest and social ambition. The precariousness of life at the time is well conveyed by Dati's record of bankruptcies, losses due to piracy at sea, and sudden death—three of his children died in a single day during the plague of 1420. Dati was also prominent in city government and wrote a notable history of Florence.

JOURNAL D'UN BOURGEOIS DE PARIS

FRENCH (1405–1449)

Despite its customary French title, modern research has established that this anonymous journal of Parisian life in the 15th century was not the work of a "bourgeois"—an ordinary citizen or burgher—but of some unidentified priest linked to the University of Paris and the cathedral of Notre Dame. Written during a troubled period of the Hundred Years' War, when France was riven by civil

conflict and partially occupied by English armies, the diary chronicles public events and everyday life, often in vivid detail. Its graphic accounts of mass burials in the plague of 1418 or starving children begging in the streets during the famine of 1420 are clearly the work of an eyewitness. Other elements of the journal, such as its references to the trial of Joan of Arc in 1431, are interesting as they provide a picture of what was rumored or believed by people at the time. The journal is known from manuscript copies made in the 15th and 16th centuries. The first complete printed version appeared in 1729.

▲ THE RECORD OF CHOE BU

KOREAN (1488)

A Record of Drifting across the Southern Brocade Sea, known in Korean as *Geumnam Pyohaerok*, is an account of an unplanned visit to

China by an official of Korea's Joseon Dynasty. Sailing for Korea from an offshore island in February 1488, Choe Bu and his party were blown off course during a violent storm and eventually washed ashore on the Chinese coast near Ningbo. The Chinese authorities escorted the Koreans on a 49-day trip along the Grand Canal to Beijing, the capital of the Ming Empire. From there, they returned to Korea by road, reaching the border in July.

Choe Bu kept detailed notes during this eventful journey, observing many fascinating and previously unknown details of Ming commerce, society, laws, and customs. After he had returned to Korea, at the request of the Korean king, Seonjong, he wrote up his travel journal in literary Chinese, the language that was used by scholars and the elite.

A printed edition of the work had already became well known by the 16th century. Today, it is regarded as an outstanding eyewitness account of Ming-era China.

2

1500—1700

Keeping a diary became more common in Europe during this time as a result of increasing literacy and the rise of Puritanism, which encouraged believers to examine their consciences by recording their daily thoughts and actions. Unknown in their day, the 17th-century journals of Samuel Pepys and John Evelyn established the English tradition of keeping a diary. In France the self-conscious elite of society under Louis XIV penned letters and memoirs rich in sophisticated wit and insight. Meanwhile, voyages of discovery provided a wide range of exotic adventures for European travelers and settlers to record. In Asia, a lively tradition of personal writing was sustained, from the war diaries of the Korean Admiral Yi to the refined travel journal of the Japanese poet Matsuo Bashō.

Magellan's Voyage

1519–1522 ▪ MANUSCRIPT AND WATERCOLOR ON PARCHMENT ▪ 98 PAGES ▪ ITALIAN

ANTONIO PIGAFETTA: EXPLORER AND SCHOLAR

The journal of Antonio Pigafetta (c.1492–1531) is one of the most fascinating early travel narratives. Filled with drama and excitement, it reads like an adventure novel, full of mutinies, shipwrecks, hostile islanders, dancing giants, and all kinds of strange and exotic creatures. Pigafetta captures both the highs and lows of discovery. But this is not a fabulous concoction. Pigafetta was a scientific observer and his writings contain valuable information about the geography and wildlife of the Pacific islands, and the harmful effects of the voyage on the islanders.

On September 20, 1519, five ships set sail from Seville, Spain, for what was to become the first known circumnavigation of the globe. The leader of the expedition was the Portuguese explorer Ferdinand Magellan, who would achieve lasting fame even though he did not complete the voyage. Magellan's exploits are known because of the diaries kept by Pigafetta, an Italian scholar from Vicenza who had volunteered for the expedition, prompted, in his own words, by a craving for experience and glory. During the three years at sea, he made detailed notes on the flora, fauna, and native inhabitants of the places they visited and recounted the tragic events that befell the ships and their crew. Of the 270 men who set out on the expedition, only 18 returned.

Pigafetta's original journal has been lost, but between 1522 and 1525, he wrote an account based on it, entitled *The First Voyage around the World,* and presented copies to various European dignitaries, including one to the Holy Roman Emperor Charles V. The immodest Pigafetta described these gifts as something to be prized above gold and silver, "a book written by my hand, concerning all the matters that had occurred from day to day during our voyage." The text of *The First Voyage* survives in four manuscripts, one in Italian and three in French. These manuscripts have provided the basis for numerous published versions of Pigafetta's journal. In 1800, the first complete edition was published in Italian; the English translation followed in 1874.

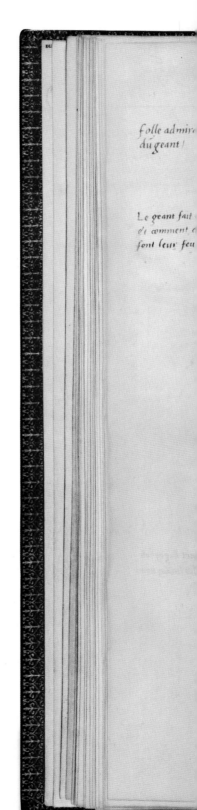

➤ **MAPPING THE WORLD** The manuscripts of *The First Voyage* all include 23 beautiful, hand-painted watercolor maps. This map, from one of the French manuscripts, shows the southern tip of South America and the stretch of water between this and Tierra del Fuego that provides a natural, navigable sea route between the Atlantic and Pacific oceans. It is now known as the Strait of Magellan.

◄ **FERDINAND MAGELLAN** When the King of Portugal refused to support his search for a new route to India, the Portuguese explorer Ferdinand Magellan offered his services to his country's great rival, Charles I of Spain. The nations were in fierce competition to control the global trade in spices. Charles authorized Magellan to search for a westward route to the Spice Islands.

" The natives continued to pursue us, and picking up the same spear four or six times, hurled it at us again and again. Recognizing the captain, so many turned upon him that they knocked his helmet off his head twice... Trying to lay hand on sword, he could draw it out but halfway, because he had been wounded in the arm with a bamboo spear. When the natives saw that, they... rushed upon him with iron and bamboo spears and with their cutlasses, until they killed our mirror, our light, our comfort, and our true guide. "

THE DEATH OF MAGELLAN RECOUNTED IN PIGAFETTA'S JOURNAL

ndoit auecq la plume en main [] Vne aultre fois ie feis
roix, et la baisay en la luy monstrant. Mais soudain cria
bos Et me feist signe que si plus ie faisoys la croix quelle
treroit en lestommach et me feroit creuer. [] Quand ce
t se trouuoit mal, demandoit la croix, et lambrassoit et
oit fort. Et se voulut faire chrestien deuant sa mort. Le
nous nommasmes Paul [] Alors que ces gens veullet
e du feu, ilz mectent vng boys poinctu quilz frottent auecq
aultre tant quilz font prendre le feu en vne moelle darbre
est comme cotton entre ces deux boys

figure du destroict Pathagomique. De la region de
agomie. Mer oceane. De la mer Pacifique. Et aultres

Le capitaine seiournant en la mer Pacificque : Les maulx
uy et ses gens y souffrirent. De linconuenient a leurs gensiues
nartz et malades. Des isles infortunees. Et en quel degre elles

Chapitre xii.

Destroict Patagonicque. — Cap de Seade. — Mer occean. — Cap de onze mille vierges. — Port de Sainct Iulien. — Mer Pacificque. — Region Patagonicque. — Cap de saincte Marie. — Flume de leha de Solis.

The text of *The First Voyage* is divided into 57 numbered chapters

Magellan named the sea on the far side of South America the Mar Pacífico, which means "peaceful sea"

In detail

Pigafetta's journal is a straightforward chronological account of the expedition. Many paragraphs begin with a date. The style of writing is factual and free of personal opinion yet full of color and detail: "Wednesday, the twenty-eighth of November, 1520, we came forth out of the said strait, and entered into the Pacific sea, where we remained three months and twenty days without taking in provisions or other refreshments, and we only ate old biscuit reduced to powder, and full of grubs, and stinking from the dirt which the rats had made on it."

Pigafetta records unusual animals sighted, notably a flock of penguins in Patagonia now named after Magellan. The text is also full of observations about the people they met, who they

sometimes treated with cruelty. Pigafetta tried to entertain: "The people of this place … thought that the small boats of the ships were the children of the ships, and that the said ships gave birth to them when the boats were lowered to send the men hither and yon. And when the boats were lying alongside a ship, they thought that the ships were suckling them."

▼ **A VISUAL ACCOUNT** Each of the 23 maps is closely linked to a particular passage in the book so that they act as illustrations to the narrative. Scrolls identify the names of the places depicted, and there are sometimes topographical features or buildings, too. The scroll below, on the island of Mactan in the Philippines, reads: "Here the captain-general died." It is referring to Magellan.

▲ **FIRST ENCOUNTERS** The Marianas were the first islands that Magellan's ships encountered in the Pacific Ocean. Pigafetta records that when the expedition dropped anchor, the islanders came aboard and stole everything they could lay their hands on. He therefore named the islands the *Islas de los Ladrones* (Islands of Thieves).

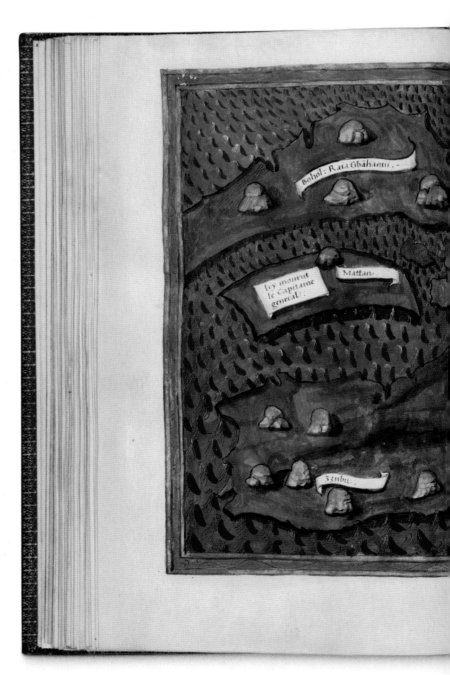

AROUND THE WORLD BY ACCIDENT

When the five small ships under his command left Spain in 1519, Ferdinand Magellan did not set out to make a voyage around the world. His goal was to find a western route to the Spice Islands, a source of valuable spices in present-day Indonesia. On the way, Magellan unintentionally discovered many of the Pacific Ocean's archipelagos and peoples but was subsequently killed in a skirmish on the island of Mactan. A new captain led the expedition onward, and it eventually reached the Spice Islands, but only one ship, the *Victoria*, made it home, thus completing the first circumnavigation of the globe on September 6, 1522. The treasure that it yielded was not the cargo of fragrant cloves in its hold, but the information that it brought back about the seas, and previously unknown animals and peoples, in the journal of Antonio Pigafetta.

► *The Discovery of the Strait of Magellan,*
Oswald Walters Brierly, 1873

The numerous islands of the Philippines are indicated on the maps

This note refers to burning a ship, since there was not enough crew for it to sail onward

Each of the Moluccas or Spice Islands bears its name in an elaborate scroll

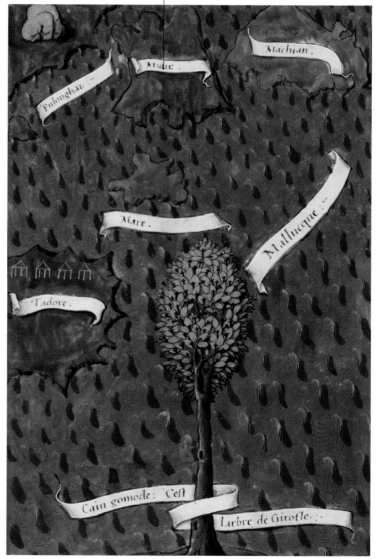

▲ **THE LAND OF CLOVES** The tree standing proud on this map is a clove tree and represents the goal of the expedition. "Wednesday, the 6th of November," writes Pigafetta, "we discovered four ... rather high islands at a distance of fourteen leagues towards the east. The pilot ... told us those were the Maluco islands, for which we gave thanks to God."

Admiral Yi gave each volume of the diary a title based on the zodiac name of the year covered

A Testament of War

1592-1598 ▪ INK ON MULBERRY PAPER ▪ SEVEN VOLUMES ▪ KOREAN

YI SUN-SHIN: ADMIRAL

Known as *Nanjung Ilji*, the diary of Korea's most renowned naval commander, Yi Sun-shin, provides a remarkable self-portrait of a patriotic hero at war. Sometimes referred to as "the Korean Nelson", Yi kept a record of his life from his appointment as an admiral on January 1, 1592, to his death during a sea battle on November 19, 1598. During this period, the Korean Joseon kingdom was waging a desperate struggle to uphold its independence against Japanese invaders. Yi's war diary provides vivid descriptions of his sea battles and strategic

conferences but also takes you into his private world, describing details of his daily life and expressing his feelings for his family and his concerns about political issues.

Born into a noble clan in 1545, Yi had made a reputation as a successful army general before being appointed to command a fleet as the conflict with Japan loomed. His diary describes the painstaking preparations that transformed his fleet into a supremely effective fighting force and the tactics that won him victory in nearly all of his 23 naval battles. But as an honest patriot, Yi also frequently expresses criticism of his country's divided and corrupt political leadership. He found himself the target of machinations and false accusations that led, in 1597,

Written in Chinese script, the diary is considered a work of art because of the fine calligraphy

> The heavens and the earth are dark, and even the sun has lost its color. Ah, how sad! My son, where are you now, having deserted me? Is it because you are such an outstanding figure that the heavens are unwilling to leave you in this world, or is it because of my sin, that this great misfortune has befallen you. Even if I hold out in this world, now on whom can I lean my heart? I wish to follow you to the grave, to stay and weep with you together under the ground, but if I do, your brothers, sisters and your mother will have no one to lean their hearts on. Thus I endure, but my mind that wails is already dead, soulless.

WAR DIARY, AFTER THE DEATH OF HIS YOUNGEST SON, OCTOBER 14, 1597

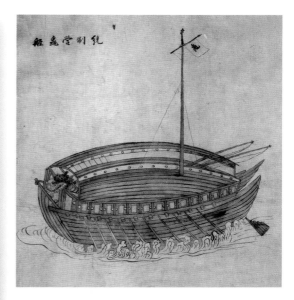

▲ **TURTLE SHIP** Yi is credited with developing the *kŏbuksŏn* (turtle ship), an armored warship. Its upper deck was shielded with spiked iron plates to defend the crew against missiles and prevent the enemy from boarding. Korean warships had gunpowder weapons, but more damage was often inflicted by firing flaming arrows.

▲ **NAVAL JOURNAL** Admiral Yi's diary has 2,539 entries, covering almost the entire period of the Imjin War between Korea and Japan. Written with brush and ink on traditional mulberry paper, the journal consists of seven volumes, one for each year. The original manuscript copy, much admired for its bold calligraphy, was kept safe by the admiral's descendants through four centuries of Korean history.

to his arrest, torture, and demotion to the rank of common soldier. This disgrace naturally led to a pause in the diary. The entries resume with Yi's restoration to command at a moment of supreme national danger, when the Japanese returned, and his victory at Myongyang on September 16, 1597, which effectively decided the war in Korea's favor.

After his death in 1598, Admiral Yi was consecrated as a Korean national hero. *Nanjung Ilji* was first published in 1795 and has become a classic text studied in Korean schools. Admired for the clarity and directness of its style, the diary serves as an exemplary text expressing the values of true patriotism and upright public service.

THE **IMJIN WAR**

In 1592, Japanese leader Toyotomi Hideyoshi launched a seaborne invasion of Korea as a prelude to an attack on China. Japanese troops captured the Korean port of Pusan, but Yi's warships crushed a Japanese fleet at Hansando. With his sea link to Japan insecure, Hideyoshi evacuated his forces.

In 1597, the Japanese returned and, with Yi absent, won control of the sea. Restored to command, Yi inflicted a miraculous defeat on a superior Japanese fleet at Myongyang. When Chinese land forces entered the war on the side of Korea, the Japanese decided to abandon the invasion and Yi won his final victory at Noryang in 1598, the battle in which he died.

▲ *The Siege of Pusan Fortress*, Byeon Bak, 1709

A Soldier's Tale

1624–1649 ▪ PEN AND INK ON PAPER ▪ 176 PAGES ▪ GERMAN

PETER HAGENDORF: MERCENARY SOLDIER

In 1988, an anonymous record of the experiences of an ordinary soldier in the Thirty Years' War was discovered in a Berlin archive. Historical detective work tracked down the author of this unique document, identifying him as Peter Hagendorf, a mercenary from Saxony-Anhalt in Germany. Hagendorf's account of his life paints a graphic picture of the miseries of military service in the first half of the 17th century.

Born around 1601, Hagendorf signed on with the Catholic League infantry in 1627 to escape poverty. Holding the rank of *Gefreiter*, one step up from an ordinary foot soldier, he served for two decades of continuous warfare in Germany. Alongside eyewitness accounts of major battles and historic events such as the Sack of Magdeburg, the book describes the daily struggle for survival in a world racked by violence, starvation, and disease. It relates acts of brutality by soldiers but shows the soldiers' own condition as hardly preferable to that of the civilians they preyed upon. Hagendorf vividly describes how, straggling behind the army with a hangover, he was attacked and robbed by peasants. The soldiers were often cold, wet, and hungry, but there are hints of warmth in Hagendorf's bleak world. Whether on the march or in camp, he was accompanied by his successive wives and their children.

◀ **SILVER COINAGE** The standard currency circulating during the period of the Thirty Years' War was the silver thaler. This example bears the image of the Gonzaga ruler of Mantua. The lowest rank of mercenary was in theory paid four thalers a month, though the pay often failed to materialize.

He mentions his first wife caring for him after he was wounded in battle and his concern for his ailing offspring, but death was everywhere. His first wife died in 1633, and he lost eight of his ten children. Hagendorf himself was a survivor. After the onset of peace in 1648, unwelcome as it made him unemployed, he put his memoirs in order and lived through to old age.

▶ **DAMAGED MANUSCRIPT** The manuscript of Hagendorf's memoirs that has survived is probably a clean copy that he wrote up after his war service ended, based on rough notes made at the time. Originally a 192-page book, it has suffered water damage, and its final section has been lost. The pages shown here describe the battle of Nördlingen, in which Hagendorf fought in 1634.

THE THIRTY YEARS' WAR

Fought mostly in Germany from 1618–1648, the Thirty Years' War was one of the most destructive conflicts in European history. It resulted from the breakdown of a compromise that had allowed Catholic and Protestant states to coexist peacefully within the Catholic Holy Roman Empire.

The Imperial army and a league of Catholic states crushed Protestant forces at the battle of the White Mountain, in Bohemia, in 1620, but first Sweden and then France intervened in support of the Protestants. With neither side able to prevail, the war was eventually ended by the compromise Treaty of Westphalia, which left Germany divided between Protestants and Catholics. The death toll in this ultimately futile conflict may have reached as much as eight million, with victims dying in combat, in massacres, and from famine and disease.

▶ *The Battle of White Mountain*, Pieter Sneyers, 1620

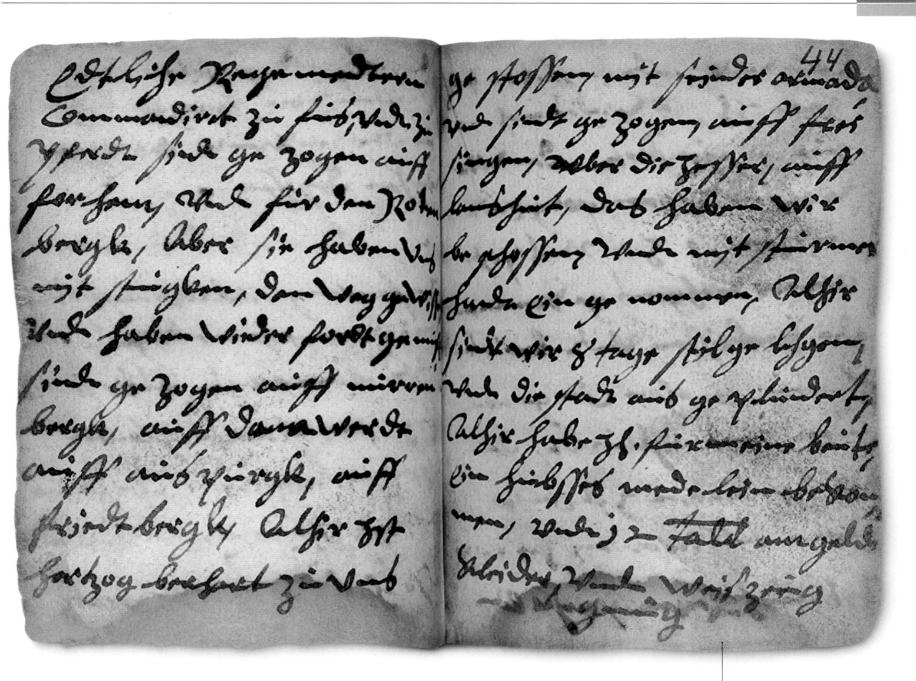

Water damage at the bottom of the page

> I entered the city [Magdeburg] by storm without incurring any injury. But once in the city, at the Neustadt Gate, I was shot twice through the body—that was my body!... The army doctor bound my hands behind my back so he could use the gouge on me. Thus I was brought back to my tent, half dead. Nevertheless, I was deeply saddened that the city burned so horribly, both on account of the city's beauty and because it is my fatherland. As I was now bandaged up, my wife went into the city, even though it was completely on fire... to fetch a cushion and cloth for me to lie on and for the dressings.

HAGENDORF'S DIARY, MAY 20, 1631

◄ **SACK OF MAGDEBURG**
On May 20, 1631, after a two-month siege, the Protestant city of Magdeburg fell to Catholic forces, Hagendorf among them. Fires were started and quickly spread from house to house. Amid the flames, the troops, unleashed upon the civilian population, engaged in an orgy of looting, rape, torture, and murder. Some 20,000 people were killed.

A Pilgrim's Journal

1630-1651 ■ PEN AND INK ON PAPER ■ 270 PAGES IN TWO VOLUMES ■ ENGLISH

WILLIAM BRADFORD: COLONIST

The group of religious dissenters, who came to be known as the Pilgrims, set sail in the *Mayflower* in 1620 to found the first long-lasting European colony in North America. One of their leaders, William Bradford, kept a journal describing their escape from persecution in Europe, and the formative years of their settlement—Plimoth Plantation—in what is now Massachusetts.

Bradford kept his journal for 21 years. The first part is a record of the 1620 journey and the struggle to set up the colony; the rest was written in stages, as events unfolded. Although Bradford wrote in the third person, the account is a record of daily events, like a diary. It is an outstanding eyewitness account of the settlers' lives, motives, and their historic settlement. The book has become a primary source of information about the early history of the Europeans in North America, covering everything from their religious faith to their government and farming methods. Its description of their difficult journey across the Atlantic includes the bouts of seasickness many endured, the storms at sea, and the rescue of one man who fell overboard. The journal continues with moving accounts of the hardships of the early years in New England, with many dying in the first winter, local people catching smallpox from the colonists, and the survivors' efforts to grow food. It pays tribute to the help that the settlers received from the Native Americans, who were often poorly repaid or treated with cruelty, and Bradford insisted that colonists who killed and robbed a local man should be properly punished.

Bradford wrote because he wanted the Pilgrims' descendants to understand both the hardships that their ancestors faced and their belief that they would receive God's help. However, his journal was lost after the American War of Independence, turning up eventually at Fulham Palace in the UK. Published in 1856, it is now kept at the State Library of Massachusetts.

In context

◄ **INTERPRETER AND GUIDE** In the journal, Bradford pays tribute to Squanto, a native who was able to help the Pilgrims because he had learned English when he visited England with an earlier group of settlers. Squanto not only acted as their interpreter but also taught the settlers how to cultivate local crops and where to fish.

▲ **THE FIRST THANKSGIVING** In November 1621, Bradford helped organize a three-day feast to celebrate the settlers' first harvest and to thank the Natives Americans for their help. Squanto's advice about which crops to grow ensured that the Pilgrims had enough food to survive. This feast became the first American Thanksgiving.

Of plimoth plantation

And first of y occasion, and jndusments ther vnto; the which that y may truly vnfould, y must begine at y very roote & rise of y same. The which y shall endeuor to manefest in a plaine Stile; with singuler regard vnto y simple trueth in all things, at least as near as my slender judgmente can attaine the same.

1. Chapter

It is well knowne vnto y godly, and judicious; how euer since y first breaking out of y lighte of y gospell, in our Honourable Nation of England (which was y first of nations, whom y Lord adorned ther with, after y grose darknes of popery which had couered, & ouerspred y Christian worled) what warrs & oppssions euer since, satan hath raised, maintained, and continued against the saincts, from time, to time, in one sorte, or other. Some times by bloody death & cruell torments; other whiles ymprisonments, banishments, & other hard vsages. As being loath his kingdom should goe downe, the trueth preuaile; and y Churches of God reuerte to their anciente puritie; and recouer, their primatiue order, libertie, & bewtie. But when he could not preuaile by these means, against the maine trueths of y gospell; but that they began to take rooting in many places; being watered with y blooud of y martires, and blessed from heauen with a gracious encrease. He then begane to take him to his anciente stratagemes, vsed of old against the first Christians. That when by y bloody, & barbarous persecutions of y Heathen Emperours, he could not stoppe, & subuerte the course of y gospell; but that it speedily ouerspred, with a wounderfull celeritie, the then best known parts of y world. He then begane to sow errours, heresies, and wounderfull dissentions amongst y professours them selues (working vpon their pride, & ambition, with other corrupte pasions, yncidente to all mortall men; yea to y saints them selues in some measure) By which wofull effects followed; as not only bitter contentions, & hartburnings, schismes, with other horrible confusions. But satan tooke occasion & aduantage therby to foyst in a number of vile coremoneys, with many vnprofitable cannons, & decrees, which haue since been as snares, to many poore, & peaceable souls, euen to this day. So as in y anciente times, the persecuti-

Bradford used very neat handwriting—he clearly wanted others to read and understand his journal

◄ **THE TRUE STORY** Writing in a plain but expressive style, Bradford used his journal to tell the story of the Pilgrims, from their problems in Europe, where they were forbidden to practice their religion freely, to the creation of their settlement in New England. Here, on the first page, Bradford explains how the Church of England had become corrupt, leading the Pilgrims to "purify" the way in which they worshipped.

> ❝ It was winter, and they that know the winters of that cuntrie know them to be sharp & violent, & subjecte to cruell & feirce stormes, deangerous to travill to known places, much more to serch an unknown coast. Besids, what could they see but a hidious & desolate wildernes, full of wild beasts & willd men … which way soever they turnd their eys (save upward to the heavens) they could have litle solace or content in respecte of any outward objects. For sumer being done, all things stand upon them with a wetherbeaten face, and the whole countrie, full of woods & thickets, represented a wild & savage heiw [hue]. ❞

OF PLIMOTH PLANTATION, CHAPTER 9

▲ **THE MAYFLOWER COMPACT** In 1620, the Pilgrims drew up and ratified the Mayflower Compact, a document about their government, saying that they would enact their own laws but remain loyal to the king of England. It was the first set of laws to establish self-governance in their new country. Bradford, one of the 41 settlers who signed the Compact, made a copy of it in his journal.

Into the Unknown

1642-1644 ■ MANUSCRIPT ON PARCHMENT ■ 192 PAGES ■ DUTCH

ABEL JANSZOON TASMAN: EXPLORER

It is no surprise that the journal of a seafaring captain should be filled with entries noting winds, the weather, the courses set, and the configuration of sails. These brief, almost terse daily notes were made by Abel Janszoon Tasman (1603–1659) for the owners of the Dutch East India Company. They had commissioned him to undertake a voyage in search of the legendary southern continent *Terra Australis* (Southern Land), and to determine whether the west coast of New Guinea was connected to it.

The idea of setting off on a voyage into the unknown would lend a sense of drama and expectation to even the most prosaic of entries, and the very first lines that Tasman wrote could be the opening of a novel. "This day August 14, A.D. 1642, we set sail from the roads of Batavia with two ships, the Yacht *Heemskerk* and the Flute *Zeehaan*, the wind being northeast with good weather." The journal charts the ships' progress, noting, for example, repairs and stocking up on wood, animals, and supplies at Mauritius (September) and a meeting of the ships' officers (October). On November 24, Tasman notes: "In the afternoon about 4 o'clock we saw land bearing east by north of us at about 10 miles distance from us by estimation; the land we sighted was very high." This is what made his name: the discovery of a new, uncharted land, which the expedition named after the Dutch colonial governor Anthony van Diemen, but was later renamed Tasmania. The expedition sailed on and the crews became the first Europeans to sight New Zealand. The ships arrived back at Batavia, the capital of the Dutch East Indies, on June 15, 1643, and Tasman's journal was handed over to Company officials.

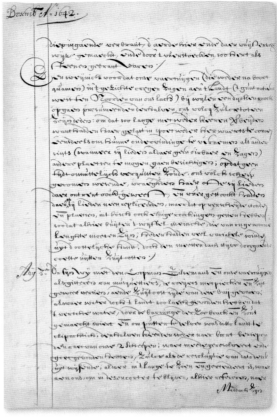

▲ **THE MANUSCRIPTS**
Two manuscripts of Tasman's journal have survived. Both were probably copied from the original in Batavia soon after the voyage. One manuscript is now in the Netherlands State Archive and the other in the Mitchell Library in Sydney. Neither was copied out by Tasman, but both of them are signed by him to confirm their accuracy.

THE **DUTCH EAST INDIA COMPANY**

In 1602, the Dutch formed the East India Company, which was known as the *Vereenigde Oost-Indische Compagnie* (VOC). Until then, Portugal had controlled the lucrative trade in spices in the Southeast Asian seas, but its empire was in decline, and other European powers were now vying for control of the valuable market. The Dutch established a fortified base at Batavia (present-day Jakarta, Indonesia), with hundreds of subsidiary posts around the region. Tasman was one of many captains that the VOC sent out to discover new shipping routes and possible trading opportunities. They also wanted to locate the fabled, vast southern continent that people thought must exist to correspond with the continental landmass in the northern hemisphere.

▲ *The trading post of the Dutch East India Company beside the Ganges in Hooghly, Bengal,* Hendrik van Schuylenburgh, 1665

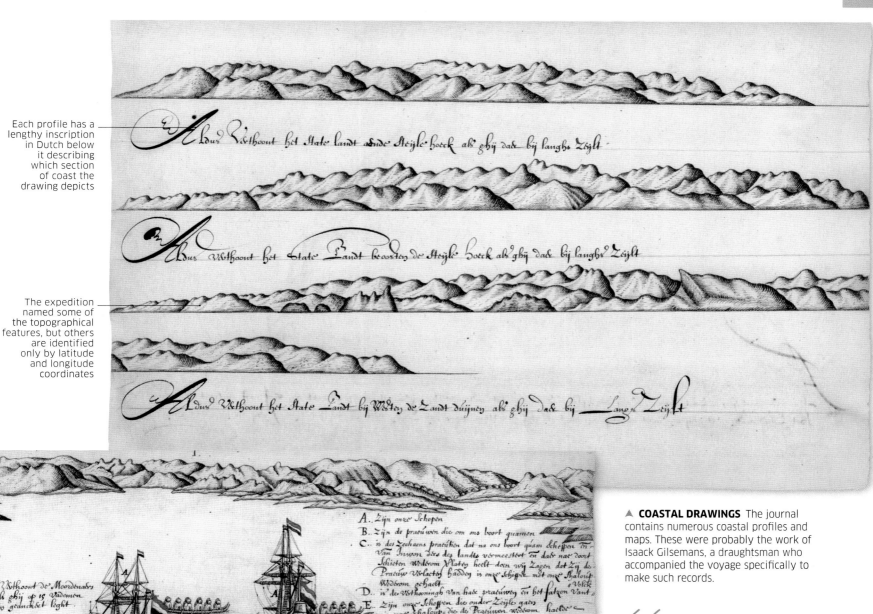

Each profile has a lengthy inscription in Dutch below it describing which section of coast the drawing depicts

The expedition named some of the topographical features, but others are identified only by latitude and longitude coordinates

A. Zijn onze Schepen
B. Zijn de prauwen die om ons boort quamen
C. is des Zeehaens prauw die na ons boort quam Schepen in Van Inwon des landts vermeestert en dat nae 'doort Schieten Weldrom Platye heelt doen wij Zagen dat Zij de Prauw Verlaeten hadden is onze Schipp met onze Schaloup Weldrom gehaelt
D. in de Usthooningh Van hate prauwen en het faizon Vant Vblick
E. Zijn onze Schepen die onder Zeijle gaen
F. is onze Schaloup die de Prauwen weldrom haelde

Us Usthoont de Moordenaers als ghij op is Vrdemon is gedruckt teght

▲ COASTAL DRAWINGS The journal contains numerous coastal profiles and maps. These were probably the work of Isaack Gilsemans, a draughtsman who accompanied the voyage specifically to make such records.

" When we had come close inshore in a small inlet which bore west-south-west of the ships, the surf ran so high that we could not get near the shore without running the risk of having our pinnace [ship's boat] dashed to pieces. We then ordered the carpenter to swim to the shore alone, with the pole and the flag ... we made him plant the said pole with the flag at top into the earth, about the center of the bay near four trees easily recognizable and standing in the form of a crescent. This work having been duly executed, we pulled back to the ships, leaving the above mentioned as a memorial for those who shall come after us. "

TASMAN'S JOURNAL, DECEMBER 3, 1642

▲ CONFLICT AT MURDERERS' BAY The Maori saw the Dutch as invaders, coming for their land. Two boats of Maori challenged them with incantations and trumpet blasts, and the Dutch responded by firing their cannons at them. The Maori people rammed one of the Dutch boats and four sailors were killed. Tasman named the place Moordenaars' (Murderers') Bay.

Gilsemans labeled this drawing "A view of the native prow with the appearance of the people"

Adventures at Sea

1659–1703 ▪ INK AND WATERCOLOR ON PARCHMENT ▪ ENGLISH

EDWARD BARLOW: SAILOR

After working as a farm boy and in a cotton mill, Edward Barlow (1642–1705) ran away to sea at the age of 17. He became an apprentice on board HMS *Naseby*, an 80-gun, three-deck English naval ship commanded by Sir Edward Montagu. During Barlow's second year at sea, the *Naseby* sailed over to the Netherlands to bring Charles II back to England, thereby restoring the monarchy after the English Civil War.

Barlow enjoyed a long career of adventure, surviving several shipwrecks, skirmishing with Barbary pirates, and fighting in the Second Dutch War. He traveled to Brazil, Jamaica, and China and was captured by the Dutch in Batavia (modern-day Jakarta, Indonesia) in 1671. While in captivity, he began to write the first installments of his journal.

Far from romanticizing a sailor's life, Barlow writes of "abuse, hardships and a life little better than a slave." He describes the difficulty of finding work in England, and at times struggles to afford even shelter. In a small town near Falmouth, he spends a night knocking on strangers' doors begging for lodging. His gritty written account is supplemented by wonderful illustrations of

> ❝ At last there arrived a ship which had loaded at Barbados … and having been out of Barbados for two days, did meet with a "harey-cane" or storm of wind, which blew so fiercely, and continued so long that she was forced to cut her mainmast and mizenmast by the board, having much water in the hold, which had spoil'd all the lower tier of sugar and done them a great deal of damage; and she was forced to bear up for Jamaica to repair again and get a new mast. ❞

DIARY OF EDWARD BARLOW

lands beyond English shores and of sea creatures that he encounters. Although he was not the most skilled of artists, his drawings have great charm and dynamism, with ships being capsized, sharks devouring men, and natives riding elephants.

In 1705, when he was the captain of his own ship, Barlow died in the same dramatic fashion in which he had lived, lost with his ship off Mozambique. His journal survived because he had left it with his wife before setting sail for the last time.

In context

▲ **ACTION ON THE BARBARY COAST** In 1661, Barlow sailed again under Sir Edward Montagu to Algiers, one of the home ports of the Barbary pirates. These raiders captured merchant ships, stealing their goods and selling their crews into slavery. The expedition intended to halt the pirates, whether by negotiation or force.

▶ **LIFE AT SEA** Barlow makes it clear that being a sailor was a risky profession. Injuries and fatalities could be caused by falls from the rigging, and even minor cuts might lead to infections and possible amputations. Poor diet often resulted in disease, particularly scurvy.

hauing: but Downe ouer Mison Mast and The Shipe by godes great Marcey
bearing vp and the windes and waues Somthing abating wee Looked out for the other
Two Shipes the Loyall Suggett and the honiball but wee Could not See aney
of them and geting ouer Maine Top Mast Doune vp on Deak for to fish and
Mende it by Reason that wee had: Cut into it before Shee bore vp to Cut it down
and hoising ouer Maine yard wee Set ouer Maine Saile and brought ouer Shipe to the winde
and Sett in ouer Sprit Saile and fore Saile and Let her Lie a trie vnder ouer Maine Saile
and pumping all the water out hauing had fiue fote water in the houlde and it begining to
bee More Moerate wether and wee Still Looking out for the other Shipes but wee Coulse
haue noe Sight of them and Two dayes after wee had a faire winde and geting ouer Top mast
vp againe wee Steard away ouer Cours for the Cape of good hope west South west and Onoor
three Dayes after wee got vp another Mison mast which wee had made of a Spare top mast

► STORMY SEAS Barlow's
account is full of the perils of
the seas. He recounts many
instances of men dying from
sickness, in accidents, or during
sea battles. Here, he depicts
the *Experiment* losing one of
its masts in a storm while
traveling to the East Indies.

The text above the
illustration is a ballad
proclaiming the strength
of the tempest

This is an imagined
view of the *Experiment*
as Barlow was on
board the ship during
the storm

Which wee had me torde but wee faire winde Continiued not Longe with vs for one the Munday
folowing wee Met with a hard gale of winde which Continiued with vs three or fore Day es and
otherwise three Mondayes one after an other wee had very foure wether at Sea: hauing more
Capable winde wee Came into the Latitude of thertey Six Degrees and Judging that wee were
vp on the Sounings that Lie of from the Cape Lande wee Sounded and founde nintey fadons
So wee knowe that wee wwere not far from the Cape but hauing Crost windes wee Coulse
not haue the Sight of it and not Longe after wee had a faire winde againe and being soe
To the northward of the Cape wee Steard ouer Cours north west and by north and north
west for the Ilande of Saint helena for there wee did intende to Touch and goe Soe

Barlow's handwriting
is remarkably neat
despite his lack
of education

▶ **FIRST PAGE** Pepys's diary, written in shorthand, opens at the start of 1660 with a preamble that covers a range of topics, from the state of his health and finances to the delay of his wife's period and the troubled English political scene. It was written in a notebook bought at a stationer's, and the top and left margins were drawn by Pepys himself with red ink and a ruler.

The entry is dual dated "1659/60" since the start of the year was not always recognized as January 1. Another "Civil Year" started later on March 25

The general "Lord Lambert" is written in a combination of both shorthand and ordinary handwriting

> " Blessed be God, at the end of last year I was in very good health, without any sense of my old pain but upon taking of cold. I lived in Axe yard, having my wife and servant Jane, and no more in family than us three. My wife, after the absence of her terms for seven weeks, gave me hopes of her being with child, but on the last day of the year she hath them again.… The new Common Council of the City doth speak very high; and hath sent to Monke their sword-bearer, to acquaint him with their desire for a free and full Parliament.… My own private condition very handsome; and esteemed rich, but endeed [indeed] very poor.… "

PEPYS'S DIARY, PREAMBLE, 1660

A Private Eye

1660–1669 ▪ PEN AND INK ON PAPER ▪ SIX MANUSCRIPTS ▪ ENGLISH

SAMUEL PEPYS: NAVAL ADMINISTRATOR

The daily journal kept by Samuel Pepys from January 1, 1660, to May 31, 1669, is both a remarkable record of a turbulent period in English history and a frank self-portrait of unparalleled honesty. Pepys takes us into the most intimate secrets of his childless marriage and his sordid infidelities in the same plain manner that he describes encounters with the king or major public events. Typically, a fine narrative description of the coronation of Charles II in 1661 ends with Pepys blind drunk, waking up the next morning covered in his own vomit.

The man who kept this unique journal was born in 1633, the son of a modest London tailor. Equipped with a good education from St. Paul's School and Cambridge University, he made a marriage of love in 1655 to a 15-year-old Huguenot exile from France, Elizabeth Marchant de Saint Michel. The couple's early years were penurious, but Pepys's energy and talent—and the patronage of his distant cousin, Edward Montagu, the Earl of Sandwich, eventually helped him rise to an important administrative position at the navy board.

No one knows why Pepys chose to begin a diary in 1660, but he certainly wrote for his own eyes only. We are plunged into the minutiae of his daily routines of work and leisure, the details of his household and his finances, his worries, and his pleasures. His frankness about delighting in his growing wealth, for which he regularly thanks God, is almost as startling as his detailed descriptions of his sex life. There are no formal character portraits, but sudden flashes of significant observation make individuals leap out from the pages.

Public events are especially prominent in the first years in which Pepys kept the diary, when he was able to observe at close quarters the end of the Commonwealth and the restoration of the monarchy. By 1665, when London was gripped by a plague of smallpox that killed about a quarter of the population, the diary is so absorbed in Pepys's buoyant career and active private life that the epidemic appears as little more than a grim background. In July 1665, he writes of "the greatest glut of success that ever I had; only, under some difficulty because of the plague."

> " **The truth is,** I do **indulge myself** a little the more **in pleasure,** knowing that **this is the proper age** of my life to do it. "
>
> **PEPYS'S DIARY, MARCH 10, 1666**

THE RESTORATION OF CHARLES II

In 1649, King Charles I was executed after being defeated in a civil war, and England became a republican Commonwealth, ruled from 1653–1658 by Lord Protector Oliver Cromwell. The death of Cromwell in 1658 left a power vacuum uncomfortably filled by his weak son, Richard. Plots were soon afoot to restore the monarchy. In 1660, Pepys traveled with a deputation sent to bring Charles I's eldest son back from exile in the Netherlands. Installed on the throne as Charles II, the new king set the tone for the Restoration period, a hedonistic reaction against Puritanism. Although Pepys was often critical of the king's frivolity, he benefitted from royal favor and faithfully served the restored monarchy.

▲ *Charles II Processing from the Tower of London to Westminster, 22 April 1661,* Dirck Stoop

Later years

In 1666, Pepys witnessed the Great Fire that destroyed much of the city of London. The following year brought naval disaster in the Dutch raid on Chatham. Pepys's diary condemns the king, described as "a lazy prince" who only "doth follow the women," his whole family "in horrible disorder by being in debt." But Pepys's own home life was not a model one. In October 1668, he was caught by his wife in intimate embrace with a young housemaid—an event that had a dramatic impact on their marriage.

At the end of May 1669, Pepys stopped writing in his diary, believing that the strain of the writing was making him go blind. But he did not lose his sight and continued to pursue an eventful career. He was promoted to Chief Secretary of the Admiralty and elected president of the Royal Society; twice he was imprisoned by his political enemies on trumped-up charges; and he was definitively sidelined after the fall of the Stuart monarchy in 1688. After Pepys's death in 1703, his diary languished forgotten in a Cambridge library until it was transcribed in 1819. A complete, uncensored edition did not appear until 1970. An important historical document, the manuscript of the diary is now housed at Magdalene College, Cambridge University.

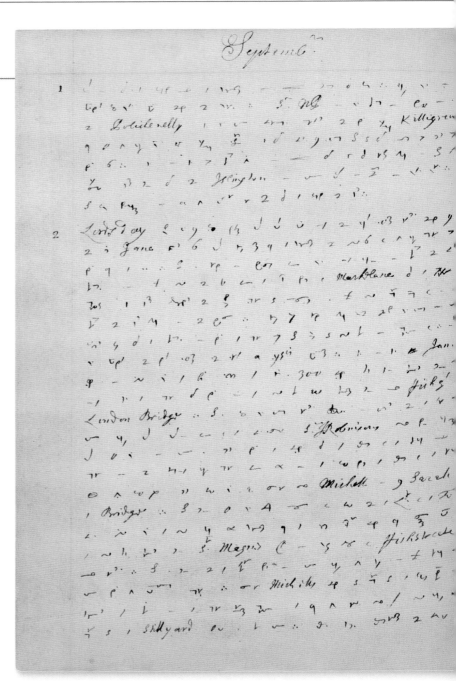

▶ **WITNESS OF THE FIRE** Pepys's vivid eyewitness account of the last day of the Great Fire, September 6, 1666, is written in the same neat, precise hand as the rest of his diary. The use of shorthand served to protect the startlingly frank journal from prying eyes, although Pepys also resorted to foreign words to cloak his most sexually explicit passages.

ENGLAND FIGHTING THE DUTCH

In the mid-17th century, England and the Dutch Republic were competing for command of the seas. Open warfare broke out in 1665, bringing major engagements such as the Four Days' Battle in which more than 150 ships took part. The war ended in disaster for the English in 1667, when Dutch ships successfully raided the naval docks at Chatham, raising fears of an attack on London. Only a humiliating peace agreement saved England from further losses. As a senior figure in naval administration, Pepys had to rebut accusations of incompetence and corruption. In his diary, he blames the defeat on the king's refusal to fund the fleet adequately. Later raised to Chief Secretary of the Admiralty, Pepys is credited with placing the navy on a more professional footing.

▶ *The Battle of Terheide*, Jan Abraham, 1653–66

▲ **THE GREAT FIRE** In the first week of September 1666, a fire that started at a bakery on Pudding Lane swept through the closely packed old city of London, destroying the medieval St. Paul's Cathedral, almost 90 other churches, and 13,000 houses. Pepys was the first person to report the fire to the king and urged that buildings should be demolished to create firebreaks.

Much of the diary is written in shorthand, making it hard to read

Some words, written in full, denote names, places, or words that were difficult to convert into shorthand

❝ So I down to the waterside, and there got a boat and through the bridge, and there saw a lamentable fire.... Everybody endeavouring to remove their goods, and flinging into the River or bringing them into lighters that lay off. Poor people staying in their houses as long as till the very fire touched them, and then running into boats or clambering from one pair of stair by the waterside to another. And among other things, the poor pigeons I perceive were loath to leave their houses, but hovered about the windows and balconies till they were some of them burned, their wings, and fell down. ❞

PEPYS'S DIARY, SEPTEMBER 2, 1666

▲ **COFFEE HOUSE CULTURE** In Pepys's day, coffee houses were a novelty in London life. From the 1650s onward, they provided civilized venues where the city's male elite could meet to gossip and discuss ideas. Pepys visited coffee houses several times a week, but he also continued to frequent old-style taverns, which were notorious sites of drunkenness and dissipation.

The Kangxi Emperor's Diary

1671–1722 ▪ INK ON PAPER ▪ CHINESE

VARIOUS SCRIBES

For most of China's long history, there was only one diary of significance: the account of the daily activities of the Chinese emperor. In Chinese society, the emperor was considered the Son of Heaven and the absolute ruler of all on Earth. His daily words and actions, large and small, constituted the official history of China. The tradition of the imperial diaries, or *qijuzhu*, began as early as the Han Dynasty (206BCE–9CE and 25–220CE), and it was maintained into the 20th century. The emperor never wrote the diaries himself; instead, there were scribes (*shi*) who recorded his daily activities. At one point during the Han era, the task was taken over by female officials, while the Tang court (618–90CE, 705–907CE) employed an imperial diarist. During the Ming period (1368–1644), the duty passed to members of the Hanlin Academy, a group of scholars who served the court.

In 1671, during the early years of the reign of the Kangxi Emperor, officials founded the Office of the Imperial Diary. The Kangxi Emperor was the fourth emperor of the Qing Dynasty (1636–1912), and his reign of 61 years (1661–1722) was one of the longest in Chinese history. His rule was marked by territorial expansion, relative wealth and stability, and a flourishing literary tradition. The activities of the Kangxi Emperor, like those of the emperors who came before him, were assiduously recorded. The records covered not only the emperor's private life but also details of ministerial meetings, diplomatic activities, and all other affairs of state. The term used for these documents was "diaries of action and repose."

After the emperor's death, the notes were edited into an official history of his reign, known as the "Veritable Records." The diaries of action and repose of the Qing Dynasty, including those of the Kangxi Emperor, are relatively complete, but those of most of the other dynasties have been lost.

In context

▲ **TOUR OF THE SOUTHERN PROVINCES** In 1689, the Kangxi Emperor embarked on a tour of the southern provinces of China, a journey of more than 2,000 miles (3,200 km), to inspect the territory. As part of the tour, he climbed to the top of Mount Tai, a site sacred to adherents of Buddhism, Confucianism, and Daoism. The tour was recorded in the official diaries and commemorated in a series of 12 finely detailed painted scrolls.

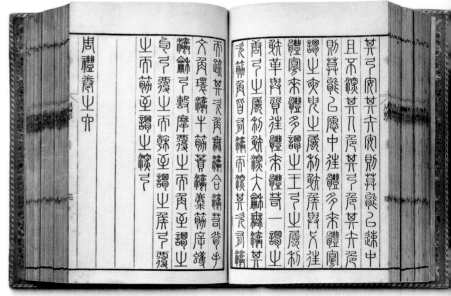

▲ **A LITERARY COURT** During his reign, the Kangxi Emperor, an enduring supporter of literature, commissioned many books. The most notable of these was the Kangxi Dictionary, which served as the standard Chinese dictionary during the 18th and 19th centuries. The book shown here is an imperial edition of the "Six Classics" commissioned by the Kangxi Emperor, which is a collection of foundational Confucian texts.

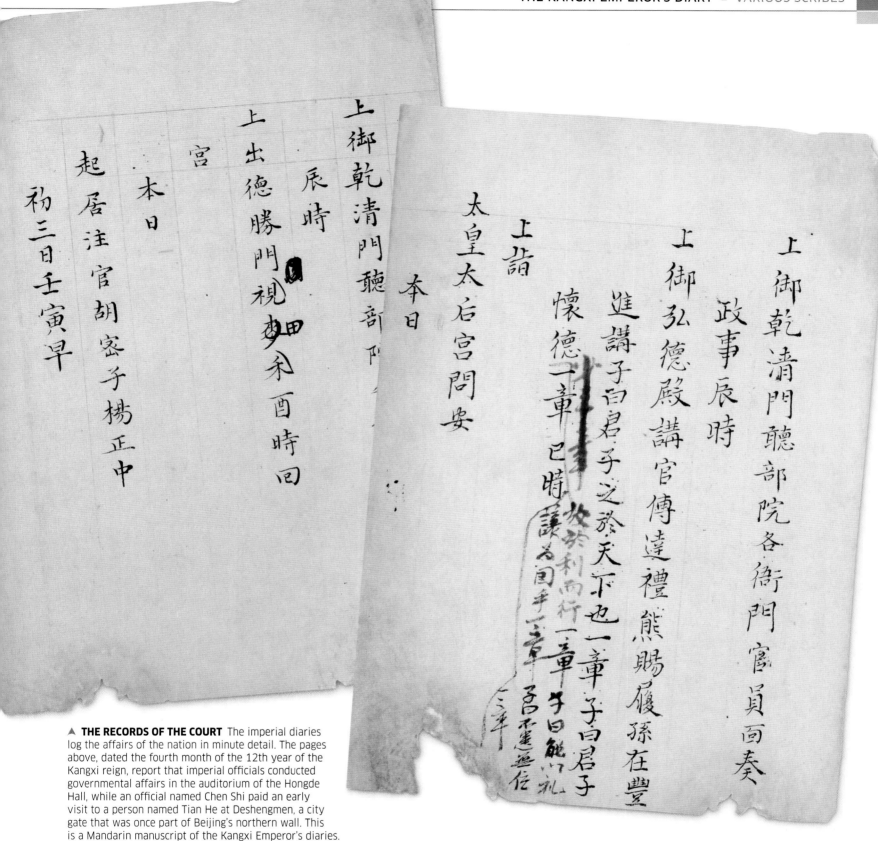

初三日壬寅早

起居注官胡密子楊正中

本日

宮

上出德勝門視◻田禾百時回

辰時

上御乾清門聽部阮

本日

太皇太后宮問安

上詣

懷德一章巳時議為回手一章

進講子曰君子之於天下也一章

上御弘德殿講官傅達禮熊賜履孫在豐

政事辰時

上御乾清門聽部院各衙門官員面奏

▲ **THE RECORDS OF THE COURT** The imperial diaries log the affairs of the nation in minute detail. The pages above, dated the fourth month of the 12th year of the Kangxi reign, report that imperial officials conducted governmental affairs in the auditorium of the Hongde Hall, while an official named Chen Shi paid an early visit to a person named Tian He at Deshengmen, a city gate that was once part of Beijing's northern wall. This is a Mandarin manuscript of the Kangxi Emperor's diaries.

" Now seeing its social customs, in general they [merely] valorize empty ostentation and leisurely ease. Those who engage in commerce are legion, while those who till the fields are few, all of which results in lavish and wealthy households, but also superficial and duplicitous social relations. Those serving as local officials should encourage the elimination of extravagance and a return to simplicity. All attention and energy should be devoted to agriculture, only then will each houseful have sufficient means and the decadent mood be reversed. Then gradually after some time, there will be happiness and harmony. "

THE KANGXI EMPEROR ON SUZHOU CITY, QUOTED IN HIS IMPERIAL DIARIES, DECEMBER 3, 1684

Letters of a Devoted Mother

1671–1696 ▪ PEN AND INK ON PAPER ▪ 1,120 KNOWN LETTERS ▪ FRENCH

MADAME DE SÉVIGNÉ: ARISTOCRAT

Warm, witty, and wise, the letters of Madame de Sévigné paint an engaging portrait of aristocratic life in the age of Louis XIV, the Sun King. The writer, born Marie de Rabutin-Chantal in Paris in 1626, came from a distinguished family and had an excellent education. At the age of 18, she married the Marquis de Sévigné, who proved a violent and unfaithful husband. After his death in a duel in 1651, she was not tempted to marry again and devoted herself to raising her son and daughter.

Letters written by de Sévigné to her Parisian friends and relatives date as far back as 1648, but her correspondence took on its full dimensions only after her daughter, Madame de Grignan, moved with her husband to distant Provence in 1671. A doting mother, de Sévigné wrote a stream of letters to her daughter expressing not only her maternal anxieties but also her wider interests and sentiments. Philosophical and moral reflections jostle with anecdotes about marital infidelity, mistresses, impotence, and homosexuality. Spending much of her time at Livry, outside Paris, or in Brittany, she expresses her great delight in nature and solitude with a sensibility that foreshadows Romanticism. She also recounts dramatic events of the day, including some she witnessed herself, such as the execution of the notorious poisoner the Marquise de Brinvilliers

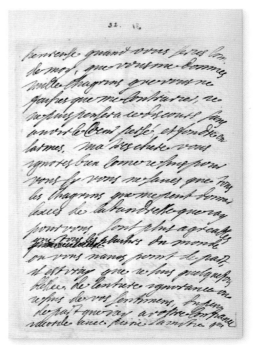

◀ **WRITTEN WITH ÉLAN**
Madame de Sévigné dashed off her correspondence in a spontaneous style, writing as she spoke. She sometimes apologizes for the length of her letters, which move effortlessly from personal matters to descriptions of public events. She wrote that she broke five or six quill pens a day and bemoaned her lack of expertise at sharpening them.

in 1676. De Sévigné's correspondence with her daughter continued until the writer's death in 1696. Copies of her letters were circulated to select readers during her lifetime, and her granddaughter published the first substantial posthumous selection of them in 1734. They have been admired ever since as models of French prose, and a brilliantly witty and incisive portrayal of 17th-century France.

In context

◀ **PORTRAIT OF A DAUGHTER**
Madame de Sévigné's beloved daughter Françoise-Marguerite (1646–1705) was considered a great beauty when she was presented at court in her youth. In contrast to her mother, she was vain and unemotional. In 1669, she married the Comte de Grignan, twice widowed and 14 years her senior, after which she lived at his castle in Provence in the South of France.

◀ **DE SÉVIGNÉ'S DESK**
When she was staying at Les Rochers in Brittany, Madame de Sévigné wrote her letters at this exquisite Chinese lacquered desk. Its quality reflects the refined taste of her milieu, which included such notable figures as the Duc de la Rochefoucauld, author of famous maxims, and Madame de la Fayette, France's first novelist.

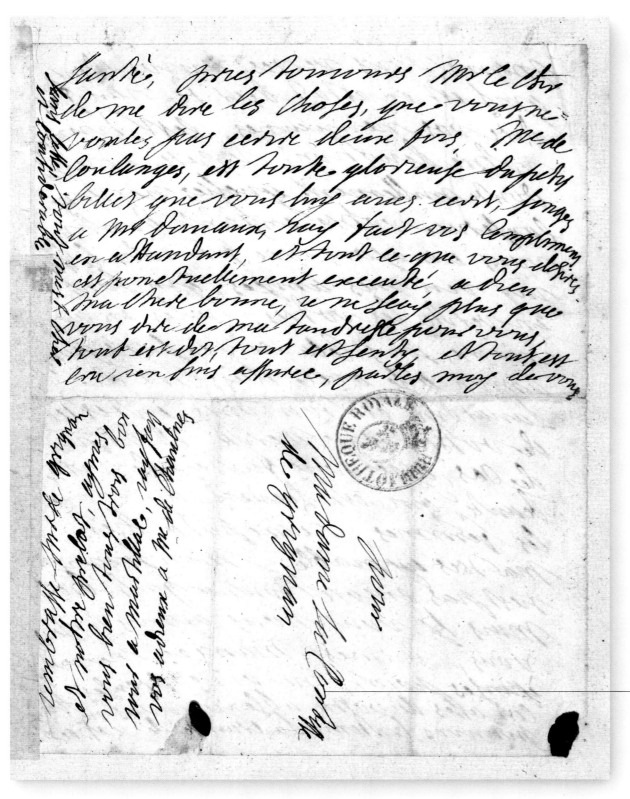

> **My life** and **sole pleasure** is the **correspondence** I **keep up** with you; all other things are far behind.

LETTER TO MADAME DE GRIGNAN, JANUARY 20, 1672

◄ **LETTER TO A DAUGHTER** Of the 1,120 letters currently known to have been written by Madame de Sévigné, 764 were addressed to her daughter, Madame de Grignan. This is one of the few original letters signed by de Sévigné that have survived. A large stash of manuscript copies of the correspondence was found in an antique shop in 1873.

De Sévigné included her daughter's nobility title, *Comtesse* (Countess), in the letter's address

> Long journeys are strange things. If we were always feeling as we do at the end of them we should never leave the spot where we are. But Providence bestows forgetfulness, the same that helps women over childbirth. God bestows this forgetfulness so that the world should not come to an end and one should undertake journeys to Provence. The one I shall make will give me the greatest joy I can have in my life, but how sad a thought to see no end to your stay there … Sometimes in these woods I go off into reveries of such gloom that I come back more shaken than if I had had the fever.

LETTER TO MADAME DE GRIGNAN, MAY 31, 1671

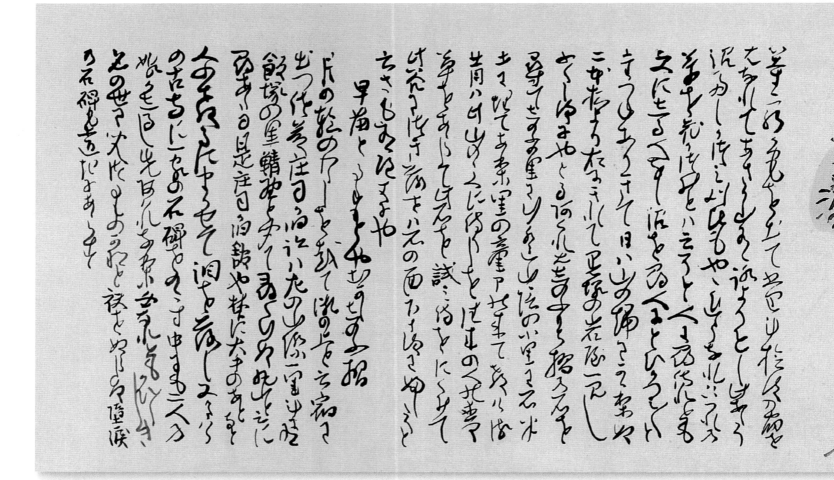

A Poet's Journey

1689-1694 ■ INK ON PAPER ■ JAPANESE

MATSUO BASHŌ: POET

One of the greatest poets of the Edo period in Japan, Matsuo Bashō (1644–1694) devoted himself to poetry after working as a servant to a young samurai. In the 1680s and '90s, he set out on a series of journeys by foot through the Japanese countryside. His most famous trips were to northern Japan, a region that few people knew at the time. Bashō's main reason for traveling was to follow in the steps of earlier great poets, in the hope of improving his own work.

Bashō wrote accounts of these trips, creating a series of journals or travelogues written in a combination of prose and poetry. *Oku no Hosomichi* (*The Narrow Road to the Deep North*), his best-known journal, conveys his reactions and poetic responses to the beauty of the often remote countryside. His verses describe birds such as the cuckoo and the crane, evoke the blossom of chestnut and cherry trees, and recount the

weather, from the gathering rains to the faint smell of the snow. Bashō also talks about the people he comes across along the way, from workers in a silkworm nursery and rice farmers to other writers, and mentions numerous historical figures connected with the places that he visits—the noble occupants of a house, for example, or the founders of temples. He was often in isolated areas and recorded the difficulties of traveling on foot in the mountains, and the uncomfortable accommodations— one haiku describes being bitten by fleas and sleeping in a bed next to a urinating horse. Episodes like this are told with gentle humor, but Bashō also meets a local man who tells him that he has been lucky to travel through the mountains safely, without having had an accident. Bashō revised his travel journals for five years after returning home so that other people could read them. They are now recognized as classics around the world.

◄ **OKU NO HOSOMICHI** Bashō's work has inspired many other poets and artists, including the 18th-century calligrapher Yosa Buson, who made this illustrated copy of it. The section shown describes Bashō's visit to a rock where cloth workers dyed their fabric. Bashō was told that the rock had been moved from another site because visitors trampled on the nearby rice crop. The text contains a haiku about the rice planters.

Bashō passed a place where a priest lived in a house in a remote spot beneath a chestnut tree

> 66
> I was told that the old seed of linked verse once strewn [in Ōishida] by the scattering winds had taken root, still bearing its own flowers each year and thus softening the minds of the rough villagers like the clear notes of a reed pipe, but that these rural poets were now struggling to find their way in the forest of error ... for there was no one to guide them. At their request, therefore, I sat with them to compose a book of linked verse, and left it behind me as a gift. It was indeed a great pleasure for me to be of such help during my wandering journey.
> 99

BASHŌ, *THE NARROW ROAD TO THE DEEP NORTH*

◄ **SORA** The poet Kawai Sora (1649–1710), a friend of Bashō's, joined him on his journey to northern Japan. Sora kept his own diary, recording both this expedition and another journey that he later made, and transcribed some of Bashō's poems in his book. It is important because it preserved Bashō's work and fleshed out the details of their travels.

Sora is standing on the right in this illustration

BASHŌ'S **POETRY**

Bashō is best known for his haikus—three-line poems in which the first and last lines have five syllables and the middle line seven. This was already an established form, but with Bashō it reached new heights. He could sum up a landscape and his emotional response to it in very few words and was able to condense his thoughts about the meaning of life into simple verses. He became famous for collaborating with other poets to create linked verses known as *renga*. In the travel journals, Bashō combined haiku with prose to create a new form, called *haibun*. The prose passages gave Bashō more space to reflect about landscapes, people, and the passing of time, as symbolized by the eternal but ever-changing beauty of natural phenomena such as the moon.

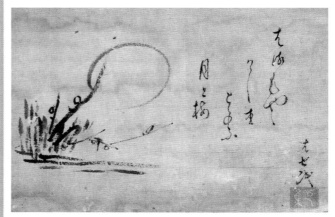

▲ **Tsuki to Ume** (*Moon and Plum Blossoms*) with haiku, Matsuo Bashō, 1693

At the Court of the Sun King

1694-1723 ▪ PEN AND INK ON PAPER ▪ 2,300 PAGES ▪ FRENCH

DUC DE SAINT-SIMON: ARISTOCRAT

The Duc de Saint-Simon's *Memoirs of Louis XIV and His Court and of the Regency* presents a critical insider view of the French monarchy and court aristocracy in the age of the Sun King. Covering the period from 1694 to 1723, the memoirs revel in the follies and vices of a court obsessed by minutiae of status, rife with political and sexual intrigue, and subject to the whims of an absolute monarch.

Born Louis de Rouvroy in 1675, Saint-Simon inherited the ducal title at the age of 18, admitting him to the cream of the French nobility. He served with the king's elite musketeers before settling into a luxurious apartment at the newly-built royal Palace of Versailles with an adored wife. There he set down the shrewd, merciless observations of court life that would later form the basis for his memoirs, keeping his notes a close secret as they would certainly have displeased the king.

Never one of Louis XIV's favorites, Saint-Simon found opportunity for advancement after the king's death in 1715. During the regency of the Duc d'Orléans, he served as a member of the ruling council and as an ambassador to Spain. In 1723, he retired to his chateau at La Ferté-Vidame, north of Paris, to concentrate on his memoirs. He died in 1755 with the work finished but unpublished.

Writing in a lively, vigorous style much admired as an example of French prose, Saint-Simon combined a astute chronicle of major historical events with vivid character portraits, details of everyday life at court, accounts of public scandals, and scurrilous gossip. His anecdotes of the eccentricities, petty cruelties, and snobberies of his cast of royals and courtiers are often outrageously funny, but he never loses his moral perspective, based on Catholic values and the traditional social order, which lends weight to his satirical barbs. When the memoirs were first published in their entirety in 1829, they were hailed as an unequalled portrayal of a lost age.

In context

◄ **ROYAL RESIDENCE** The vast royal Palace of Versailles, with its formal gardens and fountains, was created by Louis XIV as a setting for his court and a tribute to his own greatness. Saint-Simon dismisses it as "the dullest and most ungrateful of all palaces," writing that "the gardens astonish by their magnificence, but cause regret by their bad taste."

► **THE SUN KING** Coming to the throne as an infant in 1643, Louis XIV reigned for 72 years. He created a strong, centralized state that he ruled as an absolute monarch, but his extravagance and his wars impoverished the country. Although a harsh critic of the Sun King, Saint-Simon nonetheless praises his appearance—"the majestic and natural charm of all his person."

Each volume is bound in a leather portfolio

I will … speak of myself with the same truthfulness I speak of others.

***MEMOIRS OF LOUIS XIV AND HIS COURT AND OF THE REGENCY*, CHAPTER 56**

Occasional notes in the margins summarize the contents of each section

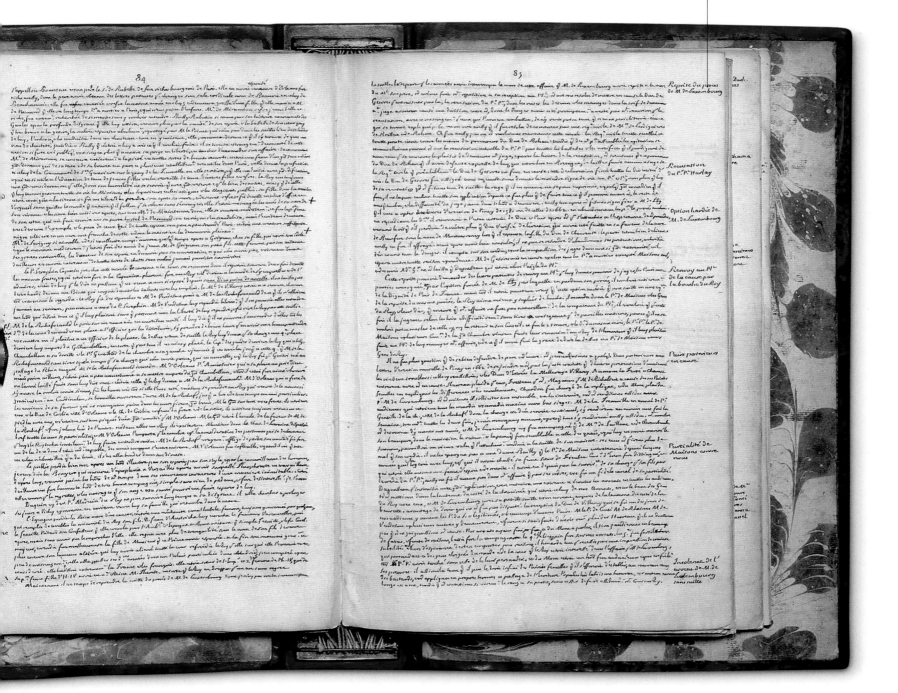

▲ **SUBVERSIVE TEXT** The original manuscript of Saint-Simon's *Memoirs* consists of 2,300 pages enclosed in 11 leather portfolios. Written in a small, neat hand, the text is remarkably clean and legible, with few erasures or insertions. Considered potentially damaging to the monarchy, the manuscript was seized by the state after Saint-Simon's death and kept under lock and key until it was returned to his heirs in 1819.

[The King] liked nobody to be in any way superior to him. Thus he chose his ministers, not for their knowledge, but for their ignorance…. He unceasingly occupied himself with the most petty details of his troops, his household, his mansions; would even instruct his cooks, who received, like novices, lessons they had known … for years. This vanity, this unmeasured and unreasonable love of admiration, was his ruin.

***MEMOIRS OF LOUIS XIV AND HIS COURT AND OF THE REGENCY*, CHAPTER 73**

Directory: 1500-1700

▼ ADRIAEN COENEN'S FISH BOOK

DUTCH (1577-1579)

Adriaen Coenen (1514-1587) lived in the coastal village of Scheveningen. Throughout his life, he earned his living as a fisherman, a fish trader, and a salvager—he sold things that he found washed up on the shore. In the 1570s, by then an old man, Coenen started to produce illustrated manuscripts, combining handwritten text with watercolor paintings. Their subject was the creatures of the sea.

The largest and most famous of his books, the *Fish Book (Visboek)*, consists of 412 folio sheets and is preserved in The Hague. Coenen's manuscripts profile a wide range of sea creatures both real and imaginary—not only fish, invertebrates, and whales but mermaids and monsters, too. He earned considerable local renown, presenting one of his manuscripts to the Prince of Orange and exhibiting

others at fairs, where visitors paid to see them. Despite its fanciful element, his work was always grounded in the notes he took of his own experience of the sea and its creatures.

MONTAIGNE'S TRAVEL JOURNAL

FRENCH (1580-1581)

In June 1580, the humanist essayist and philosopher Michel de Montaigne (1533-1592) set off on a meandering trip to Italy via eastern France, Germany, Austria, and Switzerland. He was partly motivated by the search for a cure for painful kidney stones, requiring visits to spas, but chiefly by curiosity about the world. At first, he entrusted the task of recording the trip to a secretary, but later he wrote the journal himself, alternating between French and Italian. Ignoring the renowned beauties of art and nature, Montaigne sought out the

peculiarities of foreign customs and manners. His journal records local eating habits, the design of Swiss beds and stoves, and the conversation of Roman prostitutes. He describes a Jewish circumcision, a Protestant christening, a public execution, and an exorcism. After a lengthy stay in Italy, he returned to France in the fall of 1588 to take up the post of mayor of Bordeaux. His travel journal lay unnoticed in his chateau in the Dordogne until it was discovered in 1772. The original manuscript was then lost during the French Revolution, but fortunately printed editions had been published by then.

HENSLOWE'S DIARY

ENGLISH (1591-1609)

Philip Henslowe (c.1550-1616) was an entrepreneur who became the driving force behind the growth of the theater as an entertainment in

Elizabethan and Jacobean London. He built the Rose Theatre on Bankside, Southwark, in 1587 and, in 1600, founded the acting company known as the Admiral's Men, along with his son-in-law, the actor Edward Alleyn. From 1592 to 1609, Henslowe kept a record of his theatrical business activities. Economical with paper, he wrote it on the reverse side of the accounts of an ironworks in which he also had an interest. It includes personal comments on business matters as well as a record of payments and loans to playwrights and actors, purchases of costumes and props, and box-office receipts.

Famous dramatists who appear in his accounts include Christopher Marlowe, Ben Jonson, and John Webster, but not William Shakespeare. Highly practical, Henslowe's record provides an extraordinary insight into the practicalities of the stage at a period when theater blossomed in England. The papers were preserved in the library of Dulwich College, a school founded by Alleyn, and first published in the early 20th century.

THOMAS DALLAM'S DIARY

ENGLISH (1599-1600)

Lancashire-born Thomas Dallam was a young organ builder living in London when, in 1599, he was selected for an important diplomatic mission. He was to deliver a mechanical organ to Sultan Mehmet III, the ruler of the Turkish Ottoman Empire, as a gift from Elizabeth I. Departing on board the armed merchantman *Hector*, Dallam kept a diary of his eventful journey to the Ottoman capital Constantinople (Istanbul). He recorded a sea fight, sightings of whales and dolphins, a stay in the port of Algiers, and hobnobbing with shepherds on the Greek island of Zante. Once at the sultan's court, he assembled the remarkable organ, which played automatically four times a day and was topped by clockwork birds that sang in a silver holly bush. The sultan

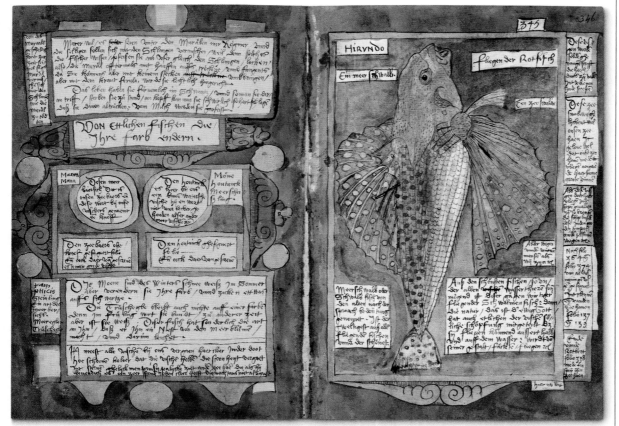

Illustration and description of a flying fish from Adriaen Coenen's *Visboek*

was so pleased with it that he offered Dallam two wives from his harem, a gift the organ builder reluctantly refused. On his return to England, Dallam wrote up his diary as "Travels with an Organ to the Grand Signieur." He went on to build some famous organs in England, but his travelogue was not published until 1893.

DIARY OF JOHN EVELYN

ENGLISH (1640–1706)

John Evelyn was a contemporary and friend of Samuel Pepys, England's most famous diarist, to whom he is often compared. Evelyn came from a higher social class than Pepys and was more learned. He began his diary as a Royalist exile living in Europe during the English Civil War. After the Restoration of the monarchy in 1660, he became a favorite of Charles II, a founding member of the Royal Society and the author of books on topics as diverse as forestry and architecture.

His diary's accounts of the historic events of this period, including the plague of 1665 and the Great Fire of London, are written in a clear, informative style, based on personal observation but lacking Pepys's immediacy. His character portraits of prominent personalities, including monarchs and royal mistresses, are always perceptive. The most personal element in Evelyn's diary is his moving expression of grief at the death of his 19-year-old daughter Mary in 1685. Continued until his death in 1706, the diary was first published in 1818 as *Memoirs Illustrative of the Life and Writings of John Evelyn*.

NEWTON'S NOTEBOOKS

ENGLISH (1661–1669)

The founder of modern physics, Isaac Newton, was born in eastern England in 1642. Admitted to the University of Cambridge in June 1661, he began keeping notes of his studies in a calf-bound writing book. Along with other notebooks, he wrote during his student years up to 1669, it provides an insight into the early development of his ideas about mathematics, physics, alchemy, and metaphysics.

Map depicting the island of Juan Fernandez, Chile, from *Journal of a South Sea Voyage* (1683)

Written in Latin, Greek, and English, the notebooks also have a personal side. A list of accounts shows how Newton spent his money, from buying a chamber pot and a chessboard to oranges and beer. A section in cryptic shorthand—not deciphered until 1964—reveals the religious, guilt-ridden side of his nature, listing sins that include "robbing my mother's box of plums and sugar" and "caring for worldly things more than God." Kept in various archives, the notebooks were made available online in 2011.

▲ BARTHOLOMEW SHARP'S DIARY

ENGLISH (1680–1682)

Bartholomew Sharp (c.1650–1702) was a buccaneering English sailor engaged in piracy in the West Indies. In 1680, he was among 331 men who set out to plunder the Spanish-held Pacific coast of South America. Sharp kept a daily log of the expedition, which he eventually led. He recorded how the buccaneers crossed Central

America on foot and then sailed southward in stolen Spanish ships. They failed to seize a hoard of Spanish treasure but caused mayhem by killing, burning, and pillaging along their way. When Sharp arrived back in the West Indies, having sailed around Cape Horn, he was arrested by the English authorities for piracy, as England was not at war with Spain at the time. Tried in England, he seemed destined to be hanged but succeeded in buying his freedom by handing over an invaluable Spanish sea chart. Sharp's diary was then written up in florid prose and circulated in various manuscript copies, one of which was presented to Charles II. Sharp returned to the West Indies and eventually died in prison.

THE JOURNAL OF FATHER SAMUEL FRITZ

CZECH (1689–1723)

Born in Bohemia in 1651, Samuel Fritz joined the Jesuit order and, in 1686, was sent as a missionary to

the Native Americans of the upper Amazon. From 1689, he kept a journal of his experiences living among the Omagua people, including an account of a 3,728-mile (6,000 km) trip that he made down the Amazon in a canoe in search of a treatment for malaria. His missionary task was complicated by conflict between the Spanish Viceroyalty of Peru, to which he gave allegiance, and Portuguese-ruled Brazil, which contested the Omagua territory. He was at one time imprisoned by the Portuguese.

Fritz describes how the Omaguas worshipped him as a figure with magical powers to begin with but then revolted against his authority. In 1704, he was promoted to Jesuit Superior and left the Omaguas, whose society was destroyed over the following years. In 1712, he returned to South America as a missionary and lived with Native Americans until his death in around 1725. Excerpts from his journal, with a commentary by an anonymous Jesuit, were first published in 1738. Fritz is also famous for having drafted the first accurate map of the Amazon.

3

1700—1800

During the Enlightenment, there was a crop of journals from distinguished figures such as the German writer Goethe, Spanish artist Goya, and Austrian composer Mozart. In Britain, James Boswell wrote an intimate diary of London life in which he portrayed many of the leading figures of the time. Curiosity about the world inspired expeditions of scientific discovery, such as Captain Cook's voyages in the Pacific and Alexander von Humboldt's journeys through the Americas, which required accurate records. As Europeans colonized the world, Asian observers, including Ananda Ranga Pillai, an Indian official, recorded their own view of these momentous changes. The American War of Independence and people's experience of everyday life in the newly founded United States inspired diaries at all levels of society.

A Journey to Lapland

1732-1741 ▪ PEN AND INK ON PAPER ▪ 191 PAGES ▪ SWEDISH

CARL LINNAEUS: BOTANIST

In May 1732, the botanist Carl Linnaeus (1707–1778) began a 1,423-mile (2,000-km) journey to Lapland in northern Scandinavia. Over the course of more than five months' traveling, he hoped to find species of plants and animals that were new to science, locate valuable minerals, and observe the life and customs of the local Sami people.

Linnaeus kept a journal all the while, describing three expeditions that he made inland during his journey. Each one involved a long trek, traveling by horse and on foot from a town on the coast of the Gulf of Bothnia, the northern arm of the Baltic Sea. The journal details the discovery of around 100 plants that had not previously been recorded, an impressive total because Lapland is not especially biodiverse. It also describes encounters with the Sami, whose remote home meant that little was known about them and their culture in the world outside.

Linnaeus had a clear, direct style of writing and recorded the facts precisely, but he also included evocative passages, describing the blossom of the bog rosemary, for example, as having the

color of "a fine female complexion." This blend of objective, scientific clarity and subjective, picturesque language conveys a strong sense of Linnaeus as an individual, one thing that makes the journal so interesting.

Another special feature is the careful, closely observed drawings of plants and animals and the topographical maps that Linnaeus made of his travels, marking mountains, rivers, and lakes. The Lapland journal was groundbreaking because of Linnaeus's precise observations, his meticulous drawings, and the new information that he collated about the people who lived in the region. He used this data in his important scientific work, both in his book *Flora Lapponica*, about the plants of Lapland, and when he was developing his famous system of classification for living organisms, which scientists still use to name plants and animals today.

> ➤ **CLOSE OBSERVATIONS** Although Linnaeus drew swiftly, using relatively few marks, the illustrations in the journal capture the essential characteristics of their subjects well. Linnaeus made quick sketches of birds, insects, leaves, flowers, seed heads, and interesting tools or artifacts that he came across. The bird on the right-hand page is a northern hawk-owl (*Surnia ulula*) that he shot down.

Linnaeus wrote fast, and his italic handwriting is sometimes difficult to decipher—he wrote the journal primarily for his own personal use

> 66 We observed a dense cloud to the northeast. It was visible both above and below us, and at length approached us in the form of a thick mist, which moistened our clothes, and rendered even our hair thoroughly wet.... We could neither see sun nor moon, nor the summits of the neighboring hills. We knew not whither to turn our steps, fearing on the one hand to fall down a precipice and lose our lives, as actually happened, a few years ago, to a Laplander under the same circumstances; or on the other to be plunged into the alpine torrent, which had worn so deep a channel through the snow, as to make any one giddy, looking upon it from above. We could now not distinguish any thing a couple of ells [meters] before us. Our situation was like that of an unskillful mariner at sea without a compass, out of sight of land, and surrounded by hidden rocks on every side. 99

CARL LINNAEUS, *LACHESIS LAPPONICA*, 1811

► FLORA LAPPONICA Linnaeus's book about the plants of Lapland was published in 1737. Compiled from the information he had gathered on his journey to northern Scandinavia, it contains details of around 540 plants. It is sometimes called the first modern botanical work because it names plants using the system of classification that Linnaeus had developed.

The journal contains sketches of tools used by the Sami, like this cylindrical trap made of twigs for catching fish

In context

Linnaeus did not publish his Lapland journal but used it as reference for the scientific works that he did publish, such as the *Flora Lapponica*. He kept the manuscript of the journal in his library, together with his other manuscripts and the books, letters, and numerous specimens of plants that he had collected on his travels. In 1787, a few years after Linnaeus's death, a British medical student, James Edward Smith, recognized the importance of the scientist's collection and was concerned that part of it had been inadequately cared for. Linnaeus had been unable to look after it properly in his old age, and some of the specimens had been damaged by moths and mice.

Smith bought almost the entire collection from Linnaeus's widow and took it to London. A year later, he founded the Linnaean Society of London (now the world's oldest natural history society) and passed the scientist's papers on to the society, which still preserves them today. Smith was also responsible for publishing the Lapland journal. He made an English translation, which came out in 1811, making it possible at last for many people to appreciate its unique contribution to science.

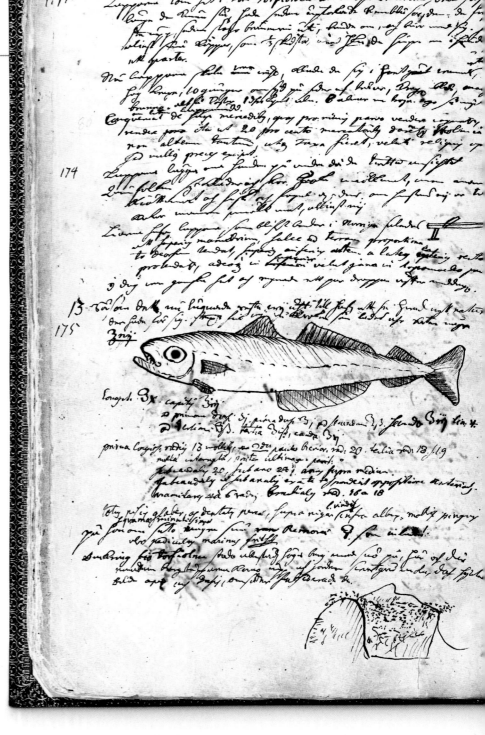

◀ **PERSONAL EMBLEM** En route to Lapland, Linnaeus gathered an elegant specimen of the twinflower—a plant he was particularly fond of and which would later be named after him, *Linnaea borealis*. The flower was said to resemble him because it was small and often overlooked. When he became a member of the Swedish nobility in 1757, he decided to adopt the plant as his personal emblem.

▶ **THE SAMI** Linnaeus spent a lot of time with the Sami on his journey. The journal records how he employed them as guides and interpreters and contains many notes about Sami houses, clothing, crafts, and boats. Linnaeus was also interested in the Sami's methods of healing and the medicines that they used.

◀ **ON THE COAST** On one of his expeditions, Linnaeus reached the coast of Norway. Here, the journal records that he fished from a boat and caught a number of saithe *(Gadus virens)*. His sketch of one of these fish appears on this page of the journal, and the clarity of the drawing makes the fish easy to identify. He reported that several specimens had remora (suckerfish) attached to them.

This sketch shows how the local people trapped salmon in the mouth of a small cove

LINNAEAN **CLASSIFICATION**

Linnaeus developed a system of classifying the natural world by using different groupings arranged in a hierarchy. Three large groups, called kingdoms, contained all the animals, plants, and minerals, respectively. The plant kingdom, for example, was then divided into smaller groups, called classes, each of which contained several orders, made up of genera composed of separate species. Linnaeus gave each species a unique Latin name made up of two parts, one denoting the genus and the other the species. He classified species by studying how they differed. For plants, for example, he looked at the number and the arrangement of their sexual parts (stamens). Although the system has evolved since Linnaeus's time, scientists still use a similar method of classification.

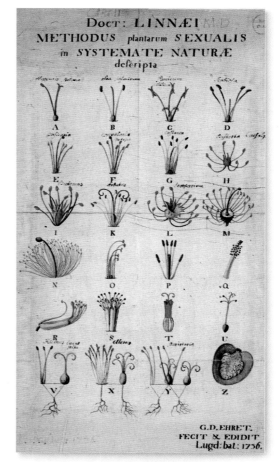

▲ **The sexual system of plants,** illustrated by Georg Ehret in *Genera Plantarum,* 1737

> ❝ I do **not know** how **the world** could **persist gracefully** if but a **single animal** species were to **vanish** from it. ❞

LINNAEUS'S JOURNAL, c.1760

Life in Pondicherry

1736-1761 ▪ PEN AND INK ON PAPER ▪ 12 PUBLISHED VOLUMES ▪ TAMIL

ANANDA RANGA PILLAI: CHIEF DUBASH

In the 17th century, European powers were vying for lucrative trade in India, but by the mid-18th century, only the English and French were still competing. As a child, Ananda Ranga Pillai (1709–1761) moved to the French settlement of Pondicherry in southeast India, where he later worked for the French East India Company and rose to become chief dubash (translator/administrator) to four French governors, including Joseph Marquis Dupleix.

Pillai began to keep a diary in 1736, 11 years before becoming chief dubash, and wrote entries in it every day for 25 years. His diary provides a unique portrait of life in 18th-century Pondicherry, as it describes the European colonization of India from an Indian point of view. Pillai valued his special status, which went far beyond just translating and involved him acting as administrator, supervisor, and general secretary. He negotiated with senior French officials and had considerable influence, of which he was proud. His diary is not a conventional diary in the Western sense but rather a blend of trade accounts, a record of correspondence, and a chronicle. Pillai is sometimes waspish about his French employers, depicting the constant skirmishes between the French and English in a near farcical

> One cannot understand what M. de la Bourdonnais means by writing one thing, one day, to the council at Pondicherry, and the next another, as if he was joking. Knowing as we do that there is generally concord and good understanding among Europeans, and that they never disagree, we cannot see what he means by saying at one time that he has restored Madras, and at another that he has not. The ways of Europeans, who used always to act in unison, have apparently now become like those of natives and Muhammadans.

ANANDA RANGA PILLAI'S DIARY, 16 OCTOBER 1746

manner. He witnessed numerous struggles for power, naval bombardments, the French capture of Madras from the English, and the Carnatic Wars. He was a careful and diligent administrator. When jars of filth are thrown into a temple, allegedly from the Christian church, he conducts a sensitive investigation and receives reports on exactly where the broken jars are found.

Pillai maintained his flair for the dramatic right up until the end. The entry for January 12, 1761, suddenly breaks off in the middle of a sentence. He died just four days later.

In context

◀ **COLONIAL OUTPOST** The French East India Company set up an outpost on the coast at Pondicherry in 1674, and it remained the main port and settlement of the French in India during the 18th century. The streets were laid out on a grid pattern and surrounded by fortified walls. The canal seen here separated the French Quarter from the Tamil Quarter, where the native population lived.

▶ **FRENCH COINAGE** Often short of funds, the French sought permission to mint their own coinage, in the form of local rupees, stamped with the French fleur-de-Lys. Ananda Ranga Pillai records in his diary how he oversaw the minting on behalf of the French governor.

[Two facing pages of handwritten Tamil manuscript]

▲ **WINDOW ON INDIA**
The left-hand page of this handwritten copy of Pillai's diary describes the maneuvers of an army unit and the confusion that results from a false alarm: "The storekeepers did not know what was happening and the false news spread very fast. The drum was beaten and the army was called to assemble. After some time, someone declared that they had gone".

Pillai wrote in his native Tamil, which has also been used in this manuscript copy

The paper is so thin that the text from the following page shows through

THE CARNATIC WARS

Joseph Marquis Dupleix arrived in India with the French East India Company in 1715. In 1742, he was made Governor General of all the French settlements in India, and based in Pondicherry, where Ananda Ranga Pillai worked for him.

Dupleix wanted to advance the interests of the French in India, and this brought him into conflict with the English, who were intent on doing the same thing. The Carnatic Wars were a series of battles fought between the two European powers for control of India's trading ports. The wars effectively ended when the British captured Pondicherry in 1761, making them the dominant foreign power in India.

▶ *Fort St. George on the Coromandel Coast*, Jan van Ryne, 1754

Recording a Revolution

1758-1807 ▪ PEN AND INK ON PAPER ▪ 2,100 PAGES ▪ AMERICAN

ELIZABETH SANDWITH DRINKER: QUAKER

The diary of Elizabeth Drinker (c.1735–1807) is the longest firsthand account of the life of a middle-class woman in 18th-century North America. The diary starts two years before Elizabeth's marriage to Henry, a prosperous Philadelphia merchant, and traces her progress from a young mother to a grandmother, recording details of family life and the couple's contacts with a wide circle of friends. Elizabeth's gripping reporting of the American War of Independence (see far right) paints a vivid picture of life during turbulent times.

The Drinkers were members of the Society of Friends (Quakers), and the diary reveals the difficulties that they experienced during the war because of their religious beliefs. Quakers were pacifists and would not swear oaths, and so Henry Drinker's refusal either to fight or to swear allegiance to the revolutionary cause led to his imprisonment for "aiding and abetting the enemy." The diary describes the distress and trouble that this caused Elizabeth. She was persecuted for her friendship with other Quakers, her house was attacked, and soldiers of both sides attempted to steal her property.

Alongside this, Elizabeth relates how she helped her family through outbreaks of dysentery, measles, and malaria and records the introduction of smallpox vaccination. She also movingly describes the effects of the 1793 epidemic of yellow fever that forced the family to flee Philadelphia. Because Elizabeth was a keen observer who recorded every event that happened around her, and how they affected her family, her diary is not only a valuable source of reference for early American history but also a lively portrayal of the time.

> ❝ The Sending off our Friends is put of[f] till 3 this Afternoon, they find it difficult to procure Waggons and Men. My Henry Breakfasted with us; then went to the Lodge. I went there about 10 o'clock ... the Town is in great Confusion at present a great fireing heard below it is supos'd the Armies are Engag'd, 'tis also reported that several Men of War are up the River.... Some time after dinner Harry came in a hurry for his Master's Horse for a Servant to ride, informing me that the waggons were waiting at the Lodge to take our dear friends away. ❞

ELIZABETH DRINKER'S DIARY, SEPTEMBER 11, 1777

▲ **A FULL LIFE** Most pages of the diary, like this one, are packed with different kinds of incidents. They include a wide range of jottings, from lists of books that Drinker has read to Quaker meetings, or from her children's illnesses to her thoughts about the French Revolution. Drinker recorded a mass of detail in handwriting that is clear, but not very tidy. Her text also includes many abbreviations, as if she was writing very fast.

The text records a meeting of several Quakers, including Henry Drinker (HD), who are awaiting trial

> 66 We had near 70 panes of Glass broken … when they threw Stones into the House. 99

ELIZABETH DRINKER'S DIARY, DESCRIBING AN ANTI-LOYALIST ATTACK, OCTOBER 24, 1781

"Friends" means members of the Society of Friends (Quakers)

... the apostates, Nich.ˢ Wale... r out Friends — they broke... p before dinner — are to meet... gain on fourth Day: —... y Committee of Friends went... cording to appointment to the... tate-House, were inform'd, the... se was put off till the next... ession —... y Woods have been on Fire... y Jersys, for some weeks past... nd done considerable damage... e have had a remarkable long... y spell of weather —... ally and Nancy went this... ternoon to y Burial of James... inghurst. Second wife —... xth day even? and no friends... t come to y Yearly meeting... awrence Salter was married... Sally Howard y 22 Ult.ᵒ —

AMERICAN **WAR OF INDEPENDENCE**

In this conflict (1775–1783), Great Britain fought North America's colonists, who declared independence and formed the United States of America in 1776. The war pitted Britain's enemies against fellow colonists who wanted to stay loyal to the British crown and posed particular problems for Quakers, who would not fight. As pacifists and loyalists, the Drinkers faced huge difficulties, which are recorded in Elizabeth's diary. She also reports, with great immediacy, occasions when she hears heavy firing as the two sides clash and describes her encounters with the military—from times when she sees one of the armies marching past, to an episode in which she travels 70 miles (113 km) to visit George Washington to plead for her husband's release from prison. Washington was unable to help, but Drinker was released soon afterward anyway.

▲ *Battle of Lexington,* William Barnes Wollen, 1910

▶ **A TRADING CITY** Philadelphia was an important port, with many ships carrying grain, wood, and other products, docking at its wharves. From their house, the Drinkers looked out onto the Delaware River and buildings that included Henry's warehouse. Elizabeth could see cargo being unloaded and merchants and dock workers coming and going.

Adventures in London

1762-1763 ▪ PEN AND INK ON PAPER ▪ 736 PAGES ▪ SCOTTISH

JAMES BOSWELL: WRITER

For a long time, James Boswell (1740-1795) was known mainly for *The Life of Samuel Johnson*, one of the greatest biographies in the English language. In the 1920s, however, two collections of his manuscript journals were discovered and were later published. They contain fascinating insights into Boswell's character and unique descriptions of 18th-century life. The most revealing manuscript of all was his London journal, written in 1762-1763 during his first visit to the British capital.

Its pages are crammed with lively descriptions of writers, aristocrats, soldiers, politicians, storekeepers, laborers, and prostitutes. They reveal the contradictory aspects of Boswell's character: his enthusiastic discovery of "the melting and transporting rites of love" and his encounters with London prostitutes, together with his feelings of guilt at his profligacy. They describe his pivotal first meeting with the writer Samuel Johnson, his passionate affair with the actress Louisa Lewis, and his discovery that he had caught gonorrhoea. They reflect his love of life but also record his bouts of depression. The daily entries were often accompanied by "memoranda," notes

> " London is undoubtedly a Place where Men & Manners may be seen to the greatest advantage. The liberty & the whim that reigns there occasions a variety of perfect & curious characters. Then the immense crowd & hurry and bustle of business & diversion, the great number of public places of entertainment, the noble churches and the superb buildings ... agitate, amuse and elevate the mind. Besides, the satisfaction of pursuing whatever plan is most agreable, without being known or look'd at, is very great. "

LONDON JOURNAL, DECEMBER 5, 1762

that Boswell made about how he should behave and what he should do on the following day. He wrote on loose sheets of paper in his flowing italic handwriting, then gathered together a weekly batch and sent them to a friend, with instructions to preserve them carefully. He did not intend to publish the London journal—the contents were far too frank—but used it as source material for *The Life of Samuel Johnson*. The passages that he quotes in the biography were all that was known of the London journal until it was published in 1950, when it was recognized as a classic of English literature.

In context

◄ **THE MITRE TAVERN** Boswell (left) is shown here with Samuel Johnson (right). After their meetings, Boswell carefully noted what Johnson had said. It was unusual at the time to quote a person. Boswell changed the course of biography by using conversations as evidence of his subject's opinions and character.

► **LOW LIFE** Boswell's journal describes many of his encounters with London's large number of prostitutes, one of whom is shown here with her madam. Although he expresses his lust with frankness, he also shows compassion for the women's dangerous and dismal lives.

(562)

this morning with the illustrious Donaldson. In the evening I went to Temple's: he brought me acquainted with a Mr. Claxton a very good sort of a young man tho' reserved at first. Mr. Nichols was there too. Our conversation was sensible & lively. I wish I could spend my time allways in such company.

Monday 16 May. Temple & his Brother breakfasted with me. I went to Love's to try to recover some of the money which he owes me. But alas a single guinea was all I could get. He was just going to dinner, so I stayed & eat a bit, tho' I was angry at myself afterwards. I drank tea at Davies's in Russel Street and about seven came in the great Mr. Samuel Johnson, whom I have so long wished to see. Mr. Davies introduced me to him. As I knew his mortal antipathy at the Scotch, I cried ... great humour and is a worthy ... But his dogmatical rough ... of manners is disagreable.

◄ **FATEFUL MEETING** The entry for May 16, 1763, describes Boswell's first meeting with Samuel Johnson. Although it did not start well, Johnson enjoyed the meeting, and the pair soon became firm friends. Boswell admired Johnson's knowledge and his expressive way with words: "I shall mark what I remember of his conversation," he says. True to his word, he wrote his great biography using information gathered from his conversations with Johnson.

The day begins unpromisingly, when Boswell tries to recover a debt, but then the chance meeting with Johnson changes his life

RECORDING A LIFE

After the London journal, Boswell kept journals for much of the rest of his life. The complete journals (which run to many printed volumes) record the events of a rich life—his travels in France, Switzerland, Germany, and Scotland; his often unwilling efforts to qualify and practice as a lawyer in Scotland; his meetings and friendships with 18th-century luminaries such as the actor David Garrick and the artist Joshua Reynolds; and his visit to Corsica when the island was fighting for independence from Genoa. Boswell published only his Corsica journal and an account of his tour of the Scottish Highlands with Johnson during his lifetime.

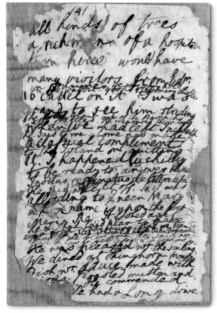

▲ **Tattered page** from Boswell's journal of the tour to the Hebrides, 1773

The Voyages of Captain Cook

1768-1779 ■ PEN AND INK ON PAPER ■ TWO VOLUMES ■ BRITISH

JAMES COOK: EXPLORER

Naval officer James Cook (1728–1779) was the leader of the expedition that first circumnavigated New Zealand and made the first European charts of the east coast of Australia in 1768–1771. Cook had also been secretly instructed to look for the Southern Continent that was thought to surround the South Pole. During his command of HMS *Endeavour*, he kept a daily journal. Cook's early entries, as the ship crossed the Atlantic Ocean, are brief, but those describing his experiences and impressions in Tahiti, New Zealand, and Australia are immensely detailed. As well as providing information on chart positions and the weather, Cook recorded the birds, animals, and butterflies that he saw and described the expedition's meetings with the indigenous peoples. On their first encounter with the people of Tahiti on April 13, 1769, for example, he notes the rules that the expedition had to observe. The first was:

"To endeavour by every fair means to cultivate a friendship with the Natives and to treat them with all imaginable humanity." These rules were incompatible with his orders to take possession of the fabled Southern Continent. During their first encounter with the Maori people on October 5, 1769, one of Cook's men shot and killed the leader of the Ngati Oneone group. The group were throwing spears to fend off the ship and protect their land, and the British retaliated with force.

The journal that Cook kept on the first of his three great voyages is full of observations and discoveries. He notes the effectiveness of a diet that includes "Sour krout" (sauerkraut) in combating scurvy, the scourge of long-distance journeys. He also notes historically significant dates. On August 22, 1770, he writes: "I … took possession of the whole Eastern Coast from the above Latitude down to this place by the Name of New South Wales together with all the Bays, Harbours, Rivers and Islands situate upon the same said coast."

In context

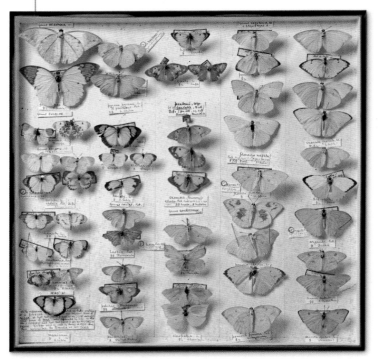

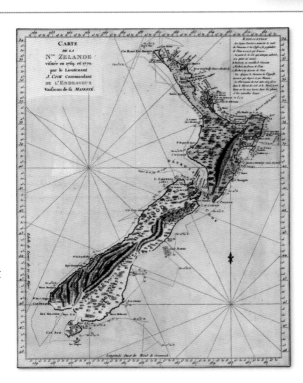

◄ **WINGED SPECIMENS** Also on board the *Endeavour* was the botanist Joseph Banks, who was accompanied by a select team of scientists and artists. Between them they collected approximately 30,000 plant specimens, more than half of which were new to science. Banks also wrote a 200,000-word journal of his own.

► **CHARTING NEW ZEALAND** On October 7, 1769, Cook sighted the coast of New Zealand. Abel Tasman had visited the west coast in 1642, but otherwise, the land was unknown to Europeans. On March 10, 1770, the *Endeavour* passed the southern tip of the South Island, proving that New Zealand did not form part of a great southern continent.

▲ **THE FIRST VOYAGE** On these pages of the journal from April 19 and 20, 1770, Cook records his first sighting of Australia. Cook's journal from his first Pacific voyage was kept by his wife, Elizabeth. When she died in 1835, at the age of 94, it went to a cousin. Eventually, this 753-page volume, the only document of the expedition entirely in Cook's own hand, was bought by what is now the National Library of Australia.

▲ **A GANGURRU** On June 23, 1770, Cook reports in his journal that one of the men "saw an Animal of the Deer kind something less than a grey hound. It was of a Mouse Colour very slender made and swift of foot." The expedition's artist, Sydney Parkinson, later saw one of these animals and drew it. He learned from the local Guugu Yimithirr people that it was called a "Gangurru"–a kangaroo.

> 66
>
> A few minutes before 11... the Ship Struck and stuck fast. Immediately upon this we took in all our Sails, hoisted out the Boats and Sounded round the Ship and found that we had got upon the South East Edge of a reef of Coral Rocks.... We went to work to lighten her as fast as possible, which seem'd to be the only means we had left to get her off.... We... threw over board our Guns, Iron and Stone Ballast, Casks, Hoop, Staves, Oil Jars, decay'd Stores etc..... We try'd to heave her off without success... notwithstanding by this time we had thrown over board 40 or 50 Tun weight.
>
> 99

THE *ENDEAVOUR* STRIKES THE GREAT BARRIER REEF, JUNE 11, 1770

In detail

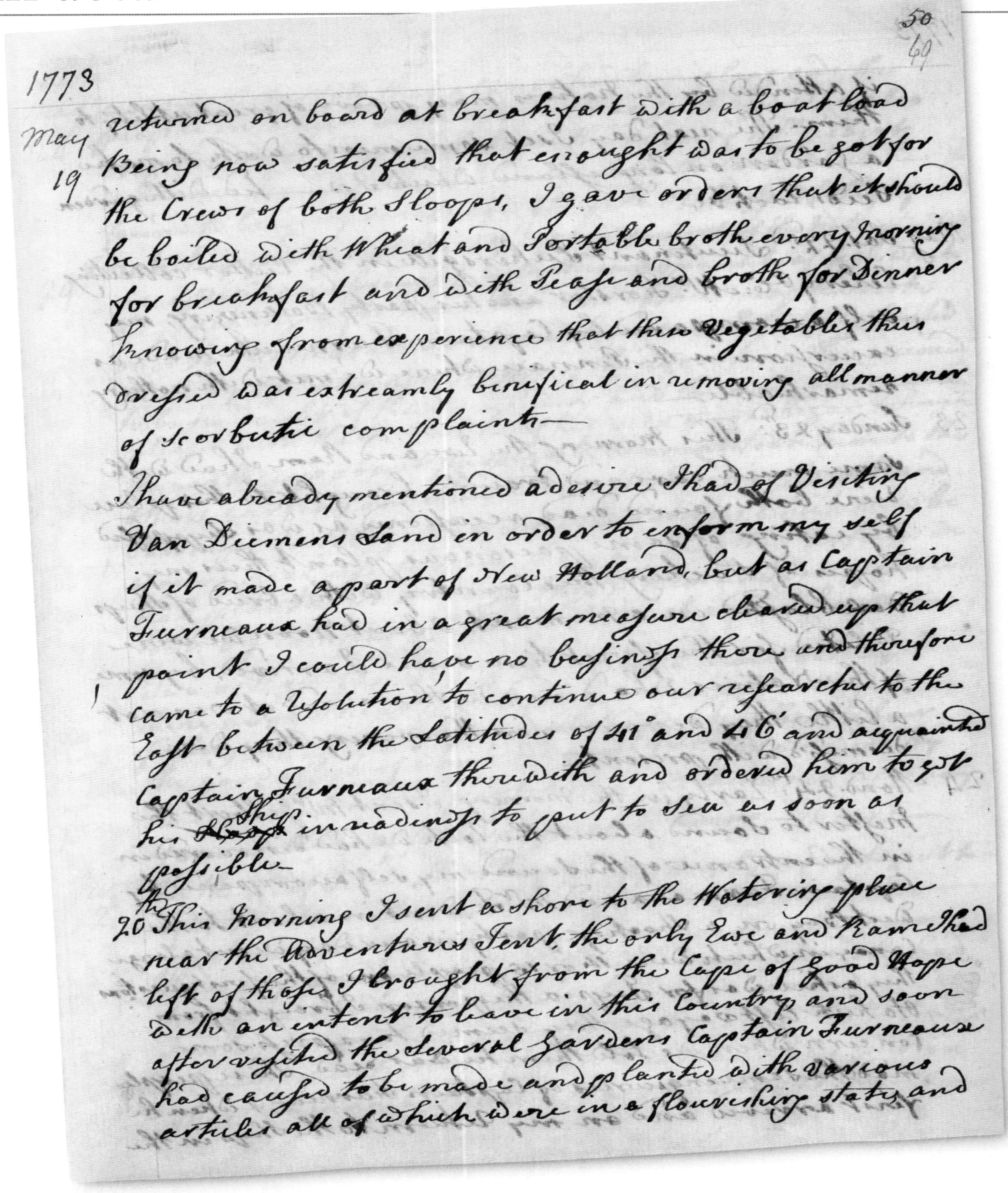

50
60

1773

May
19

returned on board at breakfast with a boat load
Being now satisfied that enought was to be got for
the Crews of both Sloops, I gave orders that it should
be boiled with Wheat and Portable broth every morning
for breakfast and with Peas and broth for Dinner
knowing from experience that these Vegetables thus
dresed was extreamly benifical in removing all manner
of scorbutic complaints—

I have already mentioned a desire I had of Visiting
Van Diemens Land in order to inform my self
if it made a part of New Holland, but as Captain
Furneaux had in a great measure cleared up that
point I could have no besiness there and therefore
came to a Resolution to continue our researches to the
East between the Latitudes of 41° and 46° and acquainted
Captain Furneaux therewith and ordered him to get
his Ship in readiness to put to sea as soon as
possible.

20 This morning I sent a shore to the Watering place
near the Adventures Tent, the only Ewe and Ram I had
left of those I brought from the Cape of Good Hope
with an intent to leave in this Country and soon
after visited the several Gardens Captain Furneaux
had caused to be made and planted with various
articles all of which were in a flourishing state and

Cook began the journal of his second voyage on July 13, 1772: "At 6 o'clock in the morning we sail'd from Plymouth." In command of HMS *Resolution*, and accompanied by the *Adventure*, Cook's purpose was again to explore the South Pacific to find out whether there really was a great Southern Continent. The expedition crossed the Antarctic Circle three times, made circuits of the South Pacific, and charted the islands that it visited. On board, it had copies of John Harrison's chronometer, an instrument designed to keep accurate time at sea. This made it much easier to calculate longitude than the method of lunar distances used on the previous voyage. Many of the places that Cook came across had already been visited by earlier explorers, but their positions had never been charted with any accuracy. Cook's expedition was able to remedy this.

Once again, Cook's journal is full of descriptions of the Pacific islands and their inhabitants. He was ultimately killed during an encounter with native people on a later expedition and his actions are now regarded by many as controversial. Cook's journals were first published in two volumes in 1777.

◄ **JOURNAL OF THE SECOND VOYAGE** Cook's entry for May 19, 1773, shows his continuing concern with the crew's diet, instructing the cooks to serve vegetables "beneficial in removing all manner of scorbutic [scurvy] complaints." He also records his decision not to visit Van Diemen's Land (Tasmania) to confirm whether or not it formed a part of New Holland (Australia), as this had already been done by the HMS *Adventure*, the sister ship of the *Resolution* on this second great voyage.

▲ **TALES FROM TAHITI** On April 22, 1774, the *Resolution* arrived at Tahiti, which Cook had visited on his first voyage. "At 8 Anchored in Matavai Bay," he writes in his journal, "which was no sooner done than we were visited by several of our old friends, who express'd not a little joy at seeing us." While they were there, expedition artist William Hodge made a sketch, which he later worked up into this painting.

▲ **IN THE ANTARCTIC** On January 17, 1773, Captain James Cook sailed further south than any ship had ever been before. In the ship's journal, now held by the British Library, Cook confirms: "At about a quarter past 11 o'clock we cross'd the Antarctic Circle, for at Noon we were by observation four miles and a half south of it and are undoubtedly the first and only ship that ever cross'd that line."

TERRA *AUSTRALIS*

Since the time of the ancient Greeks, geographers had theorized that there must be a great *Terra Australis* (Latin for "South Land") that mirrored the landmass of the northern hemisphere. Captain Cook was the latest in a long line of seafarers who had attempted to find this land. His second voyage settled the matter once and for all: "I had now made the circuit of the Southern Ocean," he wrote. "Thus I flatter myself that the intention of the Voyage has in every respect been fully Answered, the Southern Hemisphere sufficiently explored and a final end put to the searching after a Southern Continent, which has at times ingrossed the attention of some of the Maritime Powers for near two Centuries past and the Geographers of all ages."

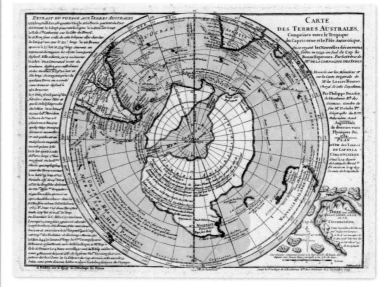

▲ *Carte des Terres Australes*, Philippe Buache, 1757

The Italian Notebook

C.1771-1780 ▪ PENCIL, INK, AND SANGUINE ON PAPER ▪ 83 SHEETS ▪ SPANISH

FRANCISCO JOSÉ DE GOYA: ARTIST

The greatest Spanish painter of the Romantic era, Francisco Goya (1746–1828) was renowned internationally for his perceptive royal portraits, his powerful anti-war etchings, and the intensity of his "Black Paintings." There are few hints of his glittering future in his first, fully documented work, *Hannibal the Conqueror Seeing Italy from the Alps for the First Time*. Painted in the Neoclassical style fashionable at the time, this picture was produced by Goya specifically for a competition held at the Academy of Fine Arts in Parma in 1771.

Goya was studying in Italy from 1769 to 1771. Very little is known about this period of his life, although early biographers concocted some fanciful anecdotes. The only solid information comes from Goya's Italian Notebook, which he kept throughout his stay and used for the rest of the decade, after his return to Spain.

The written sections of the Notebook contain a miscellany of practical information. There are lists of places that he visited and the paintings that impressed him most; receipts for pigments and other artistic materials; useful addresses, general accounts, and personal, family records.

The visual sections are much more interesting, revealing how the artist spent his time. Working in pencil, ink, or sanguine (red chalk), Goya drew copies of ancient, classical sculptures, such as the Farnese Hercules and the Belvedere Torso. He also kept a number of student figure–studies, drawn from live models, and a beautiful series of biblical scenes, including *Absalom's Death*. In addition, Goya devoted several pages of the Notebook to sketches relating to *Hannibal*. The finished painting was much admired, but it did not win the competition. Even so, the drawings in the Notebook remained useful and Goya referred to them throughout his career.

◄ **ABSALOM'S DEATH** In this masterly pencil drawing, Goya tackled an unusual biblical subject from the Book of Samuel, in which Absalom rebelled against his father, King David. In the ensuing battle, Absalom's head got caught in the branches of a great oak. His mount bolted, leaving Absalom dangling in the air, whereupon he was slain by David's commander, Joab.

In the biblical narrative, Absalom was riding a mule; Goya has changed this to a horse

This bland list of statistics conceals a history of personal tragedy in Goya's life

► **FAMILY RECORDS** Important personal details were often inscribed in the family Bible, but Goya used his Notebook for this purpose. Here, he records the birth of his first three sons, the places where they were baptized, and the names of their godparents. Poignantly, these records may also have been memorials. The artist and his wife, Josefa Bayeu, had seven (or possibly eight) children, but only one of them survived infancy.

◀ **EARLY EXPERIMENTS**
Traditionally, a river god was either portrayed as a reclining figure overturning a huge urn of water or as a large, masklike face with a torrent of water gushing through its mouth. Here, Goya appears to have been toying with using the latter option in his *Hannibal*. Sculptures of this kind were popular in ancient Rome, and Goya may have sketched one of these.

The fierce expression on the mask hints at Goya's taste for horror, which would later play a major role in his art

This figure presages Hannibal's success in Italy. Seated on a military chariot, she holds out a laurel wreath, which symbolizes victory

▲ **EVOLUTION OF A MASTERPIECE** The Notebook contains this very early sketch for *Hannibal* (the final painting is to the right). Goya initially based the composition on the strong, diagonal axis created by the main figures on the left. Later, he turned this into a pyramid by adding soldiers descending the mountain. Some critics have seen faint echoes of the Apollo Belvedere in the figure of Hannibal.

This allegorical figure represents the River Po in northern Italy. Two of Hannibal's greatest victories were on tributaries of the Po

The Kingdom of Bone

1775-1795 ▪ PEN AND INK ON PAPER ▪ 200 PAGES ▪ SULAWESIAN

SULTAN AHMAD AL-SALIH: RULER

In his diary, Ahmad al-Salih (1757–1812) chronicled his reign as the 22nd sultan of Bone, which lasted from 1775 until his death. Bone was once the most powerful of the five major kingdoms of the Bugis people in South Sulawesi (now part of Indonesia), having gained its supremacy partly by means of a strategic alliance with the colonial Dutch. It was probably as a result of European influence that the rulers and senior court officials began to keep diaries, as no one in the other kingdoms in Southeast Asia appears to have kept records in this way. Of those that have survived, Ahmad al-Salih's royal Bugis diary provides a unique insight into how such a kingdom was run in the late 18th century.

It starts on January 1, 1775, stating: "There is no god but God, Muhammad is His Messenger." Al-Salih was known for his religious learning, and this is the *shahada,* the basic statement of the Islamic faith, often recited before an important event. What follows is a record of political events, with many notes on private, family, and state affairs, and information about economic activities. The diary documents meetings with the Dutch governor and officials of the neighboring Bugis states, lists the births and deaths in court circles, and describes

> " The king passed away and was posthumously named 'Matinroe ri Mallimongang' (He who lies at Mallimongang). Yarji u'ila rahmatillah. I was appointed with the confirmation of the people of Bone as the legitimate ruler [of Bone] as the [deceased] king wished. [And] I reside in the palace [of the late king]. "

THE BUGIS DIARY, JUNE 5, 1775

dealings with slaves. Slaves played an important part in the Bugis economy and denoted status. In one entry, the sultan records a gift of 12 slaves—one for each of his children. He also celebrates Bugis culture; the diary is peppered with verses and songs, one of which is dedicated to war, along with many transcriptions of poems he admired.

The entries are matter-of-fact and mostly free of personal comment, but they do reveal that the sultan's hobbies included deer hunting, crocodile shooting, fishing, boating, picnicking, and collecting seashells. Covering an almost unbroken period of 20 years, the diaries provide a wealth of fascinating information about the history of Indonesia.

OTHER **DIARIES**

Ahmad al-Salih's diary is one of more than 20 diaries that have survived from the court of Bone. This tradition of keeping diaries began in the early 17th century and lasted into the first decade of the 20th century. The earliest was written between 1660 and 1696 by Arung Palakka, who allied himself with the Dutch East India Company to defeat the kingdom of Makassar in 1669 and become king of Bone. After his death, most of the subsequent rulers of Bone kept diaries, as did senior officials and, later, senior ministers of state. All the Bugis diaries were written on paper imported from Europe and then bound into book form. They are now housed in several institutions, including the British Library in London, the Royal Institute of Linguistics and Anthropology in the Netherlands, and the National Library of Indonesia.

▶ **Painting of a winged horse** found in the diary of Muhammad Ramadan, a high-ranking official under Sultan Ahmad al-Salih

▼ **TWO LANGUAGES** The entries in the diary are written in Buginese, with occasional pious phrases in Arabic, such as *Baraka Allah* (God's blessing). It was difficult to combine the two languages because Buginese is written from left to right, and Arabic from right to left. Each month was allocated a single page containing around 22 entries. These two pages show the entries for January and February 1789.

The name of the month is written in Arabic and in red at the top left of each page

The number of the year according to the Christian calendar is written here

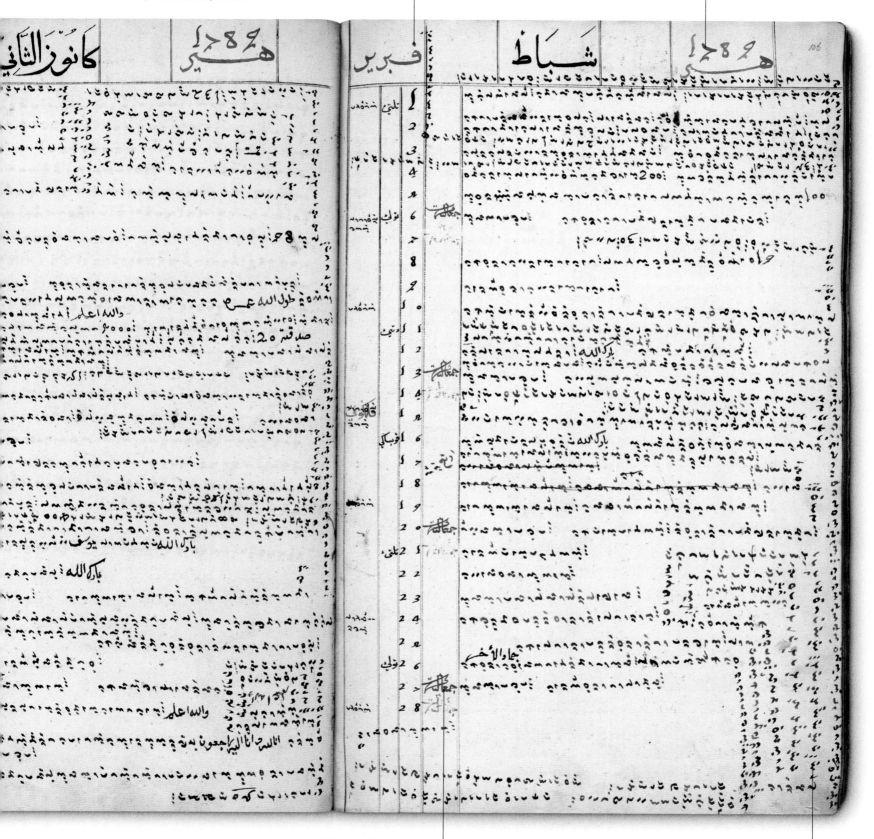

The holy day of Friday is written in an elaborate form of Arabic and highlighted in red

Some text is written at right angles to the original text to fit in additional information and comments

A Musical Catalogue

1784-1791 ■ PEN AND INK ON PAPER ■ 30 PAGES ■ AUSTRIAN

WOLFGANG AMADEUS MOZART: COMPOSER

For the last seven years of his life, the great Austrian composer Wolfgang Amadeus Mozart (1756–1791) kept a notebook of his compositions. This record, which is now known as the Thematic Catalogue, is in a hardcover book with a label on the front. On the label, Mozart wrote that he would include all of his works. The diary therefore lists an enormous variety of compositions: five of Mozart's best-known operas, including *The Marriage of Figaro* and *Don Giovanni*, along with several arias, piano concertos, his last three great symphonies, masterpieces such as the concerto that he wrote for his friend, the clarinetist Anton Stadler, and even some pieces that have been lost in the years since he died.

Mozart listed the works in the catalogue in the order in which he completed them. Each left-hand page contains entries for five pieces, giving their titles, dates of completion, and the instruments to be used. Sometimes Mozart also provided additional information, such as where the first performance was to be held or the names of singers or the person who commissioned the work. On each right-hand page, there are five pairs of musical staves, on which Mozart wrote the opening theme of each piece. Everything is in Mozart's handwriting, and the catalogue gives the reader a fascinating insight into how he operated. It not only provides information about the musicians with whom he worked but also shows how busy he was both with new compositions and adaptations of older works, such as his opera *Idomeneo,* for which he wrote additional music for a new production. It also shows how he regarded some of his works. He describes one piano piece as "a short piano sonata for beginners," for example, which explains why the music that he wrote for it is considerably simpler than that of his other sonatas.

It is not known why Mozart started to keep this musical diary, but he may have been trying to create some order in his life, as he needed more money to support his family and was also frantically busy with concerts and traveling. He obviously meant to carry on listing his works in this way, because the book contains many blank pages with ruled staves, ready for entries that Mozart would have written, had he not died, tragically, at the early age of 35.

In context

◀ **ROYAL THEATER** The Burgtheater in Vienna was where several of Mozart's operas, including *The Marriage of Figaro* and *Cosi fan Tutte*, were premiered, as well as many of his instrumental works. It was the theater of the imperial court, and although Mozart was a court composer for only a few months, his music was popular with the emperor and his family.

▶ **THE MAGIC FLUTE** Mozart's much-loved final opera (one of five listed in the diary) is full of colorful characters and sublime melodies and blends high drama with occasional humor. It tells of the triumph of the forces of good over evil and the journeys of the main characters toward fulfillment and love.

This duet for *Idomeneo* is for soprano and tenor voices

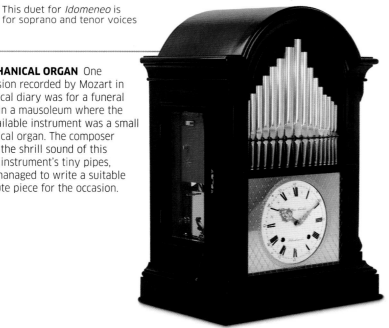

➤ **MECHANICAL ORGAN** One commission recorded by Mozart in his musical diary was for a funeral service in a mausoleum where the only available instrument was a small mechanical organ. The composer disliked the shrill sound of this unusual instrument's tiny pipes, but he managed to write a suitable 10-minute piece for the occasion.

▲ **COMPOSER'S NOTES** These two pages of the Thematic Catalogue cover the period from December 1785 to March 1786, during which Mozart completed a short opera, *The Impresario*, two piano concertos, and several pieces for the revised version of his opera *Idomeneo*. He was also writing *The Marriage of Figaro*, another opera, which was to have its first performance in May 1786.

Each staff is ruled neatly, using a special five-nibbed pen

A Poet's Discovery of Italy

1786-1788 ▪ PEN AND INK ON PAPER ▪ GERMAN

JOHANN WOLFGANG VON GOETHE: WRITER

In 1786, Johann Wolfgang von Goethe (1749-1832) took extended leave from his work as the Duke of Weimar's adviser and went on a long tour of Italy. As he traveled, he recorded his journey and impressions in a journal. This document, together with many of the letters he wrote at the time, became the basis of the book he later wrote, *Italienische Reise* (*Italian Journey*).

The journal records Goethe's travels through Italy, taking in the scenic beauty of Lake Garda in the north and the grandeur of cities such as Verona, Vicenza, Assisi, and Naples. He visited the ruined Roman town of Pompeii, climbed to the summit of Vesuvius, and explored the island of Sicily. There are also accounts of the friends he made en route, including the artists Angelika Kauffmann and Johann Wilhelm Tischbein. Already famous as a poet, Goethe traveled under the pseudonym Johann Philipp Möller to avoid attention and retain his privacy.

He spent a long time in Rome and Venice, where he marveled at the ancient architecture, which was little known to northern Europeans at the time. Impressed by the luminous southern landscape, he also wrote numerous descriptions of trees, scenery, and rocks (he was an excellent geologist).

Goethe's aim was not only to explore Italy but also "to discover myself in the objects I see." As he traveled, his experiences led to a form of spiritual rebirth: "Although I am still the same, I believe to have changed to the bones." His journal lays great emphasis on personal expression and his appreciation of nature, making it a milestone in the history of Romanticism, despite Goethe's reservations about the literary movement.

Much of the journal's content found its way into the book *Italian Journey*. Compiled 30 years after Goethe went to Italy, his travelogue became a classic of German literature. It is a moving record of a great writer exploring Italy's culture and landscape and finding a source of inspiration that would help him write many of his most famous works.

In context

◄ **ANCIENT ROME** Goethe first arrived in Rome in November 1786. Many of the ancient buildings impressed him, especially the Colosseum, which he is shown admiring in this painting by the German artist Jacob Philipp Hackert. He wrote that the Colosseum was so big that he was amazed by its size each time he went back to it.

▲ **VISUAL RECORD** Spending much of his time attending drawing classes, Goethe enjoyed practicing his watercolors during his travels. This one was done in the Villa Borghese, a landscape garden created in the 17th century by Cardinal Scipione Borghese. The park's informal blend of picturesque pine trees, water, and buildings appealed to him.

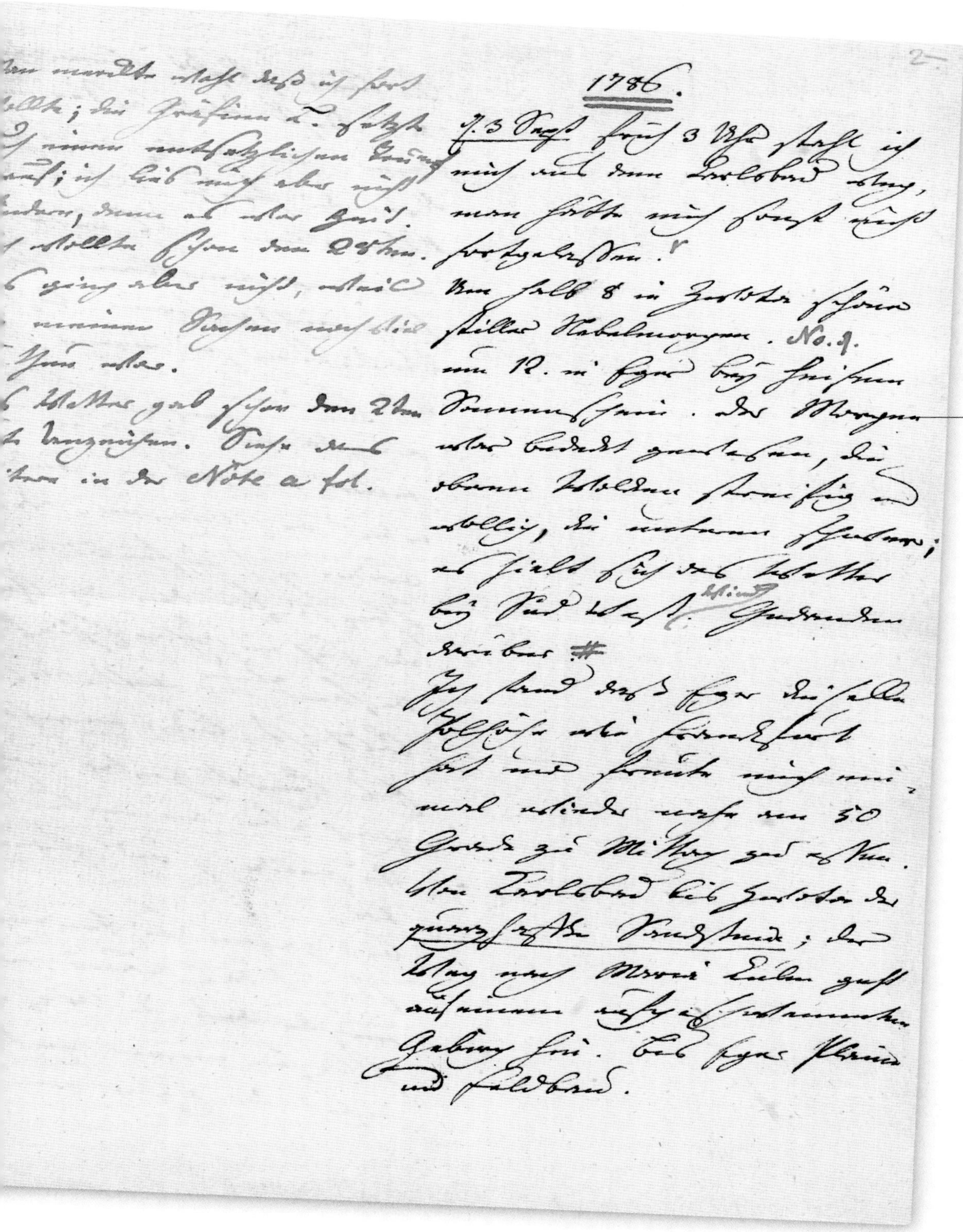

◄ **EN ROUTE** Goethe secretly set off on September 3, 1786, at 3 a.m. from the spa town of Karlsbad, Germany, to Italy. This page from his travel journal records the start of his famous journey in search of "rejuvenation and rebirth." The early entries reveal Goethe's excitement as he heads south through the Alps. Before he even reaches Verona, his first destination in Italy, he has already started to think about publishing his journal.

Written in note form, the entry was heavily revised and extended for *Italian Journey*

GOETHE'S **PUBLISHED WORKS**

Although best known as a poet, Goethe was one of the most versatile writers of his time. He wrote plays, novels, such as *The Sorrows of Young Werther* (1774) and *Elective Affinities* (1809), essays, philosophical works, and scientific studies, such as *Theory of Colors* (1810). His most famous work is *Faust* (1829), a long drama in two parts that was designed to be read like a novel rather than staged in a theater. Many of Goethe's books feature a central character who finds himself at odds with society. These Romantic heroes and anti-heroes sometimes take extreme measures to express their sense of alienation. Werther commits suicide, and Faust makes his notorious pact with the devil.

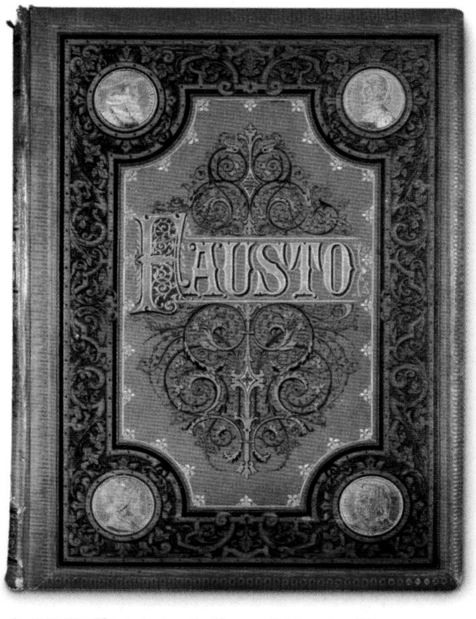

▲ **An Italian translation** of *Faust* with an ornate 19th-century binding

> Naples is a paradise: in it every one lives in a sort of intoxicated self-forgetfulness. It is even so with me: I scarcely know myself; I seem to myself quite an altered man. Yesterday I said to myself, "Either you have always been mad, or you are so now." I have paid a visit to the ruins of ancient Capua, and all that is connected with it. In this country one first begins to have a true idea of what vegetation is, and why man tills the fields. The flax here is already near to blossoming, and the wheat a span and a half high. Around Caserta the land is perfectly level, the fields worked as clean and as fine as the beds of a garden.... What will they be when the spring shall come in power?

***ITALIAN JOURNEY*, MARCH 16, 1787**

March the 9 1787

March with the detachment from the Barracks to the dock yard at ten in the morning and Embarkd on board the Friendship Transport with Captain Lieutenant Meredith and 2 Lieut Faddey 2 Sergeants 3 Corporals 1 Drummer 36 Privates 9 Woman and ⟨with greater reluctance⟩ Children; never did a poor Criminal goe to meet the ⟨than I leave the⟩ best of Woman and Sweetest of Boys god out of his gracious goodness my leaving them may turn out to our advantage, never did poor Mortal feel hemselve So unhappy as I doe at this present moment I werh to god that I was returning home again to the best of hir Sex oh what goodness doe she my belovd Betsey posses She is come on board to stay with her fond Clark untill Mr Faddey returns on board to Releive me

March the 12 liceived on board ⟨t yesterday⟩ Male and Female Convicts with Children can never forgive the unkindness of Capt in refusing me leave to Sleep out of the Ship last night oh did he love as well as I doe he would never have Refused me,

March the 13 ot Sea Oh gracious God what as such have I gone throuw last night in takeing leave of the dearest and best of Wives and not Sing my boy god grant them health and welfare is the most Sincere wishes of an affectiond husband and fond father Shuld ever I am restored to them again will never leave them. Bless thy both

EMBARCATION On the first page of the diary, dated March 9, 12, and 13, 1787, Clark describes boarding the *Friendship* and receiving the first convicts. Desperate about leaving his wife and son, he bemoans his fate: "Never did poor Mortal feel themselves Soe unhappy as I doe at this present moment...." The writing is even but dotted with blank spaces and spelling mistakes.

Life in the Colonies

1787-1792 ▪ PEN AND INK ON PAPER ▪ 312 PAGES ▪ BRITISH

RALPH CLARK: MARINE OFFICER

Rarely has the birth of a nation been written about firsthand in such an intimate fashion. Ralph Clark (c.1755–1794) was a British officer in the Royal Marines, who accompanied the first shipment of convicts from Portsmouth, UK, in May 1787 to their exile on the shores of what would become Australia. Clark's diaries begin two months before the sailing and cover more than five years, ending in June 1792. They are a deeply personal account of the long voyage out (on which Clark was often sick), and then of life in the new British colony. Clark does not seem well educated (his spelling is bad), and his journal is far from official, often dwelling on thoughts of his wife and his one-year-old son, but it provides a wealth of information about life in the early penal colony.

On arrival in Botany Bay, Clark was dismayed by the unsuitable conditions: "If we are oblige to Settle here … there will not a Soul be a life in the course of a Year" (January 23, 1788). A new site for settlement—Port Jackson—was chosen, but life was brutal. Food was scarce, so when three convicts were accused of stealing "butter pease and pork," Clark records that one received a sentence of 300 lashes while the other two were hung. Clark shows little sympathy for their charges and seems to take pleasure in recording the punishments that were meted out.

The first part of Clark's diaries is addressed to the wife he left at home, Betsey Alicia Trevan, but she is scarcely mentioned in the second part. Both husband and wife died soon after Clark's return to England in 1791. Betsey's family preserved the diaries, and they were later sold to the State Library of New South Wales.

JOURNALS OF THE **FIRST FLEET**

Ralph Clark's is just one of several contemporary accounts written by people who sailed with the First Fleet, as the 11 ships that left England for Australia in May 1787 were known. Of the 1,000 or so convicts, seamen, and soldiers on board, 12 other people also kept a journal, including Captain Arthur Phillip, who was in command of the expedition. Only one of the convicts wrote an account—James Martin, an Irishman who had been sentenced to transportation for stealing a few screws. Three years after landing in Australia, he and two accomplices stole the colony's fishing boat and escaped to Dutch-controlled Timor. Martin's manuscript was found many years later, in the 1930s, and was published as *Memorandoms*.

▲ **The First Fleet entering Port Jackson on January 26, 1788,** Edmund Le Bihan, 1888

In context

◄ **THE LAND OF ABORIGINES** The colonists made contact with the local Aborigine tribes. If his journal is to be believed, Clark became quite friendly with them, but they were often treated brutally. At one point, he was asked by the governor to "capture" two Aborigines who he had traded with, but Clark refused because he feared their children would starve.

► **NEW WORLD BIRD** Arthur Bowes Smyth (1750–1790) was a surgeon with the First Fleet. He also kept a journal of the voyage and the first 18 months of life in the new colony. He was interested in natural history, and this drawing in his journal depicts an emu, the first sighting of the bird recorded by a European.

Into South America

1799–1804 ▪ PEN AND INK ON PAPER ▪ NINE VOLUMES ▪ PRUSSIAN

ALEXANDER VON HUMBOLDT: SCIENTIST

Passionate about scientific observation, Alexander von Humboldt (1769–1859) was a visionary. His all-embracing, interdisciplinary approach to science, and the rigorous observations that he made on his travels, gave him a holistic view of nature that paved the way for how people perceive the natural world today. So much so that the journals in which he recorded a huge amount of detailed data, as well as his own thoughts, continue to provide a rich source of information for researchers today.

The American travel journals document Humboldt's five-year journey through Central and South America with the French botanist Aimé Bonpland, during which they covered more than 5,993 miles (9,650 km) canoeing up rivers, trekking with mules through tropical forests, and climbing some of the highest peaks in the Andes. The first entry in the journals, dated June 3, 1799, was written onboard the ship *Pizarro* shortly after leaving La Coruña in Spain ("The night of the 3rd to the 4th was spent very restlessly"). The last, questioning whether limewashing ships would lower the risk of epidemics, was on May 22, 1804.

Between these two entries, Humboldt recounts numerous reckless adventures (trekking barefoot when his shoes disintegrate and riding horses into a river to bring electric eels to the surface). These tales are interspersed with Humboldt's observations about the natural world and his concern about the hardships endured by the people he met—he rails against injustices such as slavery and inhumane working conditions in the mines in colonial Mexico.

Shortly before he died, Humboldt had his journals and notes bound into nine volumes. Although he requested in his will that they should be made available to science, they remained in the possession of his descendants until they were taken away to the Soviet Union at the end of World War II. In 1958, they were returned to Germany and are now held in the Berlin State Library.

Humboldt added and deleted notes right up to his death

◀ **THE SCIENTIFIC TRAVELER**
Humboldt (left) is seen here with Aimé Bonpland and many of their scientific instruments. Charles Darwin called Humboldt the "greatest scientific traveler who ever lived," and he has more natural phenomena named after him than anyone else. His most significant contribution to science may be as a prophet of climate change, when he warned that humans had the power to upset the delicate balance of nature.

" The yellowish and livid eels, resembling large aquatic serpents, swim on the surface of the water and crowd under the bellies of the horses and mules. A contest between animals of so different an organization presents a very striking spectacle.... The eels, stunned by the noise, defend themselves by the repeated discharge of their electric batteries. For a long interval they seem likely to prove victorious. Several horses sink beneath the violence of the invisible strokes which they receive from all sides in organs the most essential to life; and stunned by the force and frequency of the shocks, they disappear under water. "

JOURNAL III, 1799-1800

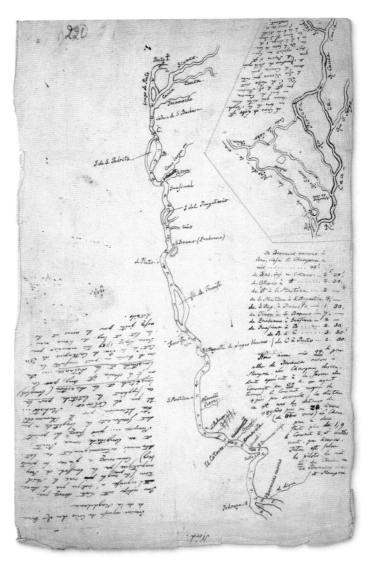

▲ **MAGDALENA RIVER** The first part of Journal VII describes the expedition that Humboldt and his companions made from April 19 to June 15, 1801, along the Río Magdalena, the main river of Colombia. As the party made its way from Cartagena up the river, Humboldt drew the sketch map above.

This drawing of a piranha comes from Journal IV, which charts Humboldt's exploration of the Orinoco River

◀ **THE JOURNALS** Humboldt wrote in German and French, and even in Spanish. The text is often not written in chronological order, and dated entries on daily events alternate with general notes. Humboldt also drew many of the things that he saw, such as the fish on the left. The journals are dotted with maps and drawings, ranging from Inca ruins, animals, and plants to diagrams of ocean currents and calculations of the curvature of the Earth.

In detail

One of the most famous sections of Humboldt's journals describes the team's ascent of Mount Chimborazo, an inactive volcano in present-day Ecuador, thought at the time to be the tallest mountain in the world. The team set off with numerous scientific instruments and stopped at regular intervals during the ascent to take measurements and readings. Humboldt also sketched many of the plants and animals that he saw. But the expedition was ill-prepared. Their clothing and equipment were inadequate, the weather conditions were poor, and they had problems breathing. Then a huge crevasse blocked any further progress: "Our stay at this immense height was most sad and gloomy. We had been labouring in a mist which only allowed us to see at intervals the abyss that surrounded us. No living creatures, no insects, not even the Condor that hovered over our heads in Antisana, enlivened the airs."

The expedition was forced to descend, but they had climbed higher than anyone ever before. Humboldt had also learnt a great deal on his way up the mountain. When he compared the notes and measurements that he had made with what he had seen on his travels elsewhere, he realized that there were corresponding climate zones at different latitudes across the continents. He saw that nature around the world is closely interconnected—a view that has had a profound influence on the way that people perceive the natural world today.

> " ... whilst the **number** of **accurate instruments** was **daily increasing,** we were **still ignorant...** "

ALEXANDER VON HUMBOLDT, INTRODUCTION TO *PERSONAL NARRATIVE* VOL. 1, 1819

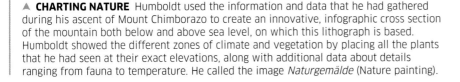

▲ **CHARTING NATURE** Humboldt used the information and data that he had gathered during his ascent of Mount Chimborazo to create an innovative, infographic cross section of the mountain both below and above sea level, on which this lithograph is based. Humboldt showed the different zones of climate and vegetation by placing all the plants that he had seen at their exact elevations, along with additional data about details ranging from fauna to temperature. He called the image *Naturgemälde* (Nature painting).

▲ **BOTANICAL ART** Humboldt and Aimé Bonpland collected thousands of plant specimens, such as this rare lupin, *Lupinus nubigenus*, found only in Ecuador, then pressed them and sent them back to Europe for further study. From these, scholars and artists produced 15 volumes on the plants of Spanish America, which were printed between 1805 and 1834.

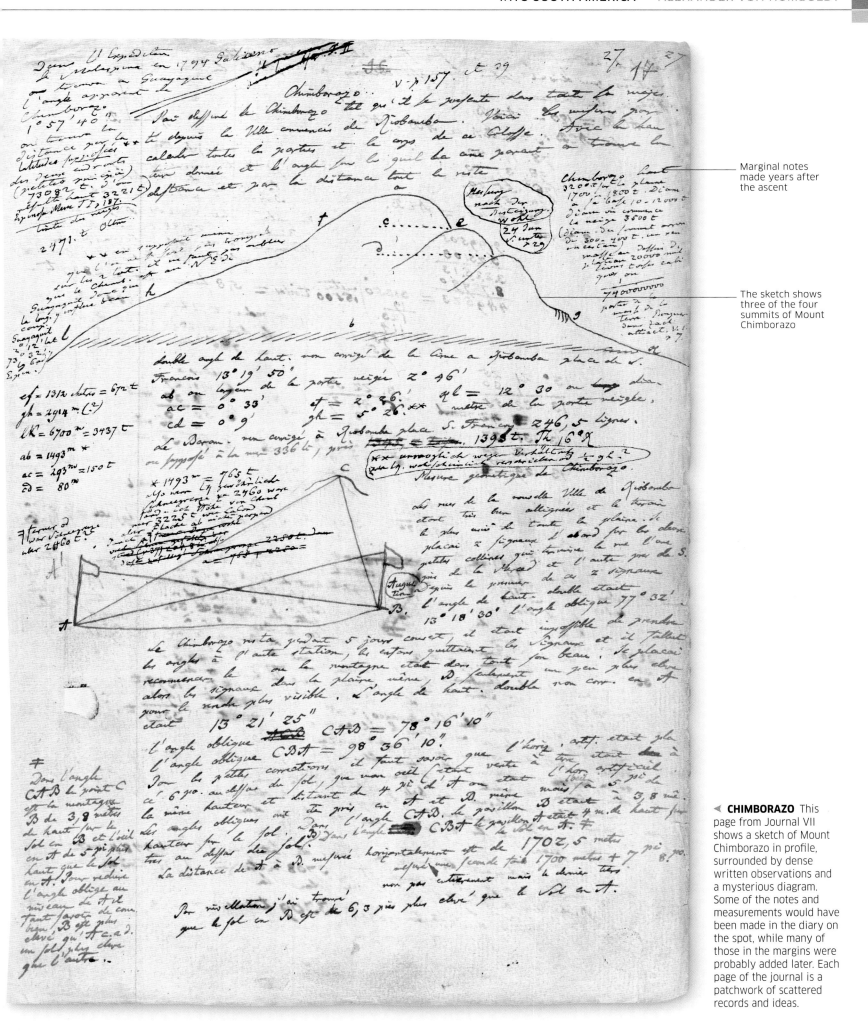

Marginal notes made years after the ascent

The sketch shows three of the four summits of Mount Chimborazo

◄ CHIMBORAZO This page from Journal VII shows a sketch of Mount Chimborazo in profile, surrounded by dense written observations and a mysterious diagram. Some of the notes and measurements would have been made in the diary on the spot, while many of those in the margins were probably added later. Each page of the journal is a patchwork of scattered records and ideas.

Directory: 1700-1800

JOHN ADAMS'S DIARY

AMERICAN (1753-1804)

The second president of the United States, John Adams (1735-1826) kept a diary for half of a century of his long life. A total of 51 manuscript volumes survive, including not only diary entries but also financial accounts, copies of correspondence, and notes.

Adams first kept a diary when he was a student at Harvard. The early volumes cover his life as a teacher in Massachusetts and his career as a lawyer. From 1774, when he was elected to the Continental Congress contesting British rule over the North American colonies, the journals provide an insider's account of the dramatic events that led to the independence of the United States. Adams then served as a diplomat in France, Britain, and the Netherlands. After 1788, when he returned home, his diary entries became more sparse; there are none at all for his presidency from 1797 to 1801. The final entries cover the routines of life on his farm at Quincy, Massachusetts, in the summer of 1804. The diaries present an intimate picture of the mindset of one of the Founding Fathers of the United States.

OLAUDAH EQUIANO

AFRICAN (c.1765-1787)

Olaudah Equiano (c.1745-1797), a former enslaved person, wrote a vivid account of his experiences in servitude and his later adventures as a free man. According to his autobiography, *The Interesting Narrative of the Life of Olaudah Equiano*, he was born in a village in West Africa, abducted by slave traders when he was a child, and transported across the Atlantic to work in bondage in the West Indies and North America. There he was given the name Gustavus Vassa.

A young man of exceptional ability and character, he taught himself to read and write. Traveling widely in the service of an English sea captain, he was able to trade in his own right, making enough money to purchase his freedom. Living in England, he became a Methodist and a respected public figure, defending the welfare of black people and campaigning to abolish the slave trade. He adopted the name Olaudah Equiano to emphasize his African origins. His *Interesting Narrative*, enlivened by his adventure-packed existence, was a sensation when published in London in 1789, going through nine editions.

◀ THE DIARY OF FANNY BURNEY

BRITISH (1768-1840)

Frances Burney (1752-1840), also known by her married name Mme d'Arblay, achieved renown as a novelist and playwright in 18th-century England. Between 1786 and 1791, she resided at the royal court of George III, acting as a Keeper of the Robes to Queen Charlotte. With her French husband, whom she married in 1793, she lived for a time in France under Napoleon Bonaparte. Most of her later years were spent at the English spa town of Bath.

Fanny Burney kept a diary from the age of 15 until the end of her life, recycling material from her journal in copious letters. Her shrewd, satirical pages are filled with many of the eminent figures of the day, including Dr. Samuel Johnson, the politician Edmund Burke, and the actor David Garrick. Her observations of the British court during the "madness" of George III are rightly famous, as is her horrific description of the mastectomy she underwent, without anesthetic,

in 1811. Burney heavily edited her diaries and letters for posthumous publication, which was carried out by her niece in 1842-1846. Some of the material she cut from her early diaries has since been rediscovered.

THE ACLAND JOURNAL

BRITISH (1776-1777)

In 1776, Lady Harriet Acland (1749-1815), a fashionable member of the British nobility, took the bold decision to accompany her husband to North America, where he was traveling as an infantry officer to fight American colonists rebelling against British rule. The journal that recounts her subsequent experiences was written partly in her own hand and partly by an anonymous male assistant, perhaps a chaplain.

The grueling journey across the Atlantic on board a military transport ship and into the interior of Canada is described in precise detail. Traveling with the forces transporting the army's artillery and baggage, Acland then participated in the disastrous British march south from Canada that ended in surrender at Saratoga in October 1777. She behaved with remarkable courage, tending the wounded and rowing to the American lines, while six months pregnant, to obtain her wounded husband's release from captivity after the British defeat. In addition to providing a record of military operations, Acland's journal is notable for its observations of life in the North American wilderness, including the customs of the Native American Ottawa people.

THE JEHOL DIARY

KOREAN (1780)

Yeolha ilgi, translated into English as *The Jehol Diary*, is a travelogue written by Pak Chiwon (1737-1805), a Korean scholar-official. In 1780, Pak accompanied an embassy sent by King Chongjo of Korea to pay homage

Fanny Burney, Edward Francisco Burney, c.1784-1785

to the Qianlong Emperor of China on the occasion of the emperor's 70th birthday. Writing in classical Chinese, Pak describes the visit to the imperial summer residence in Jehol Province and extensive travels on horseback through northern China. He vividly evokes the hardships and chance discoveries of travel—fording the Yalu River, encountering a funeral, and meeting a merchant skilled at faking antiques. His text has a clear purpose, however; he believed that Qing-Dynasty China was superior to Korea in its technology and learning.

He reports on how the Chinese went about doing things, from firing kilns to piling horse dung neatly, hoping to persuade his home country to adopt practical social and technological reforms that could improve his countrymen's everyday lives. The complete book comprises 26 chapters arranged in 30 volumes. There are several versions of the original text, none of which is authoritative.

MARTHA BALLARD'S DIARY

AMERICAN (1785-1812)

A midwife living at Hallowell on the Kennebec River in Maine, Martha Moore Ballard (1735-1812) began to keep a diary on January 1, 1785, when she was aged 50. She continued noting the minutiae of daily life in her family and rural community for 27 years, writing by candlelight with a quill pen in small diary books that she stitched together herself.

Her journal records her daily work as a midwife, traveling on horseback or by canoe to deliver babies at isolated farms, attending autopsies, and administering her own homemade remedies. It covers the occasional dramatic event, including a mass murder and a rape trial at which Ballard gave testimony, but it is mostly filled with the humdrum joys and tragedies of courtship and marriage, fever epidemics, pregnancies of unmarried women, and personal financial problems—Ballard's husband was imprisoned for debt in 1804.

The diaries were kept by Ballard's family until a descendant left them to Maine State Library in 1930. It was only in the 1980s that their historical and human interest was recognized as

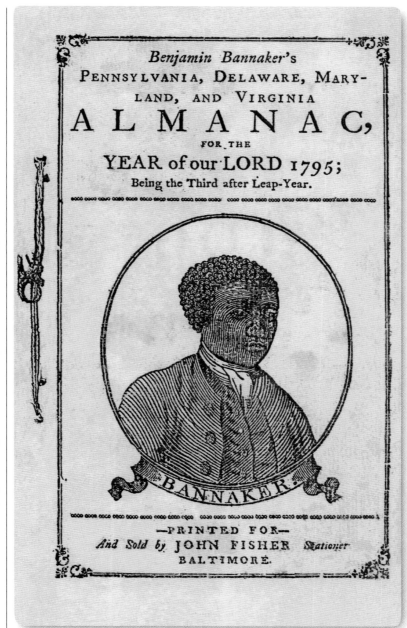

Front cover of Benjamin Banneker's *Almanac*, published 1795

a unique record of a working woman's life in the pioneering years of the United States.

JOVELLANOS'S DIARIES

SPANISH (1790-1810)

A prominent figure in Spain's literary, intellectual, and political life, Gaspar Melchor de Jovellanos (1744-1811) wanted to bring the rational progress of the Enlightenment to what he felt was Spain's backward economy and society, an ambition that brought him into conflict with conservative forces during a troubled period in Spanish history. He began a diary in 1790 when, for political reasons, he had

been banished to his native province of Asturias, in northwest Spain. Driven by an insatiable curiosity, he traveled the countryside commenting on the condition of roads and inns—which he considered mostly abysmal— the local customs and antiquities, landscape and weather, food and drink.

After Jovellanos was recalled to the center of power in 1797, his diary became more intermittent, and it stopped altogether in 1801, when he was imprisoned by his enemies. Released in 1808, he played a leading role in the attempt to establish a liberal Spanish regime while the country faced French occupation. His last diary entry was made in March 1810. He died the following year while fleeing French forces.

◀ THE JOURNALS OF BENJAMIN BANNEKER

AMERICAN (C.1791-1806)

Benjamin Banneker (1731-1806) was a free black man who farmed tobacco outside Baltimore, Maryland. Despite receiving little education, he had an exceptional ability for mathematics and sciences. He attracted attention as a young man by building a wooden clock and was involved in the survey work for constructing Washington, DC.

From 1792 to 1797, he published a popular almanac incorporating his astronomical calculations, accurately predicting eclipses and other celestial phenomena. Banneker kept journals primarily to record his astronomical observations, but he included other matters, from accounts of his dreams to copies of his correspondence with Thomas Jefferson, then US Secretary of State, in which he argued for the abolition of slavery. After Banneker died in 1806, most of his papers were destroyed in a fire. One of the journals on astronomy and some loose papers survived and have been preserved by the Maryland Historical Society since 1844.

THE ÅRSTA DIARY

SWEDISH (1793-1839)

The journal known as *The Årsta Diary* was written by Märta Helena Reenstierna (1753-1841), the wife of a Swedish cavalry officer. It is named after the Årsta Manor, the estate south of Stockholm where Reenstierna and her husband lived. She began the diary at the age of 40, by which time she had borne eight children, only one of whom—a son—survived.

Sober and industrious, Reenstierna describes in a charmingly concise and objective style the daily management of both the domestic and agricultural sides of the manor and describes a social life that encompassed cultured circles in Stockholm. The Swedish songwriter Carl Michael Bellman was one of her friends. Her husband died in 1811 and her son in 1812, but she continued to write in her diary until two years before her own death, eventually filling more than 5,000 folio pages. *The Årsta Diary* was not published until the mid-20th century.

4

1800—1860

The Romantic movement, which dominated European culture in the 19th century, promoted individualism, rebellion, and the demonstration of emotion. Diarists filled their pages with expressions of idealistic love and angst. Writers such as Dorothy Wordsworth and Henry Thoreau were inspired by the Romantic reverence for nature. French literary figures such as the Goncourt brothers produced journals in a more cynical vein. Traveling around the world continued to provide Europeans with material for journals, none more important than Charles Darwin's record of the voyage of the *Beagle*, which later led him to formulate the theory of evolution. Women's diaries, such as those of Charlotte Brontë, reflected an increasingly restless female sensibility at odds with the social restrictions of the times.

The Grasmere Journals

1800-1803 ▪ PEN AND INK ON PAPER ▪ FOUR NOTEBOOKS ▪ BRITISH

DOROTHY WORDSWORTH: DIARIST

The Romantic poet William Wordsworth and his sister, Dorothy (1771-1855), were very close. They moved to Dove Cottage in Grasmere in the English Lake District after the death of their father and continued to live together even after William married. He was already famous as a poet during his lifetime, and Dorothy was there when he wrote many of his masterpieces. She kept journals, not published until after her death, that describe their lives together and reveal the inspiration behind many of his poems. The Grasmere journals cover the first few years.

Although she was modest about her writing ability, Dorothy had a talent for description and a memory for detail that bring her journals to life. They reveal a woman who loved nature, read widely—especially poetry—relished the speech patterns of local people, and was friends with other writers, notably Samuel Taylor Coleridge. Most fascinating of all, the Grasmere journals record the experiences the Wordsworths shared—the walks they took together, their daily life, and the books they read. Dorothy tells how her brother loved walking, even at night, and how hard he worked on his poetry. She also notes

> 66 But as we went along there were more and yet more [daffodils close to the water] and at last under the boughs of the trees, we saw that there was a long belt of them along the shore, about the breadth of a country turnpike road. I never saw daffodils so beautiful they grew among the mossy stones about and about them, some rested their heads upon these stones as on a pillow for weariness; and the rest tossed and reeled and danced, and seemed as if they verily laughed with the wind that blew upon them over the lake, they looked so gay, ever glancing, ever changing. 99

THE GRASMERE JOURNALS, APRIL 15, 1802

incidents that led to some of his most famous poems, such as the meeting with a beggar woman that inspired "The Beggars." She often watched her brother at work, describing how he wrote the "Poem to a Butterfly" at breakfast, with his waistcoat unbuttoned as he concentrated on getting the words right, and records how he composed parts of his famous "Immortality Ode." Dorothy was a unique eyewitness and contributed in her quiet way to the birth of English Romantic poetry.

In context

◄ **WILLIAM WORDSWORTH** One of the major Romantic poets, William Wordsworth wrote poems celebrating the beauties of the natural world and describing the people he met on his walks. He was born in the Lake District and spent much of his life there, living at Dove Cottage from 1799 to 1808. He described life there as one of "plain living, but high thinking."

► **THE LAKE DISTRICT** Romantic writers, such as the Wordsworths and their friend Samuel Coleridge, were some of the first to admire the wild, dramatic scenery of the Lake District, especially its mountains and lakes. Most earlier writers had felt more at home in places where nature had been tamed or shaped by people.

There are many scribbled amendments, deletions, and splodges of ink

Dorothy imagines that the daffodils danced and laughed, an idea that her brother later used in his poem

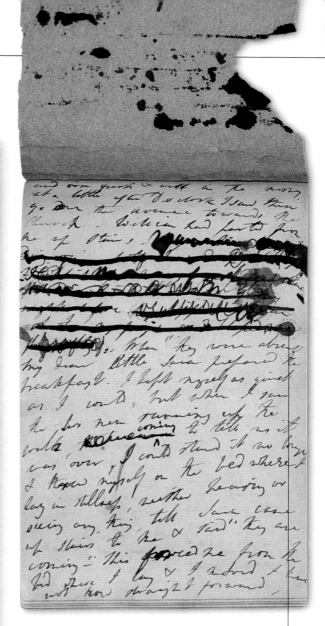

A MOMENT OF INTIMACY

The Wordsworths were devoted siblings. Here, Dorothy writes that on the night before William was married, he gave her the wedding ring, which she wore all night for safekeeping before returning it to him. Someone crossed out this part of the page, perhaps because it suggested that William and Dorothy were too intimate.

The offending lines have been struck through

◀ **POETIC INSPIRATION** This 1802 entry in the journal describes daffodils that Dorothy and William saw growing on one of their regular lakeside walks. These flowers and their movement in the breeze inspired William's famous poem "I Wandered Lonely as a Cloud," which he wrote two years later. He borrowed details of Dorothy's diary entry describing the daffodils (see above left) for the poem.

> ❝ Grasmere looked so beautiful that my heart almost melted away. ❞
>
> **THE GRASMERE JOURNALS, JUNE 21, 1800**

A Route to the Pacific

1804-1806 ▪ PEN AND INK ON PAPER ▪ 18 NOTEBOOKS ▪ AMERICAN

LEWIS AND CLARK: EXPLORERS

Captain Meriwether Lewis (1774-1809), the personal assistant of President Thomas Jefferson, and William Clark (1770-1838), a frontiersman, led a pioneering scientific expedition across the uncharted wilderness of the American West in 1804-1806. They had been dispatched by Thomas Jefferson to explore the Louisiana Territory, land newly acquired from France that makes up what is now the central third of the United States. The expedition was then to carry on west, through uncharted and maybe hostile territory, to find a navigable route through the "great rock mountains" to the Pacific Ocean. On the way, it was to map the course of the Missouri River and any other rivers; study the geology, flora, and fauna of the new lands; and make alliances with indigenous tribes it met.

Lewis and Clark assembled a team of around 30 men, known as the Corps of Discovery, and set out west on the Missouri River in May 1804. The journey was long and arduous. Both men, and the other members of the expedition, kept journals, which they wrote in regularly, describing the courses and widths of the rivers that they sailed and the terrain that they covered, backed up with detailed weather charts, compass readings, and notes of the distances traveled each day. Neither Lewis nor Clark was particularly literate—their spelling and grammar are unconventional—but both of them were expert observers, giving readers a fascinating insight into the challenges faced by the expedition.

Lewis and Clark eventually reached the Pacific in 1805, with the aid of a French-Canadian trapper who acted as a translator, his Native American wife, and the tribes that they met along the way. They had traveled 8,000 miles (13,000 km) from the mouth of the Missouri River to the mouth of the Columbia River on the northern Pacific coast. The following spring, they headed back east, returning to St. Louis in September 1806. In their journals, they had recorded not only a remarkable story of exploration but also a pivotal moment in American history.

▼ **THE GREAT FALLS** On June 13, 1805, the expedition reached the Great Falls of the Missouri River, an obstacle that would take a month to bypass. This sketch, made by Clark on July 4, 1805, shows the five waterfalls and the portage (routes for carrying a boat overland) that the expedition planned to use.

▶ **REACHING THE PACIFIC** This battered book bound in elkskin was kept by William Clark and covers the period from September 11 to December 15, 1805. On the second of these two pages, written on November 7, 1805, he describes the moment when they first caught a glimpse of their long-awaited goal, the Pacific Ocean. This was confirmation that the United States now stretched from the Atlantic to the Pacific.

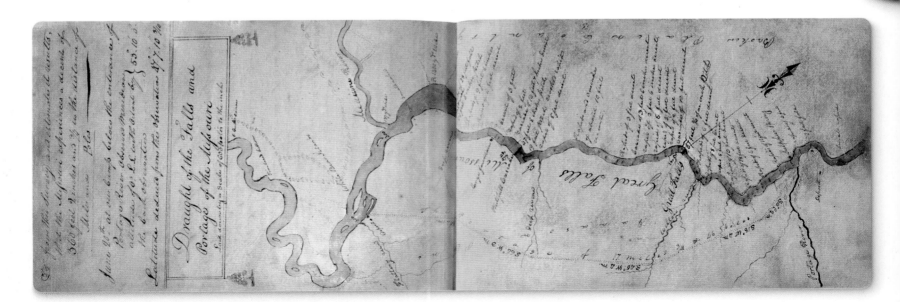

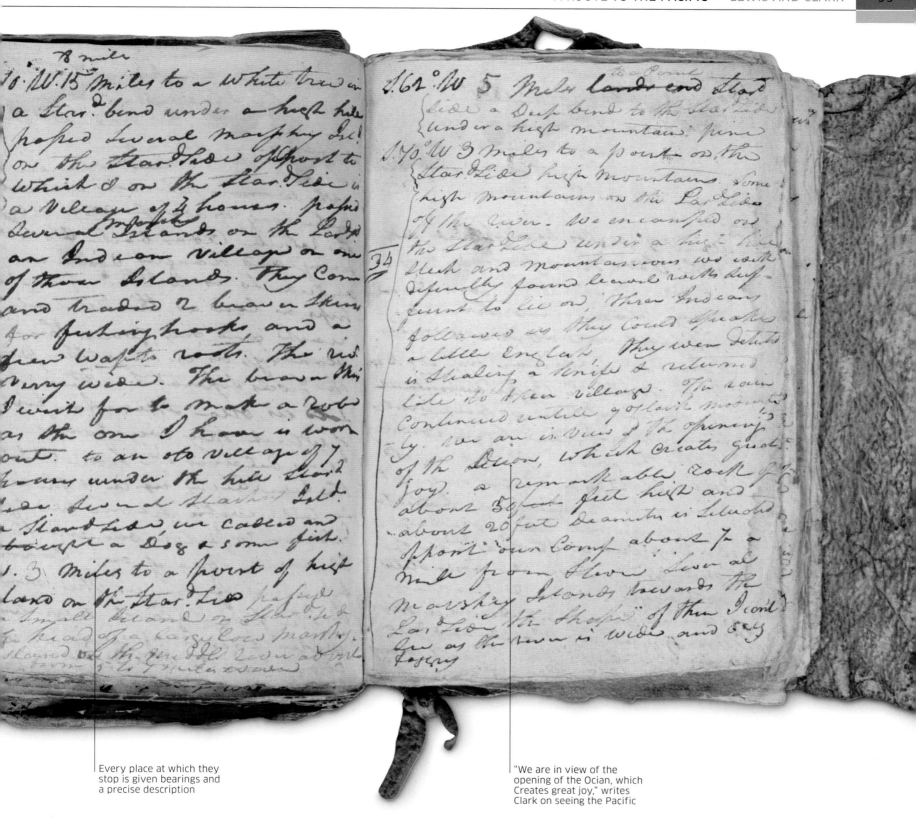

Every place at which they stop is given bearings and a precise description

"We are in view of the opening of the Ocian, which Creates great joy," writes Clark on seeing the Pacific

> ❝ … my ears were saluted with the agreeable sound of a fall of water and advancing a little further I saw the spray arrise above the plain like a collumn of smoke…. I did not however loose my direction to this point which soon began to make a roaring too tremendious [sic] to be mistaken for any cause short of the great falls of the Missouri….
>
> I hurryed down the hill which was about 200 feet high and difficult of access, to gaze on this sublimely grand spectcile … immediately at the cascade the river is about 300 yds. wide … a smoth even sheet of water falling over a precipice of at least eighty feet, the remaining part of about 200 yards … formes the grandest sight I ever beheld…. ❞

MERIWETHER LEWIS ON FIRST SEEING THE GREAT FALLS OF THE MISSOURI, JUNE 13, 1805

In detail

Lewis and Clark have been described by an American historian as "the writingest explorers of their time." They both filled many notebooks during the expedition, probably carrying them sealed in tins to protect them from damage. Thomas Jefferson had told them to detail "the animals of the country ... especially those not known in the US." Their journals are full of notes and drawings of plants and animals that they had not come across before. By the end of the expedition, they had discovered more than 300 new species. Lewis and Clark were also asked to document where Native Americans lived in the newly acquired territory and their encounters with them. They met around 50 different tribes, with whom they tried to trade, realizing how important it was to create good relationships with them. The expedition notebooks record the clothes and customs of the people they met, with a great attention to detail.

   The Lewis and Clark journals are held by the American Philosophical Society library. They fill 18 notebooks, 13 of which are bound in red leather, four in boards covered in marbled paper, and one in elkskin. They are also available to read online.

◄ **PIPE TOMAHAWK** Lewis and Clark took pipe tomahawks with them on the expedition to trade or present as gifts to Native American chiefs. Symbolizing both war and peace, the pipe (or "smoak") tomahawk was used both as a weapon and for smoking tobacco.

▲ **NATIVE AMERICANS** When the expedition met a new tribe, they would parade in uniform and demonstrate an air gun, then request to meet the chief and offer gifts. This usually helped establish friendly relations, but not always. The Teton Sioux, for example, realized that the Americans would try to take control of the trade in the region.

➤ **STATION CAMP** Lewis and Clark reached the mouth of the Columbia River on the Pacific Ocean one and a half years after setting out from St. Louis, Missouri. They established a camp on the northern side of the estuary and spent 10 days there in the rain—Clark called it "the most disagreeable time I have experienced." This is the map of the area he made on November 19, 1805.

“ It would be **distressing** to a feeling person to See our Situation at this time.... ”

WILLIAM CLARK'S JOURNAL, NOVEMBER 12, 1805

▼ **ANIMAL WATCH** Both Lewis and Clark made extensive notes on the animals that they saw. Clark also drew many of them. He was not an artist, but his drawings successfully capture the characteristics of each animal. Below is a drawing of a white salmon trout, drawn on March 16, 1806. "This is a likeness of it," writes Clark, "it was 2 feet 8 inches long."

A sage grouse, first spotted at the mouth of the Marias River and later drawn by Clark on March 2, 1806

Gentleman Jack

1806-1840 ▪ PEN AND INK ON PAPER ▪ 26 NOTEBOOKS ▪ BRITISH

ANNE LISTER: LANDOWNER

The British landowner Anne Lister (1791-1840) kept a secret diary describing her struggles as a businesswoman, her travels (in France, Spain, Russia, and other countries), and her life as a lesbian. During her lifetime, same-sex relationships were rarely discussed openly, and any mention of them met with disapproval or outright condemnation. Lister turned to her diary to express her most private thoughts–about how she found women attractive, how she flirted with female friends, and how, in later life, she was able to live openly as a lesbian with a long-term partner. She also wrote about the prejudice that she encountered because she had dared to enter the "male" sphere of industry by opening a coal mine on her land in competition with local male mine owners. Instead of trying to hide her differences from other women, Lister expressed herself in what she wore, dressing in black at a time when pale colors were fashionable for women. As a result, some people gave her the nickname "Gentleman Jack."

In the diary, passages about Lister's struggles occur alongside fascinating details about her daily life. It covers topics ranging from local social events to national news, making a document of some four million words in total. Lister hid her diary from her family and friends and wrote the most intimate parts in code. No one cracked the code until a relative, John Lister, deciphered it in the 1890s with the help of a local schoolmaster. As homosexuality was illegal in the UK at the time, John Lister did not want to draw attention to his ancestor's sexuality, and so he hid the diary. Extracts from it were published for the first time in only 1988.

▲ **ROMANTIC OVERTURES** These pages of the diary date from June 1818, when Lister was attracted to Maria Browne. The coded passage tells how she gave Maria the nickname Kallista (after a nymph loved by the goddess Diana in Roman mythology) and how Maria seems to respond well to her advances. Later, however, Maria became engaged to a man, and Lister turned her attentions elsewhere.

▲ **SHIBDEN HALL** When Lister's uncle died in 1826, she inherited Shibden Hall, a large house outside Halifax, in Yorkshire, as well as investments that gave her a substantial income. At last she had a private space and greater freedom to live as she pleased. She later extended the house and modified it to suit her needs.

> ❝ I have not exactly given [Maria] a promise in a set form of words but I have done nearly, in fact, the same thing, so that I cannot now retract with honour.... I love her & her heart is mine in return. Liberty & wavering made us both wretched & why throw away our happiness so foolishly? She is my wife in honour & in love & why not acknowledge her such openly & at once? I am satisfied to have her mind, & my own, at ease. The chain is golden & shared with [Maria]. I love it better than any liberty. ❞

ANNE LISTER'S DIARY, JUNE 13, 1821

The code used in parts of the diary is made up of a mixture of numbers, English letters, symbols, and letters of the Greek alphabet

The code used in Anne Lister's journal

▲ **CRYPTHAND** Around one-sixth of the diary is written in Lister's own code, which she called her "crypthand." She was so adept at it that she could write it quickly. She did not leave any spaces between the words, making it hard to crack. When John Lister deciphered it, he left the diary and a copy of the key to the code with a librarian in Halifax, who locked it away.

SECRET PASSIONS

In Lister's time, it was extremely difficult for a female couple to live openly in a long-term, intimate relationship. Lesbians who were able to live together usually concealed their true relationship. They claimed to live as chaste companions, and talk of homosexuality was disguised by allusions to gay couples in classical mythology. Lister's diary describes a visit in 1822 to Sarah Ponsonby and Eleanor Butler, a famous Irish couple known as the "Ladies of Llangollen," who lived in North Wales. Like Lister, these ladies dressed distinctively in black. They were said to live together as a couple but were unable to talk openly about it. Perhaps encouraged by their example, Lister began to regard herself as married to her long-term partner, Ann Walker.

➤ *Sappho and Erinna in a Garden at Mytilene,* Simeon Solomon, 1864

> " I love, & only love, the fairer sex … my heart revolts from any other love than theirs. "

ANNE LISTER'S DIARY, JANUARY 29, 1821

Diary of a Slave

1813-1869 ▪ PEN AND INK ON PAPER ▪ 186 PAGES ▪ AMERICAN

MICHAEL SHINER: NAVY YARD WORKER

The diary of Michael Shiner (1805–1880), which the US Library of Congress now holds, is extraordinary in many ways. Covering the years from 1813 to 1869, Shiner described all the major public events that took place in Washington, DC, where he lived. He gave a firsthand account of the War of 1812 that was fought between the US and the UK and documented the racial tensions, strikes, and riots that he witnessed in the Washington Navy Yard, where he worked. He also, shockingly, described the abduction of his wife and children by slave dealers, who transported them to a slave pen in Alexandria, Virginia—for one of the most remarkable aspects of the diary is that Shiner himself was originally an enslaved man, who was later made a free man.

Michael Shiner, an African American, was born enslaved in Maryland, Virginia, and was sent to Washington, DC, to work in around 1812. For most of his life, he worked as a laborer in the Navy Yard paint shop. As an enslaved man, he had no formal education, but he learned to read and write, probably at church Sunday school lessons. This was the only type of school that African Americans were permitted to attend at the time. At some point, Shiner began to keep a journal, which he called "his book."

He wrote in a small shop notebook, filling each page right to the edges with his elegant, sloping script. His writing is idiosyncratic. He had his own style of spelling, capitalization, and punctuation, which makes the text colorful and distinctive: "the time the colery [cholera] broke out in about June and July august and September 1832 it Raged in the City of washington and evry day they wher twelve or 13 carried out to they graves a day."

Part of the book is in different handwriting and may have been written by Shiner's grandson at a later date. Some of the information in the diary could have been added only after the events described, which suggests that parts of it were not a day-to-day journal but a memoir of an eventful life that was written up later. At one point, Shiner writes proudly, "I was an eyewitness to all this."

▶ **SOLD INTO SLAVERY** Halfway down the right-hand page, Shiner writes: "the 5 day of June 1833 on wensday my Wife and Childdren philis Shiner wher sold to couple of gentelman Mr Franklin and mr John armfield and wher caried down to alexandria." He describes how he traveled to Alexandria, south of Washington, three days earlier and eventually managed "with the assistance of god" to have them freed.

In context

◀ **WASHINGTON BURNS** During the War of 1812, British forces defeated the Americans at the Battle of Bladensburg on August 24, 1814. They then marched to the capital and set fire to many buildings, including the White House and Capitol Building. "As we got a sight of British armmy raising that hill they looked like flames of fier all red coats," writes Michael Shiner.

▶ **NAVY YARD LABOR STRIKE**
The Washington Navy Yard was the US Navy's largest shipbuilding yard. Shiner describes the working conditions there and the 1835 strike that erupted when management limited workers' lunch privileges. The strike triggered a bitter race riot, known as the Snow Riot, led by mechanics from the Navy Yard.

[Handwritten diary pages — Michael Shiner's diary, 1833]

WASHINGTON **SLAVE TRADE**

When Michael Shiner started work at the Navy Yard, a third of the workers were enslaved African Americans. The US capital had moved from Philadelphia to Washington, DC, in 1800, and enslaved people built the infrastructure for the new city. Alexandria, just to the south of Washington, became one of the largest slave markets in the US. After Congress outlawed the importation of new enslaved people in 1808, the city's enslaved were gradually granted their freedom. Michael Shiner filed a petition for freedom in 1836, and he and his wife and family were made free a few years later. Slavery was finally abolished in the District in 1862.

▲ **The Slave Market,** Friedrich Schulz, 19th century

> i am under ten thousand oblagation to the Hon major genral Ham lin for his kindness to me and my Wife and Children on the 7 day of June 1833 on friday the General laid a Detachment on my Wife and 3 childdren at mr armfield Jail and takein them from ther and put them in the county Jail of alexandria to wait action of the court and my wife and childdren Reemained in the county Jail in alexandria from the 7 of June 1833 until the eleven of June 1833 … all the people … appeard to be wiling to Relieve me of my disstress.

MICHAEL SHINER'S DIARY, JUNE 1833

A Voyage Around the World

1817–1820 ▪ PEN AND INK ON PAPER ▪ THREE VOLUMES ▪ FRENCH

ROSE DE SAULCES DE FREYCINET: ARISTOCRAT

At the age of 19, Rose Pinon (1794–1832), a young woman from a humble background, married 35-year-old Louis Claude de Saulces de Freycinet, a French aristocrat. Three years later, in 1816, the French Navy gave her husband command of a scientific around-the-world expedition. Unwilling to be parted, the couple hatched a plan. The night before the expedition ship *Uranie* left Toulon in southern France in September 1817, in breach of naval regulations prohibiting women sailing on state vessels, Rose was smuggled aboard dressed as a man. At first she stayed hidden in her cabin, but once the ship had made its last stop in Europe, the captain revealed his secret.

On what was to be one of the last great scientific voyages of the age, the *Uranie* spent three years circumnavigating the globe. Despite being shipwrecked off the coast of the Falklands Islands on the return voyage, the Freycinets and crew were able to return home safely with their findings and collections. There is no mention of Madame de Freycinet in any of the official expedition reports, but Rose kept her own account of the voyage in a journal that she wrote for a friend and letters to her mother. "Having far more spare time here than my husband has, I can chat with you at length," she wrote. Her journal gives impressions of the places she visited, the people

> " I shall begin my journal from the moment when, leaving my home in Toulon at midnight, I made my way alone to the house of one of my friends. There I spent a very restless night thinking of the somewhat daring adventure which I was to embark upon and the dear ones I was about to leave behind for so long and whom I might never see again…. I spent the whole of the following day writing my farewell letters and that night, around 11:30 p.m., I donned my male attire. Accompanied by Louis and one of his friends, I headed for the harbor to go aboard the ship. "

THE JOURNAL OF ROSE DE FREYCINET, SEPTEMBER 1817

whom she met, and her husband's scientific work. She describes battling through treacherous seas, placating understandably hostile islanders, and attending balls in Mauritius and Sydney.

Rose's life was tragically cut short when she died of cholera at the tender age of 38. Parts of her extraordinary journal and letters, the first written account by a woman who circumnavigated the globe, were published in 1927, some 93 years later. The journal is now kept in the State Library of New South Wales, Australia.

In context

▲ **SHARK BAY** There were two artists on board the *Uranie*, whose job was to provide illustrations of the expedition. In this painting of a camp at Shark Bay on the west coast of Australia, Rose can be seen standing outside the entrance of the tepee on the far right. When the painting was reproduced in the official report, however, Rose was painted out.

▲ **IN TIMOR** Although Rose was part of the expedition in an unofficial capacity, she always accompanied her husband ashore. This painting shows the couple arriving at Dili, in Timor, where they are greeted by the governor. His servants hold umbrellas to protect Rose, resplendent in a feathered headdress, from the sun.

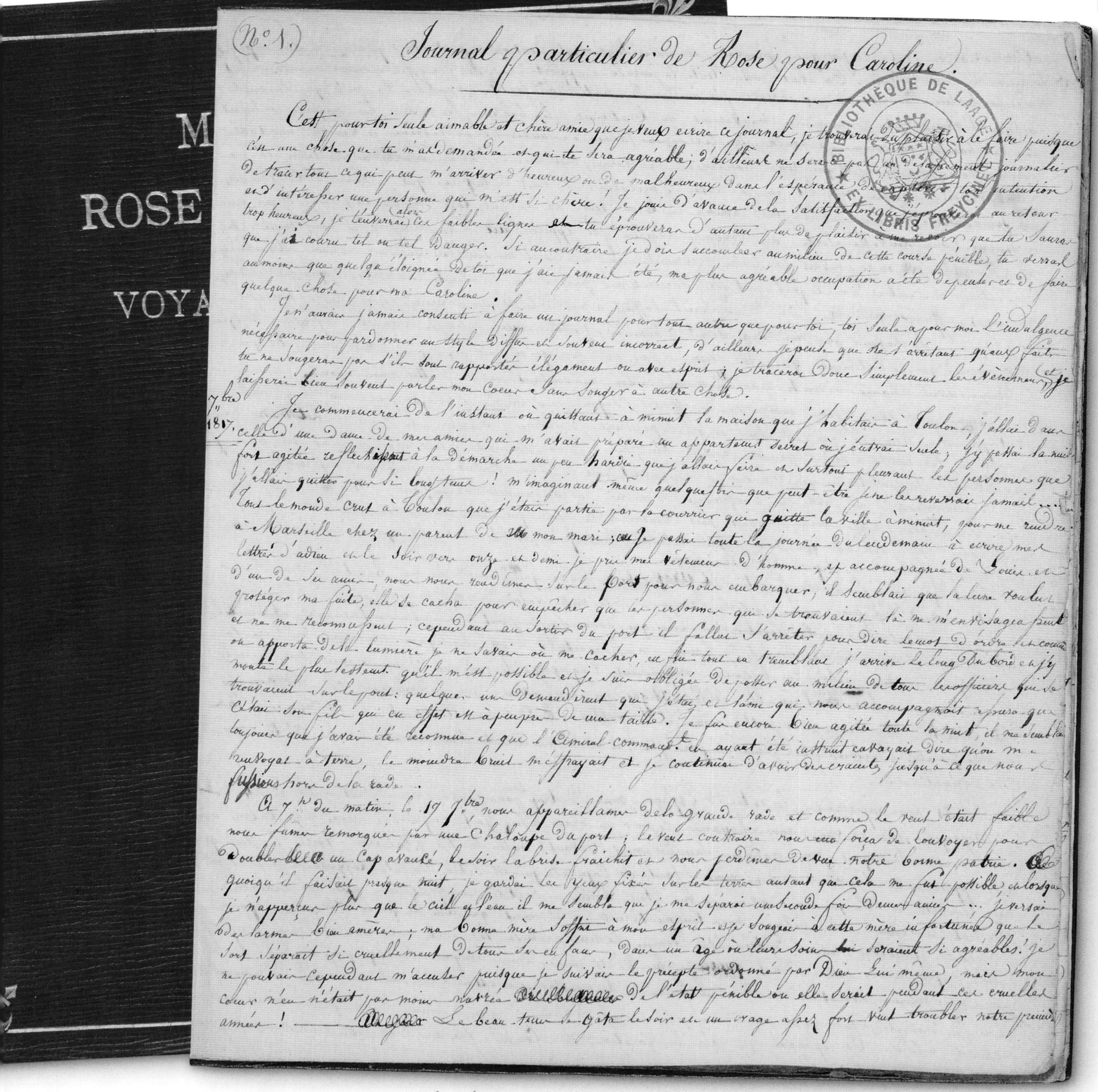

Journal particulier de Rose pour Caroline.

▲ **PRIVATE JOURNAL** Rose did not intend to have her journal published. She had promised her friend, Caroline de Nanteuil, that she would write it. "Rose's private journal for Caroline," it says at the top of the first page, shown here. There are some 132 handwritten pages of the journal altogether. Rose also wrote 15 letters to her mother, Madame Pinon, which make up an additional 200 pages.

> 66 What **saved us from peril** was our **gaiety!**… I got out my **castanets** and box of **magic tricks**. 99

THE JOURNAL OF ROSE DE FREYCINET, 1818

An Artist's Journal

1822–1824; 1847–1863 ■ INK AND WATERCOLOR ON PAPER ■ SEVEN SKETCHBOOKS; 20 NOTEBOOKS ■ FRENCH

EUGÈNE DELACROIX: ARTIST

Delacroix's Journal presents a unique portrait of one of France's greatest painters. It provides revealing insights into his character and temperament and highlights the technical skills that made him an artistic genius.

The Journal falls into two major sections: the first, which runs from 1822 to 1824, portrays a young man, nervous and excitable, on the brink of greatness; while the second begins in 1847 and continues until the end of his life. By then, Delacroix had achieved both fame and success and could write with much greater authority. Along with his lively accounts of the social whirl, he gives fascinating details of his approach to his own work and his opinions on the value of other artists. Although brief, the earlier section tells us more about the painter's personality. At the outset, Delacroix wrote that the Journal was for his eyes alone, hoping that it would help him understand his sudden shifts of mood, from exaltation to despair. Delacroix was always a man of contrasts. He loved painting scenes of savagery and violence—horses and lions fighting each other, despots butchering their concubines, victims cowering pitiably after a massacre—but his own way of life was refined and civilized. His friend, the poet Charles Baudelaire, put it succinctly: "Delacroix was passionately in love with passion, but coldly determined to express this passion as clearly as possible."

Delacroix was born into a wealthy upper middle-class background (he is thought to have been the illegitimate son of Maurice Talleyrand, a high-ranking politician). In public, he could be confident, something of a dandy, and a brilliant conversationalist with a dazzling turn of wit, but in private he was more reticent. He shrank from commitment and craved inner solitude. "The mask is everything" is a phrase that he repeated several times in the Journal.

▶ **MOROCCO DIARY** Delacroix filled seven sketchbooks during a six-month visit to Morocco. They are crammed with hundreds of tiny, rapid pencil-and-watercolor sketches, accompanied by brief notes detailing the colors, forms, and movements of anything that caught his eye. He used the sketchbooks as source material for his famous paintings of North African scenes.

◀ **HORSEMEN OUTSIDE CITY GATES** Delacroix was hugely impressed by his travels in Morocco. He did not encounter the colorful, exotic details that feature in some Orientalist paintings, but a more sober and dignified way of life that reminded him of the Classical world: "The Greeks and Romans are here at my door, in the Arabs who wrap themselves in white blankets and look like Cato or Brutus with their aristocratic bearing...."

Sketches of a mounted soldier and Arabs cloaked in their voluminous white robes

Delacroix made a point of sketching costume details, using them in his paintings for years afterward

As well as people, Delacroix recorded glimpses of the countryside that he saw, noting the shapes and colors of any unusual vegetation

> Nothing is so real to me as the illusions I create with my painting. The rest is shifting sand.

DELACROIX'S JOURNAL, FEBRUARY 27, 1824

In detail

The main body of the Journal was written in tall, narrow notebooks, similar to those that were used for housekeeping accounts. Several handwritten copies of the document were made after the artist's death, while the originals passed to the Verninac family, the descendants of Delacroix's sister. The first published edition of the Journal, based on one of the copies, appeared in 1893, but this was not a complete version of the manuscript. The diary for 1848 was lost for good after Delacroix left it in a carriage when he was traveling to Paris. Some individual pages were also torn out. Bookstores near the Seine were selling these for a few francs in the 1890s. Eventually, the surviving documents were donated to the Art Library of Paris University in 1924. Collating these with the earlier edition of the diaries, André Joubin, the Keeper at the Library, published the definitive, three-volume edition of the Journal in 1932.

Delacroix's diary of his travels in North Africa is an adjunct to the Journal. In 1832, the artist was invited to join a diplomatic mission, led by the Comte de Mornay, to the Sultan of Morocco. Delacroix's scribbled notes and sketches relating to this visit were always intended to be *aides-mémoire*, to help him compose paintings inspired by the experience.

Most of this side relates to aspects of the Sublime. "Terrible" in this context means "awe-inspiring". The section heads are written in capitals

◀ **LOVE LETTERS** Joséphine de Forget and Delacroix became lovers after she was widowed at the age of 34. The pair later separated but remained close friends for the rest of his life. Delacroix's executors destroyed the most personal letters to Joséphine, dating from 1834–1844, but she was often mentioned in the Journal.

▶ **DICTIONARY OF THE FINE ARTS** Throughout the later part of the Journal, there are notes for an art dictionary. Delacroix probably meant to publish these, but the project never materialized. They were mostly written when Delacroix was ill and so was unable to paint. Divided into brief, thematic sections, the notes provide a fascinating insight into the painter's working practices and his theories about art.

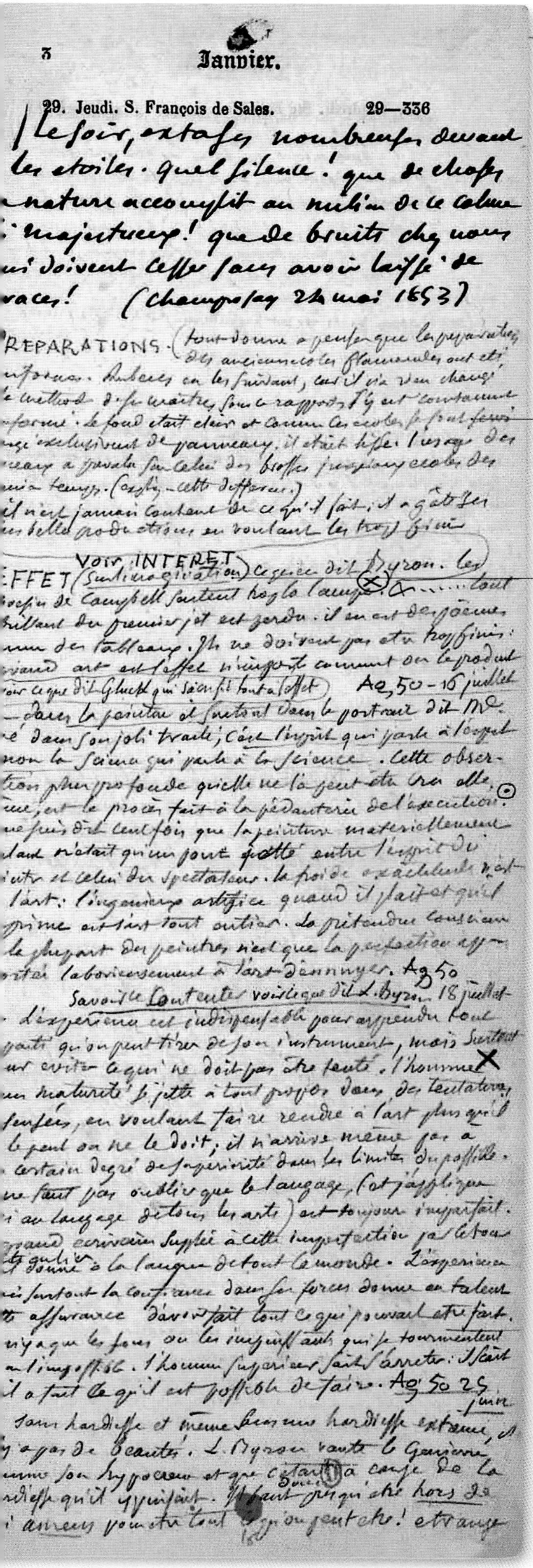
3 Janvier.

29. Jeudi. S. François de Sales. 29—336

Le soir, extases nombreuses devant les étoiles. quel silence! que de choses la nature accomplit au milieu de ce calme majestueux! que de bruits chez nous qui doivent cesser sans avoir laissé de traces! (Champrosay 24 mai 1853)

> I confess that I have worked logically. I, who have no love for logical painting, I see now that my turbulent mind needs activity, that it must break out and try a hundred different ways before reaching the goal toward which I am always straining. There is in me an old leaven, some black depth which must be appeased. If I am not quivering and excited like a serpent in the coils of a pythoness [i.e., a female soothsayer] I am without inspiration. I must recognize this and accept it. Everything good that I have done has come to me in this way.

DELACROIX'S JOURNAL, MAY 7, 1824

Description of how Rubens and the early Flemish painters adopted a uniform system of preparation

This entry details the effect of art on the imagination: "painting is nothing but a bridge ... between the mind of the artist and that of the beholder"

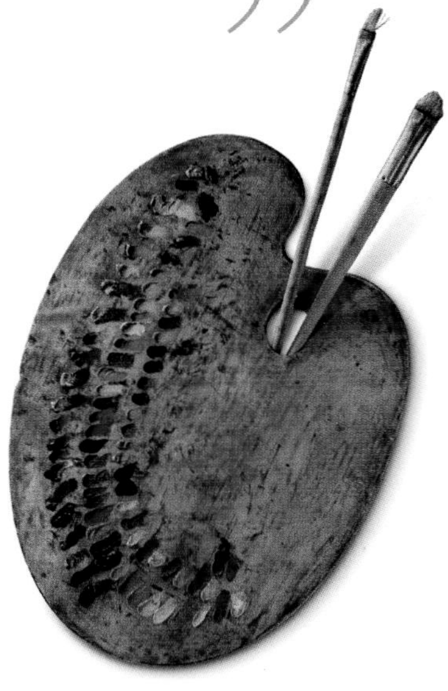

▸ **DELACROIX'S PALETTE**
Delacroix was a magnificent colorist and juxtaposed pure, complementary colors in a way that inspired later generations of painters. He spent hours experimenting with pigments and laid out his palette with care. The sight of it alone, "freshly set out with the colors all shining," fired his enthusiasm.

DELACROIX'S **ART**

Delacroix was the greatest painter of the French Romantic movement. During the 1820s, his paintings were highly controversial. Critics found his themes too modern and violent and were appalled by the apparent roughness of his style. They were accustomed to paintings that had well-ordered compositions, firm contours, and smooth surfaces. To them, Delacroix's canvases seemed chaotic and unfinished. Tantalizingly, the first section of the Journal draws to a close just as the controversy was breaking. *Liberty Leading the People* is typical of Delacroix's early style. It is a dynamic image of rebels storming the barricades in the July Revolution of 1830. They are urged on by a daringly updated version of Marianne, the symbol of the French Republic, bare-breasted and carrying a modern rifle.

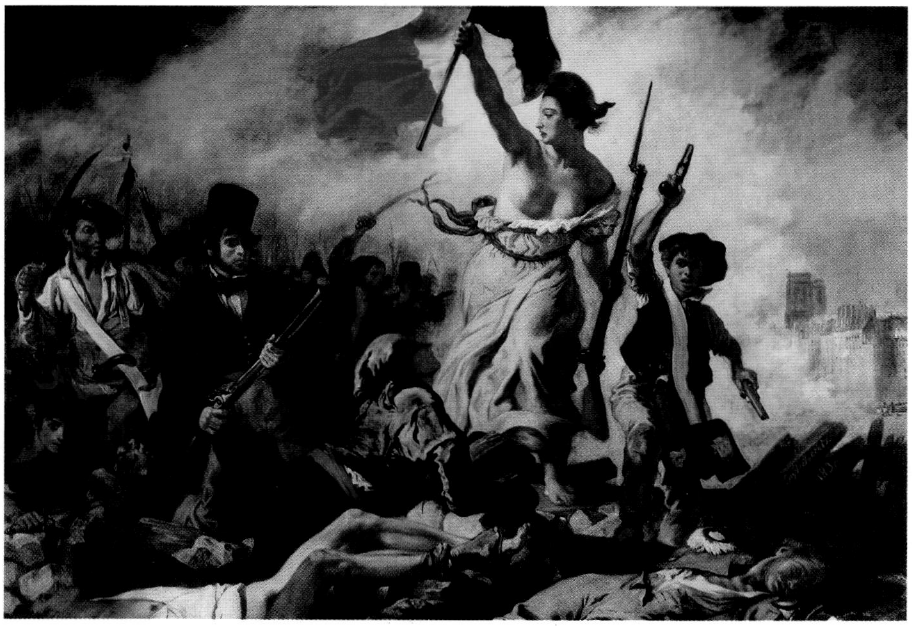

▲ ***Liberty Leading the People,*** Eugène Delacroix, 1830

A Writer in Crisis

1825-1832 ■ PEN AND INK ON PAPER ■ TWO VOLUMES ■ SCOTTISH

SIR WALTER SCOTT: NOVELIST

In the mid-1820s, the historical novelist and poet Sir Walter Scott (1771-1832) faced a crisis in his life. Already successful and famous, he had invested a lot of his money in a printing company, James Ballantyne and Co., which collapsed as the result of a banking crash. Deeply in debt, Scott recorded the profound effects of this disaster in his journal, which he began to keep in 1825 and continued writing in almost daily until shortly before his death, when the text ends midsentence.

In his journal, he describes how he resolved to work intensively to produce bestselling books so that he could pay off all his creditors. He also recounts how hard work and stress led to a series of strokes that incapacitated him. He records his day-to-day life, the death of his wife in 1826, his progress on his books, his earnings, and the travels he made to Naples, Pompeii, and Malta in the hope of improving his health. He talks about famous people he met and national events such as the riots before the 1832 Reform Bill, but he also describes his occasional depression and the country walks that helped him overcome it.

Scott writes in a pacy, fluent style much influenced by that of earlier diaries, such as those of Samuel Pepys, which had recently been published. He hoped to publish the parts of the journal that covered his travels, so he made his accounts as entertaining as he could, but he did not live to see the journal in print as he died unexpectedly in a typhus epidemic. However, Scott's first biographer, James Lockhart, found the text to an excellent source when writing about the author's life, and many later biographers have followed suit, valuing its vivid account of a writer's determined efforts to work his way out of a crisis.

In context

▲ **FINANCIAL RUIN** In 1825, a financial crisis triggered by unwise investments in South America spread around the country and led to the closure of numerous banks. Many investors went bankrupt, and Scott, as the sole investor in Ballantyne's, faced debts of around £120,000 (more than £6 million today). However, his huge income from his books enabled his relatives to repay the debts soon after he died.

Pencil annotations highlight some of the key themes and people in the diary

◄ **HISTORICAL NOVELS** Scott produced a stream of new books and short stories in the last years of his life. Popular tales such as *Woodstock* (1826) and *Anne of Geierstein* (1829) were part of his series of Waverley novels, some of the best-loved books in Europe. He also wrote successful nonfiction, including a biography of Napoleon.

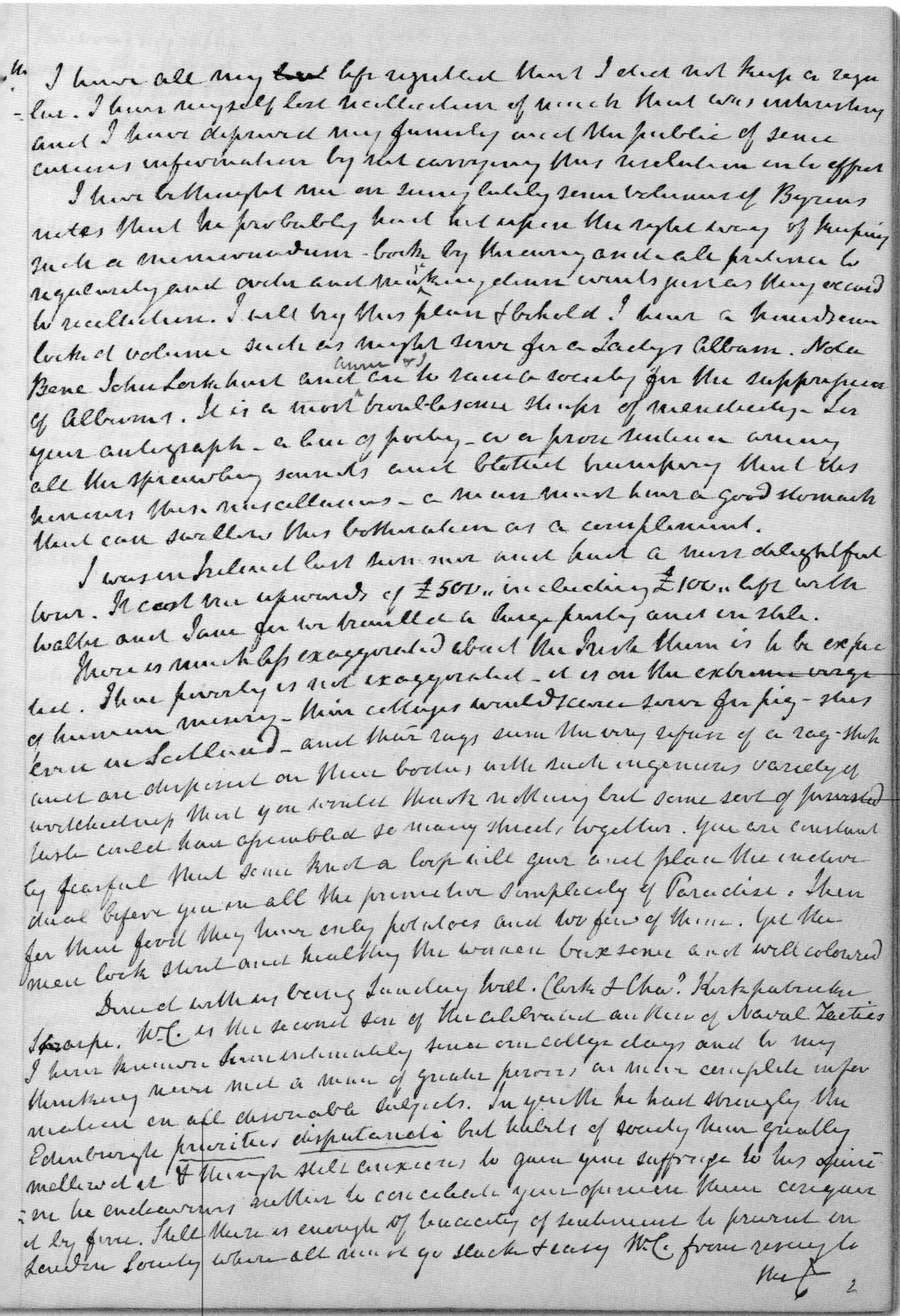

The journal records Scott's impressions of Ireland and the great poverty of many people there

The rapid handwriting, although regular and evenly spaced, is often difficult to read

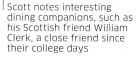

Scott notes interesting dining companions, such as his Scottish friend William Clerk, a close friend since their college days

▲ **THE FIRST PAGE** Scott begins his journal in 1825 by recalling his regret that he had never kept a regular diary. Inspired by Lord Byron's journals, he notes that Byron did not write every day but recorded events that came to mind, making his descriptions as lively and entertaining as possible. Just two days later, Scott reveals the financial worries that will dominate the rest of his life.

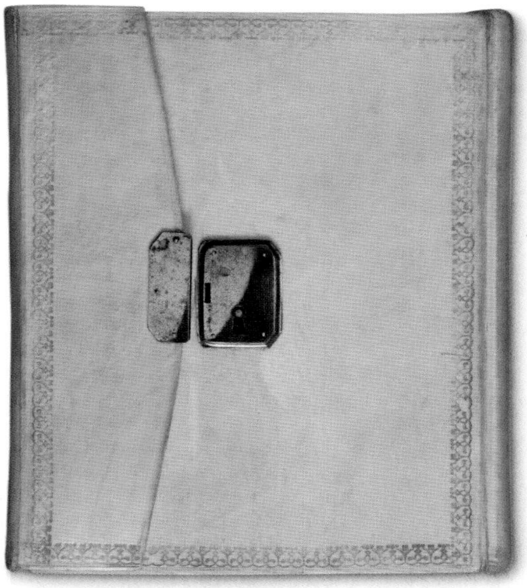

▲ **UNDER LOCK AND KEY** Scott wrote his journal in two vellum-bound volumes that he could lock. He described them as the type of book used by ladies to collect autographs and memorable sayings. Although he probably did not intend the journal to be kept secret, he valued it greatly.

> What a life mine has been!—half educated, almost wholly neglected or left to myself, stuffing my head with most nonsensical trash, and undervalued in society for a time by most of my companions, getting forward and held a bold and clever fellow, contrary to the opinion of all who thought me a mere dreamer.... Rich and poor four or five times, once on the verge of ruin, yet opened new sources of wealth almost overflowing. Now taken in my pitch of pride, and nearly winged ... because London chooses to be in an uproar, and in the tumult of bulls and bears, a poor inoffensive lion like myself is pushed to the wall.

SIR WALTER SCOTT'S JOURNAL, DECEMBER 18, 1825

The Voyage of the *Beagle*

1831–1836 ■ PEN AND INK ON PAPER ■ 800 PAGES ■ BRITISH

CHARLES DARWIN: NATURALIST

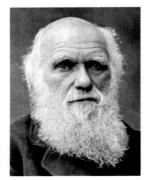

Various documents have survived from the voyage of the *Beagle*, which set out across the Atlantic Ocean to chart the coastline of South America in December 1831. Among them are 18 small notebooks filled with copious observations by the graduate Charles Darwin, who was then only 22 years of age. He was on board as a "gentleman" naturalist and carried these notebooks everywhere, notably whenever the ship anchored and he was able to venture on land. Once back on board, he transcribed the field notes into a large diary, which, over the course of the five years of the expedition, grew to some 800 pages.

In a letter to his sisters, Darwin refers to the content of his notebooks and diary as "chit-chat" and plays down its value, writing that "it is a most dangerous task, in these days, to publish accounts of parts of the world which have so frequently been visited." He was, however, being unduly modest, and his diary is full of engaging descriptions of faraway places. It is also often surprisingly funny. Take the entry for September 8, 1832, for example, when Darwin was in Argentina: "I hired a Gaucho to accompany me on my ride to Buenos Ayres, though with some difficulty, as the father of one man was afraid to let him go, and another, who seemed willing, was described to me as so fearful, that I was afraid to take him, for I was told that even if he saw an ostrich at a distance, he would mistake it for an Indian, and would fly like the wind away." It is little wonder that when Darwin's diaries were later revised and published, they became very popular with readers.

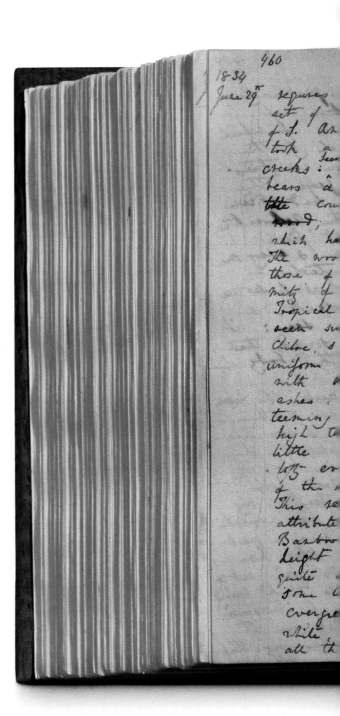

◄ **THE *BEAGLE*** Originally a twin-masted warship, HMS *Beagle* was adapted as a survey vessel and sent off in 1826 to explore the coastline of South America. Darwin joined her second voyage, invited along by the ship's captain, Robert FitzRoy, to help with the surveying. Darwin had neither scientific credentials nor experience but was invited along for his enquiring mind, enthusiasm, and gentlemanly nature. His presence on board ultimately made the *Beagle* one of the most famous ships in history.

" … nothing can be more improving to a young naturalist, than a journey in distant countries. "

CHARLES DARWIN, *VOYAGE OF THE BEAGLE*, 1839

Darwin wrote this entry in his diary from Chiloé, an island off the coast of Chile

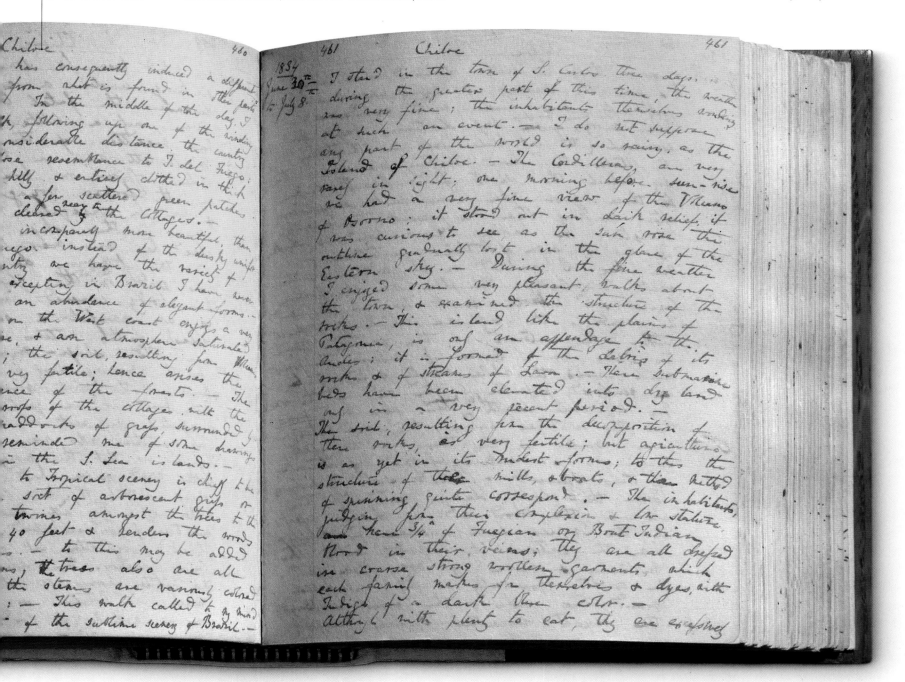

" About 9 o'clock we were near to the coast of Brazil…. The delight one experiences in such times bewilders the mind; if the eye attempts to follow the flight of a gaudy butter-fly, it is arrested by some strange tree or fruit; if watching an insect one forgets it in the stranger flower it is crawling over; if turning to admire the splendour of the scenery, the individual character of the foreground fixes the attention. The mind is a chaos of delight, out of which a world of future & more quiet pleasure will arise. "

CHARLES DARWIN'S JOURNAL, FEBRUARY 8, 1832

▲ **OBSERVATIONS FROM HMS *BEAGLE*** Each page of the diary opens with the date at the top left in the margin and the place at the top center. Darwin normally caught up with his diary during periods of inactivity aboard the *Beagle*. The text always reads as though it was written immediately after the events described, but there are instances where it is clear that many weeks had elapsed before he was able to bring the diary up to date.

In detail

In September 1835, the *Beagle* reached the Galápagos Islands, a volcanic archipelago in the Pacific Ocean, around 620 miles (1,000 km) off the coast of Ecuador. Here, Darwin was intrigued to learn that the giant tortoises native to the islands had shells shaped differently from each other and that the islanders were able to tell from these which island each one came from. The extreme isolation of the islands meant that the species of plants and animals were unlike any that Darwin had ever encountered elsewhere. "The birds are strangers to man," he wrote on September 17, "and think him as innocent as their countrymen, the huge tortoises. Little birds, within three or four feet, quietly hopped about the bushes and were not frightened by stones thrown at them. Mr. King killed one with his hat and I pushed off a branch with the end of my gun a large Hawk." Darwin records that he "industriously collected all the animals, plants, insects and reptiles from this island," adding, "It will be very interesting to find from future comparison to what district or 'centre of creation' the organized beings of this archipelago must be attached."

He had already begun to wonder why the creatures on the islands had developed in such different ways—triggering a train of thought that would later lead him to formulate his theory of evolution by natural selection, which he outlined more than 20 years later in *On the Origin of Species* (1859).

> ❝ [A naturalist] ought to acquire the habit of writing very copious notes, not all for publication, but as a guide for himself. ❞
>
> **CHARLES DARWIN, *ADMIRALTY MANUAL*, 1849**

▲ **COLLECTION OF FINDS** As the expedition's naturalist, Darwin's role was to collect specimens and make observations. Although he had some expertise in geology, he was a novice in all other areas. The numerous items that he gathered, including plants, animals, fossils, and seashells, were therefore sent back to Cambridge in the UK at intervals during the voyage so that they could be identified and classified.

▲ **GALÁPAGOS FINCHES** Darwin noticed that the beaks of finches on the islands varied, an observation that proved crucial to the development of his theories. He wrote: "Seeing this ... diversity of structure in one small, intimately related group of birds, one might really fancy that from an original paucity of birds ... one species had been taken and modified for different ends."

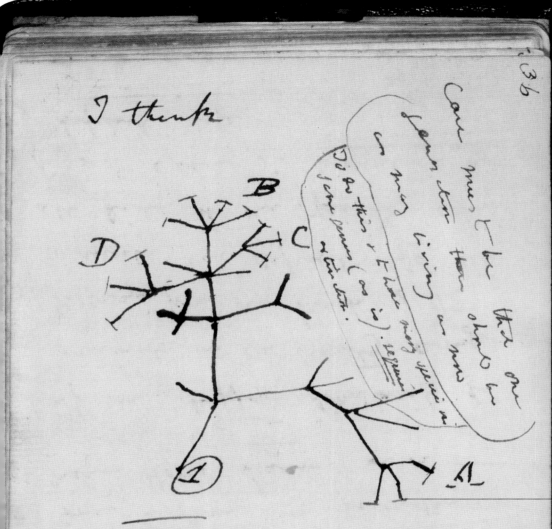

▲ **FIELD NOTES** Darwin had a series of small notebooks like this that he used on his excursions ashore during the voyage of the *Beagle*, to record his "on the spot" observations in pencil. He later stressed the importance of making notes in the field: "Let the collector's motto be, 'Trust nothing to the memory,' for the memory becomes a fickle guardian when one interesting object is succeeded by another still more interesting."

Darwin represented surviving lineages of species with a line at the end of a branch

Each letter corresponds to a different set of descendants from the common ancestor, which is marked "1" at the base of the tree sketch

◀ **TREE OF LIFE** In this notebook page–titled "I think"–Darwin first sketched how species might diversify and evolve like the branches of an imaginary tree. The idea soon came to symbolize his theory of evolution by natural selection. The main text reads: "Thus between A & B immense gap of relation. C & B the finest gradation, B & D rather greater distinction. Thus genera would be formed ... bearing relation...."

A Royal Life

1832–1836 ■ MANUSCRIPTS AND TYPESCRIPTS ■ 140 VOLUMES ■ BRITISH

QUEEN VICTORIA: MONARCH

Even before she became ruler of Great Britain, Queen Victoria (1819–1901) kept a daily journal. She began in 1832 when just 13 years old and carried on, with a few breaks, until the end of her life. The text that survives consists of 13 early volumes in Victoria's handwriting, some additional drafts, 111 volumes of transcriptions made by her daughter, Princess Beatrice, and some typed, unedited copies made for the historian Lord Esher. Beatrice made her transcriptions because Victoria wanted the diaries to be preserved without passages that might upset members of the royal family and for the originals to be destroyed. Beatrice therefore cut many passages, especially those describing Victoria's relationship with her husband, Prince Albert, and her friendships of her later years, such as that with her Indian attendant, Mohammed Abdul Karim.

Even without these passages, the diaries provide a fascinating, personal account of the monarch's life, covering wars, political events, meetings with prime ministers, and travels, as well as glimpses into her private life, such as her love for Prince Albert and the births of her children. The events described range from joyous occasions such as Victoria's coronation to tragedies such as the fall of the city of Khartoum and Victoria's grief when Albert died. Victoria was a fast, fluent writer. She described people and situations vividly, conveying her enthusiasm with extensive underlinings and exclamation marks. Until recently, only selections from the diaries had been published, but in 2012, the entire series was made available online.

▲ **FAMILY SKETCHES** Queen Victoria was an accomplished artist and illustrated many pages of her diary with sketches of her family or people she met. Princess Beatrice cut many of these drawings out of the pages of the queen's original diaries before destroying them. Queen Victoria's sketch above, dated June 13, 1851, shows herself and Prince Albert (left) at the Stuart Ball. The drawing has been inserted into Princess Beatrice's copy of the queen's diary.

In context

◄ **QUEEN AND CONSORT** Albert was the queen's constant companion. A loving husband who gave her nine children, he was also her political advisor, deputized for her when she was ill, and personally designed Osborne House, their family home on the Isle of Wight. Victoria was devastated when Albert died in 1860 and wore black for the rest of her life.

▶ **THE GREAT EXHIBITION** The 1851 Great Exhibition of Arts and Industry, held in the Crystal Palace in Hyde Park, London, included objects from all over the world. Prince Albert played a major part in organizing it, and the queen visited in June. Her diary records how impressed she was with the hundreds of machines on display.

Biblical Keepsake", "Friendship's offering"; a book called
"Tyrol" with beautiful views
of that fine country, 3 very
pretty New year's wishes,
the Gotha Almanack & a
very little almanack. I also
got a very pretty drawing
done by dearest Feodore &
a letter from Späth. I gave
Mamma, an Annual,
a drawing I had done, a
tray of my own work, & a
New-year's-wish, & a nosegay.
Got up at 8. Received
from my dear Lehzen
a lovely seal made of a

Tunbridge Pebble, with V. and a
coronet on it, a New-year's-
wish, and a little instrument for unpicking work, of
Tunbridge Ware. I gave her,
a box and a New-year's-wish.
Dressed & had my hair
done. Received a most
kind letter from dearest
Aunt Louise, & a note from
Aunt Sophia. We break-
fasted after 9. Read in
the Exposition while my
feet were rubbing. I received
also a very pretty peach-
coloured, poplin dress from
dear Mamma. Wrote my
journal. Received from

▲ **A PRINCESS'S WORLD** This page is from one of the handwritten journals that survive from the period before Victoria became queen. Dated January 1, 1836, it lists the New Year presents that the princess gave and received. Most of the gifts are quite modest. Among those Victoria gave her mother were a drawing she had done herself and "a tray of my own work."

The young Victoria's handwriting is regular, with a confident slant to the right and bold flourishes

> I never, NEVER spent such an evening!! MY DEAREST DEAREST DEAR Albert … his excessive love & affection gave me feelings of heavenly love & happiness, I never could have hoped to have felt before! He clasped me in his arms, & we kissed each other again & again!
>
> His beauty, his sweetness & gentleness—really how can I ever be thankful enough to have such a Husband! … to be called by names of tenderness, I have never yet heard used to me before—was bliss beyond belief! Oh! This was the happiest day of my life!

QUEEN VICTORIA'S JOURNAL, FEBRUARY 10, 1840 (HER WEDDING DAY)

Existential Journals

1833-1855 ▪ PEN AND INK ON PAPER ▪ 36 VOLUMES ▪ DANISH

SØREN KIERKEGAARD: PHILOSOPHER

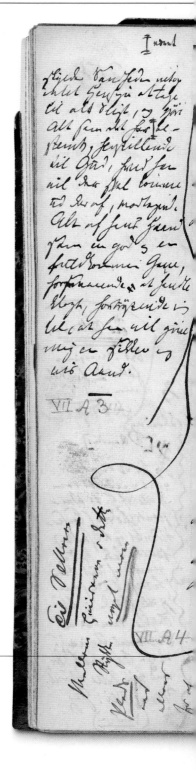

In late 1833, 20-year-old Søren Kierkegaard (1813–1855), a pensive young man in rebellion against a strict Protestant upbringing, began to write his daily thoughts and feelings in a notebook. By the time he died in 1855, having become a celebrated author and thinker, his reflections filled more than 7,000 pages of journals and notebooks. These provide an insight into the intellectual and spiritual ferment of one of the most enigmatic writers of the 19th century.

Kierkegaard lived in Copenhagen, Denmark, all his life. His copious output of published works included fiction, critical essays, and theology, but he is best known as an existentialist philosopher engaged in an anguished quest for a personal truth, "the idea for which I am willing to live and die." His journals do not consist of entries with dates, recording the incidents of his day-to-day existence. Instead, he dashed down whatever occurred to him at any time of the day or night—a vast outpouring of ideas, sketches for future works, fragments of autobiography, impassioned polemics, and provocative epigrams. He once said that it was only through writing that he was able to retain his sanity.

Some of the journals' most moving passages are about the author's doom-laden father, a domineering, self-made man who had risen from poverty and was possessed by an ineradicable sense of sin. Many entries express Kierkegaard's views on philosophy and religion, calling for an authentic Christianity based on personal experience and a leap of faith. There is a dramatic account of his failed relationship with Regine Olsen, the woman he adored but backed out of marrying. He writes, as a kind of explanation for rejecting her: "There is something spectral about me, something that makes it impossible for anyone to have to endure seeing me every day." Work began on preparing Kierkegaard's journals and notebooks for publication 10 years after his death. Their sheer length and complexity has kept editors busy ever since.

Most pages are roughly divided into two sections, indicated on this page by a wavy line

◄ **SPURNED MUSE** Regine Olsen, the daughter of a prominent government official in Copenhagen, was 18 years old when she became engaged to marry Kierkegaard in 1840. His unexplained decision to break off the engagement a year later caused a public scandal and much emotional distress, but he continued to regard Regine as his muse.

> " What I really need is to be clear about *what I am to do,* not what I must know, except insofar as knowledge must precede every action... It is a question of understanding my destiny, of seeing what the Deity really wants *me* to do; the thing is to find a truth which is true *for me,* to find *the idea for which I am willing to live and die...* What use would it be to be able to propound the meaning of Christianity... if it had *no* deeper meaning for *myself* and *my* life?... What use would it be if truth were to stand before me, cold and naked, not caring whether I acknowledged it or not...? "

KIERKEGAARD'S JOURNALS, AUGUST 1, 1835

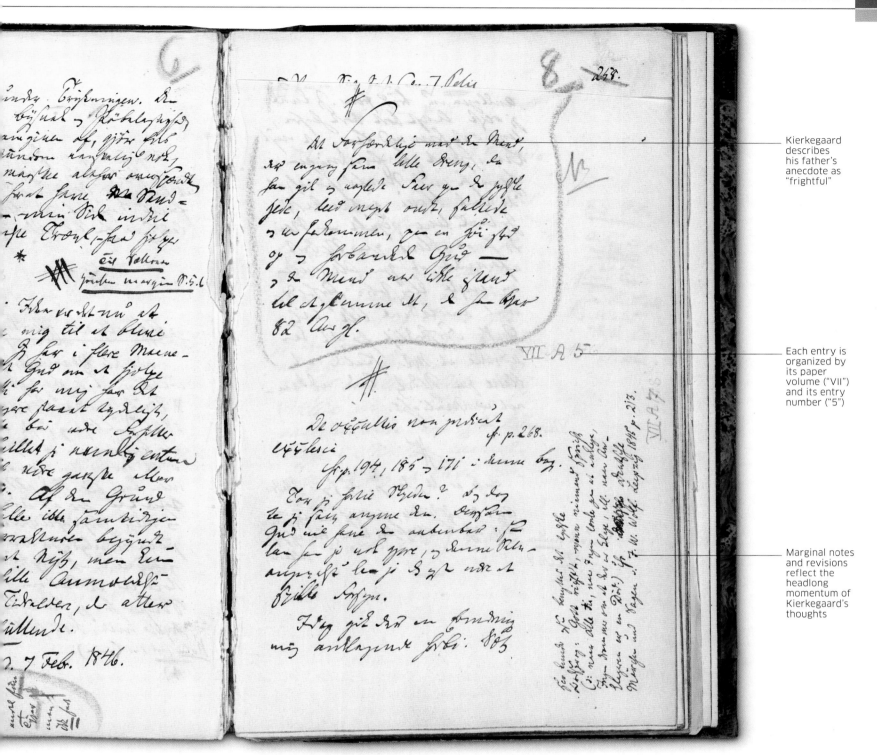

Kierkegaard describes his father's anecdote as "frightful"

Each entry is organized by its paper volume ("VII") and its entry number ("5")

Marginal notes and revisions reflect the headlong momentum of Kierkegaard's thoughts

▲ **CURSING GOD** In these pages of his journal, written in February 1846, Kierkegaard describes how his father, "as a small boy tending sheep on the Jutland heath, suffering many ills, famished and exhausted, stood up on a hill and cursed God. And that man was never able to forget it, not even at the age of 82."

◄ **WRITER'S NOTEBOOKS** Kierkegaard kept his journal in simple notebooks such as these. When the material was edited for publication after his death, many of the originals from his earlier years were destroyed or lost. He always expected the journals to be published one day.

A Victorian Sage

1835-1887 ■ PEN, INK, AND WATERCOLOR ON PAPER ■ BRITISH

JOHN RUSKIN: WRITER

The art critic, artist, social reformer, and philanthropist John Ruskin (1819-1900) traveled a great deal in Europe and was interested in many subjects, from painting to political economy. Throughout much of his life, he kept a diary and notebooks in which he drew the things that he saw on his travels—landscapes, flowers, and ancient buildings in particular. He used his diaries and sketchbooks as reference for the many books that he wrote and for the lectures he gave regularly. Ruskin's best-known books are about painting, the history of architecture, and the art and history of Venice, but he also wrote about social reform, botany, and mythology among other subjects, and his diaries and notebooks also touch on these themes.

His observations on the plight of the working man, and on nature and the environment, anticipate the ideas of socialists and environmentalists.

Ruskin's diaries also cover many subjects: his visits to France, Italy, and Switzerland; the people he met; sermons that he heard in church; notes about books he was reading; and rocks and flowers that he saw. His descriptions of scenery, especially in the Alps, are vivid, recording the fleeting effects of the light and clouds. His notes about buildings are minutely detailed: with his sketches, they form a fascinating record of the architecture of Rouen, Paris, Milan, and Venice. Ruskin drew on this research when he wrote *The Seven Lamps of Architecture* and *The Stones of Venice,* so the diaries were not published during his lifetime. When they were, in the 1950s, they provided an insight into Ruskin's character and powers of observation.

In context

◄ **EFFIE GRAY** Ruskin married Effie Gray, a young woman from a family that the Ruskins knew, in 1848. Gray described Ruskin as an "oppressive" husband and the marriage was never consummated. The union was annulled in 1854, and Gray married the Pre-Raphaelite painter John Everett Millais.

► **LETTER TO JOAN SEVERN** Among Ruskin's many surviving letters are several to his second cousin, Joan Severn (also known as Joanna). Severn became Ruskin's housekeeper and nurse in his final, troubled years at Brantwood. This jewel-like study of a milk thistle, done "in the morning, early," shows that his eye for detail and his drawing skills were as strong as ever.

> But at the end of the range, right over Murano ... burning crests of snow were seen mingled among bars of cloud and gaps of sky, relieved against grey sea cloud behind. The sun was near setting; the calm space of sky changed not; the clouds, as motionless as the hills, and as defined, held up their waved curtain from off the field of gold; and the dark mountain chain, countless in its serrations and gathering together of pointed peaks, lay as sharp and shattered against the amber air, as if it had been a mass of near Highland hills.

JOHN RUSKIN'S DIARY, NOVEMBER 20, 1849

▲ **VENETIAN SKETCHBOOKS** In the 1840s, Ruskin made many drawings of the buildings of Venice, especially details such as the ornamental carvings and stone tracery in the windows of Gothic churches and palaces. He valued these details both because of their fine craftsmanship and because they showed that medieval masons were allowed to produce work of great beauty–they were not mere drudges like many Victorian laborers.

This is a cross section of the tracery and surrounding stonework of the window shown on the opposite page

Each sketch is accompanied by explanatory notes and a label saying where it was made

Detail of part of a window in a building in the Campo Sant'Agostin, near the medieval Basilica dei Frari in Venice

In detail

Although much of Ruskin's diaries is about art, architecture, and scenery, there are passages that are intensely personal, especially those that he wrote late in his life at Brantwood, his home in the Lake District. Some entries record minor illnesses; others reveal his obsession with Rose La Touche, a woman nearly 30 years younger than him, who turned down his marriage proposals. Some mention his troubles with depression, which became worse over time and led to a series of debilitating nervous breakdowns. These psychotic episodes, thought to be related to the death of Rose at the early age of 27, led to long periods of inactivity, which were unusual for a man who spent most of his days working. Ruskin tried to analyze the episodes, going back through the pages of his diaries to look for possible symptoms and causes.

In the early 1880s, he came to the end of one of the volumes in which he kept his diary. Since he had written only on the right-hand pages, he went back to the beginning of the book and wrote new entries on the left. This means that entries from the late 1870s and early 1880s appear side by side. Some of these facing pages reveal the startling contrast between Ruskin's sane and lucid normality and his periods of mental instability.

▲ **COLOR AND DETAIL** Ruskin made this watercolor study of a kingfisher in around 1870. He captured the colors of the bird's vibrant plumage meticulously, creating an image as bright as the work of the Pre-Raphaelites, whom he admired. Ruskin gave the study to the School of Drawing that he founded in Oxford, hoping it would inspire students to do similarly observant and painstaking work.

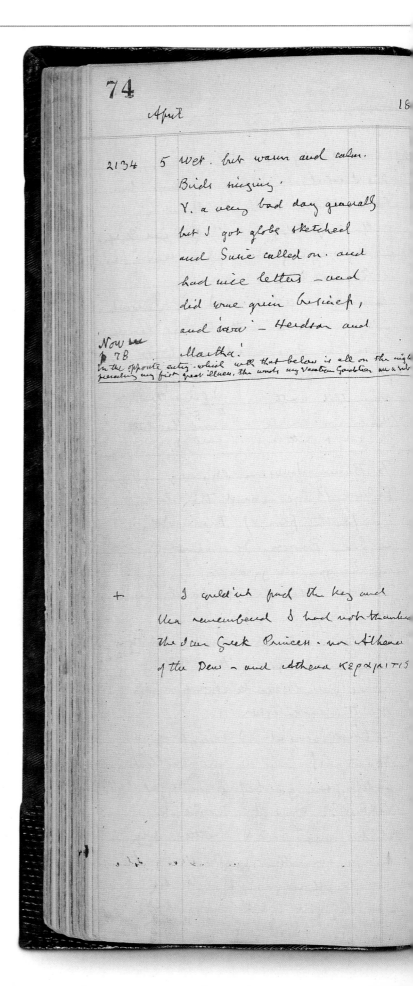

74

◄ **LOOKING BACK** These two pages contain diary entries written five years apart. The paragraph from April 1883 (top left) records a day when Ruskin was apparently in good health, receiving letters, visiting friends, and doing some drawing. The opposite page was written in February 1878, when he had his first mental breakdown. The handwriting here looks fast and fluent, but Ruskin's prose is disconnected and far less coherent.

The text is rambling and refers piecemeal to Raphael and Tintoretto, the doges of Venice, and Shakespeare

> 66 **Let me see** that I don't **thaw away** into waste myself, now the **Spring's come** again for me, **once more!** 99
>
> **JOHN RUSKIN'S DIARY, JANUARY 1879**

ART CRITIC

Ruskin wrote tirelessly about the artists he liked. His great passions were the English landscape painter J. M. W. Turner and the Pre-Raphaelites, a group of British painters that included John Everett Millais, William Holman-Hunt, and Dante Gabriel Rossetti. The Pre-Raphaelites adhered to Ruskin's belief that artists should be true to nature and produce work directly from life and created vibrant images. Ruskin praised their work, although they were sometimes attacked for blasphemy and crudity. In *Lorenzo and Isabella*, depicting an episode from Boccaccio's *Decameron*, Millais used the bright palette and slightly stilted poses characteristic of the Pre-Raphaelites. These features were typical of the early Italian painters (those who lived before Raphael), whom both Ruskin and the Pre-Raphaelites admired.

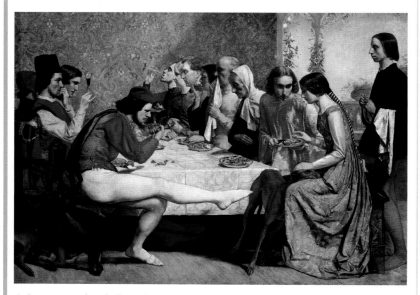

▲ *Lorenzo and Isabella*, John Everett Millais, 1848–49

The Roe Head Journal

1836-1837 ▪ PEN AND INK ON PAPER ▪ BRITISH

CHARLOTTE BRONTË: NOVELIST

Famous as the author of *Jane Eyre*, Charlotte Brontë (1816–1855) grew up in the family home at Haworth, Yorkshire, with her father, brother Branwell, and two sisters, Emily and Anne, who were also writers. In 1831, she left home to go to school at Roe Head, about 20 miles away, and in 1835, at the age of 19, she returned to the school to work for three years as a teacher. Here, Charlotte kept a journal, writing in tiny but clear letters on small sheets of paper, which she folded in four to make pages around 4½ × 7 in (12 × 18 cm) in size. She and her siblings had made miniature books like this when young and had filled them with stories about imaginary worlds.

Charlotte's Roe Head journal mixes descriptions of her daily life with further episodes of these fantasy stories. Her accounts of Roe Head are quite bleak, and it is clear that although she was a good teacher and was liked by the school's head, she felt suffocated and lonely. She describes the extreme local weather, which she likes, but expresses her loneliness, her struggles to adjust to life as teacher, and her frustration at being stuck at remote Roe Head. There is a marked contrast between the place in which Charlotte finds herself and the imaginary

worlds of Angria, Glass Town, and Verdopolis that Charlotte and Branwell had created. Angria was full of exotic, dashing heroes and romantic young women, of revolutions and battles. Charlotte continued these stories in her journal, and this gave her a form of escape from the tedium of her daily life and a way of maintaining a connection with the family she loved.

> " All this day I have been in a dream, half miserable and half ecstatic: miserable because I could not follow it out uninterruptedly; ecstatic because it shewed almost in the vivid light of reality the ongoings of the infernal world.... Then came on me, rushing impetuously, all the mighty phantasm that we had conjured from nothing to a system strong as some religious creed. I felt as if I could have written gloriously— I longed to write. The spirit of all Verdopolis, of all the mountainous North, of all the woodland West, of all the river-watered East came crowding into my mind. If I had had time ... I felt that the vague sensations of that moment would have settled down into some narrative better at least than any thing I ever produced before ... I thought I should have vomited. "

THE ROE HEAD JOURNAL, AUGUST 1836

In context

◄ **CHILDHOOD BOOK** All the Brontë sisters began writing as children. Charlotte's first handwritten book dates from around 1828, when she was only 12. It contains a story, beautifully illustrated in watercolor, that begins, "There once was a little girl and her name was Ane [sic]...." Many of these early stories are very dramatic. One features a fire that seems to predict the fire at the end of *Jane Eyre*.

▶ **ROE HEAD SCHOOL** At Roe Head, the teachers and girls lived in the school house. There was little opportunity for travel, except for country walks, and the atmosphere could be stifling. Charlotte probably based Lowood, the dour boarding school in *Jane Eyre*, on Roe Head. Her life there was made bearable by two friends she had made while a pupil.

> **"** Must I from **day to day** sit **chained** to this chair **prisoned** within these **four bare walls? "**

THE ROE HEAD JOURNAL, AUGUST 1836

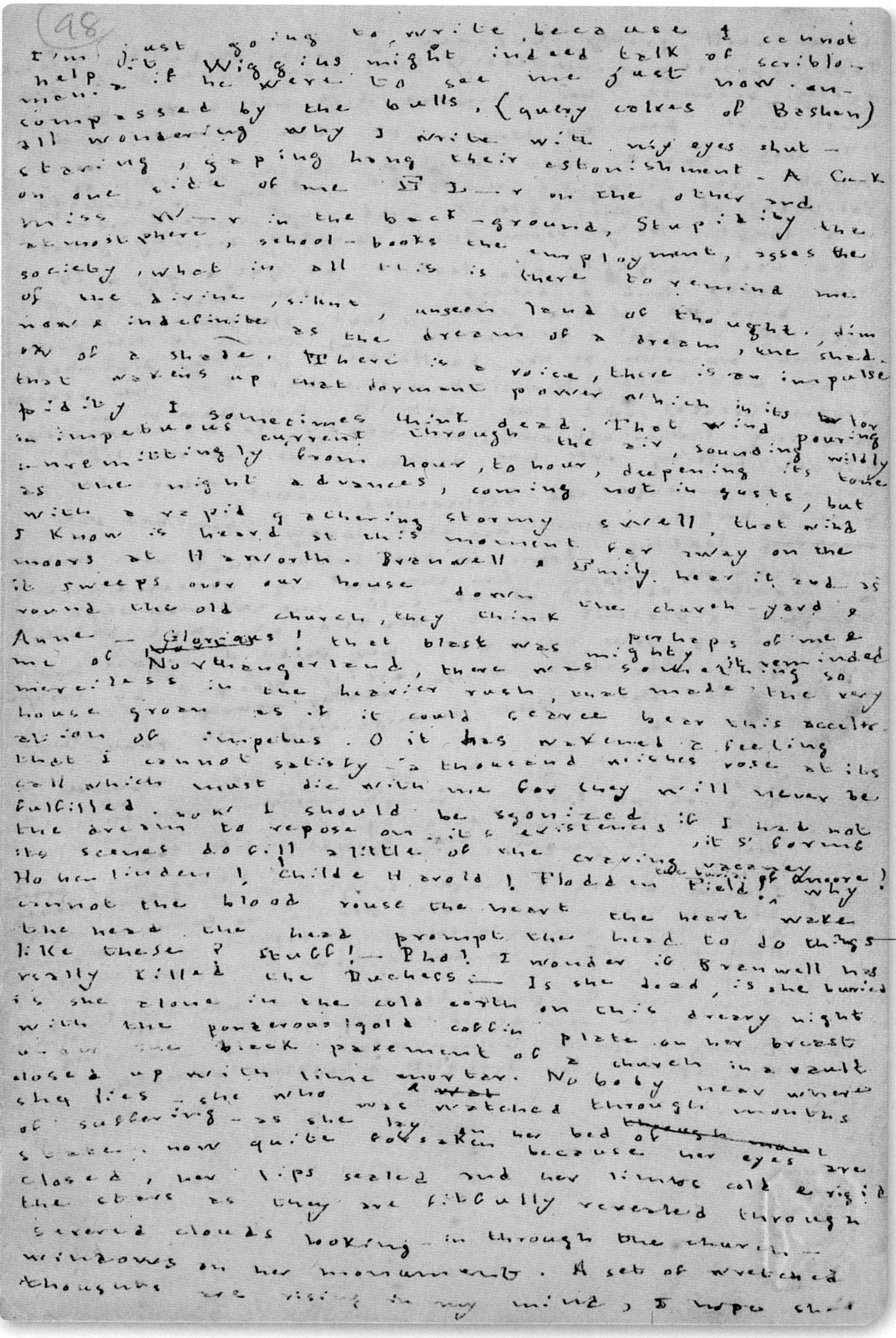

(98) I'm just going to write because I cannot help it. Wiggins might indeed talk of scribblemania if he were to see me just now. encompassed by the bulls, (query calves of Bashan) all wondering why I write with my eyes shut — staring, gaping long their astonishment. A C—k on one side of me E— L—r on the other and Miss W—r in the back-ground, Stupidity the atmosphere, school-books the employment, asses the society, what in all this is there to remind me of the divine, silent, unseen land of thought, dim now & indefinite as the dream of a dream, the shadow of a shade. There is a voice, there is an impulse that wakens up that dormant power which in its torpidity I sometimes think dead. That wind pouring in impetuous current through the air, sounding wildly unremittingly from hour to hour, deepening its tone as the night advances, coming not in gusts, but with a rapid gathering stormy swell, that wind I know is heard at this moment far away on the moors at Haworth. Branwell & Emily hear it and as it sweeps over our house down the church-yard & round the old church, they think perhaps of me & Anne — Glorious! that blast was mighty it reminded me of Northangerland, there was something so merciless in the heavier rush, that made the very house groan as if it could scarce bear this acceleration of impetus. O it has wakened a feeling that I cannot satisfy — a thousand wishes rose at its call which must die with me for they will never be fulfilled. now I should be agonized if I had not the dream to repose on — its existences, its forms, its scenes do fill a little of the craving vacancy. Hohenlinden! Childe Harold! Flodden Field! the burial of Moore! why cannot the blood rouse the heart the heart wake the head the head prompt the hand to do things like these? Stuff! — Pho! I wonder if Branwell has really killed the Duchess. — Is she dead, is she buried is she alone in the cold earth on this dreary night with the ponderous gold coffin plate on her breast under the black pavement of a church in a vault closed up with lime mortar. Nobody near where she lies — she who was watched through months of suffering — as she lay on her bed of state, now quite forsaken because her eyes are closed, her lips sealed and her limbs cold & rigid the stars as they are fitfully revealed through severed clouds looking in through the church-windows on her monument. A set of wretched thoughts are rising in my mind, I hope she

EMILY BRONTË'S DIARY

Charlotte's sister Emily, author of the novel *Wuthering Heights*, also wrote a diary for four years in the 1830s. Emily's diary blends accounts of daily life with events from a fictional world, Gondal, which she and Anne had invented together. Emily illustrated some pages and this drawing shows the two sisters at work. Spread out on the table are the small sheets of paper on which they wrote the diary and their Gondal stories and poems, as well as the tin in which they kept their papers. Each sheet was carefully folded in four when put away in the tin, and the sheets are still creased as a result.

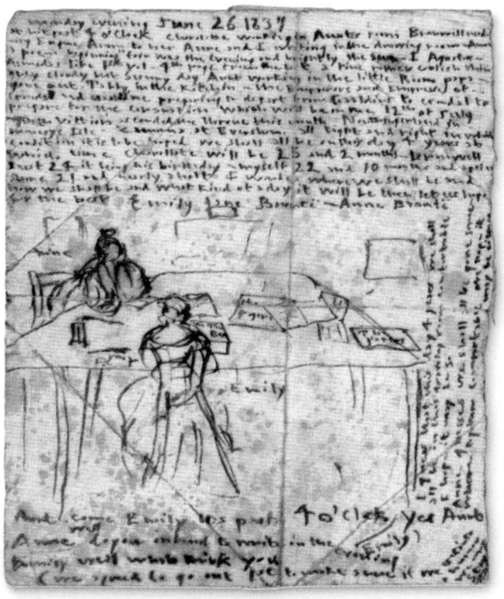

▲ **Illustrated entry** from Emily Brontë's diary dated June 26, 1834

Charlotte's handwriting is so small that some people need a magnifying glass to read it

◄ **THE URGE TO WRITE** This entry of 1836 is typical of the Roe Head journal. "I am just going to write because I can't help it," says Charlotte, and she describes where she is and what she is doing. Her frustration with her situation at Roe Head then gives way to yearning for Haworth and her family. This in turn segues into fantasizing about the imaginary subjects of the stories that she and Branwell wrote together when she was still at home.

The Chronicler of Nature

1837-1861 ▪ PEN AND INK ON PAPER ▪ 47 VOLUMES ▪ AMERICAN

HENRY DAVID THOREAU: WRITER

Thoreau (1817-1862) was a genuine all-arounder. He once described his occupation as "literary and scientific, combined with land-surveying," but his talents extended far beyond that. He was an innovative naturalist, a philosopher, and a campaigner for civil liberties. Many of his concerns seem even more relevant today than they did in his own time. He was passionate about preserving natural habitats and the environment: "Let us keep the New World new," he said. He promoted the idea of community parks and, leading by example, showed how to live a simpler life in an increasingly complex world.

Born in Concord, Massachusetts, Thoreau spent most of his life in New England. In his youth, he ran a private school with his brother, but the defining influence on his career was his friendship with the transcendentalist philosopher, Ralph Waldo Emerson. Thoreau worked in Emerson's household

> " Live in each season as it passes; breathe the air, drink the drink, taste the fruit and resign yourself to the influences of each. Let them be your only diet…. In August live on berries, not dried meats and pemmican, as if you were on shipboard making your way through a waste ocean, or in a northern desert. Be blown on by all the winds. Open all your pores and bathe in all the tides of Nature, in all her streams and oceans, at all seasons. "

THOREAU'S JOURNAL, 23 AUGUST 1853

for a couple of years and lived in a cabin on his land from 1845 to 1847. During this solitary existence, Thoreau developed his unique skills as a writer and a chronicler of nature. His journal played an important part in this process. It was meant to be a private testing ground for his ideas and his literary skills, but many people now prefer it to the books and essays that Thoreau actually published.

In context

▲ **WALDEN POND** In 1844, Emerson bought some woodland at Walden Pond, outside Concord, to save it from destruction. Thoreau asked if he could build a cabin there, in return for working the land. This was agreed, so he constructed a one-room shack from the remains of an old railroad shanty. Here, he could write in seclusion, observing nature at close quarters.

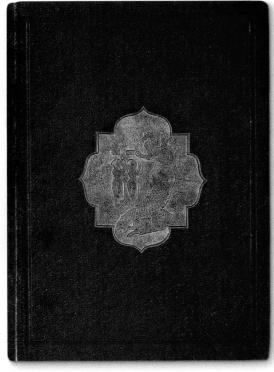

▶ **SACRED TEXTS** Many transcendentalist ideas stemmed from sacred Indian texts. Emerson had a large collection of Oriental books that Thoreau read when staying with him, notably the *Bhagavad Gita*. "In the morning, I bathe my intellect in the stupendous and cosmogonal philosophy of the *Bhagavad Gita*," he wrote.

▼ **TRANSCENDENTALISM** Thoreau was a devoted follower of transcendentalism, a spiritual form of philosophy that gained popularity in the US in the early 19th century. Its adherents believed social institutions had become corrupt and that individuals reached their full potential only when they were self-reliant. They also believed in the healing power of nature. Thoreau writes about transcendentalism in this entry for March 5, 1853.

Here, Thoreau laments that he could not be totally honest about his beliefs, fearing that they would make him a laughing stock

> The fact is I am a mystic—a transcendentalist—and a natural philosopher to boot.

THOREAU'S JOURNAL, MARCH 5, 1853

In detail

Thoreau began to keep his handwritten journal in 1837 and continued until his death in 1862. The results eventually filled 47 manuscript volumes. The journal begins conventionally enough, as a diary of daily events, but it grew into something far more complex—a repository of the author's ideas, projects, and observations. Thoreau recognized from early on the value of "writing for my own eye only," using the journal as a place to hone and develop the books he hoped to publish. The 1853 volume, for example, contains lengthy draft sections of *Walden*, his account of an excursion that would later be published as an essay ("The Maine Woods") and notes for an unpublished article intended for an anti-slavery magazine.

For many modern readers, however, the most interesting sections of the journal are probably Thoreau's accounts of his long, sauntering walks and boating trips, coupled with his acute observations on "Nature in her everyday mood and dress."

He usually wrote at home in the morning and set off on his walks in the afternoon. While he was out, he took copious "field notes," which he later worked up into journal entries, often composing the entries for several different days at a single sitting. He intended to organize his material in a scientific manner. In his manuscript, he marked passages relating to the changing of the seasons with parallel lines in ink or pencil. In 1860, Thoreau began to compile this information into a series of lists and charts, but he did not live long enough to complete the task. Wherever possible, he also backed up his findings with quotations from other writers. These quotations came from a bewildering variety of sources, ranging from the Reverend William Gilpin's writings on the "picturesque" and Roman agricultural authors, such as Varro, Cato, and Columella, to the account books of Ephraim Jones, an 18th-century shopkeeper in Concord.

▲ **BIRD LOVER** Thoreau was particularly interested in the way that birds coped with the changing seasons. He described snow buntings, for example, as "true winter birds ... these winged snowballs. I could hardly see them in ... the driving snow." He backed up his observations with quotes from noted authorities, such as Wilson's *American Ornithology*.

▼ **BOTANICAL NOTES** Thoreau became a very knowledgeable botanist over the years. He collected leaves, plants, and seeds on his many excursions. He stuck a few of these into the pages of his journal but most ended up in his herbarium. This eventually contained around 900 labeled specimens, which are now housed at Harvard University.

▶ **WINTER SCENE** On November 11, 1858, Thoreau went out rowing, delighting in the reds of the pitcher plants and cranberry vines that stood out against the frost. He also brought home a dead hen hawk that a neighbor had shot. Thoreau identified the species, admiring its taste for seclusion. "The same thing which keeps it in the woods—away from the cities—also keeps me here."

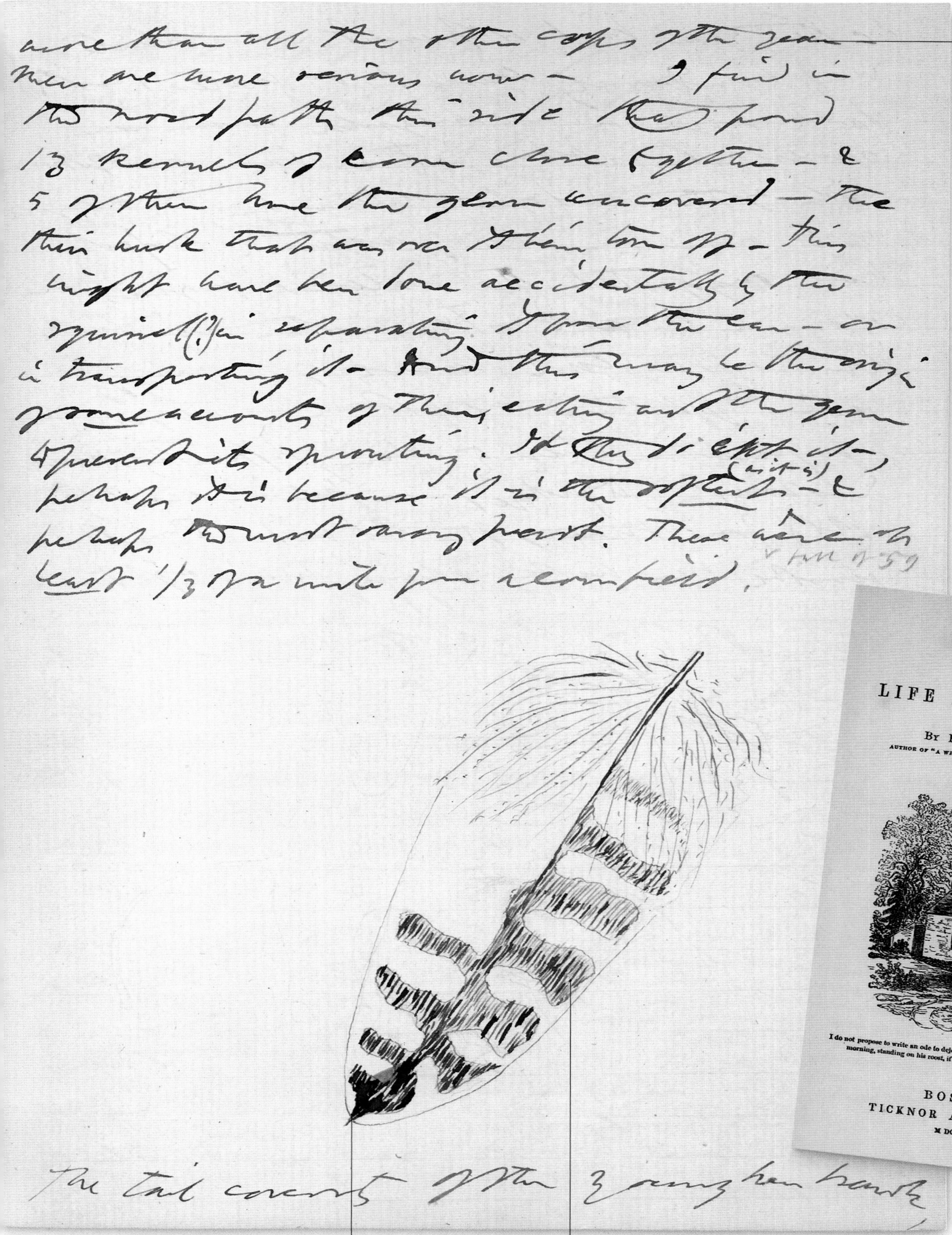
more than all the other crops of the year. [...] are more serious now— I find in the wood path this side the pond 13 kernels of corn close together— & 5 of them have the germ uncovered—the thin husk that was over it having been torn off—this might have been done accidentally by the squirrel (?) in separating it from the ear—or in transporting it. And this may be the origin of some accounts of their eating out the germ to prevent its sprouting. If they do eat it, perhaps it is because it is the softest (as it is) & perhaps the most savory part. These were at least 1/3 of a mile from a cornfield.

The tail coverts of the young hen hawk

Thoreau loved the winter chill: "Its harvest of thought is worth more than all the other crops of the year"

Thoreau's drawing shows a tail feather from a young hen hawk (a type of buzzard)

Thoreau was impressed by the feather's markings, which are "very handsomely barred or watered with dark brown"

▼ ***WALDEN*** Generally regarded as Thoreau's masterpiece, *Walden* describes his experiences during the two years from 1845 to 1847 that he spent living in a cabin at Walden Pond. Thoreau produced several drafts, revising and expanding the text, before it was finally published in 1854.

WALDEN;

OR,

LIFE IN THE WOODS.

By HENRY D. THOREAU,

AUTHOR OF "A WEEK ON THE CONCORD AND MERRIMACK RIVERS."

I do not propose to write an ode to dejection, but to brag as lustily as chanticleer in the morning, standing on his roost, if only to wake my neighbors up.—Page 92.

BOSTON:

TICKNOR AND FIELDS.

M DCCC LIV.

A Musical Marriage

1840-1844 ▪ PEN AND INK ON PAPER ▪ GERMAN

ROBERT AND CLARA SCHUMANN: MUSICIANS

On the day after their wedding in September 1840, Robert Schumann (1810-1856) and his new wife, Clara (1819-1896), started writing a joint marriage diary. It was their intention, Robert wrote, to record "all the joys and sorrows of marital life." The Schumanns were a formidably talented couple. Clara, née Wieck, already had an established reputation as a concert pianist with an inimitable expressive touch, and Robert was an innovative composer, appreciated by a small musical elite, and a noted music critic. They had fought for the right to marry against fierce opposition from Clara's father, Friedrich Wieck, who thought Robert was a wastrel and that marriage would ruin his daughter's musical career.

The couple originally agreed to write alternate weeks of the diary, although in practice, Clara did more. Their styles are quite distinct—Robert was an experienced writer, sometimes pedantic, and Clara more relaxed and chatty. They describe their busy lives in Leipzig, exploring music together, meeting friends, attending concerts, arranging performances, and making ends meet. Clara's appearances as a pianist are their main source of income, but she is also responsible for running the home and looking after the children—she eventually bore eight of them. She accepts inequality, dedicated to nurturing the career of her adored husband. Her only serious complaint is when she cannot practice piano because it disturbs Robert's composing. The overall impression is of a loving, harmonious marriage.

The last section of the marriage diary covers Clara's concert tour in Russia in 1844. Robert accompanied her, taking notes on life there that she later wrote up as a travelogue. Their return from Russia marked the end of the marriage diary. It is given special poignancy by what followed—Robert Schumann's descent into madness, attempted suicide, and eventual death in an asylum. Clara outlived him by 40 years but never remarried.

▶ **SELF-SACRIFICING WIFE** These pages of the diary were written by Clara Schumann in January 1841, when her husband was composing his Spring Symphony. The couple were supposed to write alternate entries, but Clara authored five consecutive weeks at this time, on the grounds that "when a man composes a symphony ... even his wife must accept herself as set aside!"

In context

◀ **YOUTHFUL PRODIGY** Clara Wieck, Schumann's future wife, gave a piano recital in Leipzig at the age of nine and set off on her first successful European concert tour two years later. She became one of the most celebrated piano virtuosi of her day, credited with more than 1,300 performances.

▶ **CLARA'S MUSIC** A gifted composer, Clara wrote a piano concerto at the age of 14 and composed notable chamber works and songs during her marriage. She was discouraged by the lack of precedent for this: "A woman must not desire to compose, there has never yet been one able to do it."

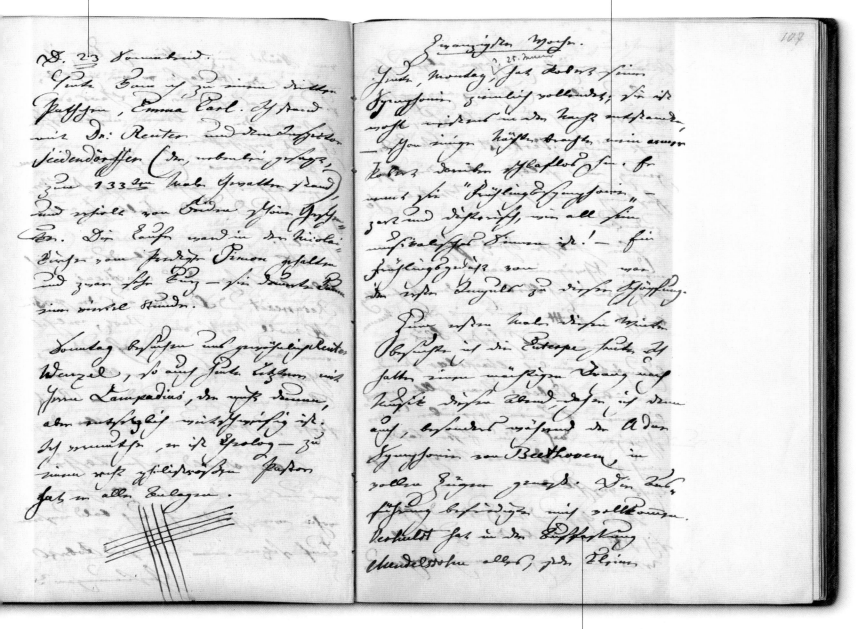

These pages begin with an entry written in Clara's hand, dated "23 Saturday"

Clara notes that Robert calls the nearly finished piece his "Spring Symphony," named after a poem by Adolf Böttger

Clara wrote quickly and added flourishes to many letters, making her handwriting difficult to read

◄ **THE YOUNG BRAHMS**
In 1853, Johannes Brahms, then an unknown 20-year-old, became a friend of the Schumanns. When Robert was confined in an asylum at the end of his life, Brahms developed a close relationship with Clara; they may even have been lovers. After her husband's death, Clara gave first performances of several of Brahms's works as he grew to be a famous composer.

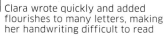

First of all let, me kiss you most tenderly on this day, your first day as a wife, the first of your 22nd year. This little book, which I inaugurate today, has a very intimate meaning; it shall be a diary about everything that touches us mutually in our household and marriage; our wishes, our hopes shall be recorded therein; it should also be a little book of requests that we direct toward one another ... also one of mediation and reconciliation whenever we have had a misunderstanding; in short, it shall be our good, true friend, to whom we entrust everything, to whom we open our hearts.

ROBERT SCHUMANN, MARRIAGE DIARY, SEPTEMBER 13, 1840

A Lifetime's Thoughts

1846-1910 ■ PEN AND INK ON PAPER ■ 32 VOLUMES ■ RUSSIAN

LEO TOLSTOY: WRITER

The great Russian novelist Leo Tolstoy (1828-1910) was born into a long line of nobles at his family's country estate and kept diaries for most of his adult life. He started when he was 18 years old, had to spend time in the hospital being treated for venereal disease, and carried on until just before he died, by which time he had written some four million words. Early on, he specified why he wanted to keep a diary and how he intended to use it. He wanted to combine reflections on human life and its purpose with the aim of self-improvement. He chides himself for his personal failings: "I am intemperate, indecisive, inconstant, stupidly conceited and ardent, like all characterless people," he says, and accuses himself of cowardice, impracticality, and idleness.

Initially, Tolstoy tried to address these weaknesses by keeping a journal of his daily tasks. He divided each page into two columns, setting targets for each day in the first column and recording what he had achieved in the other. Later, he simply wrote narrative diaries packed with his thoughts and opinions on a huge range of topics—social problems in Russia, rural life, industrialization, education, and spiritual questions. Although he was a member of the aristocracy, which enjoyed great privilege and wealth in 19th-century Russia, Tolstoy showed unusual concern for members of the lower classes. He came to believe over time that his social position was so unfair that he wanted to give most of his wealth away. He also had idiosyncratic views on religion: while he was serving in the Russian army during the Crimean War (1853-1856), he wrote that he would like to start a new kind of Christianity based on reason, without the dogma or mysticism that had come to be associated with it.

Tolstoy's distinctive opinions, together with his evocative descriptions of people and places, and the insights into how he worked on his great novels make his diaries a fascinating read.

➤ **EMOTIONAL WHIRL** The pages of the diaries from August to September 1862 were written when Tolstoy was first married to his wife Sofia and was experiencing the ups and downs of conjugal life. He wrote at great speed, right to the edges of the pages, crossing many things out. His handwriting was notoriously hard to read—only Sofia was able to decipher it easily.

TOLSTOY **THE NOVELIST**

After a trilogy of semiautobiographical novels, Tolstoy started work on the books that sealed his reputation. *War and Peace* (1869) is a vast epic about the lives of five Russian families during the Napoleonic Wars (1803-1815). Tolstoy seamlessly blends scenes of domestic life with descriptions of great battles, such as Austerlitz and Borodino, and lengthy philosophical discussions. He did an enormous amount of historical research and also drew on the experiences of army life that he had recorded in his diary. He wanted to blur the boundaries between history and fiction, to get closer to the truth.

War and Peace was followed by *Anna Karenina* (1878), a tragic love story about a married heroine's affair with a count that touches on many issues of the day, such as politics, class, religion, and the role of women. These two novels are Tolstoy's greatest works, but *Resurrection* (1899), a late novel that criticizes the Russian church, is also widely read.

LEON TOLSTOÏ
ANNA KARÉNINE

➤ **French edition** cover of Tolstoy's acclaimed novel *Anna Karenina*, 1949

> ## To write the genuine history of present-day Europe: there is an aim for the whole of one's life.

THE DIARIES OF LEO TOLSTOY, SEPTEMBER 22, 1852

> I had counted much upon this period, yet, to my sorrow, find that I remain always the same: within a few days I have done all the things of which I disapproved. Abrupt changes are impossible. Several times recently I have shown myself weak, both in ordinary relations with men, and in danger, and in card play—and still am held back by false shame. I have told many lies ... I have been idling away my time, and even now cannot collect my thoughts, and, although writing, I feel no inclination to write.

THE DIARIES OF LEO TOLSTOY, SEPTEMBER 4, 1851

In detail

▲ **LATER YEARS** Tolstoy's diary became more philosophical (and dour) in the last 10 years of his life. This entry was written in 1910, just two months before he died. He comments on his health and the visits of friends. He also records letters he has sent and received. Among these are ones that he wrote to the Indian political leader Gandhi, whom he refers to as "the Hindu."

Tolstoy's first books, *Childhood*, *Boyhood*, and *Youth*, are semiautobiographical. His diary reflects these fictional accounts of an upper-class young man growing up and his gradual realization of the plight of the peasants who work for him. Although Tolstoy did not intend to publish the diary, he also did not try to keep it secret. When he married Sofia in 1862, he showed her his diary, and some of what she read must have shocked her—especially the frank descriptions of her husband's love life and the son he had fathered with one of the serfs on his estate. Stoically, Sofia was able to accept this side of him.

In 1863, Tolstoy began to write the first of his great novels, *War and Peace*. *Anna Karenina* followed soon after, and he recorded his progress on both novels in his diary. When he had finished *Anna Karenina*, his thoughts turned increasingly to social reform and, later still, to spiritual matters. After Tolstoy died, Sofia began to read the diaries, many of which she had not opened before. They gripped her attention and she made neat copies of the text. On reading some of his entries, she reproached herself in her diary: "Why did I never read and copy it before?"

When Tolstoy's diaries were finally published in the 20th century, they were widely read and valued for their penetrating insights into the character and mind of one of history's greatest novelists.

▲ **EMANCIPATION OF THE SERFS** In the first half of the 19th century, Russian serfs were not allowed to own property or businesses and had to seek permission to marry. The Emancipation Edict of 1861 abolished serfdom and granted them these rights. This gave them freedom and the right to buy land, but many could still not afford enough land to make a living and so were scarcely better off.

> ❝ A true work of art … is produced only when the artist seeks, strives. ❞
>
> **THE DIARIES OF LEO TOLSTOY, JANUARY 23, 1896**

SOFIA TOLSTOY'S DIARY

Sofia kept a diary throughout her long married life. At first, she paints a seemingly idyllic picture of a privileged life at the Tolstoy's country estate: dinner parties, picnics with her children, and meetings with other aristocrats and famous writers, such as Chekhov. However, as Tolstoy became more obsessed with his religious views and was determined to give away his wealth, Sofia felt alienated. She feared losing their wealth, mainly because she wanted to educate her large family well, and resented the crowds of cranks and "hysterical" women who wanted to meet her husband. Sofia was a talented writer herself, so her diary is a poignant record of her deteriorating marriage. It ended in 1910, when the 82-year-old Tolstoy left her. He died a few weeks later.

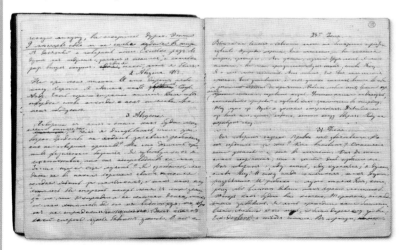

▲ **Pages from Sofia Tolstoy's diary,** written July 31, 1863

▲ **CREATIVE PARTNERSHIP** In 1862, Tolstoy married Sofia Behrs, the daughter of a German physician and a Russian mother, 16 years his junior. The marriage was a creative partnership as well as an emotional one. Along with running the home and estate, Sofia dutifully helped Tolstoy with his work, making fair copies of his drafts and helping him with editing.

In the Amazon

1848–1859 ▪ PEN AND INK ON PAPER ▪ TWO VOLUMES ▪ BRITISH

HENRY BATES: ENTOMOLOGIST

As a young man, amateur naturalist Henry Walter Bates (1825–1892) spent most of his spare time studying the insects near his home town of Leicester and became a skilled entomologist. After meeting the scientist Alfred Russel Wallace, the two men decided to go on a trip to Brazil to research the wildlife of the Amazon, a region scarcely known to scientists. Bates ended up staying in Brazil for 11 years and kept field journals of his discoveries. He used small pocketbooks that he could carry with him, meticulously recording both daily details such as the weather and describing the wildlife that he saw.

His daily writings reveal the dangers that he faced during his travels in the rain forest—wild animals, floods, and deadly diseases—he caught both malaria and yellow fever in Brazil. The journals include descriptions of caimans, snakes, piranhas, and insects, especially butterflies, which were Bates's greatest interest. He made thousands of meticulous drawings of butterflies and other insects, working in Indian ink and watercolor and adding details in pencil. Studying so many butterflies over a long period of time gave him a special insight into their biology and enabled him to develop the theory of mimicry that made him famous. This was the idea that some animals evolve to look similar to more toxic species, in order to repel predators. It fascinated Charles Darwin, helping him provide proof for his theory of natural selection.

Bates published an account of his Brazilian discoveries in his book *The Naturalist on the River Amazons*. He drew extensively upon the journals when writing both the book and numerous articles on Amazonian wildlife (especially beetles and butterflies), including his studies of mimicry. Because he wrote up his research in this way, Bates felt no need to publish the journals themselves. A book containing facsimiles of the two volumes at the Natural History Museum in London was finally published in 2020.

▶ **ADVENTURES ON THE AMAZON** In *The Naturalist on the River Amazons*, Bates describes the landscape and the lives of the local tribes, as well as the wildlife that he found there. Several illustrations depict his life on and around the river and the mishaps that he endured while traveling. He often describes these as "adventures." This one is captioned "Turtle fishing and adventure with alligator."

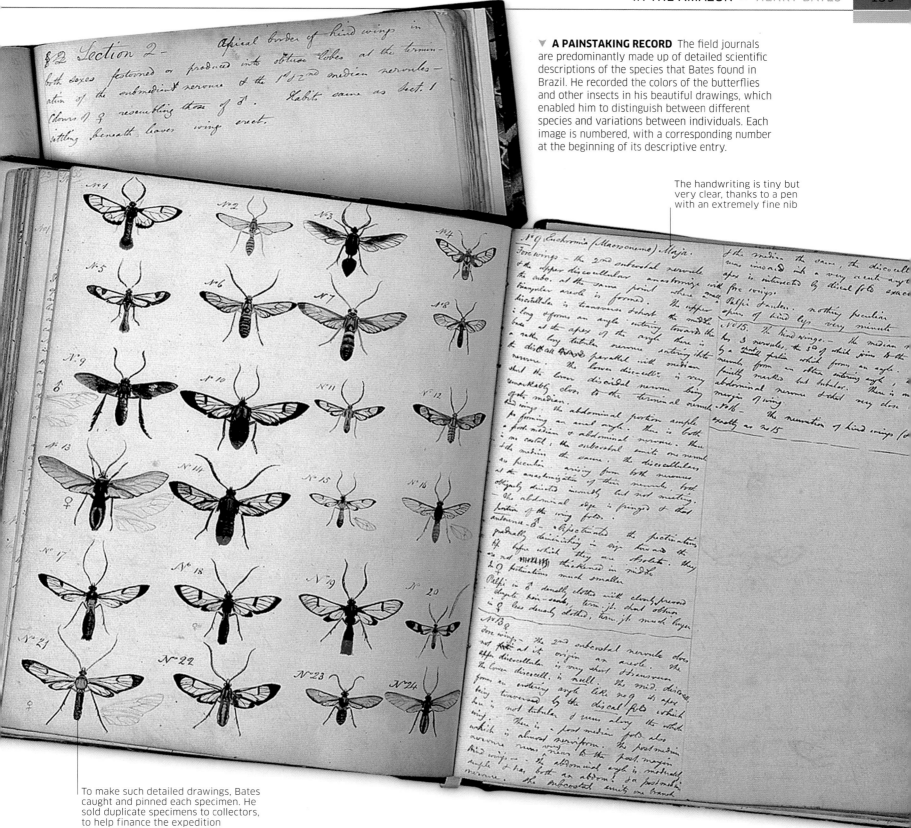

▼ **A PAINSTAKING RECORD** The field journals are predominantly made up of detailed scientific descriptions of the species that Bates found in Brazil. He recorded the colors of the butterflies and other insects in his beautiful drawings, which enabled him to distinguish between different species and variations between individuals. Each image is numbered, with a corresponding number at the beginning of its descriptive entry.

The handwriting is tiny but very clear, thanks to a pen with an extremely fine nib

To make such detailed drawings, Bates caught and pinned each specimen. He sold duplicate specimens to collectors, to help finance the expedition

> On these expanded membranes [butterfly wings] Nature writes, as on a tablet, the story of the modification of species, so truly do all changes of the organisation register themselves thereon. Moreover, the same colour-patterns of the wings generally show, with great regularity, the degrees of blood-relationship of the species. As the laws of Nature must be the same for all beings, the conclusions furnished by this group of insects must be applicable to the whole organic world; therefore, the study of butterflies—creatures selected as the types of airiness and frivolity—instead of being despised, will some day be valued as one of the most important branches of Biological science.

HENRY BATES, *NATURALIST ON THE RIVER AMAZONS*, 1863

Literary Gossip in Paris

1851–1896 ▪ PEN AND INK ON PAPER ▪ 11 NOTEBOOKS ▪ FRENCH

THE GONCOURT BROTHERS: WRITERS

Edmond and Jules de Goncourt wrote many books together and used the same technique for their journal. Until Jules (1830–1870) died, they took turns writing, with one brother correcting the text written by the other, evolving a seamless style that made it impossible to tell who had written what. After Jules's death, Edmond (1822–1896) thought about stopping the journal, but he decided to continue on his own,

to record historic events such as the Franco-Prussian War, the siege of Paris, and the suppression of the Paris Commune. The Goncourts' combined account, which covers a span of 45 years, is an entertaining, candid, and gossipy chronicle of the literary and artistic circles of Paris. No one knows why they kept the journal, but it was partly to vent their frustration at the disappointing sales and poor reviews of their books. The

▲ **KINDRED SPIRITS** The Goncourt brothers, neither of whom married, lived together and were rarely parted for more than a few hours at a time. They wrote novels, plays, histories, and a book about 18th-century French art, but their journal is now their most famous work. They state in its preface: "The journal is our nightly confession, the confession of two lives never separated in pleasure, in work or in pain ... of two twin spirits."

▶ **SOCIAL WHIRL** Each page of *The Goncourt Journal* blends social observation, spiteful gossip, and references to the brothers' wounded self-esteem. On these pages from June 1857, the brothers describe courtesans they meet at dinner with a friend: "velvety eyes with a glance like a warm caress"; the insults and criticism they have to endure; and a recurring episode of Jules's illness.

Our Paris ... in which we were born ... is disappearing.

THE GONCOURT JOURNAL, NOVEMBER 18, 1860

brothers usually wrote their entries at night, while the day's impressions were still fresh in their minds. They wrote fast, sometimes using notes Jules had jotted on his cuffs during the day. This kept their descriptions lively, and even the apparent lack of organization and the random variety of subjects (accounts of low life mixed with observations on art and books) help make their work an enjoyable read. The brothers did not publish the journal at first, but in 1886, Edmond published selections from it, and their frankness offended some of the people mentioned. When he died, he left the manuscripts to the Académie Goncourt, which he had founded, with instructions not to publish them for 20 years. Even then, however, the Académie held back. It was only in the 1930s that its first edition of *The Goncourt Journal* appeared.

NATURALISM

Although *The Goncourt Journal* is written in a plain, literary style, the language used in many of the brothers' other books is more elaborate. However, some of their novels, especially *Germinie Lacerteux* (1864) portray the lives of both the upper and lower classes in a frank, direct manner, pioneering a literary movement that became known as naturalism. This was a realistic, detached approach to writing fiction, often involving characters from the lower social classes, lurid incidents, and social commentary. The novelist most closely identified with naturalism was Émile Zola, whose realistic novels set in contemporary France tackled thorny issues of the day such as industrialization, alcoholism, prostitution, and violence. Zola's books were successful, which the Goncourts resented because they felt he had stolen a technique that they had invented but failed to profit from.

▲ **Émile Zola,** Édouard Manet, 1868

In context

The *Goncourt Journal* paints vivid pictures of French artists and writers at a time when Parisian cultural life was among the most vibrant in the world. The brothers met a huge number of interesting people in the city's cafés, at society dinner tables, in bohemian studios, and even in brothels. Their friends and acquaintances included some of the most famous novelists and poets in France–Alphonse Daudet, Théophile Gautier, and Gustave Flaubert, who they wrote about appreciatively, as well as the novelist Émile Zola, who is portrayed less sympathetically. Their descriptions are perceptive and witty–the poet Baudelaire, for example,

has an open-necked shirt and "his head shaved, just as if he were going to be guillotined." The Goncourts were also friends with leading artists, such as the Impressionist painter Edgar Degas and the sculptor Auguste Rodin, and with high-ranking socialites, such as Princess Mathilde Bonaparte. They had a keen ear for dialogue, which they jotted down verbatim in their entries for each day.

Although many of these people were worried when Edmond Goncourt began to publish parts of the journal, its sparkling blend of social cameos and literary gossip bring the society of late 19th-century Paris vividly to life.

> " Our admirer and pupil Zola came to lunch today. It was the first time we had ever seen him. Our immediate impression was of a worn-out *Normalien*, at once sturdy and puny, with Sarcey's neck and shoulders and a waxy, anemic complexion, a strapping young fellow with something of the delicate modeling of fine porcelain in his features, in the line of his eyes, in the angry planes of his nose, and in his hands. The whole of his person was built rather like his characters ... with two contrary types, mingling male and female in them....

THE GONCOURT JOURNAL, DECEMBER 14, 1868

▲ **CULTURAL LIFE** In addition to a large cast of notable writers, many artists, from Manet to Degas, make an appearance in the journal. The people that the Goncourts met at society dinners and in cafés help form a complex picture of Parisian cultural life in the period known as the belle époque, when the Impressionists transformed art, and the novel and poetry found new directions in the hands of Émile Zola and Charles Baudelaire.

Casino de Paris

LIANE DE POUGY

► **PRINCESSES AND COURTESANS** *The Goncourt Journal* depicts people from all walks of life, from princesses to prostitutes. It describes men's affairs with prostitutes in particular with great frankness. Liane de Pougy (right) was an actress, courtesan, performer at the Folies-Bergère, and the lover of several aristocrats. Edmond Goncourt described her as "the most beautiful woman of her century."

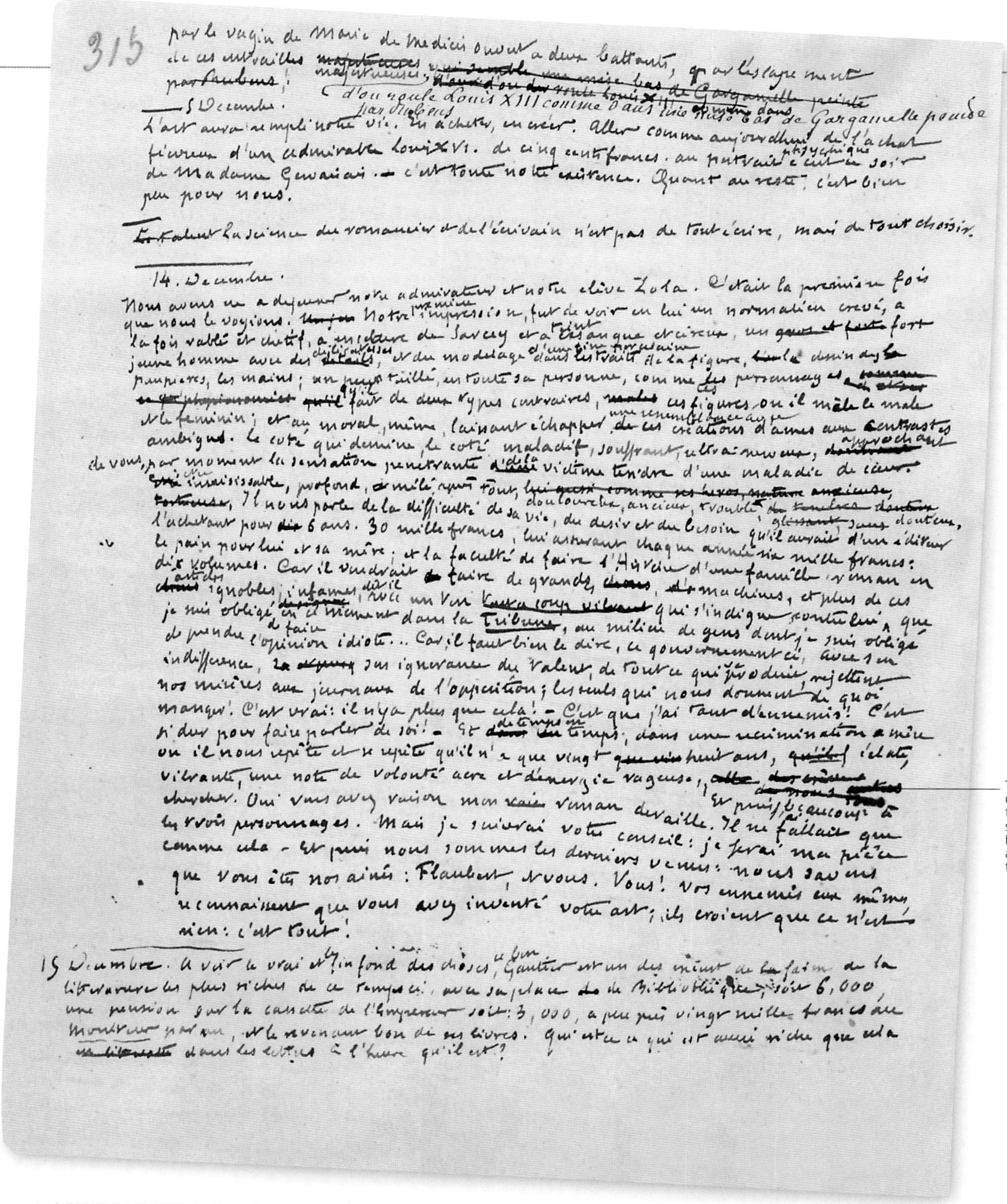

[Handwritten manuscript page in French — the Goncourt brothers' journal, with numerous crossings-out. The text is largely illegible handwriting and is not transcribed here.]

The frequent crossings-out in the manuscript show how the brothers refined and corrected their journal

▲ **A FATEFUL MEETING** On December 14, 1868, the Goncourts recorded their first meeting with the realist novelist Émile Zola. Their account of their "admirer and pupil" is far from flattering. They describe him as a sickly and hypersensitive person who looks as if he suffers from heart disease. Zola's ambition was to write a 10-volume story of a French family, the work that eventually became his Rougon-Macquart series of 20 novels.

Directory: 1800-1860

▼ BYRON'S LETTERS AND MEMOIRS

BRITISH (1798-1824)

Romantic poet Lord Byron (1788-1824) became an international celebrity at the age of 23, when his narrative poem *Childe Harold's Pilgrimage* was hailed as a work of genius. Dogged by debts and scandalous rumors about his private life—notably an alleged incestuous relationship with his half sister Augusta—he left England in 1816, going to live first in Italy and then in Greece, where he died of fever during the Greek War of Independence. More than 3,000 of Byron's letters have survived. Frank, witty, vigorous, and spontaneous, they present a vivid and intimate portrait of the poet's life, expressing his hatred of all forms of moralizing and hypocrisy.

Between 1818 and 1822, Byron also wrote his memoirs. The first part was said to be rather dull, but the second part was allegedly scandalous. After his death, his estranged wife and his friends therefore conspired to have the manuscript of the memoirs burned, claiming that publication would have ruined his posthumous reputation. The letters, which were first published in full in the 1970s and 1980s, are the nearest thing we have to his autobiography.

MARY SHELLEY'S DIARIES

BRITISH (1814-1844)

Novelist Mary Shelly (1797-1851) was born Mary Wollstonecraft Godwin, the daughter of William Godwin, a philosopher, and Mary Wollstonecraft, a famous defender of women's rights. In the summer of 1814, at the age of 17, she ran away to France with the unhappily married poet Percy Bysshe Shelley. Right from the start of their romantic escapade, Mary kept a diary, initially with Shelley, recording their penniless wandering across a continent devastated by recent warfare. The journal was later published, along with other material, as *History of a Six Weeks' Tour*.

Mary continued to keep a regular diary through the troubled years that followed. She married Shelley after his wife committed suicide, they lived together in Italy, two of their children died, she wrote her Gothic novel *Frankenstein*, and Shelley drowned at sea in 1822. Her diary entries are mostly brief and sparing—she notes the death of Shelley's first wife in a single sentence without comment. But after Shelley himself died, she poured forth her grief in what has been called the "Journal of Sorrow." She continued to keep a sporadic diary, with less intensity, until 1844.

THE JOURNALS OF MAXIMILIAN ZU WIED

GERMAN (1815-1817, 1832-1834)

Prince Maximilian zu Wied (1782-1867) was a naturalist and ethnologist from a town on the Rhine. In 1815, he embarked on a scientific mission to unmapped regions of southeastern Brazil, where he studied the local fauna, flora, and Native American peoples. After his return in 1817, he published an account of his Brazilian experiences, which he based on his travel journal.

In 1832, aged 50, Wied set out on a second epic trip, this time to the North American interior, accompanied by the artist Karl Bodmer. Most of his North American journal covers a voyage on a fur trader's steamer up the Missouri River from St. Louis to the border of Montana. Wied meticulously records the customs and culture of the different groups of Native Americans whom he encountered en route. He also observes the damage wreaked by white frontiersmen and how wildlife was being destroyed at an alarming rate by overhunting.

Wied returned home to Germany in 1834 after enduring many hardships and life-threatening illnesses. Admirably illustrated by Bodmer, his journal is an irreplaceable record of a natural world that was rapidly disappearing.

THE JOURNAL OF MRS. ARBUTHNOT

BRITISH (1820-1832)

Born into a minor branch of the British aristocracy, Harriet Fane (1793-1834) was catapulted into high political circles by her marriage in 1814 to Charles Arbuthnot, a senior Tory politician. She became a political hostess and an intimate friend of elite figures such as the foreign secretary, Lord Castlereagh, and Britain's most famous general, the Duke of Wellington.

In 1820, Mrs. Arbuthnot (as she is usually known) decided that, "living so much among the leading men of the day," she would keep a diary to record her insider's view of the political scene. Her verbatim accounts of political meetings and conversations have proved an invaluable source of reference for historians, but the journal is also a witty and passionate personal document, expressing her intense admiration for her heroes, notably Wellington, and her loathing

Portrait of Lord Byron in Greek costume, anon, c.1830

The Sphinx of Giza, photograph by Maxime du Camp, from *Égypte, Nubie, Palestine et Syrie*, 1852

of all opponents of Toryism. Despite many rumors to the contrary, she was probably not Wellington's lover, but she did in effect become his social secretary after he was made prime minister in 1828. When Wellington and the Tories fell from power in 1830, she largely lost interest in her diary, which ends midsentence two years before her death.

A MORMON MIDWIFE'S DIARY

AMERICAN (1846–1888)

The diary of Patty Bartlett Sessions (1795–1892) is a unique record of life in the early years of the Latter Day Saint movement, whose principal theology was Mormonism. Born in Maine, Bartlett married David Sessions in 1812 and took up a career as a midwife. In the mid-1830s, the couple converted to Mormon beliefs.

Patty Sessions's first diary begins in 1846, when she was chosen to join the pioneering Mormon wagon train

that forged a route from Illinois via Winter Quarters, Nebraska, to Salt Lake Valley in Utah, where they settled. After her first husband died, she married John Parry in 1851. She wrote that she was glad to have "someone to cut my wood for me." Both her husbands were polygamous, in line with their faith—a fact that she writes of with evident discomfort and an attempt at acceptance. She kept a daily diary for 20 years, recording the experience of frontier life in a blunt and practical style, as well as noting the hundreds of births she attended.

After 1866, Sessions's diary entries became more sparse; the last one was written four years before she died.

▲ GUSTAVE FLAUBERT IN EGYPT

FRENCH (1849–1850)

The celebrated French realist novelist Gustave Flaubert (1821–1880) was a copious letter writer, but he kept a diary only when he was traveling.

In October 1849, at the age of 28, he embarked on a trip to Egypt with fellow writer and photographer Maxime du Camp. Flaubert's journal describes their voyage across the Mediterranean and their experiences touring Egypt (visiting Alexandria and Cairo, climbing the pyramids, sailing up the Nile to Thebes, and crossing the desert on camels and horses). Maxime du Camp took photographs of the monuments that they visited.

Not much interested in antiquities, Flaubert revels in the exoticism of a country totally free of the dullness and restrictions of bourgeois Europe. He evokes the harsh desert landscapes, the monuments, and the people they meet with glowing attention to detail, but he also spends a considerable amount of time describing his visits to brothels and bathhouses.

When he returned to Europe in 1851, Flaubert attempted but failed to make a book out of his travel notes. An expurgated version of the journal was published after his death in 1881, but the complete text did not appear in print until the late 20th century.

MARK TWAIN'S NOTEBOOKS

AMERICAN (1855–1910)

Humorous writer Samuel Langhorne Clemens (1835–1910), better known by his pen name Mark Twain, never kept a daily diary but filled notebooks and journals from the age of 19. He first developed the habit while training to pilot steamboats on the Missouri, noting down every feature of the river. Later he used his notebooks as an aid to his professional writing, jotting down random ideas for stories, observations of the world around him, jokes, and satirical barbs as they occurred to his fertile brain.

In the 1880s, when Twain was a successful author, he sometimes dictated the notes for a secretary to transcribe. These fed into his prolific journalism, travel writing, and fiction. Chaotic and fragmentary, his notebooks are a spectacular display of mental fireworks. Selections were first published 25 years after his death, and a full edition appeared in 1975.

From Miss Martha Webb, to Ida Lois Benson

"Come, and buy Wine and Milk, without money
and without price"
Hark! It is Wisdoms voice, that spreads itself
around
Chas A Benson
Salem
Mass
The Lord my shepherd is, He will my want supply
On board Bark Glide of Salem
From Boston
Bound to the Eastward of Cape of Good Hope
1879
Broad is the road that leads to death
And thousands...

5

1860—1900

The late 19th century saw a proliferation of diaries and other personal records. Some relate to historical events, including Mary Chesnut's vivid personal account of the American Civil War and the prison diary of wrongly convicted French Jewish army officer Alfred Dreyfus. Others reflect the growing importance of science, such as those of Marie Curie and Thomas Edison. The reflections of artists Vincent van Gogh and Paul Gauguin and architect Antoni Gaudí provide a unique insight into the creative process at a turning point in Western art. Exceptional personalities such as Swiss explorer Isabelle Eberhardt, who defied social norms to live as a nomad, appear alongside accounts of everyday life from British clergyman Francis Kilvert and the humorous French author Jules Renard.

A Dixie Diary

1861-1865 ▪ PEN AND INK ON PAPER ▪ SEVEN SURVIVING VOLUMES AND TWO NOTEBOOKS ▪ AMERICAN

MARY CHESNUT: DIARIST

The diary of Mary Boykin Chesnut (1823–1886) is recognized as one of the finest personal accounts of the American Civil War. Chesnut was born in South Carolina to a family of plantation owners in the American South whose wealth depended on the work of black enslaved people. Her husband, James Chesnut, was a prominent political figure in the formation of the breakaway Confederacy in 1861, which precipitated the Civil War.

Mary Chesnut began keeping a diary in 1861, as the United States slid toward Civil War, and stopped in June 1865, soon after the war had ended with the defeat of the South. She was not a consistent diarist, having many demands on her time, and made few entries from August 1862 to October 1863, but even so she filled 12 volumes of leather-bound lockable journals with her candid thoughts and observations, whether as a hostess entertaining the elite of the Confederacy, living in cramped hotel quarters, or experiencing relative isolation on the Chesnut family's Mulberry plantation. Although she aspired to portray people and events objectively, she inadvertently reveals herself as a strong, complex personality, depressive, often bad-tempered, vain—"I can make anyone love me if I choose"—and surprisingly critical of the institution of slavery. She vividly evokes the progressive stages of the Confederacy's disastrous war, from the time of "uniforms & gay soldiers" to "practical earnest bitter fighting," culminating in her flight before the advancing forces of Union General William Sherman that laid waste to the South.

Two decades after the war, living quietly as a widow in South Carolina, Chesnut extensively rewrote her Civil War journals to produce a more coherent account of the period. A selection from this work, published in 1905 as *A Diary from Dixie*, made her posthumously famous. Since 1981, a version of the diary integrating more personal material from her original journals has been published as *Mary Chesnut's Civil War*.

In context

◄ **THE SPARK THAT LIT THE FIRE** Mary Chesnut was present on April 12, 1861, when Union-held Fort Sumter in Charleston Harbor, South Carolina, was shelled by Confederate artillery. These were the first shots of the Civil War, provoking President Lincoln into recruiting an army to subdue the South. The diarist's husband played a leading role in the attack, which Mary described as "a great day."

▼ **CONFEDERATE LEADERSHIP** Jefferson Davis, the president of the Confederacy, is shown here in military uniform at the center of his generals. Mary Chesnut was well acquainted with Davis, and her diary contains many remarks supportive of his presidency. His wife, Varina, was one of her best friends during the war. She is often caustic about other leading Confederates who frequented her drawing room.

" I wonder if it be a sin to think slavery a curse to any land... God forgive *us*, but ours is a *monstrous* system & wrong & iniquity... This *only* I see: like the patriarchs of old our men live all in one house with their wives & their concubines, & the Mulattoes one sees in every family exactly resemble the white children–& every lady tells you who is the father of all the Mulatto children in every body's household, but those in her own, she seems to think drop from the clouds or pretends so to think... My disgust sometimes is boiling over.... "

MARY CHESNUT, MARCH 18, 1861

THE AMERICAN **CIVIL WAR**

By the 1850s, the United States was sharply divided over the issue of slavery, which had been abolished in the Northern states but underpinned the economy and society of the South. When Abraham Lincoln became president in 1861, most of the slave-owning states, fearing that he intended to abolish slavery, seceded from the Union and formed an independent Confederacy. Lincoln declared it an illegal rebellion and launched a war to regain control of the South.

Ending slavery was not initially the aim of the Northern states, but the participation of African Americans in the war on the Union side swung opinion in favor of abolition. After four years of war, the Confederacy was defeated, and a constitutional amendment that outlawed slavery was passed. The Southern states were devastated by the war, which left their white elite impoverished and embittered.

▲ *Storming Fort Wagner*, Kurz & Allison, 1890

◄ **TURNING POINT** It was the excitement of political crisis that spurred Chesnut into keeping a diary. She wrote the first pages while staying with her mother (Em) in Conecuh Country, Alabama, and describes her anxiety now that Abraham Lincoln has been elected president and "our fate sealed." "This southern Confederacy must be supported both by calm determination and cool brains," she states.

Conecuh. Ems.
February 18th 1861.
I do not allow myself to vain regrets or sad foreboding. This southern Confederacy must be supported now by calm determination & cool brains – we have risked all, & we must play our best for the stake is life or death I shall always regret that I had not kept a journal during the two past delightful & eventful years. The delights having exhausted themselves in the latter part of 1860 & the events crowding

in so that it takes away ones breath to think about it all. I dare say I might have recorded with some distinctness the daily shocks – "Earthquakes as usual" Lady Sale. but now it is to me one night mare from the time I left Charleston for Florida where I remained two anxious weeks, amid hammocks & everglades oppressed & miserable & heard on the cars, returning to the world that Lincoln was elected. our fate sealed. Saw at Fernandina a few men running

Mary Chesnut refers here to being overwhelmed by the increasing pace of events at the end of 1860

Into the Wilderness

1867-1913 ▪ PEN AND INK ON PAPER ▪ 84 VOLUMES ▪ SCOTTISH

JOHN MUIR: CONSERVATIONIST

"I only went out for a walk, and finally concluded to stay out till sundown, for going out, I found, was really going in." Finding the spiritual in a hike in the great outdoors is a recurrent feature of the journals of John Muir (1838–1914). Brought up in a strict, religious family, first in Scotland and then in the American Midwest, Muir went on to become a leading conservationist, often known as the "Father of the National Parks."

In 1867, when an accident almost blinded him in one eye, Muir decided to follow his dreams of exploration and set off on a walk of about 994 miles (1,600 km) from Kentucky to Florida. He did not follow any set route but wanted to go by "the wildest, leafiest, and least trodden way." He later spent several years in Yosemite Valley, California, where he led an almost monastic life studying the local geology and plants. As he explored the wilderness, he filled notebooks with his thoughts and observations, a habit he maintained all his life.

Muir's journals, now held by the University of the Pacific Library, document his activities from 1867 until 1913, the year before he died. They cover his "Thousand-mile walk," his travels in Alaska, his 1903 world tour, and his 1911 voyage to South America and Africa. Some notebooks contain only text, but others are punctuated by Muir's delicate drawings. What shines through most strongly of all, however, is Muir's love of nature, which he writes about in an almost ecstatic manner: "The clearest way into the Universe is through a forest wilderness," he states. His writing style has been described as part Proust and part Buddha. The journals provided material for the many magazine articles and books Muir wrote. Since his death, several collections of extracts from his journals have been published.

▶ **SIERRA JOURNAL** In addition to his journals, which were written as events happened, Muir kept a number of notebooks, some of which were written retrospectively. This *Sierra Journal* describes Muir's experiences in the summer of 1869, but it was actually written 18 years later, in 1887, and is no doubt colored by hindsight.

Muir wrote in ink but made copious amendments and additions in pencil

◀ **THE "THOUSAND-MILE WALK"** On September 2, 1867, Muir set out from Louisville, Kentucky carrying a knapsack containing a few essentials, such as a Bible and a plant press with which to preserve botanical specimens. He had hardly any money and depended largely on the kindness of strangers. He recorded the details of the walk in pocket-sized journals that later formed the basis for a book.

❝ It has been said that trees are imperfect men, and seem to bemoan their imprisonment rooted in the ground. But they never seem so to me. I never saw a discontented tree. They grip the ground as though they liked it, and though fast rooted they travel about as far as we do. They go wandering forth in all directions with every wind, going and coming like ourselves, traveling with us around the sun two million miles a day, and through space heaven knows how fast and far! ❞

JOHN MUIR'S JOURNALS, JULY 11, 1890

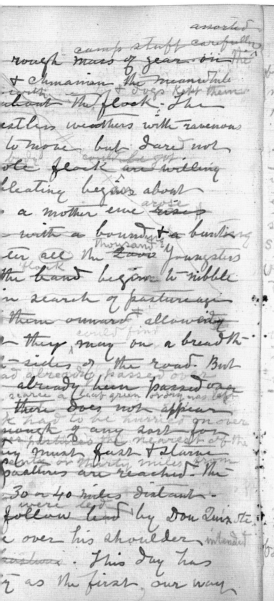

The drawing has been cut out and stuck into this notebook. It may have come from an earlier journal

In context

◄ **YOSEMITE** In 1903, President Theodore Roosevelt (left) accompanied Muir on a camping trip in Yosemite. Muir saw it as an opportunity "to do some forest good in talking freely around the campfire." He was able to persuade Roosevelt to create Yosemite National Park—the first of five such national parks that would receive the president's backing.

► **EXTENDED TRIP** Many of Muir's journals were later reworked, extended, and published as books. The months that he spent as a shepherd in the foothills of California's Sierra Nevada in 1869 later provided the material for *My First Summer in the Sierra*, which was published in 1911, just three years before Muir died.

A View from the Vicarage

1870-1879 ▪ PEN AND INK ON PAPER ▪ THREE SURVIVING NOTEBOOKS ▪ BRITISH

FRANCIS KILVERT: CLERGYMAN

The diary of Francis Kilvert (1840-1879) paints a vivid picture of rural life in Victorian Britain. It is also a striking self-portrait of a clergyman whose attitudes and behavior contradict many stereotypes of his era and his profession. Kilvert began keeping a diary in February 1870, when he was a 30-year-old curate at the village of Clyro in Radnorshire, near the border between England and Wales. After failing to marry Fanny Thomas, with whom he had fallen headlong in love—her family forbade the marriage because they considered his status and income inadequate—he returned to his clergyman father's parish in Wiltshire in 1872. Four years later, he moved back to Radnorshire, but the diary entries that have survived from this later period, up to his marriage and subsequent death in 1879, show him waning in energy.

In his journal, Kilvert comes across as sympathetic, unstuffy, modest, and good-natured, with a keen eye for the beauty of nature and the opposite sex. Conscientious in his duties, he describes harrowing visits to parishioners living in abject poverty, often blighted by loneliness, illness, or insanity. But his own world is that of the rural elite, with picnics and dinners and vacations by the sea, enjoying croquet and the new fad for lawn tennis. He can be thoroughly irreverent, as in his hilarious description of pallbearers at a funeral almost crushed by the weight of the coffin. He is also enthusiastic about swimming in the nude and enjoys flirtatious talk with young women. Modern readers might take issue with some of his attitudes.

Kilvert wrote that he kept a diary "because life appears to me such a curious and wonderful thing ... even such a humble and uneventful life as mine." From the moment a selection of the diary was first published in 1938-1940, it has been recognized as a classic evocation of a bygone age.

In context

▲ **ROMANTIC LANDSCAPE** Inheriting the sensibility of the English Romantic movement, Kilvert reveled in the beauty of the countryside, which he explored during long walks and described in lyrical passages in his diary. This painting, *A View in Radnorshire*, by William West shows one of the landscapes near Clyro that Kilvert so admired, seen with a similar Romantic eye.

▶ **CENSORIOUS WIDOW** Kilvert married Elizabeth Rowland in 1879 but died shortly after their honeymoon. His widow inherited the journals and is believed to have censored them, destroying two sections and removing any mention of herself. Her motive for this is not clear, as she left many passages in which Kilvert expressed admiration for other women.

The entry starts with the date, Friday, August 5, which is underlined

Here, Kilvert peers down into the craggy cove known as "Hells Mouth" and describes the "frightening depth below"

Friday 5 August. The last pleasant excursion. The last happy day. Martin had been sent to Falmouth overnight for a carriage & horse & brought back a very heavy horse & hooded carriage in which he drove us this morning to Godrevy. We called at Cousturne (Roseworne) to leave an Inverness Cloak which Capt. Parkin lent me to drive home in last Friday & the kind hospitable people made us promise to call on our return & have supper or something. Redruth Market, people hurrying about with conger eels. Sorrowful dreams.

We met with several sharp white squalls & had all to crowd for shelter under the head with an umbrella up in front. H. suggested that passers by would say — "There is a lady & gentleman with a child."

The road led us along the top of the cliffs. The carriage was stopped by a gate & we got out to look down "Hells Mouth." Standing on the turf edge of the cliff you look down sheer into a small narrow semicircular cavern into which the sea was & boils at a horrible depth below.

Leaving Mrs H. in the carriage to drive on to Gwythian Church Town, H & I struck across the down to see the British Church buried in the sand. We came to the place suddenly & without warning & looked down into the Church as into a long pit. The sand is drifted solid up to the very top of the outside walls. The walls are about four feet

▲ **KILVERT NOTEBOOK** Only three of the original 22 notebooks in which Kilvert wrote his diary still exist. The rest of the text has survived as a result of a transcription made in the 1930s. One of the three notebooks includes descriptions of Kilvert's vacation in Cornwall in the summer of 1870. This entry for August 5, describing the last day of the vacation, includes a typically curious detail in his observations of a market: "people hurrying about with conger eels."

❝ Bathing yesterday and today … At Shanklin one has to adopt the detestable custom of bathing in drawers. If ladies don't like to see men naked why don't they keep away from the sight? Today I had a pair of drawers given me which I could not keep on. The rough waves stripped them off and tore them down round my ancles. While thus fettered I was seized and flung down by a heavy sea which retreating suddenly left me lying naked on the sharp shingle from which I rose streaming with blood. After this I took the wretched and dangerous rag off and of course there were some ladies looking on as I came up out of the water. ❞

KILVERT'S DIARY, JUNE 12, 1874

An Artist's Letters

1872-1890 ▪ PEN AND INK ON PAPER ▪ C.800 LETTERS ▪ DUTCH

VINCENT VAN GOGH: ARTIST

Van Gogh's diary-like letters provide a fascinating record of the thoughts and personality of one of the greatest artists of the modern era. More than 800 have survived, offering an insight into Van Gogh's daily life, his struggles with his health, and his creative process. They are filled with sketches of pictures that he was working on, along with the ideas that inspired them.

Van Gogh was born to a pastor in the Dutch village of Groot Zundert in 1853. He came to art almost by default, after failed attempts to become an art dealer, a teacher, and a lay preacher. The decisive switch came in around 1880, when Van Gogh was living in the Borinage, a bleak coal-mining district in Belgium. There, he began producing drawings of the poor, empathizing deeply with their suffering.

Largely self-taught, Van Gogh concentrated initially on pictures of peasant life. He took up oils in 1882, but his paintings remained rather somber until he moved to Paris in 1886. There, his art was transformed. He discovered Impressionism and his colors became much brighter. They intensified still further after his move to Arles, in the south of France, in 1888. Here, the full measure of Vincent's artistic genius reached its zenith. Working like a man possessed, he produced more than 200 paintings in the next 18 months, including many of his most famous masterpieces.

Van Gogh hoped that other painters would join him in Arles and that they would form a new artists' colony, but his dream was soon dashed. When Paul Gauguin came—lured by financial assistance from Theo, Van Gogh's brother—it was a disaster. There was a violent quarrel. Gauguin fled, and Van Gogh, in a fit of despair, sliced off part of his left ear and delivered it to a local prostitute. His physical wound healed soon enough and he began working again at a furious pace. The mental scars remained, however, and in 1890, less than two years after his crisis in Arles, Van Gogh took his own life.

➤ **BROTHER THEO** Most of Van Gogh's letters were written to his younger brother Theo (1857-1891), who offered unfailing support to the artist throughout his life. He sent Vincent money for paints and living expenses and, through his job as an art dealer, introduced him to the Impressionists.

◄ **HOSPITAL IN ARLES** After his breakdown, Van Gogh recuperated in the hospital in Arles, where he began painting again. Epilepsy, schizophrenia, and alcoholism, exacerbated by overwork and stress, have all been suggested as causes of his illness. Van Gogh recognized sadly that he would have to work alone: "I don't dare ask other painters to come here ... they risk losing their mind."

> " Everyone here suffering either from fever or hallucinations or madness, we get along like members of the same family. "

TO THEO FROM THE HOSPITAL IN ARLES, FEBRUARY 3, 1889

> ❝
> I myself feel, to the point of being mentally crushed and physically drained, the need to produce, precisely because in short I have no other means, none, none, of ever recouping our outlay. I can do nothing about it if my paintings don't sell. The day will come, though, when people will see that they're worth more than the cost of the paint and my subsistence, very meager in fact ... But my dear brother, my debt is so great that when I've paid it ... the hardship of producing paintings will ... have taken my entire life, and it will seem to me that I haven't lived. ❞

TO THEO, AROUND OCTOBER 25, 1888

The farmworker is using a harrow to smoothen the soil after plowing. A harrow would normally have been pulled by a horse

In detail

Van Gogh's brilliant creativity and personal sufferings are fully chronicled in his remarkable letters. For much of his life, he was rootless and isolated. He moved home frequently and was unable to hold down a romantic relationship. He also had a tendency to take things to excess. He lost his job as a lay preacher when, out of sympathy for the poor, he began giving away all his own possessions. Similarly, when he was painting at Arles, he put his health at risk by working long hours outdoors, day after day, in the searing heat.

Throughout all of this, Van Gogh's letters provided a lifeline, a positive link with friends and family. The most important of these were the letters to Theo, which were often long, articulate, and thoughtful. Sadly, Van Gogh did not keep his brother's letters, so the correspondence is largely one-sided. However, it is clear enough that Theo provided moral support and encouragement, as well as financial aid. Without these, it seems very unlikely that Van Gogh could have pursued a meaningful artistic career. He certainly recognized his brother's contribution, commenting in a letter on April 30, 1889: "If I was without your friendship, I would descend without remorse to suicide."

▲ **THE BEDROOM AT ARLES** Van Gogh had been alone in Arles for several months before Gaugin's arrival and was longing for the companionship of a fellow painter. He decorated their home very simply, in a way that he hoped was both restful and conducive to painting. This painting is in a style he had learned from Japanese prints, with bold outlines and flat colors.

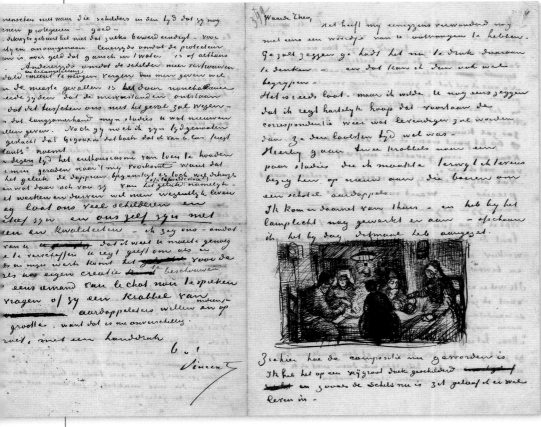

▲ **LETTER TO THEO** Van Gogh is in a buoyant mood in this letter from April 1885. He includes a sketch of *The Potato Eaters*, which is the chief masterpiece of his early period in the Netherlands. He felt that it was a "real peasant picture," showing people enjoying the food that they had dug out of the soil with their own hard labor.

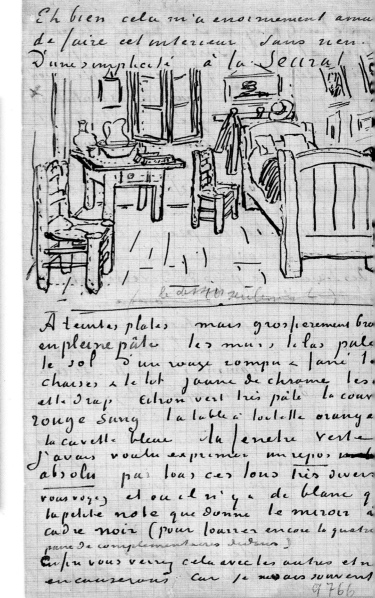

> In short, looking at the painting should rest the mind, or rather, the imagination.

TO THEO, OCTOBER 16, 1888, ABOUT
THE BEDROOM AT ARLES

In later versions of the picture, the setting sun becomes more prominent, dwarfing the sower

I heard Rodin had a beautiful head at the Salon.
I have been to the seaside for a week and very likely am going thither again soon.— That whore
Sands — fine figures there
like Cimabue — straight stylish
Am working at a Sower...

The great field all violet. The sky & sun very
yellow. It is a hard subject to treat.
Please remember me very kindly to
Mrs Russell — and in thought I heartily
shake hands... **Yours very truly**
Vincent

▲ **THE SOWER** This is from a letter written in English to the Australian artist, John Peter Russell in June 1888. Van Gogh painted several versions of *The Sower* at this time, both before and after his clash with Gauguin. He was strongly attracted by the theme. It is a peasant picture but also has biblical overtones. In later versions, the sun has swollen to an enormous size, dominating the scene.

Specifications of the colors he wanted to use—violet for the field and yellow for the sun and sky

◀ **WELCOME LETTER** Van Gogh wrote this letter to Gauguin on October 17, 1888, a few days before he arrived in Arles. The letter is full of hopefulness. Gauguin had been dragging his heels, but now he was on his way and Van Gogh was at pains to make him welcome. He included the sketch to show how attractive he had made their home, adding: "I'm sure that once here, like me, you'll be seized with a fury to paint."

The Manuscript of Reus

1873-1879 ■ PENCIL, PEN, AND INK ON PAPER ■ SPANISH

ANTONI GAUDÍ: ARCHITECT

Gaudí was one of the most extraordinary figures in 20th-century architecture: a visionary who created unique mansions, parks, and churches that were both beautiful and bizarre. Historians have long been eager to study him, to learn the secrets of his fertile imagination, but regrettably there is limited source material. During the Spanish Civil War, Gaudí's office in the Sagrada Família in Barcelona was looted and most of his records destroyed. Fortunately, his student notebook, *The Manuscript of Reus,* had been moved to safety, but it was forgotten about until the 1960s, when it was rediscovered by the biographer César Martinell.

One authority has described the *Manuscript* as "a beautiful set of handwritten notes by Gaudí, which reflect the personality of a young student, full of energy and eager to conquer the world of architectural design." However, Gaudí was no ordinary student. His family was not wealthy, so he financed his education by working as an assistant in several architectural practices. This gave him a broad range of experience at a very early age—a fact confirmed by the sheer variety of drawings in the *Manuscript.* Among other things, these include a solar clock, a glove-maker's display case, angelic figures, a hospital floor plan, and a reliquary.

Gaudí's writings in *The Manuscript of Reus* are just as interesting, although he had not yet developed his distinctive style. The most significant sections are about ornamentation, the Christian Church, and the family home. Gaudí's taste for unusual decoration became a major feature of his later work; his commitment to Catholicism has led to serious calls for his beatification; and his revolutionary approach to domestic architecture made him a figurehead of Catalan resurgence. During Gaudí's lifetime, Barcelona was transformed. Its population quadrupled, and it grew in size, assuming the proportions of a major, modern city. Gaudí's masterpieces gave it a unique character, symbolizing a renewed confidence in Catalan culture, identity, and nationalist aspirations.

CAREER AS AN **ARCHITECT**

Gaudí was Spain's greatest and most inventive architect. No fewer than seven of his works have been placed on UNESCO's World Heritage list. A native of Reus, in the Tarragona region, he was trained in Barcelona, where he spent almost his entire career. Gaudí was the greatest exponent of Catalan *Modernisme* (the Spanish equivalent of Art Nouveau). He was influenced by Gothic and Moorish styles but also drew inspiration from the natural world. His building surfaces often seem to undulate or mimic the growth of plantlike forms. Gaudí had a taste for colorful, exotic decoration, frequently using fragments of broken ceramics. He was also a fervent Catholic, devoting many years to his architectural masterpiece, the Sagrada Família.

▶ **The Expiatory Church of the Sagrada Família** is Gaudí's most celebrated work; a radical, Gothic fantasy that he never managed to complete

" The house is the small nation of the family.... The independent family has its own house; what it does not have is a house for rent. The house itself is the native country and the rental house is the land of emigration; this is why the house itself is ideal for all.... The house we imagine has two objectives: first are its hygienic conditions, which make those who grow and develop in it into strong and robust beings; and second are its artistic conditions, which endow them as much as possible with our proverbial integrity of character. "

FROM "THE MANOR HOUSE" SECTION OF *THE MANUSCRIPT OF REUS*

On this page, dated August 10, 1878, Gaudí set out some of his ideas about *hornamentacion* (ornamentation)

◄ **GAUDÍ'S PROJECTS** As a student, Gaudí tackled a wide variety of assignments, ranging from an ornamental fountain and a royal wharf to a monumental gateway for a cemetery. This design for a university assembly hall was a presentation in his final exam. In it, Gaudí demonstrated his versatility, combining a classical dome with an Early Christian ambulatory and a blend of Mudéjar and Hispano-Moresque decoration.

The Work of a Social Reformer

1873–1943 ▪ PEN AND INK ON PAPER ▪ 57 NOTEBOOKS ▪ BRITISH

BEATRICE WEBB: SOCIOLOGIST

The sociologist, economist, and leading reformer Beatrice Webb (1858–1943) was one of the most influential people in the history of English socialism. Working for most of her life with her husband Sidney, with whom she enjoyed a happy, 50-year marriage, she was one of the founders of the London School of Economics. Her research and writings in the early 20th century laid the foundations for the social welfare system introduced in Britain decades later.

Webb's extensive diaries document these activities, setting them within the framework of her personal life. They also describe her friendships with politicians, from Winston Churchill to Ramsay MacDonald, and with writers such as H. G. Wells, George Bernard Shaw, and Leonard and Virginia Woolf. Many entries cover the work the Webbs did to further the cause of socialism and of social research—from fundraising for the LSE to the books and articles she wrote. These publications, some written with Sidney and others independently, cover subjects such as the cooperative movement and the treatment of the poor in Britain.

In the diaries, Webb also records the turbulent events of the 20th century—two world wars and huge social and political changes. Her busy life and this ever-changing background are chronicled in clear, lively, and sometimes ironic language, revealing a writer who was an outstanding judge of both people and politics. Her influence was enormous, but she occasionally doubted her own abilities, a quality that helps make her even more sympathetic in her diaries. Webb used her diaries as a source for the first volume of her autobiography, *My Apprenticeship.* She did not live to publish any later volumes, so the diaries are the best account of her full life.

> Are the books we have written together worth … the babies we might have had?

BEATRICE WEBB'S DIARY, APRIL 24, 1901

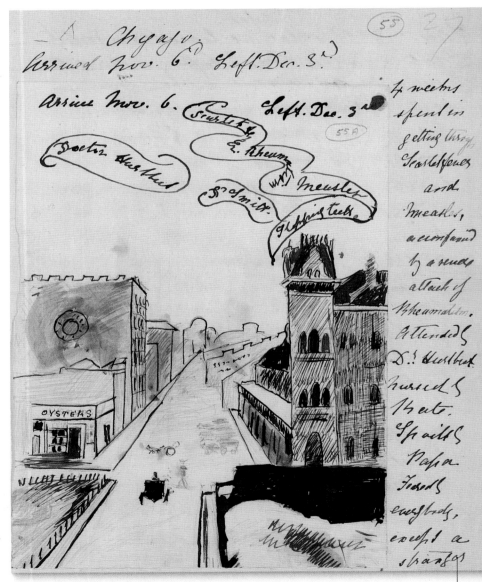

▲ **THE DIARY BEGINS** When Beatrice was 15, her father, businessman Richard Potter, took her with him on a trip to America, where she visited Chicago and New York and saw Niagara Falls. She began her diary during this trip, and its pages include this drawing of a Chicago street. The habit of diary-keeping stayed with Beatrice for the rest of her life.

The diary was written in haste, in gaps during Beatrice's busy days, and the handwriting is often hard to read

> ❝ Sometimes Sidney and I feel that we can hardly repay by our work, the happiness and joy of our life. It seems so luxurious to be able to choose what work one will do according to one's faith in its usefulness and do that work in loving comradeship. The next ten years will prove whether we are right in devoting our energies to the establishment of a science of society and whether the amount of scientific work we have mapped out for ourselves is not beyond our powers. ❞

BEATRICE WEBB'S DIARY, SEPTEMBER 25, 1900

In context

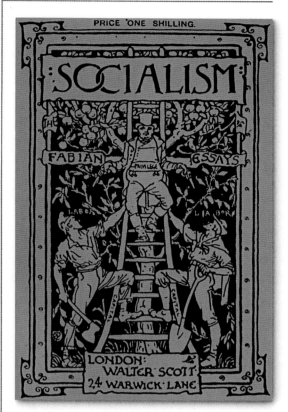

▲ **FABIAN SOCIALISM** Beatrice Webb was a leading figure in the Fabian Society, a socialist organization that campaigned for social reforms such as a universal healthcare system and a minimum wage. Fabians believe that social change should come about by evolution rather than revolution. This approach has influenced left-wing political thinking in Britain.

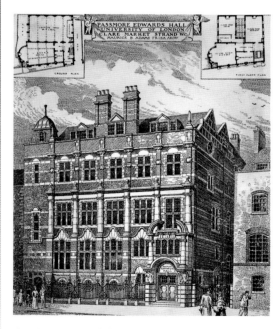

▲ **THE LSE** Founded in 1895, the London School of Economics was the first British university to offer degrees in the social sciences. Its first purpose-built premises was the Passmore Edwards Hall. In her diary, Beatrice attributed the idea for the LSE to Sidney, who conceived of an "association of students who would be directed and supported in doing original work."

▲ **MAKING IDEAS COME TO LIFE** On this page from March 26, 1896, Webb describes how the ideas for a political science library for the LSE came "in a flash across Sidney's mind." She then explains how, having tried various sources of money in vain, they had to appeal to the public for funds for the library. The effort was eventually successful and helped establish the LSE as one of the major research centers for political science.

A Whaling Diary

1880 ▪ PEN AND INK ON PAPER ▪ TWO VOLUMES ▪ BRITISH

ARTHUR CONAN DOYLE: AUTHOR

Famous as the creator of the fictional detective Sherlock Holmes, Arthur Conan Doyle (1859–1930) originally trained as a doctor in his native Edinburgh. In 1880, when still a young medical student, he was offered the chance to go on a voyage to the Arctic as a ship's surgeon. The SS *Hope* was a whaling ship, and Conan Doyle kept a journal of his experiences during the six-month journey. He used the diary to record daily life on board the ship, the Arctic scenery, and the gruesome, dangerous work of the whalers.

The diary is packed with detail, describing the young Conan Doyle's medical duties, from treating men who had fallen overboard and been injured by the ice to caring for a dying crew member. He also recounts his own experiences of work at sea, such as venturing on to the ice to hunt seals, only to tumble into the freezing sea three times. He records his reaction to the bitter cold of the ice, huddling close to the stove on returning to the ship, and how his enthusiasm for the hunt was marred by sympathy for the dying animals. He notes sightings of seals, whales, and different birds, describing his surroundings vividly, and illustrating the journal with humorous sketches and paintings of ships, sailors, birds, and animals.

Conan Doyle did not publish the diary but used it as the basis for numerous factual articles. Some of his short stories, such as *The Captain of the Pole-Star*, are also based on events that happened during his journey. He clearly treasured the diary and kept it for the rest of his life.

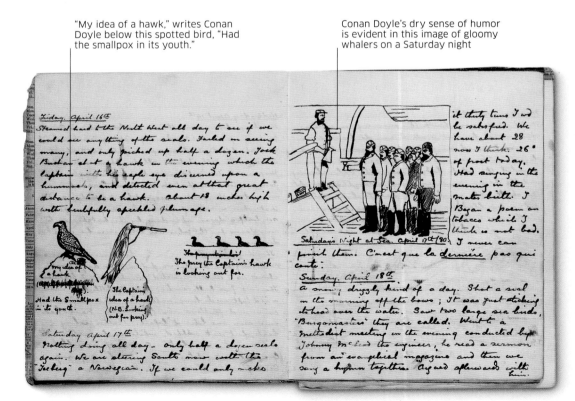

"My idea of a hawk," writes Conan Doyle below this spotted bird, "Had the smallpox in its youth."

Conan Doyle's dry sense of humor is evident in this image of gloomy whalers on a Saturday night

> When I got my head above the hatchway the very first thing I saw was the whale shooting its head out of the water and gamboling about at the other side of a large 'sconce' piece of ice. It was a beautiful night, with hardly a ripple on the deep green water. In jumped the crews into their boats, and the officers of the watch looked that their guns were primed and ready, then they pushed off and the two long whale boats went crawling away on their wooden legs.

WHALING DIARY, JUNE 26, 1880

◀ **ON THE LOOKOUT** The journey of the SS *Hope* was not a great financial success—the expedition caught only two whales, along with 2,400 seals. On April 17, Conan Doyle writes: "Nothing doing all day." His humorous pen-and-ink sketches depict not only members of the crew but also a "hawk" scouring the ocean for prey with the aid of a telescope.

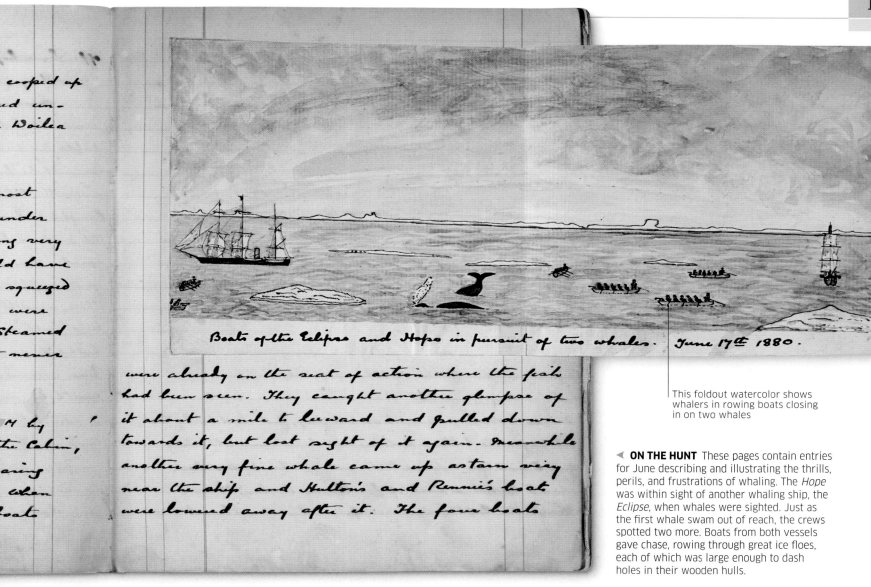

cooped up
ud un-
. Woilea

most
under
my very
ld have
squeeged
were
Steamed
never

M by
the Cabin,
aing
when
boats

were already on the seat of action where the fish had been seen. They caught another glimpse of it about a mile to leeward and pulled down towards it, but lost sight of it again. Meanwhile another very fine whale came up astern very near the ship and Hulton's and Rennie's boat were lowered away after it. The four boats

Boats of the Eclipse and Hope in pursuit of two whales. June 17th 1880.

This foldout watercolor shows whalers in rowing boats closing in on two whales

◄ **ON THE HUNT** These pages contain entries for June describing and illustrating the thrills, perils, and frustrations of whaling. The *Hope* was within sight of another whaling ship, the *Eclipse*, when whales were sighted. Just as the first whale swam out of reach, the crews spotted two more. Boats from both vessels gave chase, rowing through great ice floes, each of which was large enough to dash holes in their wooden hulls.

In context

▲ **WHALER'S BOUNTY** Whales were mainly hunted for their blubber, which was a source of valuable oil, but also for whalebone, which was used to stiffen corsets. Even in whaling ports such as Peterhead, Scotland, where the SS *Hope* was based, the vast creatures were regarded as a curiosity, and people came to ogle at the enormous carcasses when they were brought ashore.

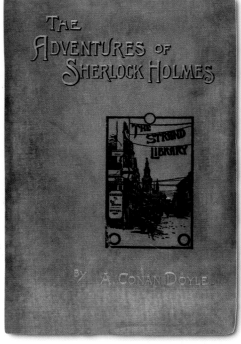

THE ADVENTURES OF SHERLOCK HOLMES

THE STRAND LIBRARY

BY A. CONAN DOYLE

◄ **SHERLOCK HOLMES** Arthur Conan Doyle's Sherlock Holmes stories, featuring the detective with an uncanny ability to solve difficult cases by dint of minute observation and relentless logic, won him a huge following. Conan Doyle eventually published 56 short stories and four novels about the detective. Holmes is still popular as a character in movies and TV series today.

Learning to Write

1881-1897 ▪ PEN AND INK ON PAPER ▪ BRITISH

BEATRIX POTTER: WRITER AND ILLUSTRATOR

The author Beatrix Potter (1866-1943) kept a journal for about 16 years, starting when she was just 14 years old. She stopped writing in it well before she published any of her famous children's books, such as *The Tale of Peter Rabbit* or *The Tailor of Gloucester*, and its entries show her feeling her way as a writer, covering topics ranging from her home life to impressions of well-known people such as the artist John Everett Millais.

Potter led a sheltered life with her parents, spending much of her time in the house where she was born in London. However, during the summer and early fall, the family regularly stayed in a rented house in the Lake District, where she walked, relaxed, lost herself in nature and developed an interest in drawing and studying mushrooms, on which she

later published scientific articles. Descriptions of the places that she visited, of the Lake District scenery that she loved, of long country walks, and of animals are among the most vivid passages of the journal. Her observations of the people she met are also astute and lively, especially when she reports things she has overheard.

Potter's journal gave her a private space, where she could reflect on her experiences without the disapproving comments of her strict mother. In fact, when Potter began to write her journal, she devised a code so that her mother could not read it. She also used the journal to hone her skills as an author. She stopped making entries soon after she began to write scientific articles, but not before she had described the often-hostile male scientists she encountered–she refers to the then director of Kew Gardens as the "botanical pope." After this, Potter's journal lay unnoticed until long after her death.

> ❝ I say fearlessly that Michelangelo is hideous and badly drawn. I wouldn't give tuppence for it except as a curiosity. ❞

THE JOURNAL OF BEATRIX POTTER, APRIL 25, 1883

◄ **PARENTS AND DAUGHTER** Potter's parents, Rupert and Helen, were well off. They had inherited money from their parents' textile businesses, and Rupert also worked as a barrister. They shared their daughter's love of nature and art, encouraging her and her brother to keep pets. The family's wealth enabled Rupert and Helen to take their children on long country vacations.

► **SECRET CODE** The code that Potter invented for her journal is based on a simple "letter substitution" system, which involves replacing one letter or symbol for another. Once she had grown used to the code, Potter could write very quickly, making her handwriting hard to decipher. It was many years before the journal was finally decoded, by Potter expert Leslie Linder. It took him several years to complete the task.

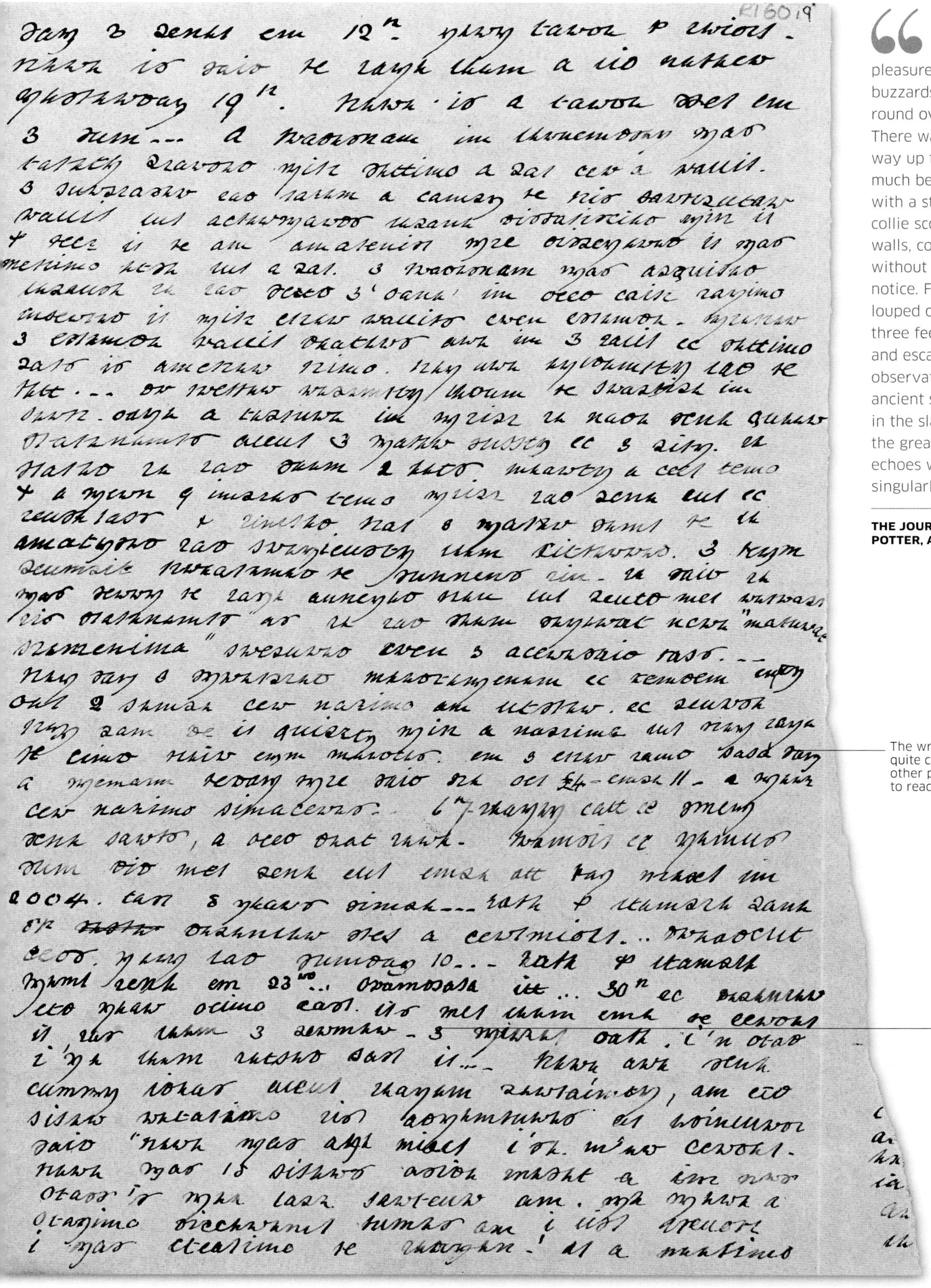

The writing on this page is quite clear, but many of the other pages are much harder to read

Potter used the number "3" for "the" or "three"

"... we had great pleasure watching a pair of buzzards sailing round and round over the top of Wansfell. There was an old shepherd half way up the side of Troutbeck, much bent and gesticulating with a stick. He watched the collie scouring round over stone walls, coming close past us without taking the slightest notice. Four or five sheep louped over a wall at least three feet high on our right and escaped the dog's observation, whereupon the ancient shepherd, a mere speck in the slanting sunlight down the great hillside, ... awoke the echoes with a flood of the most singularly bad language."

THE JOURNAL OF BEATRIX POTTER, AUGUST 10, 1885

In detail

Potter's love of animals and her fascination with their behavior shines through in her journal, which features both accounts of creatures she has seen and animal stories she has read. She was educated at home, by several governesses and an art teacher employed by her parents. Potter became attached to some of these teachers, who encouraged her to write and draw. She became good at both, although her spelling was sometimes erratic, and kept in touch with one of her governesses, Annie Moore, for many years, as well as Moore's son, Noel.

In addition to her observations of wildlife in the English countryside, Potter kept a constant watch on the pets she kept at home, which included a mouse and two rabbits. To amuse Noel Moore, she sent him entertaining illustrated letters about animals, one of which featured her pet rabbit, Peter. The letter begins by describing Peter's habits and Potter's attempts to trim his claws, which had become too long. On the second page, however, is a drawing of rabbits throwing snowballs. It is as if Potter had moved from the real world to a fictional one. This letter in effect shows the birth of the Peter Rabbit books that made her famous. Two of her other books, *The Tale of Squirrel Nutkin* and *The Tailor of Gloucester*, were also based on picture letters that she sent to the Moore children.

◀ **PET AND OWNER**
Potter's first rabbit, Benjamin Bouncer, was her constant companion. He went on vacation with the family, and Potter took him for walks on a long string leash. Benjamin's successor was Peter Piper, who followed her everywhere. Potter drew her pets all the time, and her sketches formed the basis of the illustrations that she later made for her books.

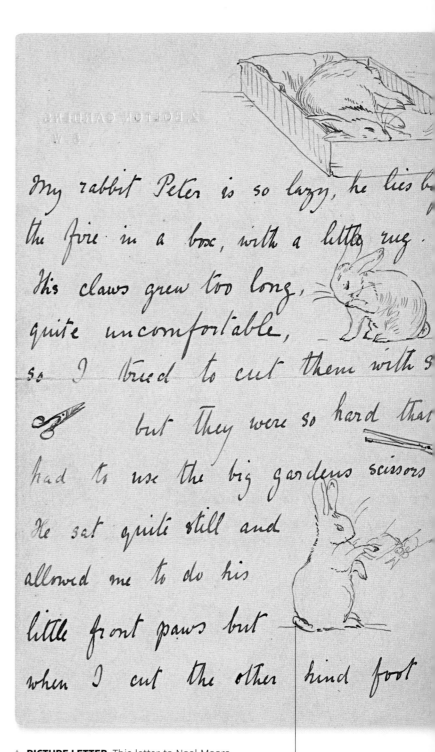

▲ **PICTURE LETTER** This letter to Noel Moore shows Potter creating the mixture of simple narrative and animal illustrations that became her trademark. When she first offered her stories to a publisher, the drawings were simple line illustrations similar to those of the snowballing rabbits in this letter. However, her publisher persuaded her to redraw them in color, which he thought would be more appealing to children.

Peter Piper, Potter's pet rabbit, has his claws trimmed

▲ **LAKELAND LANDSCAPE** Later in life, Potter left London and went to live at Hill Top, a farm in the Lake District. She bred sheep on her land and married a local solicitor, William Heelis. She loved the hills close to her home and often painted them, as here. When she died, she left her land and farms to the National Trust, preserving them for posterity.

PETER RABBIT

Although Potter sold some illustrations she made for other people's books, she could not find a publisher for *The Tale of Peter Rabbit*, the first book she wrote. She decided to publish it herself, mainly for friends and family, and illustrated it with simple line drawings of the rabbits, who act like humans and wear clothes. When her small print run came out, Warne, the publisher who had previously rejected the book, offered to publish it. Potter accepted the offer, and Warne's edition, with color illustrations, came out in 1902. It soon became a bestseller, and Potter followed it up with many more stories in the same small format. All of them sold well, but the mischievous Peter Rabbit was probably her most popular character.

▲ **Illustration from *The Tale of Peter Rabbit*,** written and illustrated by Beatrix Potter and published by Warne in 1902

> His disposition was uniformly amiable and his temper unfailingly sweet.

INSCRIPTION ON BEATRIX POTTER'S COPY OF *PETER RABBIT*

Woodside Villa July 19.th 1885

Slept as sound as a Bug in a barrell of morphine, Donned a boiled and starched emblem of respectability = Eat food for breakfast, Weather delightful — Canary seed orchestra started up with same old tune, ancestors of this bird sang the self same tune 6000 years ago to Adam down on the Euphrates, way back when Abel got a situation as the first angel — Read Sunday Herald, learned of John Roaches failure - am sorry - he has been pursued with great malignity by newspapers and others, from ignorance I think - Americans ought to be proud of Roach who started in life as a day laborer and become the giant of industry and the greatest shipbuilder in the United States Employing thousands of men and feeding innumerable families - What has he now for this 40 years of incessant work and worry   People who hound such men as these I would invent a special Hades, I would stricken them with the Chronic sciatic neuralgia and cause them to wander forever stark naked within the artic circle' — Saw in same paper account of Base ball match, this struck me as something unusual —— Read more about that immeasureable immensity of tact and beauty Madame

RIGHTEOUS ANGER The diary alternates between records of Edison's daily activities and reflections on events taking place in the US. Here, he vents his anger at the press's treatment of John Roach, who had risen from poverty to become America's largest shipbuilder, only to lose much of his fortune when the government canceled a contract and the banks blocked planned loans.

> Dot [Edison's daughter] just read to me outlines of her proposed novel, the basis seems to be a marriage under duress – I told her that in case of a marriage to put in bucketfulls of misery. This would make it realistic, speaking of realism in painting etc Steele Macaye… told us of a definition of modern realism given by some frenchman whose name I have forgotten: 'Realism, a dirty long haired painter sitting on the head of a bust of Shakespeare painting a pair of old boots covered with dung.' The bell rings for supper. I go. Sardines the principal attraction…

THE DIARY OF THOMAS ALVA EDISON, JULY 12, 1885

An Inventor on Vacation

1885 ▪ PEN AND INK ON PAPER ▪ 44 PAGES ▪ AMERICAN

THOMAS ALVA EDISON: INVENTOR

Thomas Edison (1847–1931) is the most famous American inventor of all time, known best perhaps for inventing the incandescent light bulb and phonograph. He kept a diary for only a short period, in the summer of 1885, when he took his first long break from work in many years and went to stay at the house of his friend, Ezra Gilliland, on the coast in Massachusetts.

By this time, Edison had already produced several of his famous inventions, but science and technology are scarcely mentioned in his diary. Instead, he records in a chatty tone what he has done each day, describes what he is reading, and expresses his thoughts on literature, art, and religion. Edison was also looking for a wife. For 13 years, he had been married to Mary Stilwell, who had borne him three children, but she had died in 1884, and he hoped that Gilliland would introduce him to his female friends. One of the young women he met was 20-year-old Mina Miller, and Edison notes how he thought about her so much that on one occasion he was nearly run over by a streetcar. The couple married the following year.

Although Edison's description of Mina is generally quite restrained, the diary is written in rather flowery language that suggests a practical man trying to write in a literary way.

INVENTIONS

Thomas Edison was a prolific inventor, with more than 1,000 patents to his name. His work was wide-ranging and included the phonograph and carbon microphone, the incandescent light bulb, a method of generating and distributing electricity, a way of taking clearer X-ray images, and an accumulator (a kind of rechargeable battery). He also developed a movie camera and a motion picture device called the kinetoscope. Edison was able to be so productive because he sold a number of his early patents and used the profits to set up a laboratory where he and his assistants could work together. He was the first to use a collaborative method of study on a large scale, and some say that the research laboratory was his greatest invention.

▶ **Late 19th-century replica** of Edison's lamp with a carbon filament light bulb

Edison, however, had a humble opinion of his own literary ability and called himself a barbarian because he was unable to appreciate a book by Nathaniel Hawthorne that he was reading. His diary paints a revealing portrait of a great American inventor outside his familiar environment of the laboratory, and its frequent flashes of humor, as when he describes the family parrot as having "the taciturnity of a statue, and the dirt producing capacity of a drove of buffalo," make it unexpectedly entertaining.

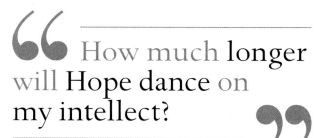

> ❝ How much **longer** will **Hope** dance on my intellect? ❞

THE DIARY OF THOMAS ALVA EDISON, JULY 19, 1885

◀ **WAR OF THE CURRENTS** Edison's power distribution system used direct current (DC), whereas his rival, the Westinghouse Company, used alternating current (AC). AC could be sent along cheaper, thinner wires, which made it more commercially viable for street lighting and domestic users over wide areas, and so Edison lost the battle over which system to use.

A Social Observer

1887-1910 ■ PRINTED ■ FOUR VOLUMES ■ FRENCH

JULES RENARD: AUTHOR

A warm, witty man with brilliant powers of observation, Jules Renard (1864–1910) began to keep a journal when he was in his early 20s and carried on until the end of his life. This was during a period known in France as the belle époque, a time of peace, prosperity, and social change during which the arts flourished, and Renard's journal provides a fascinating insight into it. Renard wrote poems, short stories, novels, and plays, but his life was unusual for a writer because, in addition to socializing with writers and critics in Paris, he spent much of his time in Chitry, a small town in Burgundy, where he became mayor like his father before him. As a result, his journal contains accounts of life in both the city and the country. He provides witty thumbnail sketches of famous writers of the day, such as the poet Paul Verlaine and the novelist Anatole France, and also of his country neighbors. He describes Paris but also notes details of the natural world. He records snatches of conversations among the literati and jots down brilliant one-liners about life and writing.

Although Renard's childhood was difficult (see below), he overcame this to enjoy a long marriage with a woman he loved and to have children. The tone of the writing is mostly happy, with much humor and a real love of life. Renard wrote the journal primarily for himself, to help him develop his writing skills and give him a source of anecdotes and dialogue on which he could draw for his fiction and plays, but when his works were published in a collected edition, the journal was included. Its evocative descriptions, witty aphorisms, and vivid picture of turn-of-the-century France make it one of Renard's best-loved works.

> ❝ I want to **create a style for myself** as clear to the eyes **as a spring morning.** ❞
>
> **THE JOURNAL OF JULES RENARD, OCTOBER 1898**

▲ **COFFEE-HOUSE LIFE** As a young man in the late 1880s, living in Paris and newly married, Renard began to visit coffee houses, where writers and actors went to meet, gossip, and read the newspapers. His friends included the writer Alfred Capus, whose popularity as a journalist was growing, and Renard was able to find useful contacts in the literary world and the theater as he lingered over coffee.

POIL DE CAROTTE

The most popular of Jules Renard's many books is *Poil de carotte* (Carrot Top), a short, semiautobiographical novel about François Lepic, an unloved redheaded child based on Renard himself. The book tells how François uses his cunning to battle his mother, who dislikes him, and his father, who takes no notice of him. It describes how François is bullied but also depicts the countryside that Renard portrays so well in his journal. The story gave Renard a chance to explore his own difficult childhood in fictional form and drew on the humor that is such a significant feature of his journal. *Poil de carotte* grew in fame when Renard adapted it for the stage in 1900. It is now regarded as a classic of French literature.

▶ **Jacket of** *Poil de Carotte*, illustrated by F. Vallotton, 1902

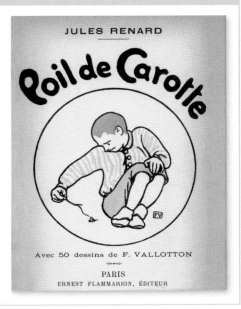

JULES RENARD

Poil de Carotte

Avec 50 dessins de F. VALLOTTON

PARIS
ERNEST FLAMMARION, ÉDITEUR

LES ŒUVRES COMPLÈTES

Jules Renard

(1864-1910)

Journal Inédit
1887 - 1895

Typographie
FRANÇOIS BERNOUARD
73, Rue des Saints-Pères, 73
A PARIS

---

182   JOURNAL 1893

La vie l'amuse le matin, l'ennuie le soir.
Tout le monde en ferait autant.
Il fut applaudi comme poète par Charles Cros.
Un monsieur, " fervent admirateur ", me de-
mande si je ne suis pas l'auteur de *l'Épouvantail*.
Mon étonnement.
— Oui, dit-il. C'est un pauvre qui vole les habits
d'un épouvantail, et soudain, pris de scrupule, lui
met ses propres habits.
Allier la plus plate réalité à la plus folle fan-
taisie.
Il eut un duel avec Mendès pour entrer à l'*Echo
de Paris*.
3 *février*. Il dit toujours oui et fait toujours non.
13 *février*. A Genève. Pissoires : défense de
s'arrêter ici.
Ernest Tissot a la voix double.
Un ministre à Taine : " S'il fait froid ici, c'est à
cause des ultramontains ".
Un autre monta sur une chaise et se mit à chanter
une chanson badoise.
Edouard Rod est le grand homme. On le dit : il
le joue. Après le dîner, il nous demanda la permission de nous faire une lecture, et, avant sa lecture,
il nous dit quelques mots qui ressemblaient fort à
un morceau de conférence. Il a le cou très court et
incline sa tête en arrière. Il a les cheveux rejetés, et
il aime fort un portrait où il ressemble à Zola. Il
voudrait bien se vendre à 100.000.
— Mettons dix mille.
Duchosal, une sorte de Scarron haineux qui fait
des vers suaves.
J'aime Maupassant parce qu'il me semble écrire
pour moi, non pour lui. Rarement il se confesse.

▲ DAYS IN THE LIFE This page from the journal demonstrates the wide variety of material Renard included. Over a few days in February 1893, he records quotations, guiding principles for writers, observations, his admiration for the French author Guy de Maupassant, and a meeting with a man who mistook him for Maurice Renard, a writer of fantasy and science-fiction stories.

◄ PUBLICATION The first complete edition of the *Journal of Jules Renard* was published in five volumes in 1925–1927, and since Renard's widow destroyed the manuscripts, this is the earliest text available. The complete edition was eventually followed by single-volume selections and translations. Other writers in particular appreciated the journals. British author W. Somerset Maugham was so taken by them that he decided to publish his own journal after reading Renard's.

" Paris is becoming fantastic. Those buses without horses ... You seem to be living in the land of shades. And this thought comes back to me: "Aren't we all dead without knowing it?" In these sounds, reflections, in this mist, you walk in anxiety, less with the fear of being run over than with the fear of no longer being alive. The impression of being in an immense cave, and your head in a pulp from the noise. All kinds of smoke: the blue, light smoke, the white, the gray, the heavy black, all go up to the azure and are lost, and the azure remains. There are no leaves left; the wind blows only to make a fuss. Year's end. Our last energy falls away like leaves. "

THE JOURNAL OF JULES RENARD, DECEMBER 1905

Noa Noa

1893-C.1903 ▪ INK, WATERCOLOR, AND COLLAGE ON PAPER ▪ C.200 PAGES ▪ FRENCH

PAUL GAUGUIN: ARTIST

For most of his career, Paul Gauguin (1848-1903) considered himself an outsider. "I have two natures," he said, "a savage and a civilized man." This idea stemmed from childhood memories of when he was living in Peru, and Gauguin tried to develop the "savage" side of himself by attempting to be at one with nature, free from what he saw as bourgeois, European restraints. For a time, he tried to pursue his dreams in Brittany, steeped in its ancient Celtic traditions, but a visit to a replica Tahitian village at the World's Fair of 1889 inspired him to look farther afield. Abandoning his Danish wife and five children, he set off for the South Seas.

In reality, Tahiti was a disappointment. It was Westernized and colonial, and missionaries were suppressing native traditions. Gauguin himself accepted government grants to fund his travels and used his privileged, colonial status to exploit young Tahitian women. In his art, however, he created the paradise he had hoped to find. He painted local girls

> " Every day gets better for me, in the end I understand the language quite well, my neighbours... regard me almost as one of themselves; my naked feet, from daily contact with the rock, have got used to the ground; my body, almost quite naked, no longer fears the sun; civilization leaves me bit by bit and I begin to think simply ... and I function in an animal way, freely—with the certainty of the morrow [being] like today ... I become carefree and calm and loving. "

SECTION IV, *NOA NOA*

in colorful fabrics, rather than the dresses that the missionaries encouraged them to wear, and introduced symbols from the island's waning culture. He had gained a reputation in Brittany but returned to France a forgotten man. His Tahitian paintings sold poorly, so he decided to write an account of his time there, to help the public understand his new work. *Noa Noa* was written as a journal, but it was really a pretext for publicizing his romanticized persona as a "savage". Begun in 1893, it remained unfinished at his death.

GAUGUIN'S **CAREER**

Gauguin started painting as a hobby, turning professional only after losing his job as a stockbroker. Mentored by Camille Pissarro, he initially worked in an Impressionist style but was soon drawn to the theories of the Symbolists. Using simplified forms and areas of flat, pure color, he aimed to convey moods and emotions rather than precise depictions of the physical world.

Gauguin's style reached maturity in Brittany, where he shared a studio with Émile Bernard. Together, they developed a form of Symbolism that incorporated elements of Japanese prints, medieval art, and stained-glass windows. This was deployed to glorious effect in Gauguin's Tahitian pictures, but their true significance was not appreciated by his contemporaries. Gauguin's status as a pioneer of modern art was not recognized until after his death.

➤ *Two Women of Tahiti*, Paul Gauguin, 1892

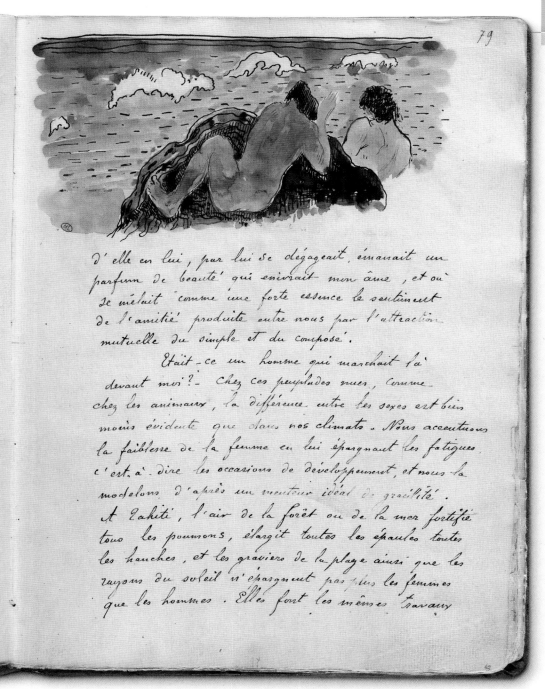

79

In context

◀ **MEMORABLE MUSE** During his first stay in Tahiti, Gauguin met Teha'amana, a 13-year-old girl. She appears in several of his paintings as well as this fine carving made from the local pua wood. Teha'amana's trancelike stare is complemented by a small, ambiguous figure on the reverse of the carving, which may represent Eve.

▶ **TIDINGS FROM TAHITI** *Noa Noa* was Gauguin's fictionalized account of his stay in Tahiti. The name means "fragrant." Gauguin chose the title to conjure up the heady, exotic quality of the island and its culture. He underlined this by illustrating the text with beautiful woodcuts and watercolors, executed in a bold and colorful "primitive" style.

▲ **PENSIVE IN POLYNESIA** In these pages, Gauguin describes an expedition into the interior of the island, to find wood for a sculpture. He was exhilarated by the physical effort of hacking down a tree, feeling that it "destroyed all the old remnant of civilized man in me." He also admired the Tahitians' perfect harmony with nature, from which "there emanated a beauty, a fragrance (*noa noa*) that enchanted my artist soul."

On Devil's Island

1894-1899 ■ PEN AND INK ON PAPER ■ 14 SURVIVING NOTEBOOKS ■ FRENCH

ALFRED DREYFUS: ARTILLERY CAPTAIN

During 1,517 days of barbaric imprisonment on a remote island, Alfred Dreyfus (1859–1935) railed against his conviction for treason using the only means available: pen and paper. He cataloged his despair in his diary and in thousands of letters to his wife, Lucie, and to the French authorities. Fearing for his survival, he hoped that his writings would clear his name.

Dreyfus's liberty had been sacrificed to maintain the prestige of the French military. As the only Jewish officer on the General Staff, he was the chief suspect when intelligence intercepted a list of minor French military secrets that had been passed to the German embassy. A faint similarity to Dreyfus's handwriting was enough to convict him. Dreyfus's writings span the five years after his conviction and include a diary that he began in April 1895 after his arrival on Devil's Island, a former leper colony off the coast of French Guyana.

In his diary, Dreyfus turns repeatedly to the pain of separation from his wife and two young children; the malarial fevers that brought him close to death; the poisonous spider crabs and biting insects in his fetid hut; and the security measures that

> ❝ They will certainly end by killing me through repeated suffering or by forcing me to seek in suicide an escape from insanity. The opprobrium of my death will be on Commandant du Paty, Bertillon, and all those who have imbrued their hands in this iniquity. Each night I dream of my wife and children. But what terrible awakenings! When I open my eyes and find myself in this hut, I have a moment of such anguish that I could close my eyes forever, never to see or think again. *Evening*: Violent heart spasms, with frequent paroxysms of suffocation…. ❞

DREYFUS'S DIARY, DECEMBER 13, 1895

deny him walks outdoors. Kept in solitary confinement with all his correspondence censored, he was unaware of the crisis in France, known as the Dreyfus Affair, that would eventually clear his name. After a revision of sentence was granted in November 1898, he was allowed to see the ocean for the first time in years.

In Rennes, France, Dreyfus was found guilty in a corrupt retrial and accepted a pardon to keep his liberty. His diary pages, notebooks, and letters were published as *Five Years of My Life* in 1901, and he was exonerated of all charges in 1906.

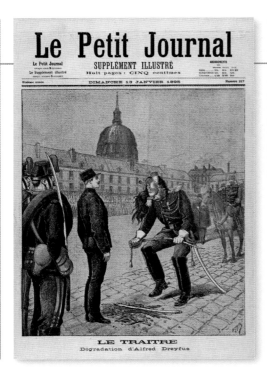

LE TRAITRE
Dégradation d'Alfred Dreyfus

In context

◀ **THE DEGRADATION** After his conviction for treason, Captain Dreyfus was publicly stripped of all signs of rank, and his sword was broken in two. He was then paraded around the military school square in front of officials and a baying mob of onlookers. The humiliating ceremony was headlined "The Traitor" in *Le Petit Journal*.

▶ **DETENTION AND ISOLATION** Kept in solitary confinement on Devil's Island, Dreyfus found solace in books, magazines, and writing materials. He wrote about his struggle to build fires to wash his linen and cook. His rations were water, rice, bread, tough meat, and condensed milk. He threw away the canned pork that was forbidden by his faith.

The case against Dreyfus rested on a disputed match between his handwriting and a memo leaking military intelligence to the Germans

Each sheet of paper was numbered and signed to prevent Dreyfus from smuggling out messages

A NATION **DIVIDED**

Anti-Semitism had been fermenting in France since the nation's humiliation in the Franco-Prussian War of 1870. In an atmosphere of paranoia and extreme nationalism, the press whipped up hysteria against an "enemy within," targeting France's 100,000 Jews in the population of 40 million. The trumped-up treason case against Dreyfus, the only Jewish officer in the army's General Staff, divided the nation. The novelist Émile Zola, at the forefront of the 400,000 Dreyfusards, exposed the deception at the heart of the affair in *J'Accuse…!* an open letter to the president. "The truth is on the march and nothing will stop it!" he wrote before naming Major Ferdinand Esterhazy as the real traitor. In the libel trial that followed, Zola was convicted and sentenced to a year in prison.

L'AURORE
Littéraire, Artistique, Sociale
J'Accuse…!
LETTRE AU PRÉSIDENT DE LA RÉPUBLIQUE
Par ÉMILE ZOLA

➤ **Émile Zola's** open letter in *L'Aurore* newspaper naming Major Ferdinand Esterhazy

▲ **HAUNTED BY INJUSTICE** Early in the diary, Dreyfus described walking outdoors and gazing at the sea through his window, but after a false rumor about his escape spread in France, he was confined for 24 hours a day and locked in irons in his bed at night. A high fence blocked his view of the outside world. What tortured Dreyfus most was his false conviction for a hateful crime. "If there is justice in the world, my untarnished name must be given back to me," he protested.

A Nomad in the Sahara

C.1897-1904 ■ PEN AND INK ON PAPER ■ SWISS

ISABELLE EBERHARDT: EXPLORER

The writings of Isabelle Eberhardt reveal a short but extraordinary life. She was the illegitimate fifth child of a Russian general's wife who eloped to Switzerland with the Russian anarchist tutor of her children. Isabelle was born soon after, in Geneva in 1877. Growing up, she and her siblings had an unconventional education, which combined intellectual learning with physical activities. Isabelle was encouraged to cut her hair short and wear boys' clothes because they were more practical for chopping wood, gardening, and riding horses.

In 1897, Isabelle and her mother sailed to Tunis, where they both converted to Islam. Her mother died six months later, but Isabelle felt reborn in North Africa and remained there. Discarding her European identity and clothes, she reinvented herself as a young male Arab, with the name Si Mahmoud Saad. She became an Islamic mystic, or Sufi; learned Arabic; lived among the poor; smoked hashish; had affairs; and traveled through the wilder, more remote regions of North Africa. In 1901, she married Slimène Ehnni, an Algerian soldier who was attached to the French Army.

Eberhardt's papers blend autobiography with travel writing. She documented her conversations with people across the Sahara, retelling their stories and sharing local customs without judgment. But her adventures were also a personal journey in search of identity and authenticity. "For me, it seems that by advancing in unknown territories," she wrote, "I enter my life."

From 1902, Eberhardt was a regular correspondent for a French newspaper in Algiers. She met Hubert Lyautey, the French general in charge of the city of Oran, and became a liaison between him and the local Arabs; she may also have spied for him. In 1904, she was staying in the garrison town of Aïn Sefra when it was hit by a flash flood, and Eberhardt was drowned. She was only 27. The editor of the newspaper for which she wrote, Victor Barrucand, completed some of her unfinished work and published it—including her travelogue *Dans l'ombre chaude de l'Islam* (1906).

In context

◄ **IN DISGUISE** Eberhardt's male attire allowed her to move freely in North Africa, since unmarried women were not expected to travel alone. However, in 1901, when a religious fanatic learned of her disguise, he attacked Eberhardt with a sword and nearly severed her left arm. When asked why she was wearing a man's clothes, she responded: "It is practical for riding."

► **RESCUED FROM THE FLOOD** This illustration from *Le Petit Journal*, dated November 6, 1904, depicts the flash flood in Aïn Sefra that took Eberhardt's life. In the aftermath, her body was found pinned under a beam in her house. Soldiers sifted through the devastation to gather all her surviving papers, which were then passed to the editor Victor Barrucand.

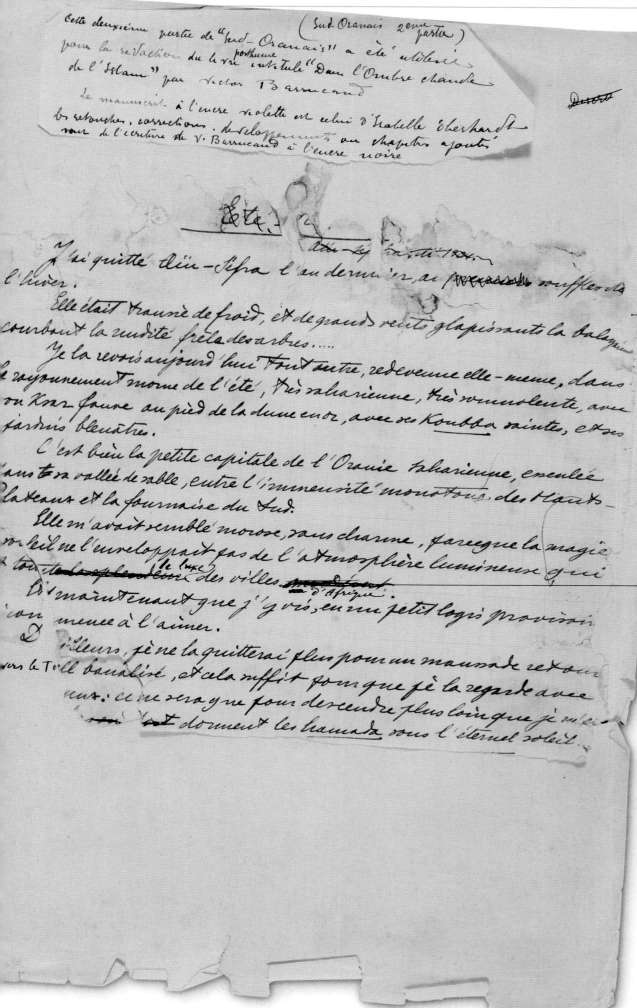

◀ **SAYING FAREWELL** This is the first page of Eberhardt's travelogue, posthumously published as *Dans l'ombre chaude de l'Islam* (*In the Shadow of Islam*). She wistfully describes leaving her temporary home in Aïn Sefra, located in the Algerian Desert, as she sets off to explore the surrounding Saharan landscape and meet its inhabitants. Starting in May 1904, it covers the last year of her uncompromising life of adventure.

Stains marking the flash flood from which Eberhardt's papers were salvaged

Deletions made by Eberhardt's literary executor, Victor Barrucand

> " Among these brave people, I am completely at ease. I entered into their midst and sat down in a corner of the courtyard. They didn't even notice me. Of course, there's nothing remarkable about me. I'm able to pass everywhere completely unobserved, an excellent position to be in for observing. If women are not good at this, it's because their costume attracts attention. Women have always been made to be looked at, and they aren't yet much bothered by the fact. This attitude, I think, gives far too much advantage to men. "

IN THE SHADOW OF ISLAM

Radioactive Notebooks

1897–1902 ▪ PEN AND INK ON PAPER ▪ THREE NOTEBOOKS ▪ POLISH/FRENCH

MARIE CURIE: PHYSICIST AND CHEMIST

One of the most influential scientists of all time, Marie Curie (1867–1934) did pioneering work on radioactivity, won Nobel prizes for Physics and Chemistry, and was the first woman to be made a professor at the University of Paris. Working initially with her husband, the French physicist Pierre Curie, she discovered the radioactive elements polonium and radium.

The couple worked in a laboratory set up in the basement of their house. Three of their laboratory notebooks have survived, covering the five years from when Marie first began to investigate the properties of pitchblende, a black mineral rich in uranium. She was furthering the research of French physicist Henri Becquerel, who had discovered in 1896 that uranium salts emitted rays. The Curies' notebooks document the laborious task of processing vast amounts of pitchblende to try to explain the radiation it emitted. They describe the methods that the Curies used to try and isolate the elements within pitchblende and track the progress they made. In July 1898, they discovered polonium, which they named after Marie's native Poland, and in December they discovered radium. It was another 12 years before Marie managed to isolate pure metal radium from pitchblende and prove its existence definitively.

The notebooks are a record of this groundbreaking work in the laboratory, material that would form the basis of the numerous scientific papers that Marie published. She often worked in appalling conditions, and the notebooks contain her occasional outbursts of frustration, as when the temperature dropped to just above freezing. No one at the time knew about the dangerous effects of radioactivity, so the Curies did not wear protective clothing or take precautions. The notebooks themselves are so radioactive that they have to be kept in lead-lined boxes. A unique record of a pioneering scientist's work, they are now held at the Bibliothèque Nationale in Paris.

In context

Le Petit Parisien
SUPPLÉMENT LITTÉRAIRE ILLUSTRÉ

UNE NOUVELLE DÉCOUVERTE. — LE RADIUM
M. ET Mme CURIE DANS LEUR LABORATOIRE

◄ **JOINT ENTERPRISE** Marie moved to Paris to study in 1891 and met Pierre Curie when he gave her working space in his laboratory. By 1896, the pair had married, and soon they began to work together on radioactive substances. Their collaboration lasted until Pierre's death in an accident in 1906. Marie carried out all her scientific work, for which she was awarded Nobel prizes in Physics (1903) and Chemistry (1911), in Paris.

The Curies determined that the radioactive element polonium was chemically similar to the element bismuth

► **RADIOACTIVITY** The Curies used instruments devised by Pierre, such as an ionization chamber, to detect radioactive substances. They realized that radiation had an effect on substances and objects—it turned this glass flask used for experiments purple, for example. Research into the effects of radiation led to Marie's pioneering work on using radioactive substances to treat cancerous tumors.

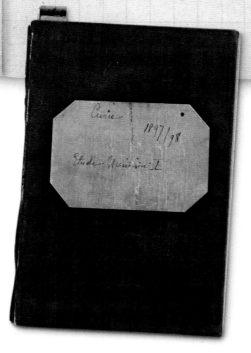

FINDING POLONIUM These diary pages from June 18, 1898, written by both Pierre and Marie Curie, describe the work that led to their discovery of polonium. Using different approaches involving techniques drawn from physics and chemistry, the couple treated a sample of pitchblende so that various elements in the mineral, such as lead, copper, and bismuth, were separated.

DANGEROUS WORK The Curies' notebooks were contaminated by the radioactive materials in the laboratory. Radium's radioactive decay is slow, so they will remain dangerous to handle for at least 1,500 years. Marie died from leukemia, contracted as the result of the dangerous environment in which she worked.

> These **minerals** may contain an **element** … more **active than uranium.**
>
> **MARIE CURIE,**
> **APRIL 12, 1898**

Directory: 1860-1900

▼ CHARLES BENSON'S JOURNAL

AMERICAN (1862–1881)

Charles Augustus Benson (1830–1881) was a free black American from rural Massachusetts. As a young man, he left his wife and moved to the port of Salem, where he found work as a cook and steward on merchant ships. He married a second time and supported a family, valuing the achievement of respectability.

Benson wrote diaries during his many voyages, illustrating them with his own drawings and images cut out of periodicals. His diaries describe the hardships of life at sea, the loneliness and homesickness he suffered, and his relationships with captains and shipmates. He also reflects on his personal ambitions and his marital problems. Abandoning his maritime career for a decade at the end of the American Civil War, he returned to sea in 1875. His final voyages were made aboard the merchant vessel *Glide*, sailing to Madagascar and Zanzibar. Benson made his last diary entry in March 1881, a few months before his death.

BELL'S NOTEBOOKS

AMERICAN (1865–1910)

The Scottish-born scientist and engineer Alexander Graham Bell (1847–1922) is best known as the inventor of the telephone. Bell kept laboratory notebooks recording his experiments at many periods of his life, illustrated with his own drawings.

The idea for a telephone grew from Bell's work with people who had speech and hearing difficulties—both his mother and his wife were deaf. He was living in Boston, Massachusetts, when he first drew a design for a telephone in his 1874 notebook. In an entry for March 10, 1876, he reports the first successful electronic transmission of speech, a message to his assistant who was sitting in a neighboring room: "Mr Watson—come here—I want to see you."

Made rich by the patent for the telephone, Bell continued to work as an inventor in various fields, ranging from sound recording to aeronautics. Highly prolific, he filled notebooks and journals with a wealth of new ideas, including his reflections on eugenics—the improvement of the human race through selective breeding—an idea to which he was strongly committed.

MATTIE J. JACKSON

AMERICAN (1866)

The memoirs of Mattie Jane Jackson (1847–1910) provide a moving insight into the insecurity of family life for black people under slavery in the American South before and during the Civil War. Jackson was born in St. Louis, Missouri. Her parents, Ellen Turner and Wesley Jackson, were enslaved to different owners. A few years after Mattie's birth, her father escaped to freedom in the North. Ellen Turner remarried and had two children by another enslaved man, George Brown, before he too escaped. Turner's own attempts at flight were repeatedly frustrated. Punished and abused, she was eventually separated from her children, who were then sold to different owners.

In 1863, Mattie Jackson escaped to Indianapolis, Indiana, where she was later reunited with her mother. After Emancipation in 1865, Jackson went to live with her stepfather and his new wife, Dr. Lucy Schuyler Thompson, in Lawrence, Massachusetts. Jackson, who could read a little but could not write, dictated her memoirs to Thompson, who wrote them down. *The Story of Mattie J. Jackson* was published in 1866. Jackson urged her readers "to buy my little book to aid me in obtaining an education, that I may be enabled to do some good in behalf of the elevation of my emancipated brothers and sisters."

▶ LIVINGSTONE'S LAST JOURNALS

SCOTTISH (1866–1873)

In 1866, the Scottish missionary Dr. David Livingstone (1813–1873) led an expedition into East Africa, searching for the source of the Nile River. Livingstone was already famous around the world for earlier trips he had made into the African interior and was in the habit of making daily notes in pocket field diaries, which he then copied out and wrote up in full in a more formal journal.

The East African expedition soon turned to disaster. Abandoned by his porters, isolated, and ill, Livingstone was forced to travel with slave traders, whose business he abhorred. In 1870, having run out of notebooks and ink, he wrote his field diary on the pages of an old newspaper, using berry juice. Witnessing his traveling companions carry out a massacre of the local Manyema people left him "crushed, devastated and spiritually broken." Soon after this, he was found by the American journalist Henry Morton Stanley, who brought him much needed supplies, including new notebooks to write in. Livingstone continued his trip, making his final diary entry four days before his death, in present-day Zambia, in 1873. His *Last Journals* were published the following year. In 2011, digital scanning techniques enabled researchers to read the original 1871 field diary, which had faded and become illegible over time.

Charles Benson's journal, with a cutout from a periodical

TCHAIKOVSKY'S DIARIES

RUSSIAN (1873–1891)

The Russian composer Pyotr Ilyich Tchaikovsky (1840–1893) kept a diary for most of his life, but only 11 of his journals have survived—he probably destroyed the others to conceal his secret—that he was gay. Although the earliest surviving diary entries were written in 1873, most of the journals cover the period from 1886 to 1891, by when Tchaikovsky had reached the height of his fame.

Many of the entries consist of an abrupt account of his daily activities in note form: "A walk. Newspapers. Whist. Supper at home." Tchaikovsky constantly rebukes himself for excessive drinking, but there are none of the overt references to his sexuality that appear in his letters. When he discusses music and aesthetics, his comments on his contemporaries are sometimes robust—he dismisses fellow composer Johann Brahms as a "scoundrel." Concert tours abroad feature prominently. The last diary records his triumphal visit to the United States in 1891.

Tchaikovsky died in 1893, probably due to the Russian cholera epidemic, but some scholars have also alleged that he might have committed suicide.

A YOUNG GIRL'S DIARY

AMERICAN (1889–1891)

Selina Richards Schroeder was the daughter of prosperous parents living in New York City. At the age of 14, she began writing a diary that she kept for three years. In it, she confided her private thoughts and feelings, occasionally resorting to code to ensure greater secrecy. Comments on "boys" form a great part of the diaries, from cynical remarks about "beardless cads" to romantic enthusiasm. A picture emerges of a privileged lifestyle, shopping at the finest New York stores, vacationing in the Hamptons, and taking dancing classes and music lessons. Schroeder provides a valuable child's eye view and an insight into the expectations of girls in late nineteenth-century America. The diaries are now kept by the Historical Society of Pennsylvania.

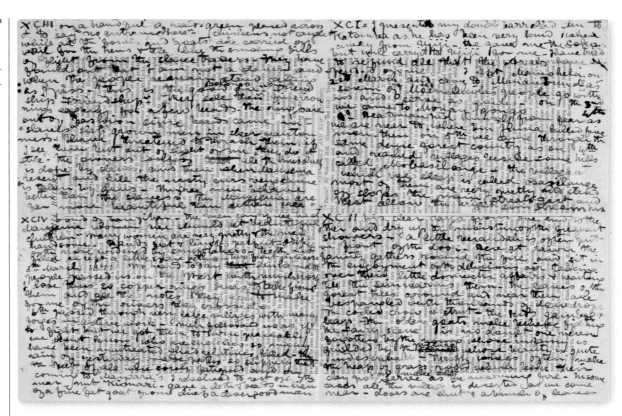

A page from David Livingstone's field diary, 1870

ALICE JAMES'S DIARY

AMERICAN (1889–1892)

The sister of two prominent Bostonian intellectuals, novelist Henry James and psychologist William James, Alice James (1848–1892) suffered disabling mental and physical illness for much of her life. Diagnosed as suffering from hysteria, she began keeping a diary while staying in England in 1889, seeking an outlet for her turbulent emotions and some escape from her "sense of loneliness and desolation." Either written in her own hand or dictated to her friend Katherine Loring, her diary continued until her death from cancer at the age of 43. Unsparing in its self-analysis, it describes her suicidal and homicidal impulses, her sense both of intense inner vitality and terrible weakness, "ground slowly on the grim grindstone of physical pain."

After Alice James's death, Loring distributed copies of the diary to her family, who admired its intelligence and literary qualities but were appalled by some of the hostile feelings that it revealed. The diary was not published until 1934. After a more authentic version was published in the 1960s, James was adopted as a hero by many feminists.

THE DIARY OF IRIS VAUGHAN

SOUTH AFRICAN (1897–1906)

First published in volume form in 1958, the childhood diary of Henrietta Emily Iris Vaughan is a South African classic. The daughter of a magistrate at Marais in the Eastern Cape, Iris Vaughan was encouraged to write a diary by her father when she was only seven, to try to distract her from making embarrassing comments in public. As she wrote, with her child's spelling mistakes: "Everyone should have a diery. Becos life is too hard with the things one must say to be perlite and the things one must not say to lie."

Observant, curious, and precocious, she produced an inimitable and often unintentionally amusing child's view of small-town life in the Cape Colony before, during, and after the Boer War. She says of Boer fighters: "They nearly all had beards like in the bible."

Vaughan continued to keep a diary until she was 16. Later on, she wrote novels, without much success, but the acclaim that greeted her diary's publication, in extracts in 1949 and then in book form in 1958, inspired her to produce two volumes of reminiscences in the late 1960s.

RILKE'S EARLY DIARIES

AUSTRO-HUNGARIAN (1898–1902)

Born in Prague, then part of Austria-Hungary, Rainer Maria Rilke (1875–1926) is recognized as one of the most distinguished lyric poets in German literature. In 1897, aged 21, he fell in love with 37-year-old Lou Andreas-Salomé, who became his intellectual and artistic mentor. Rilke made trips to Russia and Italy with Salomé, sometimes accompanied by her husband. While in Florence in spring 1898, he began a diary, addressed to Salomé, in which he expressed his response to Renaissance art and his elevated ideas on life, history, and the nature of genius.

The diarizing for Salomé, which contains many passages of symbol-laden prose, continued until the fall of 1900, when Rilke stayed at an artists' colony at Worpswede in northern Germany. There, he met and married the sculptor Clara Westhoff. His journals of this period express the wildly fluctuating emotions he experienced as a husband and then a father. The diaries break off in 1902 after his move to Paris, where his poetry rapidly began to evolve toward a new modernist aesthetic.

1915 ~ Secteur de Lorette ~

~ Au Fond de Buval ~

~ Une Nuit agitée ~

~ La Fosse aux loups ~

Seconde saignée ~

La mort de l'instituteur Mondier

~ de Pepieux.

Quelques jours plus tard le major qui était venu donner ses soins au Commandant Noirand fut décoré de la croix de guerre pour être allé panser un officier blessé en un endroit très dangereux, c'était bien, mais il est permis de remarquer que ce major était venu par ordre. Et si lui avait une croix de guerre pour être resté un ... le ... qui auraient ...

Liebster Vater,

Du hast mich letzthin einmal gefragt, warum ich behaupte, ich hätte Furcht vor Dir. Ich wußte Dir, wie gewöhnlich, nichts zu antworten, zum Teil eben aus der Furcht, die ich vor Dir habe, zum Teil deshalb, weil zur Begründung dieser Furcht viele Einzelheiten gehören, als daß ich sie im Reden halbwegs zusammenhalten könnte. Und wenn ich hier versuche, Dir schriftlich zu antworten, so wird es doch nur sehr unvollständig sein, weil auch im Schreiben die Furcht und ihre Folgen mich Dir gegenüber behindern und weil die Größe des Stoffes über mein Gedächtnis und meinen Verstand weit hinausgeht.

6

1900–1940

The early part of the 20th century was overshadowed by World War I, which scarred a generation. The many personal responses to this industrialized warfare include the diaries of German artist Käthe Kollwitz and of British poet Siegfried Sassoon. The age of European exploration drew to a close with Captain Scott's log of his tragic Antarctic expedition. The onset of literary modernism produced two of the greatest writer's diaries, by Virginia Woolf and Franz Kafka, both tortured personalities in their own ways. The notebooks of psychologist Carl Jung reveal the fascination at the time with the unconscious, as do the sexually exploratory journals of Anaïs Nin. The letters and notebooks of George Orwell and Albert Camus, meanwhile, reflect the profound social and political conflicts provoked by the economic depression of the 1930s.

New Forest   I JAN

This is at any rate a cheerful new Years
Day, as though we had turned over a new
leaf & swept the sky clean of cloud.
It was clear with frost at the turn
of the night, when the New Year came in
with the new day. T. & A. went out, with
rum punch in their hands, to salute 1905;
they shouted, & declare that innumerable
owls answered them. This may be true,
because on soft nights when I lie with my
window open I hear the mellow call
of owls repeated again & again at no
great distance, & the crude holloa of a
baby owl, who is has still to learn the call
of an owl.   The afternoon was
a beautiful specimen of winter light; the
air as clear as though sheets of
glass had been dissolved into atmosphere
& all the colours were lively & delicate.

Writing for Herself

1897–1941 ▪ PEN AND INK ON PAPER ▪ 26 VOLUMES ▪ BRITISH

VIRGINIA WOOLF: WRITER

The novelist and essayist Virginia Woolf was born Virginia Stephen in London in 1882. Her father, Leslie Stephen, was a prominent figure in the Victorian literary elite. In 1897, at the age of 14, Virginia began keeping a diary, detailing the daily life of her privileged family circle. By that time, she was already emotionally scarred. The death of her mother in 1895 had triggered the first of several terrifying mental breakdowns she was to endure. She had also probably been sexually abused by one of her half brothers. The diaries that she kept for most of her life are perceptive, full of malicious humor, curiosity, intellectual energy, and a thirst for pleasure, despite the demons that plagued her and eventually led her to suicide.

Woolf's diaries developed in parallel to her career as a writer. Early on, they provided a form of literary exercise, a training for writing fiction and essays. From 1915, by which time she was a published novelist, she kept an almost daily diary that she treated as a release from the discipline of literary writing, a chance to express observations and ideas spontaneously and carelessly, writing at a "rapid haphazard gallop," with "slapdash and vigour." Carefully preserved and bound in boards each year, the journals came to be regarded by their author as possible raw material for novels or for future memoirs.

LITERARY ACHIEVEMENT

Virginia Woolf did not publish her first novel, *The Voyage Out*, until 1915, when she was 33. It was *Mrs Dalloway* (1925) and *To the Lighthouse* (1927), which she wrote in a stream-of-consciousness narrative style, that established her as a prominent modernist novelist, Her later fiction included the spirited, gender-bending satire *Orlando* (1928) and *Between the Acts* (1941), a meditation on British history set shortly before the outbreak of World War II. She is also renowned for her nonfiction works, such as the classic feminist text *A Room of One's Own* (1929) and the semifictional anti-war essay *Three Guineas* (1938). Since her death, her diaries have been recognized as some of her finest literary works.

▲ **Front cover** of Woolf's book-length essay *Three Guineas*, 1938.

The life depicted in Woolf's diaries is rich and varied. As a member of the Bloomsbury Group (see next page), and running the Hogarth Press with her husband, Leonard Woolf, she was able to describe at firsthand many of the leading personalities and cultural events of her day. But the diaries are also intimate, covering her romantic involvement with author Vita Sackville-West, her married life, difficulties with servants, and her everyday struggle with the demands of being a writer.

◄ **STARTING OUT** The first entry of the young Virginia Stephen's diary for 1905 is a lyrical evocation of a frosty New Year's Day in the English countryside. At the time it was written, she had only recently recovered from one of her episodes of severe mental illness and was embarking on her first steps in a career as a professional writer.

► **MARRIED LOVE** In 1912, Virginia Stephen married Leonard Woolf, a Cambridge-educated Jewish intellectual who had worked as a colonial civil servant in British-ruled Ceylon (Sri Lanka). He gave up his career to become his wife's most consistent emotional support, sustaining a loving marriage despite her protracted bouts of mental illness.

> ❝ Why is life so tragic; so like a little strip of pavement over an abyss? ❞
>
> **THE DIARIES OF VIRGINIA WOOLF, OCTOBER 25, 1920**

In detail

In the 1930s, Woolf's diaries reveal her increasing preoccupation with the rise of fascism and the slide into World War II. The Woolfs made several trips abroad between the wars. There is a startling account of their traversing Nazi Germany on a road trip in 1935, accompanied by a pet marmoset. The mounting crisis was brought brutally home by the death of Virginia's young nephew, Julian Bell, in the Spanish Civil War in 1937.

Woolf advocated a feminist-based pacifism, which she had difficulty renouncing even after Britain went to war in 1939. Living mostly at Rodmell in rural Sussex, the Woolfs found themselves in the front line of the Battle of Britain.

The diary alternates accounts of playing bowls with observation of aerial warfare—Woolf describes lying facedown in the grass while bombers fly overhead. Fortunately, the diaries themselves survived the bombing of the Woolfs' Bloomsbury properties in October 1940.

There is a touch of despondency in Woolf's diaries for spring 1941, but they give no clear hint of the terminal crisis she was suffering, and she continued to make plans for future books and articles. The last entry, for March 24, tails off with "L[eonard] doing the rhododendrons...." Four days later, fearing a return of madness, she drowned herself in the nearby Ouse River.

◀ **WAR DAMAGE** During the Blitz in October 1940, while the Woolfs were living in Sussex, their Bloomsbury house in Tavistock Square was destroyed by a bomb. A year earlier, they had moved their belongings, including Virginia's diaries, to a new home in nearby Mecklenburgh Square. This was also damaged by a bomb, but Virginia managed to retrieve her diaries.

> ❝ Moreover there looms ahead of me the shadow of some kind of form which a diary might attain to. I might in the course of time learn what it is that one can make of this loose, drifting material of life; finding another use for it than the use I put it to, so much more consciously & scrupulously, in fiction. What sort of diary should I like mine to be? Something loose knit, & yet not slovenly, so elastic that it will embrace any thing ... that comes into my mind. I should like to it resemble some deep old desk, or capacious hold-all, in which one flings a mass of odds & ends, without looking them through. ❞

THE DIARIES OF VIRGINIA WOOLF, APRIL 20, 1919

THE **BLOOMSBURY GROUP**

Named after the Bloomsbury district of London, the Bloomsbury Group was a set of intellectuals and artists who met regularly as friends from 1905. As well as Virginia and Leonard Woolf, they included Vanessa Bell (Woolf's sister) and her husband, Clive Bell; artist Duncan Grant; biographer Lytton Strachey; art critic Roger Fry; economist John Maynard Keynes; and novelist E. M. Forster. A Bohemian elite in revolt against Victorian morality, they were renowned for their belief in sexual equality and freedom, their informality, and their fierce intellectual debates, as well as their cultural achievements. The Bloomsbury Group reached the peak of its influence in the 1920s, after which there was a backlash against its elitist aestheticism.

▶ **Lytton Strachey (center)** sharing tea with other members of the Bloomsbury Group at Ham Spray, Wiltshire

Writing quickly, says Woolf, forces her to be direct and shoot the words out spontaneously

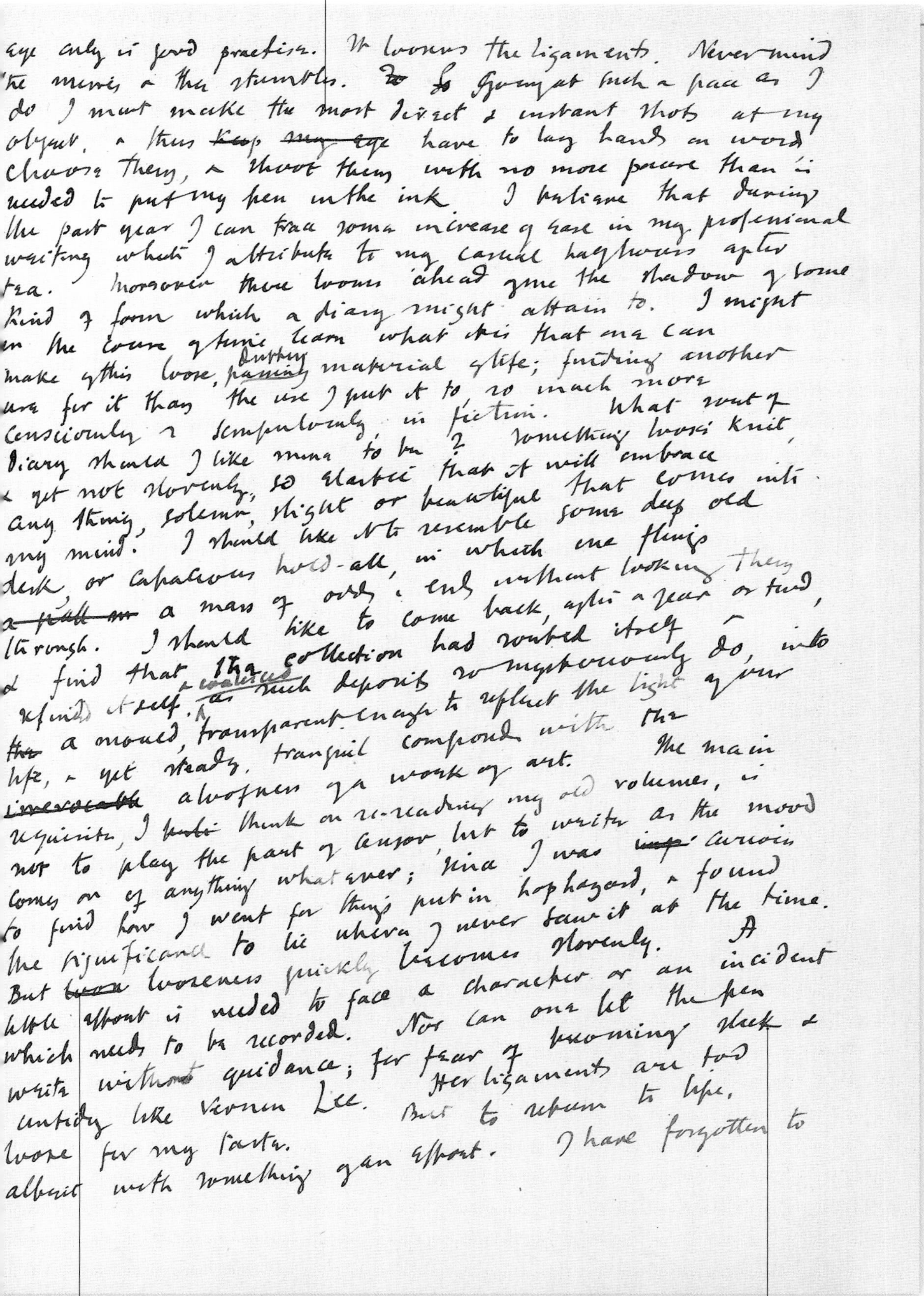

[Handwritten diary entry by Virginia Woolf, largely illegible cursive script]

THE DIARY OF VIRGINIA WOOLF

THE DIARY OF VIRGINIA WOOLF

a writer's diary

Virginia Woolf

▲ **GOING PUBLIC** In 1953, Leonard Woolf published extracts from Virginia's diaries under the title *A Writer's Diary*. The selection consisted of passages he considered relevant to her life as an author. He declared the rest "too personal to be published as a whole." The complete text of the 1915–1941 diaries was published in 1977.

Even in the diary, Woolf crosses out occasional words if she decides they do not hit the mark

Although wanting to write "as the mood comes," Woolf is aware of the dangers of text becoming "slack and untidy"

Taking a Line for a Walk

1898-1918 ▪ PEN AND INK ON PAPER ▪ FOUR VOLUMES ▪ SWISS

PAUL KLEE: PAINTER

Spanning 20 years from 1898 to 1918, the four diaries of Paul Klee (1879–1940) describe a young man's journey to artistic maturity. At the age of 19, Klee wrote the first of more than a thousand numbered entries, which record a life lived through music, theatre, literature, and art, and the gradual discovery of his "line," the abstract forms that for him underpinned a reinvention of art.

Swiss-born, Klee wrote in formal Swiss German and orchestrated the change of mood and tempo of the text of his diaries to create a symphony out of his life. He was an accomplished musician at a young age. Exploits with girls, drinking sprees, art tours in Italy and Paris, and introspective angst are punctuated with poems, transcriptions of "ear worm" musical riffs, and prophetic analyses of where his art might lead him.

When the diaries were published in 1957, 17 years after Klee's death, they were promoted as secret records, but it is known that Klee had revised them for a potential autobiography. Although in one entry he deplored public obsession with the lives of famous artists, his own biography continues to fascinate. His jottings revealed self-doubt when he proposed to pianist Lily Stumpf because his "art did not even feed one man." Lily's father, a Munich doctor, was of the same opinion. In Munich, Lily gave piano lessons to keep the family afloat, while Klee chronicled his care of their baby son, Felix; his experiments with drawing and engraving; and the rejections from exhibitions and magazines. But as the diary marched on toward World War I, seismic shifts occurred in Klee's life: critical acclaim, "new art" galleries and sponsors, and an alliance with the Russian artist who lived next door, Wassily Kandinsky, the founder of the Expressionist group *Der Blaue Reiter*.

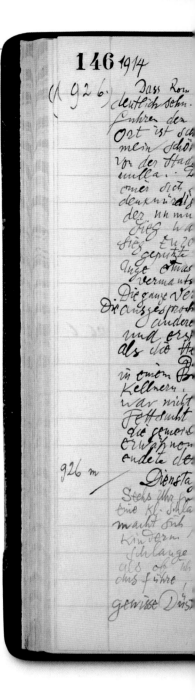

In context

◀ **COLOR POSSESSES ME** Returning home from Tunisia, Klee painted his first pure abstract—an assembly of rectangles and circles called *In the Style of Kairouan* (1914). Shortly before, he recorded an epiphany while painting in the "gently diffused light" of Kairouan: "Color possesses me. I don't have to pursue it.... Color and I are one. I am a painter."

▶ **THIS INSANE WAR** Klee (center, third row) was drafted into the infantry in Landshut, Schleisheim in 1916, two years into a conflict that he later described as "this insane war." His artistic collaborators August Macke and Franz Marc had died in battle. Klee's postings to the flying corps workshop, air force logistics, and payroll kept him far from the front.

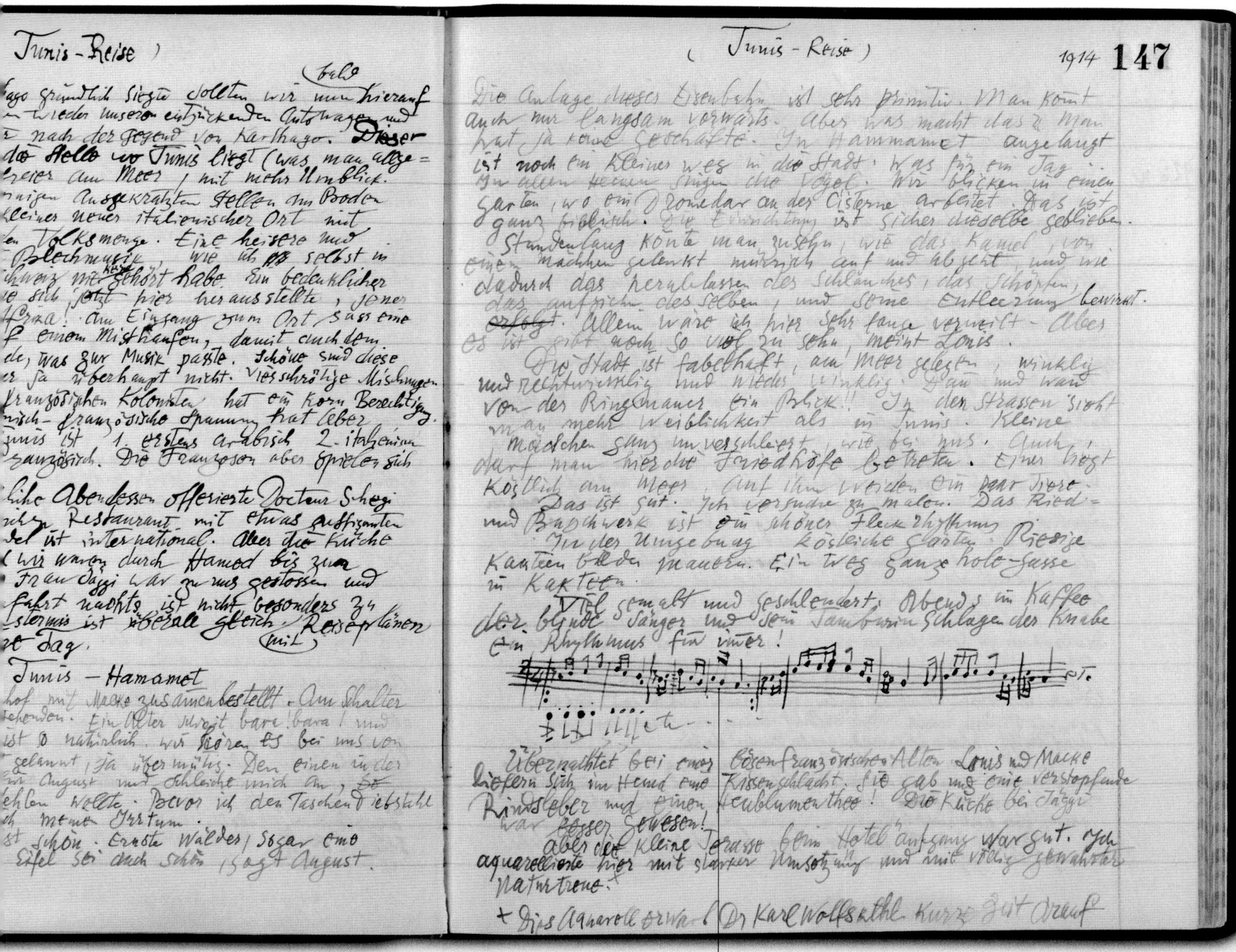
Tunis-Reise)
(Tunis - Reise)
1914 147
Tunis – Hamamet

Listening to a blind singer and a boy with a tambourine, Klee notes down “a rhythm that will stay with me forever!”

▲ **THREE GO TO TUNISIA** At times, Klee’s diary account of a trip to Tunisia in April 1914 reads like a *Boys’ Own* adventure. In his mid-30s, he traveled on a passenger steamer ship from Marseille to North Africa with fellow painters August Macke and Count Louis Moillet. Klee’s enchantment with Arabic architecture, culture, and landscape is recorded alongside tales of high jinks and abundant meals.

> What a day! Birds sang in every hedge. We looked into a garden where a dromedary was working at the cistern. Downright biblical. The set up certainly hasn’t changed....
>
> The city [Hammamet, in Tunisia] is beautiful, right by the sea, full of bends and sharp corners. Now and then I get a look at the ramparts! In the streets more women are to be seen than in Tunis: little girls without veils, as at home. Then too, one is allowed to enter the cemeteries here. There is one splendidly situated by the sea. A few animals graze in it. This is fine. I try to paint. The reeds and bushes provide a beautiful rhythm of patches.

***THE DIARIES OF PAUL KLEE*, 1898–1918**

In detail

The legacy of Paul Klee's 10 years of teaching at the Bauhaus were the theories of pictorial form and visual design that he formulated, exploring them exhaustively in more than 2,500 pages of notebooks, memoranda, diagrams, and sketches. These notes formed the backbone of two volumes that were published posthumously in German and then English between 1956 and 1973: *The Thinking Eye* (*Das bildnerische Denken*), and *The Nature of Nature* (*Unendliche Naturgeschichte*). In the first book, Klee's complex analyses of the relationships between different lines, between colors and tones, between static and dynamic, and between active and passive are held

to be as revolutionary to modern art as Leonardo da Vinci was to the Renaissance, and Isaac Newton to physics. In the second volume, Klee's focus is on process and motion in nature: how life forms spring into being—how geometry lies behind the form of a honeycomb, or how it is possible to look at a seedpod in terms of the relationship between its kernel, inner space, and shell.

Klee proposed that his theories, drawn from the creativity involved in producing a piece of work, and therefore from the subconscious, should be "a device for achieving clarity" rather than rules to be learned by heart.

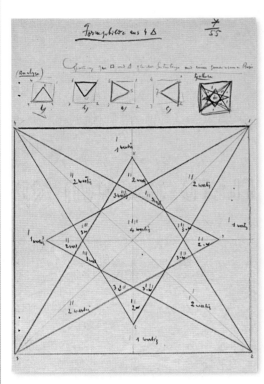

▲ **FORM USING FOUR TRIANGLES** Here, an arrangement of colored triangles creates zones of colors of different weights. Klee was fascinated by the relationship between painting and geometry. By giving lines and tones measurements, he drew attention to the fundamental relationship between the physical world and abstract art.

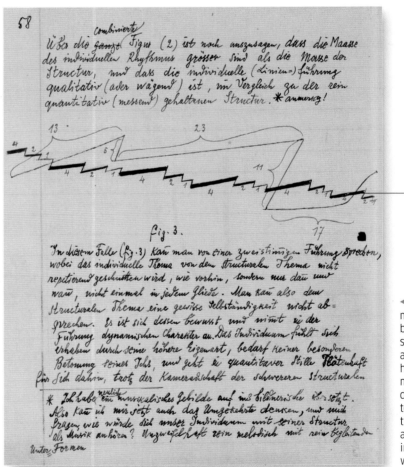

The lines representing "two voices" are given measurements of mass and quality

◀ **POLYPHONIC ART** As a musician, Klee was fascinated by polyphonic music, in which several independent melodies are heard simultaneously. In his notebook, he translates music into pictorial form to demonstrate that musical texture has a place in art. He then reverses the process to ask himself what a pen-and-ink drawing of a structure would sound like as music.

> " Art does not reproduce the visible, but makes visible. The very nature of graphic art lures us to abstraction, readily and with reason. "

PAUL KLEE, *THE THINKING EYE*

gleichen Teilen, und analog. verhalten sich orange und violett wie Wirkungen: zu ihren Ursachen Gelb Rot bezw. Rot Blau. Wir sind also wohl berechtigt, den rechts erscheinenden Farben verschiedenen Rang beizumessen.

(Darstellung)

Die Geometrische Auschauung des ganzen Geschehens wird uns dies mit noch knapperer Deutlichkeit zeigen.

			Rang
Blau	4 Blau + 0 Gelb	= Blau	I
	3 „ + 1 „	= blaugrün	III
	2 „ + 2 „	= grün	II
	1 „ + 3 „	= grüngelb	III
Gelb	0 „ + 4 „	= Gelb	I
	1 Rot + 3 „	= gelborange	
	2 „ + 2 „	= Orange	II
	3 „ + 1 „	= orangerot	
Rot	4 „ + 0 „	= Rot	I
	3 „ + 1 Blau	= rotviolett	
	2 „ + 2 „	= violett	II
	1 „ + 3 „	= violettblau	
	0 „ + 4 „	= Blau	I

fig. 11

Jetzt springt der secundäre Charakter der drei Mischungen direct ins Ange. Ihre Einordnung in die primäre Blau- Gelb- und Rot bewegung kann klarer nicht zum Ausdruck kommen. Die Ursächlichkeit der drei Primären

◄ **UNDERSTANDING COLOR**
This diagram forms part of Klee's illustrated notes for a Bauhaus lecture that he gave on color theory in December 1922. He uses overlapping squares and triangles of red, yellow, and blue (the three primary colors) to show how secondary and tertiary colors are formed. Down the right-hand side of the page, he lists the names of the variations in color: blue, blue-green, green, and so on.

Violet is shown as a secondary color, formed when equal amounts of the primary colors red and blue merge

THE **BAUHAUS**

The experimental Bauhaus school in Weimar, Germany, founded by architect Walter Gropius in 1919, brought international painters and craftsmen together to work and teach in a vibrant, inclusive community. Art, craft, technology, and materials were given equal status and taught in workshop-based classes directed by a master craftsman and an artist. Invited to join, Klee began 10 years at the Bauhaus in 1921, lecturing in theory and overseeing workshops on book binding, creative painting, glass painting, and weaving. In the mid-1920s, the Bauhaus adapted to meet the needs of the machine age and, under pressure from the right-wing government, moved to the industrial city of Dessau. The left-wing leanings of the group remained under constant scrutiny, and in 1933, the Gestapo declared the Bauhaus un-German and closed it.

➤ **Walter Gropius** (center) and Paul Klee (fourth from the right) with fellow teachers on the roof of the Bauhaus in Dessau, Germany

A Crusader for Social Justice

1908-1943 ▪ PEN AND INK ON PAPER ▪ 10 NOTEBOOKS ▪ GERMAN

KÄTHE KOLLWITZ: ARTIST

Kollwitz's diary coincides with one of the most turbulent periods in German history. While she never meant it to be an official record of her times, its wealth of anecdotal detail paints a vivid picture of the social ills and changing fortunes of her homeland during the first half of the 20th century. Käthe Schmidt (1867-1945) was born in Königsberg in East Prussia (now Kaliningrad, Russia). She grew up in a family that had strong, moral principles and a highly developed social conscience. Her artistic ambitions were encouraged by her family, but she was never very interested in exploring the latest aesthetic theories. For her, art was simply a means of highlighting the suffering and injustice that she saw all around her.

This approach intensified after she married Karl Kollwitz, a doctor working in one of the poorest areas of Berlin. Käthe drew many of his patients and wrote in her diary about the effects of deprivation on their lives. This inspired some of her most famous prints, most notably *The Downtrodden*, and her series on workers' uprisings.

When World War I began, Kollwitz focused on an even greater form of suffering. Her younger son, Peter, was killed in Flanders in October 1914, and she became a committed pacifist. She produced anti-war posters and joined the Women's International League for Peace and Freedom. In 1918, when the call went out for old men and young boys to join the fight, she wrote: "There has been enough of dying! Let not another man fall."

Creating a memorial for Peter was the all-consuming project of Kollwitz's later years. In her diary, she describes seeing her sculptures erected: "We went from the figures to Peter's grave and everything was alive and wholly felt. I stood before the Woman, looked at her—my own face—and wept and stroked her cheeks." A complete edition of Kollwitz's diary, *Die Tagebücher*, was published in 1988.

▶ **A MEMORIAL FOR PETER** Kollwitz was determined to create a memorial for Peter, but it took years for her plans to come to fruition. Here, on January 11, 1924, she describes her idea for the memorial. The result was *The Mourning Parents*—two sculptures that look out over the military cemetery near Diksmuide, in Belgium. The father stares at the grave while the mother bows her head in sorrow.

In context

◀ **THE PRISONERS** This is the final scene from "The Peasants' War" (1902-1908), a powerful set of seven etchings, which helped to forge Kollwitz's reputation. The series was based on a 16th-century uprising, but its issues were still relevant in the 20th century. Kollwitz gained financial sponsorship from the Association for Historic Art for her work on the project.

▲ **WOMAN WITH DEAD CHILD** One of Kollwitz's first major works after switching to more universal themes, this was exhibited in Berlin in 1903 and praised for its "embodiment of maternal pain." The woman's features are contorted in anguish. The model for the boy was Peter, Kollwitz's son, who was then seven years old.

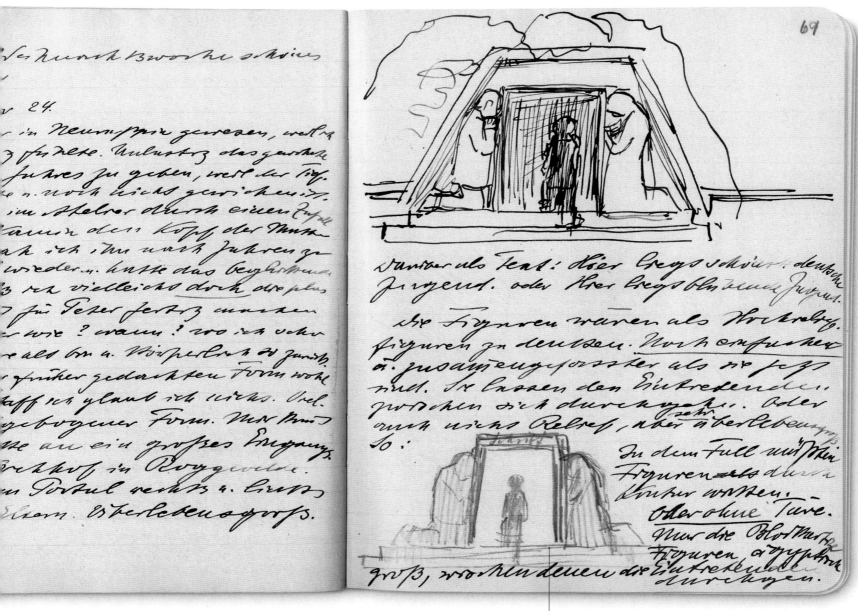

Kollwitz's plans for a memorial went through many phases. Here, she considered a form of portal

ART CAREER

Kollwitz was a remarkable graphic artist and sculptor, one of the leading lights of the German Expressionist movement. She was trained by the engraver Rudolf Mauer and attended classes at the Munich School for Women Artists. Kollwitz specialized in printmaking techniques (etching, lithography, and woodcuts), making her name with two emotive sets of etchings – "The Weavers' Revolt" (1893-1897) and "The Peasants' War" (1902-1908). Later, she took up sculpture, after studying at the Académie Julian in Paris.

Kollwitz enjoyed considerable success. She was a cofounder of the Women's Art Association (1913) and became the first female member of the Prussian Academy of Arts in Berlin (1919), teaching there as the professor of printmaking, but her later career was hampered by the rise of the Nazis.

▲ **Käthe Kollwitz at work** on the sculpture *Mutter mit zwei Kindern (Mother with two children)*, 1932-1936

❝ On the way back there was a young Silesian soldier in our compartment who was leaving the hospital for garrison service. A cheerful young man, with a childish rosy-cheeked face. He had been there from the beginning, lived through everything in Belgium and was wounded in the big battles along the Marne. Someone asked him what it was like to be under fire. 'No one speaks a word— everyone is completely silent—but when one man after another starts to fall you become so afraid that the fear pulls you forward.' ❞

DIE TAGEBÜCHER: 1908-1943, SEPTEMBER 29, 1914

A Fatal Expedition

1910-1912 ▪ PENCIL ON PAPER ▪ THREE VOLUMES ▪ BRITISH

ROBERT FALCON SCOTT: NAVAL OFFICER AND EXPLORER

The diaries of Captain Robert Falcon Scott (1868-1912), recounting his second failed attempt to be the first to reach the South Pole, contain some of the most poignant words ever written. In 1901-1904, Scott had led the *Discovery* Expedition, which set a new record for the southernmost point reached by man. He led a new expedition south aboard HMS *Terra Nova* in 1910, arriving in Antarctica in January the following year. He kept a journal throughout the expedition, recording its progress.

On October 24, after overwintering at Cape Evans, members of the expedition set off to the Pole. Two and a half months later, on January 16, 1912, Scott wrote: "the worst has happened." He and his team had found evidence that their rival, Norwegian explorer Roald Amundsen, was ahead of them. Two days later this was confirmed: when Scott's team reached the Pole, they found the Norwegians' tent with a note from Amundsen. Dejected, they had to turn around and start the grueling 700-mile (1,126 km) trek back to their winter base.

Scott and his four companions endured deteriorating weather, illness, and injuries, and their food was running out. By March 21, only three men were still alive. With two days' rations left, faint with hunger and ravaged by scurvy, they pitched their tent as a blizzard approached. They were just 11 miles (17.5 km) from a supply depot, where there was ample food.

Seven months later, a search party found the small green canvas tent. Three frozen corpses lay inside. Next to Scott's body was a sheaf of letters, as well as his journal, which he kept writing in right until the end. One of the last entries, written in the tent, reads: "We are weak, writing is difficult, but for my own sake I do not regret this journey, which has shown that Englishmen can endure hardships, help one another, and meet death with as great a fortitude as ever in the past."

In context

▲ **CAPE EVANS** The expedition spent the winter at Cape Evans in a prefabricated hut. At one point, it housed 25 men. Scott wrote: "The hut is becoming the most comfortable dwelling-place imaginable. We have made ourselves a truly seductive home, within the walls of which peace, quiet and comfort remain supreme."

► **BENEATH THE BARNE GLACIER** Herbert Ponting was the photographer on the *Terra Nova* Expedition and spent 14 months in Antarctica. Scott wrote: "No expedition has ever been illustrated so extensively, and the only difficulty will be to select from the countless subjects that have been recorded by his camera."

◄ **RACE TO THE POLE** Scott's neat penciled handwriting records progress toward the South Pole, noting the weather and the terrain. Here, on December 23, 1911, he writes: "Started at 8, steering S.W. Seemed to be rising, and went on well for about 3 hours, then got amongst bad crevasses and hard waves. We pushed on to S.W., but things went from bad to worse, and we had to haul out to the north, then west."

▲ **WRITING BY CANDLELIGHT** The hut at Cape Evans had artificial light and there were also kerosene lamps, but Scott often wrote his journal by candlelight, using the matches to light his pipe.

" The worst has happened, or nearly the worst ... About the second hour of the march Bowers' sharp eyes detected what he thought was a cairn; he was uneasy about it.... Half an hour later he detected a black speck ahead. Soon we knew that this could not be a natural snow feature. We marched on, found that it was a black flag tied to a sledge bearer; near by the remains of a camp; sledge tracks and ski tracks going and coming and the clear trace of dogs' paws—many dogs. This told us the whole story. The Norwegians have forestalled us and are first at the Pole.... Tomorrow we must march on to the Pole and then hasten home with all the speed we can compass. All the day dreams must go; it will be a wearisome return. "

**SCOTT'S JOURNAL,
JANUARY 16, 1912**

The weather conditions are marked "T. [temp.] –3°. Southerly wind, force 2"

Pencil diagrams track the expedition's progress to the Pole

In detail

"**Great God!** this is an awful place and terrible enough for us to have laboured to it without the reward of priority," wrote Scott when they reached the South Pole. They were eager to begin retracing their steps back to their base at Cape Evans, but Scott was already expressing doubts in his journal that they could do it. The weather was exceptionally bad and the men were growing weaker. On February 4, Scott writes casually: "Just before lunch unexpectedly fell into crevasses, Evans and I together." On February 17, Edgar Evans died. A month later, Lawrence Oates, realizing his frostbitten feet were slowing the others down, said with great gallantry: "I'm just going outside and may be some time." Scott writes: "He went out into the blizzard and we have not seen him since."

In his last entries, Scott knew they were unlikely to survive and he was writing for those who came after him. At the end, he says: "Had we lived, I should have had a tale to tell of the hardihood, endurance, and courage of my companions which would have stirred the heart of every Englishman. These rough notes and our dead bodies must tell the tale."

▼ **ROALD AMUNDSEN** The five-man expedition led by Norwegian explorer Roald Amundsen arrived at the South Pole on December 14, 1911, five weeks ahead of Scott and his team. The Norwegians, who wore Inuit-style fur clothing and knew that they needed to use dogs to pull their sleds, all managed to make it safely back to their base.

▲ **THE STRUGGLE BACK** Page 36 of the second volume of Scott's journal records their arrival at the South Pole. Already knowing that they had been beaten in the attempt, it was not the triumphal achievement they had hoped for: "We have had a horrible day," writes Scott. There was a harsh wind, the temperature was –7°F (–22°C), and the party was still in a state of shock as they followed in the tracks of the Norwegians.

▲ **SCOTT'S UNION JACK** Scott carried with him this silk Union Jack, which had been presented to him by Queen Alexandra of Denmark, the widow of Edward VII. He flew it at the Pole for the photograph below of the five members of the expedition. The flag was retrieved from the tent where the bodies of Scott, Wilson, and Bowers were found.

> 66 Our wreck is certainly due to this sudden advent of severe weather.... I do not think human beings ever came through such a month as we have come through, and we should have got through in spite of the weather but for the sickening of a second companion, Captain Oates, and a shortage of fuel in our depots for which I cannot account, and finally, but for the storm which has fallen on us within 11 miles of the depot at which we hoped to secure our final supplies. 99

SCOTT'S JOURNAL, MARCH 29, 1912

TERRA NOVA EXPEDITION

Sixty-five men took part in the *Terra Nova* Expedition, the aim of which was not just to reach the South Pole but also to carry out scientific research. Only 16 men set out on the march overland from the coast of Antarctica to the South Pole, accompanied by dog teams, ponies, and motor sledges. The motors broke down, the ponies had to be shot for food, and the dog teams were sent back. Scott selected four men, seen below, to make the final push to the Pole. They are, from left to right, Edward Wilson, Henry Bowers (seated), Robert Falcon Scott, Edgar Evans (seated), and Lawrence Oates.

▲ **The five members** of Captain Scott's final, ill-fated attempt to reach the South Pole

▲ **LAST WORDS** Just 11 miles (17.5 km) from the next supply depot, the three last members of the party were trapped in their tent by a blizzard that raged for nine days, making it impossible to continue. Getting weaker, Scott realized on March 29, 1912, that the end had come: "It seems a pity, but I do not think I can write more–R. Scott–Last Entry–For God's sake look after our people."

meiner Leiter nicht einmal jene Sohlen zu Ver-
fügung stehn. Es ist das natürlich nicht alles
und eine solche Anfrage bringt mich noch zum
Reden. Aber jeden Tag soll mindest eine Zeile
gegen mich gerichtet werden wie man die
Fernrohre jetzt gegen den Kometen richtet. Und
wenn ich dann einmal vor jenem Satze erscheinen
würde hergehetzt von jenem Satze so wie ich
z. B. letzte Weihnachten gewesen bin und wo
ich so weit war dass ich mich nur noch gerade
fassen konnte und wo ich wirklich auf
der letzten Stufe meiner Leiter schien, die
aber ruhig auf dem Boden stand und an
einer Wand. Aber was für ein Boden: was für
eine Wand! Und doch fiel jene Leiter nicht,
so drückten sie meine Füsse an den Boden,
so hoben sie meine Füsse an die Wand.

Kafka compared his task as a
writer to the athlete balancing on
the unstable ladder—he felt that
he could not find a firm
foundation for his ideas

▲ **QUICK DOODLES** When young, Kafka had wanted to be an artist and he illustrated
some pages of the diary with sketches and doodles. Among the most effective are the
rapid sketches of people watching Japanese acrobats in an early entry made in 1910.
Each face is drawn with a single, unbroken line, and expressive curves define the
precariously balanced bodies of the performers.

Loneliness and Angst

1910–1923 ■ PEN AND INK ON PAPER ■ 13 NOTEBOOKS ■ CZECH

FRANZ KAFKA: WRITER

The Czech Jewish novelist Franz Kafka (1883–1924) kept a diary for the last 14 years of his life. Writing in German (the language of the educated classes in Kafka's native Prague at the time), he chronicled his daily life, travels, anxieties, artistic and philosophical ideas, and dreams. Filling 13 notebooks with handwriting that became smaller and smaller as time went by, Kafka wrote about his isolation from his family (especially from his difficult, domineering father), his uncertainty about his ability to write, and his frequent illnesses. Much of this makes the tone of the diary agonizingly self-critical and intense. Although Kafka's best friend, Max Brod, insisted that both in person and in many of his letters, Kafka was far more cheerful and often witty, the diary became a conduit for his feelings about events that were hard to cope with, and dark and oppressive thoughts. Alongside the melancholy moods, however, there are pages of brilliant, detailed observation, perceptive comments about art and writing, and more upbeat passages, especially those describing his travels in Italy, France, and Switzerland.

Devotees of Kafka prize the diaries for their often vivid writing, the light they shed on the author, and for the drafts of stories that they contain. Before he died, Kafka told Brod to destroy all his manuscripts—both the fiction (little of which had been published) and the diaries. Brod was convinced that his friend's work was important so could not bring himself to do this. Instead, he preserved the papers, ensuring that Kafka's three great novels, *The Castle*, *America*, and *The Trial*, his many short stories, and eventually the diaries were published.

> " How **time flies;** another **ten days** and I have achieved **nothing.** It doesn't come off. "

THE DIARIES OF FRANZ KAFKA, MARCH 11, 1915

In context

◄ **ENGAGEMENT** The diary describes Kafka's first meeting with Felice Bauer in August 1912. Felice worked in Berlin, but they wrote to one another regularly. In 1913, they became engaged but still met only rarely. The letters continued until 1917, when Kafka broke off the engagement because he was suffering from tuberculosis and knew that it would eventually kill him.

◄ **FATHER AND SON** Kafka's father Hermann owned a fashion retail business. Disappointed that his son wanted to be a writer and would not take over the family business, he criticized Franz in a way that hurt him deeply. In this long letter to his father, Kafka accuses Hermann, quite justly, of being domineering and not caring about him.

In detail

Although he was highly educated and had a responsible job with an insurance company, as a German-speaking Jew, Kafka was an outsider in Prague. He often found it difficult to fit in, and the diary records his botched attempts to make conversation and his difficult on-off relationships with women. Much of Kafka's fiction is also about social outsiders, and some of his stories were inspired by dreams that he recorded in his diary.

It is not surprising, therefore, that he thought of the diary as his writer's notebook. He kept a record of many of his thoughts about art and writing, as well as critiques of plays he had seen at the theatre. In some entries, he is harshly critical of his own work and laments how he suffers from writer's block. The diary also contains short passages that form the beginnings of stories and longer drafts of his novel *America* and short stories such as *The Stoker* and *Investigations of a Dog*. Kafka eventually did more work on some of these drafts so that he could publish them. Others proved useful to Max Brod when he began to prepare Kafka's fiction for publication.

▲ **ORIGINAL DRAFT** One of the stories that Kafka drafted in his diary was *The Judgement*, the final paragraphs of which are shown above. Kafka notes that he wrote the story in a single sitting on September 22-23, 1912, working at it all night until six o'clock in the morning. He adds that he was so stiff from sitting that when he finished, he could hardly pull his legs out from under the desk.

◄ **JEWISH PRAGUE** Kafka's family lived in the Jewish quarter of Prague. It had several synagogues, including the Spanish Synagogue (left), near which there is now a statue of Kafka. He had a Jewish education up until the age of 13, but as an adult, he attended synagogue only on High Holidays, when he went with his father.

[Handwritten German diary/draft text of The Judgement*, page 433/27]*

This is where the draft text of *The Judgement* comes to an end and the diary resumes

KAFKAESQUE FICTION

As well as his three powerful novels, Kafka wrote the story *Metamorphosis* (1915), about a salesman who wakes up one morning to discover that he has turned into "a monstrous vermin" (usually interpreted as an insect or cockroach). Several of Kafka's works are about someone trapped in a situation they do not understand, which often involves a faceless and inaccessible bureaucracy. In the novel *The Castle* (1926), a surveyor is sent to a village to do a job but cannot gain access to the officials who govern the village from a mysterious castle. The predicament of Kafka's hero, at the mercy of bizarre, sinister forces beyond his control, has given rise to the term "Kafkaesque," to describe such situations in real life. Kafka's diaries recount how he too felt trapped in situations that he could not resolve–both at work and in his personal life.

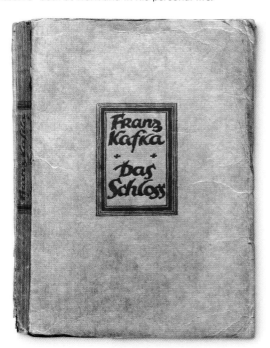

▲ **First paperback edition** of Kafka's *Das Schloss* (*The Castle*), 1926

▲ **MAX BROD** Kafka first met Max Brod at college in Prague. Both men were law students and were embarking upon careers as writers. Brod became one of Kafka's confidants and the two men discussed their work with each other. When Kafka died, Brod became his literary executor, and his regard for his friend's work was such that he did not destroy his manuscripts as Kafka wished.

❝ Didn't go home for supper, nor to Max's either, where there was a gathering tonight. Reasons: lack of appetite, fear of getting back late in the evening; but above all the thought that I wrote nothing yesterday, that I keep getting farther and farther from it, and am in danger of losing everything I have laboriously achieved these past six months. Provided proof of this by writing one and a half wretched pages of a new story that I have already decided to discard…. Occasionally I feel an unhappiness that almost dismembers me, and at the same time am convinced of its necessity and of the existence of a goal to which one makes one's way by undergoing every kind of unhappiness. ❞

THE DIARIES OF FRANZ KAFKA, MARCH 13, 1915

The Red Book

1914–1930 ▪ INK ON PARCHMENT ▪ 205 PAGES ▪ SWISS

CARL GUSTAV JUNG: PSYCHIATRIST AND PSYCHOTHERAPIST

After years at the forefront of the new science of analytical psychology, Carl Jung (1875–1961) retreated to Switzerland, abandoning his academic and professional posts. The 38-year-old psychoanalyst faced ridicule after contradicting the concepts of his former mentor and collaborator, Sigmund Freud, and found himself staring into the abyss. As a child, Jung had experienced occasional hallucinations, but now he was visited by visions of Europe ravaged by floods and rivers of blood. When World War I (1914–1918) broke out, he made connections between his private imaginings and external events; he concluded that his state of mind was not madness and warranted rigorous investigation.

In 1913, Jung began the first of seven black notebooks that chronicled "his confrontation with the unconscious." He spent his evenings evoking his fantasies while fully conscious, entering into them in order to converse with personifications of his feminine self, his dark side, his teacher, and his soul. Besieged by serpents and dragons, gods, and devils, Jung found safety in recording these "active imaginings"—he

> " To the superficial observer, it will appear like madness.

EPILOGUE TO *THE RED BOOK*, 1959

believed that writing them down freed him from their power. Over the next 16 years, he analyzed the entries in his "Black Books" and transcribed them into a red leather-bound volume that he called *Liber Novus* (*New Book*), which he illustrated himself. This became the bedrock of his future theories on extraversion and introversion, archetypes (universal role models and images), collective memory, religion, and myth creation.

The Red Book, as it is now known, was not published during Jung's lifetime—he was reluctant to expose his inner struggles to scientific scrutiny. It languished in a Swiss bank vault for 50 years after his death, until the Jung historian Sonu Shamdasani persuaded his estate to publish a facsimile in 2009.

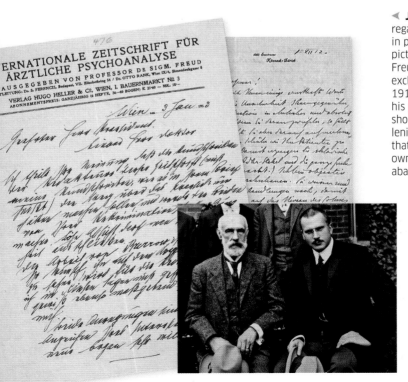

◀ **JUNG AND FREUD** Once regarded as Freud's heir apparent in psychoanalysis, Jung (right in picture) distanced himself from Freud's theories. In a bitter exchange of letters in 1912 and 1913, he accused Freud of treating his pupils as "slavish sons" and showing his patients neither leniency nor love. Freud replied that Jung lacked insight into his own "illness" and that he was abandoning their relationship.

▶ **SWALLOWER OF THE SUN** In Jung's book, dragons are used to represent either the monstrous side of the self, the unconscious, or the Antichrist. The dragon illustrated here, Jung explains, signifies the withdrawal of "Atmavictu," the breath of life. The dragon slayer is a youth who had helped Jung murder a hero in an earlier imagining.

Each chapter begins with an ornate, illuminated letter, thought to be reminiscent of the Book of Kells

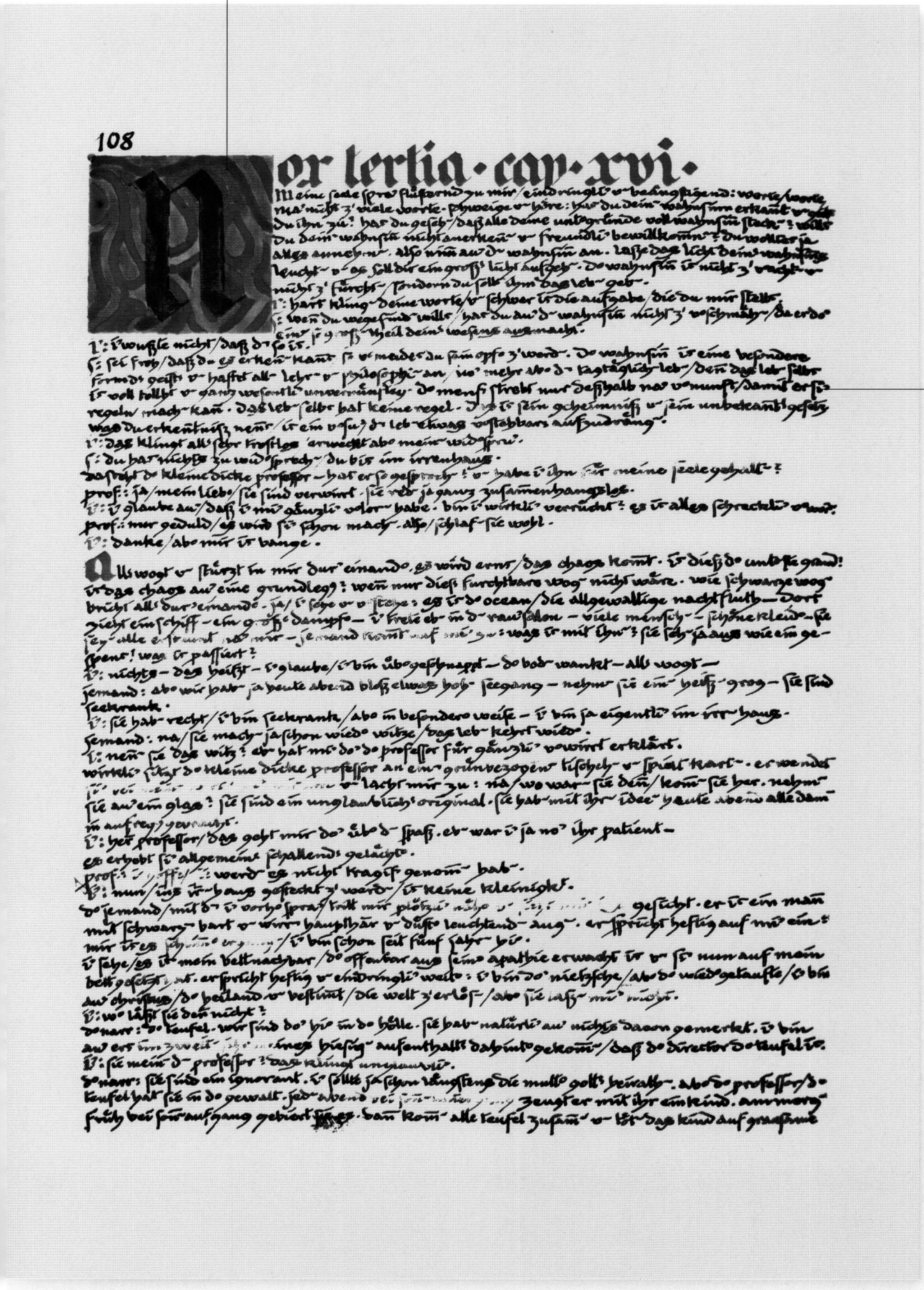

108

ox tertia · cap · xvi ·

◄ **NOX TERTIA** In the chapter *Nox tertia* (Third night), Jung has a dialogue with his soul about madness, chaos, Christ, and hell. He wrote the dense, poetic German text calligraphically on cream parchment in the original *Liber Novus* (*New Book*), which sat like a medieval manuscript on an easel in his study. The book contains more than 70 illustrations, including mandalas—circular forms that Jung regarded as the "wholeness of self."

Here, Jung converses with his soul, which is personified as a spiritual guide

> ❝ My soul spoke to me in a whisper, urgently and alarmingly: 'Words, words, do not make too many words. Be silent and listen: have you recognized your madness and do you admit it? Have you noticed that all your foundations are completely mired in madness? Do you not want to recognize your madness and welcome it in a friendly manner? You wanted to accept everything. So accept madness too. Let the light of your madness shine, and it will suddenly dawn on you. Madness is not to be despised and not to be feared, but instead you should give it life.' ❞

THE RED BOOK, NOX TERTIA, LIBER SECUNDUS

A Conscript in the Great War

1914-1918 ■ PEN AND INK ON PAPER ■ 19 NOTEBOOKS ■ FRENCH

LOUIS BARTHAS: SOLDIER

When the French Army mobilized at the start of World War I, Louis Barthas (1879-1952) was one of millions of citizens called up for military service. A 35-year-old barrel maker from southern France, Barthas was a socialist, pacifist, and trade unionist. As a corporal in the infantry, he led a squad in the trenches on the Western Front from December 1914 to April 1918. He somehow survived the slaughter in which more than a million French soldiers died, returning home with the mud-stained pocket diaries in which he had recorded his bitter experiences.

Over the following years, Barthas devoted his evenings to writing up his journals as war memoirs, incorporating material from letters he had sent home from the front. The result of his labors was more than 1,700 pages of manuscript filling 19 notebooks. His ambition was to present the ordinary soldiers' view of the war as an antidote to the lies of militarist propaganda. He describes the men's hatred of officers, their sporadic acts of collective disobedience and fraternization with the enemy, and the solidarity within the squad that helped them bear the squalor and horrors of the trenches.

Barthas never saw his work published. The notebooks languished in a drawer until one of his grandchildren sent them to publishers. When the memoirs were finally published in 1978 as *Poilu*, the French slang term for an infantry soldier, they were acclaimed as a moving and accurate account of what the author called "the accursed, infamous war, which forever dishonored our century and blighted the civilization of which we were so proud."

▼ **ILLUSTRATED JOURNAL** These pages from Barthas's Fifth Notebook cover the battle for the ridge of Notre Dame de Lorette on the Artois front. They show how Barthas used postcard pictures to illustrate his journal and wrote dramatic headings for sections of the narrative: "A lively night … Second bloodletting…." The text criticizes the award of a medal to a medic who saved an officer's life, while ordinary soldiers' daily heroism went unrecognized.

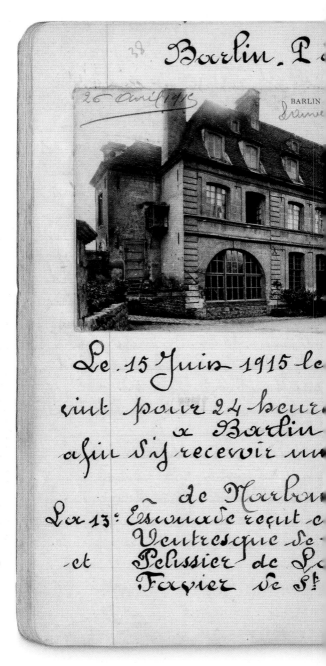

▲ **LONG-SUFFERING TROOPS** French infantry soldiers, known as the *poilus* (hairy ones), file along a trench in their steel helmets in this 1915 painting of Souchez, Artois, by François Flameng. Discontent over futile offensives, poor food, harsh discipline, and lack of leave spilled over into mutiny in the French Army in the spring of 1917.

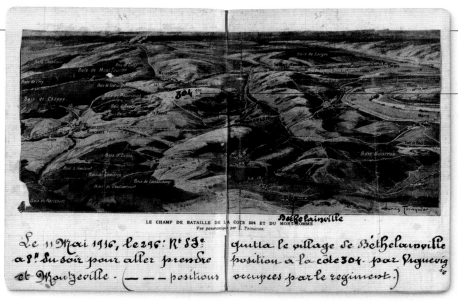

Barthas has marked the position of Côte 304

▲ **BATTLE PLAN** Barthas pasted battlefield maps clipped from magazines into his notebooks, annotating them to show the position of his own squad. This image from his Tenth Notebook shows the situation at Verdun in May 1916, when he was positioned on the notorious Côte 304, a small hill that was the scene of some of the most vicious fighting in the entire war.

▲ **FIFTH NOTEBOOK** The cover of Barthas's Fifth Notebook is decorated with one of his sketches and bears the title "The Lorette Charnel House," referring to the costly battle for Notre Dame de Lorette. Despite the care he had taken to write and illustrate his personal account of the war, Barthas made no attempt to have it published.

This heading refers to a "second bloodletting"

> ... I saw, heading toward me, three dwellers of the trenches. I looked at them with horror. They were covered in mud, from the tips of their shoes to the peaks of their képis, as if they had just waded through a sea of muck. Their hands, their faces, moustaches, eyebrows, hair, all covered with viscid mud.... In a few words they sketched out their sad fate. Every night you had to attack, patrol, or dig. The machine guns drove you mad. You had to lie in the mud for hours at a time. Daily rains, no shelters, badly fed—such was their sad fate, and such was going to be mine.

SECOND NOTEBOOK, NOVEMBER 4 TO DECEMBER 14, 1914

A Poet in the Trenches

1915–1918 ▪ PENCIL AND INK ON PAPER ▪ 10 NOTEBOOKS (WAR DIARIES) ▪ BRITISH

SIEGFRIED SASSOON: WAR POET

Born into a wealthy family, Siegfried Sassoon (1886–1967) was a minor poet, an amateur sportsman, and, in his own words, "a fox-hunting man" before he volunteered for the army at the onset of World War I (1914–1918). Sent to the French trenches in 1915, he underwent experiences that transformed his life and his poetry. His war diaries offer a vivid account of an officer who was both a brave soldier and a bold anti-war protester.

Written in notebooks small enough to fit into the pocket of an officer's tunic, the war journals open with Sassoon joining the Royal Welch Fusiliers in France. At first, he enjoys the French countryside, observed with the sensitive eye of a nature poet, but soon he is recounting the brutal experience of trench warfare. Angered by the death of a close friend, Sassoon writes "hate has come also and the lust to kill." Leading almost suicidal raids on German trenches—which earned him the nickname "Mad Jack"—he describes "laughing with my men at the fun I've had out in no-man's-land."

Alongside a reckless bravery that won him a Military Cross, Sassoon felt mounting anger at the conflict. Influenced by his fellow officer and poet Robert Graves, his verses—sometimes drafted in his diary—turned toward an increasingly realistic observation of the horrors of war. After the terrible Battle of the Somme in July 1916, he was invalided home with a fever. A second spell at the front in spring 1917 ended when he was shot in the shoulder. By now, his diaries were revealing nightmares and severe mental strain. Sent back to England to recover, Sassoon decided upon open revolt against the war.

> " Something in me keeps driving me on; I must go on till I am killed. "
>
> **SASSOON'S JOURNAL, APRIL 29, 1917**

◄ **TRENCH WARFARE** For much of the war, the opposing armies in France held static lines of trenches separated by "no-man's-land"—a strip of mud, craters, and barbed wire. The trenches were often wet and infested with rats. A courageous officer, Sassoon was noted for conducting night raids on German trenches.

The head of the German Kaiser

▶ **WOUNDED IN ACTION** In addition to writing his diary, Sassoon made vivid sketches in his notebooks, including this one of a military hospital ward. He was wounded twice in the course of the war—shot by a German sniper in April 1917 and then again, mistakenly, by one of his own men in July 1918.

July 1st. 1916.

Saty. 7.30. a.m. Last night was cloudless a starry & still — the bombardment went on steadily. We had breakfast at 6. — The morning is brilliantly fine — after a mist early. Since 6.30 there has been hell let loose. The air vibrates with the incessant din — the whole earth shakes & rocks & throbs — It is one continuous roar — Machine-guns tap & rattle — bullets whistling over head — small fry quite outdone by the gangs of hooligan-shells that dash over to. need the German lines with their demolition parties. The smoke-cloud is cancelled as the wind is wrong since yesterday. Attack should be starting now, but one can't look out as the m-g. bullets are skimming. Inferno — inferno — bang — smash!

▲ **SOMME DISASTER** Scribbling feverishly, Sassoon recorded the disastrous opening of the Somme offensive on July 1, 1916, which he witnessed from a trench dugout. He could find no adequate words for the violence of the bombardment, resorting to "Inferno–inferno–bang–smash!" More than 19,000 British soldiers were killed that day.

This rapid sketch shows a face shocked by the blasts

> Sitting on the firestep in warm weather and sunshine about 10 am with the lark above and the usual airmen. Can't remember Thursday night's show very clearly; it seems mostly rain and feeling chilled, and the flash of rifles in the gloom; and O'Brien's shattered limp body propped up down that infernal bank—face ghastly in the light of a flare, clothes torn, hair matted over the forehead.... Trying to lift him up the side of the crater, the soft earth kept giving way under one's feet.... I would have given a lot if he could have been alive, but it was a hopeless case....

SASSOON'S JOURNAL, MAY 27, 1916

In detail

While recuperating from a wound in England in July 1917, Sassoon made a public statement criticizing the conduct of the war and calling for a negotiated peace. As a serving officer, he should have faced court martial for what he himself called "an act of wilful defiance of military authority." Instead, he was diagnosed with "shell-shock" and sent to Craiglockhart military hospital for treatment. His diary is blank until December 1917, when he agreed to return to service despite his anti-war sentiments, first in Palestine and then back to France. Wounded again, he was in England at the armistice in November 1918. In the war diaries' last entry, he describes the celebrations in London as "an outburst of mob patriotism ... a loathsome ending to the loathsome tragedy of the last four years."

Ten years after the war, Sassoon used the war diaries as the basis for an acclaimed set of lightly fictionalized memoirs, known as the "George Sherston trilogy." He continued to keep diaries right up to his death in 1967, but the later journals have attracted far less interest.

> ❝ The **dead bodies** lying about the trenches … **will haunt me** till I die. ❞
>
> **SASSOON'S JOURNAL, APRIL 14, 1917**

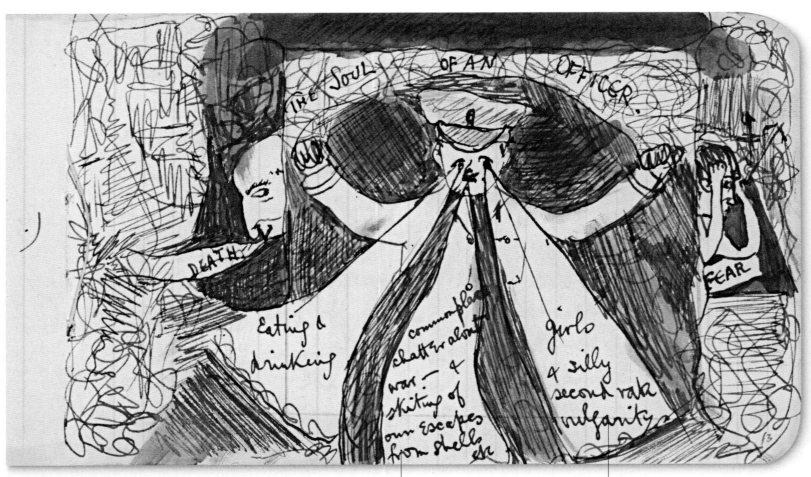

▲ **THE SOUL OF AN OFFICER** This savagely satirical image, from Sassoon's diary for June to August 1916, dissects the psychology of an officer at the front, hiding lurking thoughts of fear and death behind a vain façade of idle chatter and boasting. Sassoon was deeply conflicted about his own role in the war, which part of him found satisfying and even enjoyable.

Part of "putting on a brave face" consists of bragging about daring escapes from danger

Another ruse is to boast about sexual conquests and to be vulgar

BRITISH **WAR POETS**

The experience of World War I provoked serving soldiers into writing some of the most powerful poetry in the English language. Early in the conflict, poets such as Rupert Brooke and Julian Grenfell celebrated the war as a refreshing challenge after stagnant years of peace. Later, the horrors of trench warfare led other poets, including Sassoon, Robert Graves, and Isaac Rosenberg, to develop a new style of verse informed by gritty realism and satire. Probably the best-known war poet, Wilfred Owen, was influenced by Sassoon after the two met as patients at Craiglockhart hospital in 1917. Owen was killed a week before the armistice in November 1918. The poetry of the trenches had a profound influence on the negative way in which the war was later viewed.

▼ **A SOLDIER'S DECLARATION** Sassoon's anti-war protest statement, entitled "Finished with the War: A Soldier's Declaration," was read out by an MP in the House of Commons on July 30, 1917. Sassoon wrote out this copy of the statement in his journal. His accusation on the first page that the war was being "deliberately prolonged" by the British government in "a war of aggression and conquest" was factually incorrect.

▲ **Soldiers of the Middlesex Regiment,** the 1st Battalion, in a trench during the Battle of Bailleul, 1918

21

My only desire is to make things as easy as possible for you in dealing with my case. — I will come to Litherland immediately I hear from you, if that is your wish.

I am fully aware of what I am letting myself in for. "

_____

Copy of Statement.

This fair copy is clean. The original had deletions and passages crossed out

I am making this statement as an act of wilful defiance of military authority, because I believe that the War is being deliberately prolonged by those who have the power to end it, I believe that this war, upon which I entered as a war of defence and liberation, has now become a war of aggression and conquest. I believe that the purposes for which I and

In making this provocative statement, Sassoon knew that he was risking court martial

Sassoon's interpretation of events was not factually accurate

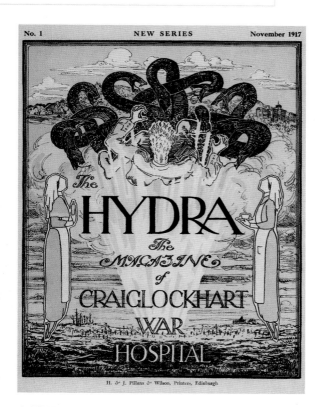

No. 1   NEW SERIES   November 1917

The HYDRA
The MAGAZINE *of* CRAIGLOCKHART WAR HOSPITAL

H. & J. Pillans & Wilson, Printers, Edinburgh.

▲ **THERAPEUTIC PUBLICATION** The *Hydra* was a magazine produced by the patients at Craiglockhart, a psychiatric hospital in Edinburgh that treated shell-shocked British officers during World War I. Both Sassoon and his fellow war poet Wilfred Owen had verses published in the *Hydra* while staying at the hospital in 1917.

22

my fellow-soldiers entered upon this war should have been so clearly stated as to have made it impossible for they

The Voice of Catalonia

1918-1919 ■ PEN AND INK ON PAPER ■ ONE NOTEBOOK ■ CATALAN

JOSEP PLA: JOURNALIST

One of the great Catalan writers, Josep Pla (1897–1981) studied law in Barcelona at the end of World War I, but his family did not have enough money to set him up as a lawyer, and he was convinced that he could make a living by writing. In 1918, a Spanish flu epidemic forced him to leave the city and go home to his parents in the village of Palafrugell on the Costa Brava. There, he began a journal, which he continued to keep when he returned to Barcelona and finished his degree.

For Pla, keeping a journal was meant to help him "learn to write." Across 20 months, he filled a gray notebook with affectionate descriptions of the people around him (his family, friends, neighbors, shopkeepers, the village priest); reflections on books that he was reading; and humorous reflections on all manner of things, from the Catalan language to hangovers. He describes the countryside of Catalonia and the atmosphere of Calella, a simple seaside town at the time. When he went back to Barcelona, he recorded debates at a club, the Atheneum, which he attended regularly, and mused on his progress as a writer. He revealed that he learned little from his teachers at the university but far more from other writers whom he met,

> 66 The Rambla is wonderful. It is one of the few streets in Barcelona where I feel completely at ease. There are always enough people to guarantee that one will meet an acquaintance or two, but there are also enough that one can lose oneself, if one feels like it. Taking a morning walk along the Rambla between forensic practice and mercantile law, is like passing from death into life.... There are three delicious things in Barcelona: bread, kidney beans, and cod. Cod cooked in any manner: baked, stewed, with potatoes, etcetera.... There are also excellent pastries—but as I don't have a sweet tooth I rarely partake— and coffee and tobacco. 99

THE GRAY NOTEBOOK, JANUARY 17, 1919

and still more from observing city life. He combined a keen eye for detail with dry irony and a passionate love of language. The journal comes to an end when Pla is offered a job as the Paris correspondent on *La Publicidad*, a Catalan newspaper.

Pla looked after the journal throughout his life and later revised and added to the text to make his coming-of-age memoir, *The Gray Notebook*, a testimony of a former age. Written in Catalan, it was one of the first modern works in prose to celebrate the language and has become a literary classic.

In context

◄ **BUSTLING CITY** When Pla was writing his journal, Barcelona was a prosperous industrial city and the largest town in Catalonia. Having expanded hugely in the 19th century, it was still growing, and the work of innovative architects, such as Antoni Gaudí, was making it even more impressive. It was home to many Catalan writers, artists, and musicians.

▶ **THE GRAY NOTEBOOK** Pla revisited his journal over the years, revising the text and adding new passages. In doing so, he reinvented it as a novel about a young man growing up and finding his vocation. This version was published in 1966 as *El Cuaderno Gris* (*The Gray Notebook*), when Pla was 69. It has since been translated and published around the world.

Josep Pla
El cuaderno gris
PRÓLOGO DE CARMEN RIGALT

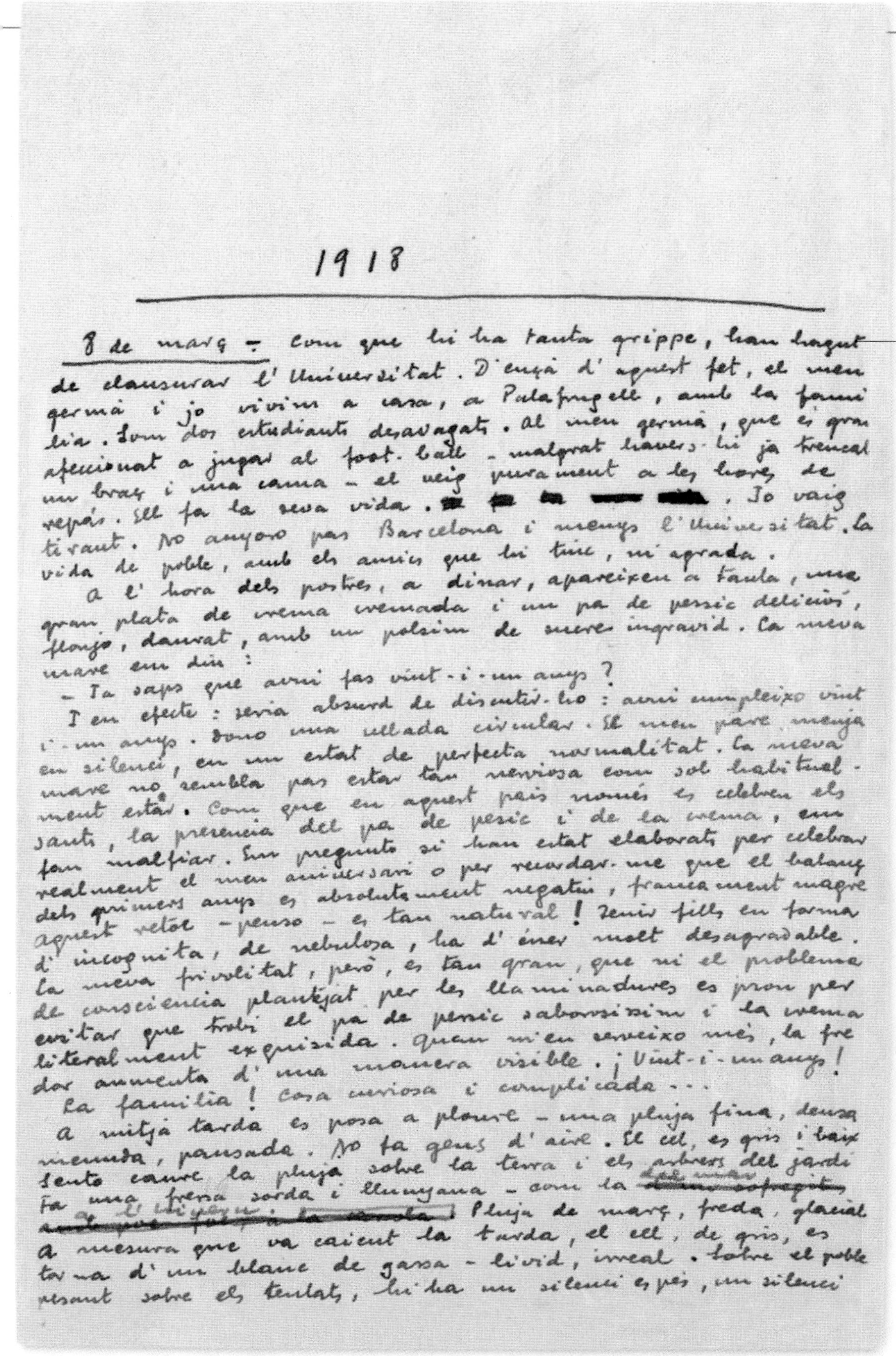

◄ **FIRST PAGE** Josep Pla began his journal on March 8, 1918, his 21st birthday, after leaving for Palafrugell, about 75 miles (120 km) northeast of Barcelona, to escape the flu epidemic. He resolves to "write whatever happens–simply to pass the time–come what may." He doubted if anyone would ever read his random thoughts, but it is his resolve to concentrate on the details of everyday life that makes the journal so interesting today.

1918

[Handwritten journal page in Catalan, beginning:]

8 de març — com que hi ha tanta grippe, han hagut de clausurar l'Universitat...

Pla writes that the university has had to close because of the flu epidemic

CATALAN LITERATURE

Catalonia is a region with a strong identity as well as its own language. By the time Pla started writing, many Catalan writers had already explored the potential of the language. Among them were modernists, who wanted to assert the region's identity and tended to focus on the darker side of life, and members of the *Noucentisme* movement, who were more conservative and wrote elaborate, rather affected poetry in traditional forms. Pla and the friends who met at the Atheneum rejected both approaches. They disliked the rhetoric of *Noucentisme* and adopted a more journalistic approach to writing. Pla aimed above all for simplicity and clarity.

▲ **The seal** of the Government of Catalonia

> " It is more difficult to write than to think, much more difficult: so everyone thinks. "

THE GRAY NOTEBOOK, MAY 11, 1918

Finding Tutankhamun

1922-1930 ▪ PEN AND INK ON PAPER ▪ NINE JOURNALS AND POCKET DIARIES ▪ BRITISH

HOWARD CARTER: EGYPTOLOGIST

In October 1922, archaeologist Howard Carter (1874–1939) began the first of nine journals covering his excavation in the Valley of the Kings in Luxor, Egypt, and within a few weeks had made the most iconic discovery in Egyptian archaeology. Anterooms of jumbled treasures led to the untouched burial chamber of Tutankhamun, an 18th-dynasty pharaoh who had died in his late teens about 3,000 years earlier. Carter's journals describe each step of the way, beginning with the sunken staircase leading to the tomb.

Carter learned his methodology working as an artist on excavations in Egypt in his teens and, by his late 40s, was financed by Lord Carnarvon, who had a concession to excavate in the valley. Carter's journal records his first cablegram to Carnarvon: "At last have made wonderful discovery in Valley. A magnificent tomb with seals intact. Re-covered same for your arrival. Congratulations." In late November, Carnarvon, his daughter, Howard, and colleague Arthur Callender entered the tomb's anteroom and were astonished by its contents—life-sized ebony-black effigies of the pharaoh, gilded couches, alabaster vases, a throne, and chariot parts glinting with gold. Carter writes: "It was a sight surpassing all precedent...."

Subsequent journals cover 10 seasons of excavation and document the opening of the burial chamber with its solid gold coffin nested in the sarcophagus. Carter's descriptions of ancient garlands, figurines, and jewelry are punctuated with accounts of lavish official openings attended by dignitaries—and battles with the Egyptian authorities. A picture emerges of a dogged perfectionist struggling to preserve and remove some 5,000 precious objects to the museum in Cairo while thousands flocked to the tomb. After an official suggests his obstinacy will disappoint tourists, Carter fumes: "As I do not work for tourists ... I have taken no notice of this futile remark."

Carter's pocket diaries of "to-do" lists give an insight into the practicalities of digs in the 1920s. He needed electric cables, a gate, cement, photographic materials, bandages, 32 bolts of calico, chemicals—and donkeys.

> " It was sometime before one could see, the hot air escaping caused the candle to flicker, but as soon as one's eyes became accustomed to the glimmer of light the interior of the chamber gradually loomed before one, with its strange and wonderful medley of extraordinary and beautiful objects heaped upon one another.... There was naturally short suspense ... when Lord Carnarvon said to me 'Can you see anything?' I replied to him 'Yes, it is wonderful.' I then with precaution made the hole sufficiently large for both of us to see. "

EXCAVATION JOURNAL, NOVEMBER 26, 1922

◄ **TUTANKHAMUN REVEALED** In this photograph by Harry Burton, an Egyptian worker is holding a torch while Carter analyses the black, pitch-like emollient that has glued the mummified body into its solid-gold coffin. Carter relied on local assistants and archaeologists for his work, including Hussein Abdel-Rasoul, who found the entrance to the tomb while looking for a spot to place water.

> **WHAT LIES BENEATH** Sketches of the king's body record bracelets, amulets, rings, and necklaces between 16 layers of cloth bandages. Each item was given a letter: P is a chased sheet-gold hawk with outspread wings and Q a black resin scarab on gold wire. Nearly 100 groups of objects were found on the body.

Each find was given a reference number to be used in all excavation records and drawings

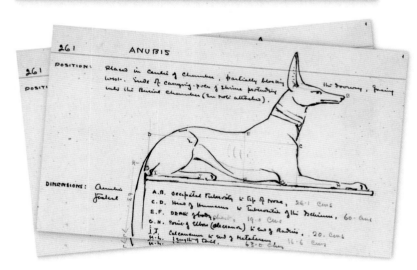

THE ANUBIS SHRINE Carter's early years as an artist stood him in good stead. His records of tomb artifacts include this beautifully executed drawing of a statue of Anubis, the god of mummification and the afterlife, in the form of a jackal. The recumbent figure on a platform with carrying poles occupied the center of the store room in the burial chamber.

On a north panel of a shrine, Carter noted the hieroglyphic "back east" and decided that the shrines were wrongly placed

Carter sketched the shape of a slab of granite, cracked in half, that formed the lid of the sarcophagus

◄ **THE SARCOPHAGUS** Four months into the second excavation, Carter's team dismantled the nest of gilded wooden shrines with folding doors in the burial chamber, using winches and hoists. Between their walls they found bows and arrows, lamps, and fans with gold handles. The magnificent crystalline sandstone sarcophagus with its four goddesses at the corners was finally revealed.

In Emotional Turmoil

1914-1977 ▪ PEN AND INK ON PAPER ▪ C.1,500 PAGES ▪ FRENCH/AMERICAN

ANAÏS NIN: AUTHOR

The journal of writer Anaïs Nin (1903-1977) is her best-known work. Nin, whose parents were Cuban but who spent her early years in France and much of her life in the US, started it when she was just 11 years old and continued it for her entire life. It is one of the frankest journals ever written by a woman and includes revelations about her numerous affairs—with her psychoanalyst Otto Rank and with her estranged father, among others. She also describes her torrid relationships with writers, such as Henry Miller and Gore Vidal, and the critic Edmund Wilson, as well as her bigamous marriages and the complicated double life in New York and California that this entailed.

Nin's diary is not, however, just about her relationships. She also recounts her struggles to be recognized as a writer and her horrified reaction to World War II. Although she regarded the diary as private, she also considered publishing it, but two things stood in her way: her explicit descriptions of sex, and the extraordinary length of the diary—it runs to about 15,000 typescript pages. In 1966, the first of a series of seven selected

> But I need a place where I can shout and weep. I have to be a Spanish savage at some time of the day. I record here the hysteria life causes in me. The overflow of an undisciplined extravagance. To hell with taste and art, with all contractions and polishings. Here I shout, I dance, I weep, I gnash my teeth, I go mad—all by myself, in bad English, in chaos. It will keep me sane for the world and for art.

INCEST: FROM "A JOURNAL OF LOVE", OCTOBER 27, 1933

volumes was published in the US. Although some of the more erotic elements had been left out, the number of Nin's affairs shocked many—but also increased interest in the diary. Many women regarded Nin as a spokesperson for feminism, a rare example of a woman who had achieved a personal freedom similar to that of men. When a new, unexpurgated edition of the diaries was published in 1986, reactions were still mixed. Some readers praised their frankness, while others complained that there was too much focus on relationships with men. Anaïs Nin continues to divide opinion but still fascinates readers.

In context

◀ **OTTO RANK** Anaïs Nin studied psychoanalysis in Paris in the 1930s and was analyzed herself by her teacher, Otto Rank (left), a colleague of Sigmund Freud (centre). The analytic sessions were clearly important to her and she discusses them frequently in the journal, hoping they will help her develop to as a writer. Rank influenced her greatly, and she duly became his lover.

▶ **SELF-PUBLISHING** In the 1940s, Nin struggled to find a publisher in the US, so she bought a small press and printed her work herself. Operating the foot pedal was hard, but she managed to print 300 copies of two books. One, *Under a Glass Bell*, was praised by the critic Edmund Wilson, and Nin's work finally became known.

148

at some time of the day.
I record here the hysteria
life causes in me. The
disbordements of an undisciplined
extravagance. To hell with
taste and art. With all
contractions and polishings—
Here I shout, I dance, I
weep, I gnash my teeth
I go mad—all by myself,
in bad English, in
chaos. In compensation for
the taste I show to the
world. Here in this
journal I run amuck
It will keep me sane
for the world and for
art.

It is like my passion
for Henry which I can't
hold in, the craving for
him...which could drive me

◄ **YEARS OF TORMENT** In the early 1930s, Nin found herself entangled in the relationship of Henry Miller and his wife, June. Nin's novella *Djuna* is based on this affair. In this entry dated October 27, 1933, she proclaims that her journal is a refuge for her deep and often confused feelings that she could never publish: "All this is out of the book [*Djuna*], the work of art, but all the more reason for preserving it here. In the book, restraint, indirectness, trickeries!"

Nin confided in her journal without "contractions and polishings" to try to preserve some sense of order in her life

LITERARY WORKS

Nin's work was very varied—novels, short stories, essays, and a critical study of the English writer D. H. Lawrence. She also wrote erotica for an anonymous 1940s "collector" that were not originally meant for wider publication. Her early fiction, including *House of Incest*, used Surrealist techniques to analyze various characters and to narrate dreams that Nin had had. Like many of her books, it features a central female character seeking fulfillment and "wholeness." *Cities of the Interior*, a five-volume sequence of novels, revolves around several female characters who resemble different facets of Nin herself—the novels draw heavily on the writing in her journal. None of the novels has proved as popular with readers as the journal itself.

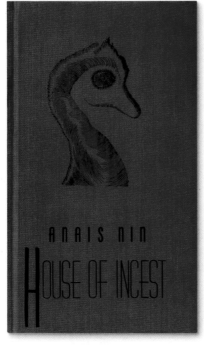

▲ **First American edition** of *House of Incest*, Anaïs Nin, 1947

> ❝ We **write** to **taste life twice,** in the moment and **in retrospection.**... We write ... to **render** all of it eternal. ❞

Notes on Hard Times

1931–1949 ▪ PEN AND INK ON PAPER ▪ 11 NOTEBOOKS ▪ BRITISH

GEORGE ORWELL: NOVELIST AND ESSAYIST

Eric Blair, better known by his pen name, George Orwell, kept diaries and notebooks for most of his life—11 of these have survived. They provided raw material for his articles and books, allowed him to vent his ideas on politics and society, and satisfied his compulsive urge to document the world around him. None of the notebooks offer information on Orwell's personal life; idle gossip and soul-searching were sternly excluded.

Born in 1903, Orwell received an elite education at Eton and then served as a police officer in British-ruled Burma (present-day Myanmar) before deciding to become a writer. In the 1930s, in revolt against his privileged background, he pursued a range of experiences, from sleeping in hostels for down-and-outs to fighting as a soldier in the Spanish Civil War (1936–1939). His earliest extant journal, the 1931 "Hop-Picking Diary," describes traveling with vagrants to rural Kent in search of casual work.

Its vivid observation of the lives of the poor is repeated in the "Road to Wigan Pier Diary," which records his fact-finding visit to industrial northern England in 1936. Expressing Orwell's passionate indignation at the conditions of life at the bottom of society, both journals formed the basis for published works.

Sadly, the notebooks of his service in the Spanish Civil War were lost. Of his other diaries, the two written in the early years of World War II (1939–1945) are the most interesting. They display Orwell's usual acute eye for detail, notably in his observation of everyday life during the London Blitz. He expresses constant irritation with the incompetence of those in power, fighting a war he absolutely believed Britain needed to win. After the war, growing in fame but with failing health, Orwell withdrew into a crofter's life on the bleak Scottish island of Jura. His Jura diaries are a record of daily facts, from the state of the weather to pulling turnips, fishing for lobster, and observing seabirds. His last notebook entry was written shortly before he died of tuberculosis in a London hospital in 1950.

In context

▲ **GREAT DEPRESSION** In the 1930s, the industrial towns and cities of northern England, including Sheffield pictured above, were blighted by poverty, mass unemployment, bad housing, and environmental problems. Orwell visited the north for two months in 1936, sharing the living conditions of the poor. He kept a diary that later provided material for his book *The Road to Wigan Pier.*

▲ **LONDON BLITZ** Britain went to war with Germany in September 1939. For eight months in 1940–1941, London and other British cities were subjected to sustained night attacks by German Luftwaffe aircraft. More than 40,000 civilians were killed in the bombing campaign. Orwell and his wife, Eileen, lived in a flat in London for most of the Blitz, from where he described the devastation firsthand.

14.3.42. I reopen this diary after an interval of abt 6 months, the war being once again in a new phase.

The actual date of Cripps's departure for India was not given out, but presumably he has gone by this time. Ordinary public opinion here seems gloomy abt his departure. A frequent comment — "They've done it to get him out of the way" (which is also one of the reasons alleged by the German wireless). This is very silly & reflects the provincialism of English people who can't grasp that India is of any importance. Better-informed people are pessimistic because the non-publication of the government's terms to India indicates almost certainly that they are not good terms. Impossible to discover what powers Cripps has got. Those who may know something will disclose nothing & one can draw hints out of them only by indirect means. Eg. I propose in my newsletters, having been instructed to give Cripps a build-up, to build him up as a political extremist. This draws the warning, "don't go too far in that direction", which raises the assumption that the higher-ups haven't much hope of full independence being offered to India.

Rumours of all descriptions flying round. Many people

The Cripps Mission was a failed attempt by the British government to secure India's collaboration in World War II

◄ **WARTIME PROPAGANDIST** This is the first manuscript page of Orwell's second wartime diary, begun on March 14, 1942. By then he was working at the BBC, which he describes as having an atmosphere "halfway between a girls' school and a lunatic asylum." His job was to broadcast propaganda to persuade India to support Britain in the war. He was not happy about this, writing: "All propaganda is lies, even when one is telling the truth."

ORWELL'S **PUBLISHED WORKS**

In the 1930s, Orwell built a modest reputation as a writer of realist novels, such as *Keep the Aspidistra Flying* (1936) and *Coming Up for Air* (1939), and of books of nonfiction reportage, namely *Down and Out in Paris and London* (1933), *The Road to Wigan Pier* (1937), and *Homage to Catalonia* (1938). Late in his short life, he wrote the two fictional works for which he is best known: the fable *Animal Farm* (1945) and the dystopian fantasy novel *Nineteen Eighty-Four* (1949), which expresses his hatred of totalitarianism. Orwell also published hundreds of essays on subjects as diverse as the political misuse of language, English socialism, boys' comics, and cheeky seaside postcards.

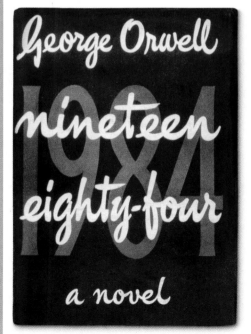

▲ **First UK edition** of *Nineteen Eighty-Four* by George Orwell, 1949

> ❝ Regular features of the time: neatly swept-up piles of glass, litter of stone and splinters of flint, smell of escaping gas, knots of sightseers waiting at the cordons.... Nondescript people wandering about, having been evacuated from their houses because of delayed-action bombs. Yesterday two girls stopping me in the street, very elegant in appearance except that their faces were filthily dirty: 'Please, sir, can you tell us where we are?' ... Withal, huge areas of London almost normal and everyone quite happy in the daytime, never seeming to think about the coming night.... ❞

WARTIME DIARY, ON LONDON DURING THE BLITZ, SEPTEMBER 21, 1940

The Impossibility of Being

1935–1959 ▪ PEN AND INK ON PAPER ▪ NINE EXERCISE BOOKS ▪ FRENCH-ALGERIAN

ALBERT CAMUS: WRITER

In his fifth notebook, Albert Camus (1913–1960) asks himself: "Why am I an artist and not a philosopher?" He answers, "Because I think according to words and not according to ideas." Words are the bedrock of the nine exercise books that he began in May 1935, at the age of 22. They are documents of a writer's craft, filled with joyous descriptions of landscape, weather, literary gems, and discussions with contemporaries. Overheard conversations and encounters on streetcars and in cinemas sit alongside scenarios and dialogues that he later used intact in his novels and plays.

The notion of the absurd—the search for meaning in a meaningless existence—is a recurring theme throughout the notebooks. Camus tries to analyze "the pull that justice and its absurd procedure has for certain minds," the theme of his own novel *L'Étranger*. Later, he notes his fight against his own cynicism and the "not difficulty, but impossibility of being."

Famous by the age of 30, Camus greets success and criticism equivocally. His unsent letter to a critic who questioned the morality of *L'Étranger* refers to censorship under dictatorship. Camus declares that no one "has the right to judge whether a work may serve or harm the nation at this moment or forever." But he is also "melancholy" when awarded the Prix des Critiques for *La Peste* because "opposition is essential" and reacts in a similarly anxious fashion when he wins the Nobel Prize for Literature in 1957.

Camus deleted most of the autobiographical events from the first six notebooks; only brief references to his bouts of tuberculosis remain. But the final three, covering the nine years before his early death in a car accident in 1960, are in diary form. Worried about his failing memory, Camus documented his travels in Greece and Italy, his falling out with the philosopher Jean-Paul Sartre and the Parisian Marxists, and his conflicted allegiance to the plight of his French-Algerian family in the Algerian War of Independence.

In context

◀ **THE RESISTANCE** Camus wrote reports for *Combat*, the clandestine newspaper of the French Resistance during the war, and became editor in chief in 1944. Witnessing the street battles during the liberation of Paris, he wrote: "freedom's barricades are once again being erected .... again justice must be redeemed with men's blood."

▶ **ALGERIA** From 1954, Arab Algeria's battle for independence from colonialist France escalated into bloody attacks by the *Front de Libération Nationale* and counter protests (right) from European Algerians. Camus's editorials called on all sides to spare civilians and campaigned against the use of torture.

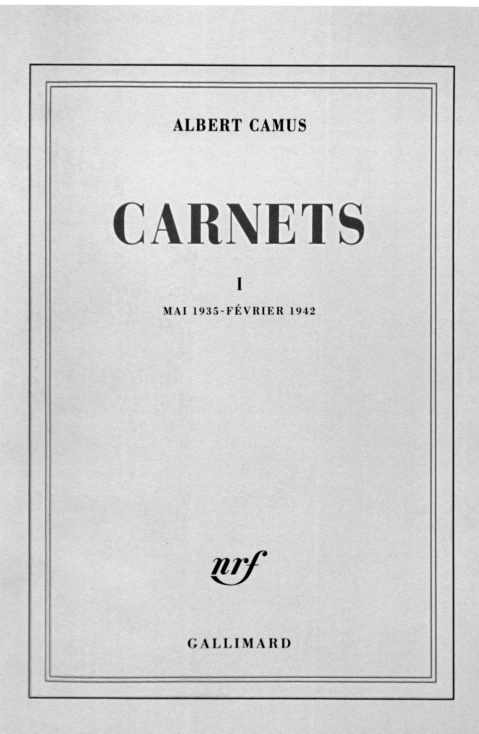

◄ **LIFE'S IDEAS** Camus called his books of ideas and impressions *cahiers* (exercise books), but they were renamed *Carnets* (notebooks) by Editions Gallimard, Paris, when published in 1962, to distinguish them from books of critical essays. Translator Philip Thody read the original books and noted how Camus's full, rounded handwriting varied with each entry and became cramped and difficult to read toward the end of his life.

LITERARY CAREER

Albert Camus's works include journalism, plays, philosophical writing, and five novels. Published in the 1940s, his best-known novels are the absurdist *L'Étranger* (*The Outsider*), about a murderer who is condemned to death for his failure to conform to social norms, and *La Peste* (*The Plague*), which explores human responses to separation and isolation in a quarantined Algerian city during a plague.

Camus's notebooks offer interesting insights into an early novel about the pursuit of happiness, which he replaced with *L'Étranger*. *La Mort Heureuse* (*A Happy Death*) was published posthumously, along with *Le Premier Homme* (*The First Man*), an unfinished autobiographical novel about childhood in Algiers.

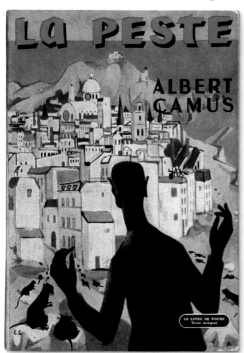

▲ **Front cover** of *La Peste* (*The Plague*), Albert Camus, first published in 1947

> 66 We lead a difficult life not always managing to fit our actions to the vision we have of the world…. We struggle and suffer to reconquer our solitude. But a day comes when the earth has its simple and primitive smile. Then, it is as if the struggles and life within us were rubbed out.
>
> Millions of eyes have looked at this landscape and for me it is like the first smile of the world. It takes me out of myself, in the deepest meaning of the expression. It assures me that nothing matters except my love, and that even this love has no value for me unless it remains innocent and free. 99

NOTEBOOK 1, SEPTEMBER 1937

Directory: 1900-1940

THE DIARY OF OLGA ROMANOV

RUSSIAN (1905-1917)

Grand Duchess Olga Nikolaevna Romanov (1895-1918) was the eldest daughter of Nicholas II, the last tsar of Russia. She began a diary at the age of 10, recording her daily routines in the enclosed world of the tsarist court: family meals, religious services, games, the weather. Keenly aware of her parents' efforts to find her a suitable royal husband, she recorded her romantic feelings for less suitable men in a private code she had devised.

From 1914, when Russia entered World War I, Olga Romanov's life and her diaries changed radically. Serving as a nurse in a military hospital, she encountered the horror of war, her emotions aroused by the wounded officers she tended. In December 1916, her diary records the murder of the mystic Grigori Rasputin, widely hated for his influence at court but, to Olga, a friendly figure known from childhood. She stopped keeping a diary in March 1917, when Tsar Nicholas abdicated at the start of the Russian Revolution. Together with the rest of the royal family, Grand Duchess Olga was murdered by Bolshevik revolutionaries in July 1918.

MILES FRANKLIN'S DIARIES

AUSTRALIAN (1909-1954)

Born in New South Wales, Australian writer and feminist Miles Franklin (1879-1954) published her best-known novel, *My Brilliant Career*, at the age of 22. Unfortunately, her own career did not match that title. While seeking in vain for further literary success, between 1906 and 1932, she lived in the US and Britain. It was in Chicago that she began to keep a daily diary in 1909, and when she eventually returned to live in the suburbs of Sydney, she continued the practice until her death.

Her pocket diaries eventually contained more than a million words, some in an almost indecipherable shorthand, and there were also literary notebooks in which she wrote in a fuller style. Like all of Franklin's writings, the diaries are energized by her robust personality, caustic sense of humor, and strong opinions. They describe her frustration at her limited commercial and critical success as an author, the menial work she undertook in order to make ends meet, and her friends and enemies on the Sydney literary scene. A selection of the diaries was published for the first time in 2004.

E. M. FORSTER'S LOCKED DIARY

BRITISH (1909-1967)

The English novelist Edward Morgan Forster (1879-1970), known as E. M. Forster, wrote in a variety of journals and notebooks from the age of 16. In 1909, he inherited a diary with a lock and key from a relative. For much of the rest of his life, he used this to record events and his thoughts with the freedom bestowed by privacy and used other notebooks as diaries that others might read.

Some of the most interesting material in the locked diary concerns Forster's homosexuality, which was illegal in Britain at the time. It includes his sometimes troubled reflections on his sexuality, noting various brief encounters and erotic fantasies. Attracted to working-class men, Forster eventually formed a long-term relationship with a married policeman. Expressing fluctuating moods and fleeting desires, often rendered obscure by private allusions, the locked diary constitutes an intimate self-portrait of a complex individual. It was first published in its entirety in 2011.

THE PATTON DIARIES

AMERICAN (1910-1945)

One of the most flamboyant American generals of the 20th century, George S. Patton (1885-1945) kept intermittent diaries from the time of his honeymoon in Europe in 1910. His journals cover his experiences of warfare from American intervention in Mexico in 1916-1917 to service as a tank commander on the Western Front in World War I to the spectacular successes in World War II that made him famous.

Patton's diaries for the period from 1942 to 1945 are especially detailed and candid. They relate on a daily basis his victorious campaigns in Tunisia, Sicily, and northern Europe, from the invasion of Normandy to the occupation of Germany. Patton gives vigorous expression to the belligerent attitudes that made people dislike as well as admire him, including his insubordinate stance toward his military superiors and his fixed dislike of America's allies—"God damn all British," he writes. Diary entries for 1945 describe Jews as "lower than animals" and Russian officers as having the appearance of "recently civilized Mongolian bandits." The diaries have been published as part of the Patton Papers.

◀ THE JOURNAL OF KATHERINE MANSFIELD

NEW ZEALAND (1914-1922)

Born in New Zealand, Katherine Mansfield (1888-1923) moved to England where she built a reputation as an outstanding writer of short stories. She died of tuberculosis at the tragically early age of 34.

The opening page of a story by Katherine Mansfield

Never a systematic diarist, Mansfield left behind 46 notebooks and piles of loose papers scrawled with sporadic diary entries, general musings, and fragments of stories, interspersed with shopping lists and recipes.

In 1927, Mansfield's husband, John Middleton Murray, published the *Journal of Katherine Mansfield*, assembled from a selection of these private writings that he had extensively edited. This work became a literary classic, exhibiting Mansfield's lucid sensibility and sharp eye for detail and evoking in a harrowing manner her desperate struggle to live with terminal illness.

A complete transcription of Mansfield's notebooks has since been published, revealing her to be more adventurous and acidly critical than implied by the *Journal* that was originally published. Along with juvenile diaries from her early life in New Zealand, the notebooks present a more rounded picture of a complex individual, but the *Journal* retains its status as a literary classic.

THOMAS MANN'S DIARIES

GERMAN (1918–1921, 1933–1955)

The celebrated German novelist Thomas Mann (1875–1955) kept diaries throughout his life, but he destroyed many of them, burning his earliest journals in 1896 and then incinerating his remaining pre-1933 diaries in 1945, except for the 1918–1921 sequence, which survived by chance.

The year 1933 was when the Nazis assumed power in Germany, making it necessary for Mann to go into political exile. He did not want the private expressions of his political opinions before that date to be known, as they may have compromised his anti-Nazi stance. When he died, Mann left his diaries in sealed boxes, with instructions that they should not be opened for 20 years. As he wrote in one diary entry: "Let the world know me, but not until everyone is dead."

When the diaries were examined in 1975, they turned out to consist primarily of meticulous daily notes, written each evening at bedtime, detailing Mann's walks, health, medication, meals, dreams, and

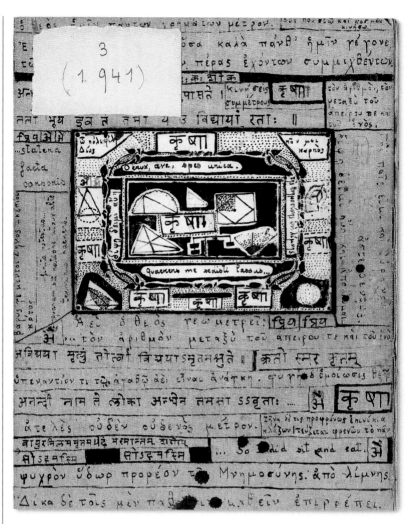

The cover of one of Simone Weil's notebooks

sexual functioning. Despite their mundanity, they clarified the central secret of Mann's life—his insatiable desire for young men. Published in Germany in 10 volumes, the diaries form a major complement to his voluminous novels and short stories.

▲ THE WEIL NOTEBOOKS

FRENCH (1934–1943)

Both a political activist and a Christian mystic, Simone Weil (1909–1943) is now widely revered, but was little known in her lifetime. Born into a secular Jewish family in Paris, she became a philosophy teacher. In 1934, the year when she began to fill her notebooks with thoughts on philosophy and politics, she took a sabbatical to experience life as a factory worker.

In 1937, she underwent a mystical revelation that made her turn to Catholicism. In World War II, Weil fled the Nazi occupation of France, ending up in England. She died, possibly of self-starvation, after insisting on eating the same minimal food rations as people in occupied France. The first selection of entries from her notebooks, published in 1948 as *Gravity and Grace*, emphasized her idiosyncratic religious views.

A more complete version of the notebooks, which was published in three volumes from 1951 to 1956, emphasized her preoccupation with the evils of state power and social injustice. Elegant, concise, and paradoxical, her abstract thoughts are infused with the pain she felt at the terrible suffering in the world, which she was determined to share.

A CIVIL WAR DIARY

SPANISH (1936–1937)

Faustino Vázquez Carril (1914–1937) was a young man from northern Spain who aspired to become a journalist but instead joined the army to escape

poverty and starvation. When Spanish generals, including Francisco Franco, launched an uprising against Spain's Republican government in 1936, Faustino found himself fighting in the ranks of the rebels, although his sympathies were with the Republic.

He kept a journal from the start of the Civil War, mixing lyrical descriptions of the countryside with accounts of the horrors of combat. He also made hostile comments on the rebel generals and their fascist allies, the Falangists. During the war, when he was hospitalized as a result of a traffic accident, another soldier noticed the subversive remarks in his diary and reported him. Tried by a military tribunal, he was executed by a firing squad on May 10, 1937, aged 23. His diary was published in 2011.

JOHN STEINBECK'S WORKING DAYS

AMERICAN (1938–1941)

In 1938, the author John Steinbeck (1902–1968) began to write *The Grapes of Wrath*, a groundbreaking novel about Oklahoma farmers driven by drought and poverty to migrate to California. As he was working on the novel, he kept journals in which he wrote entries every day, monitoring his progress, recording his gnawing self-doubts, and urging himself to keep going to the end. "This is the longest diary I ever kept," he writes, "Not a diary of course, but an attempt to map the actual working days and hours of a novel." He constantly reminds himself of the need for self-discipline and perseverance and, in fact, manages to write around 2,000 words of the novel each day.

After the novel was finished five months later, he continued to write in the diary until 1941, recording the book's critical and commercial success (it won the Pulitzer Prize for fiction in 1940) and the political attacks it drew from some quarters. Steinbeck never intended the *Grapes of Wrath* journals to be read by the public, but he said they should be shown to his sons, so they could "know to some extent what manner of man their father was."

Recognized as a unique portrayal of the creative process, the diary was first published under the title *Working Days* in 1989.

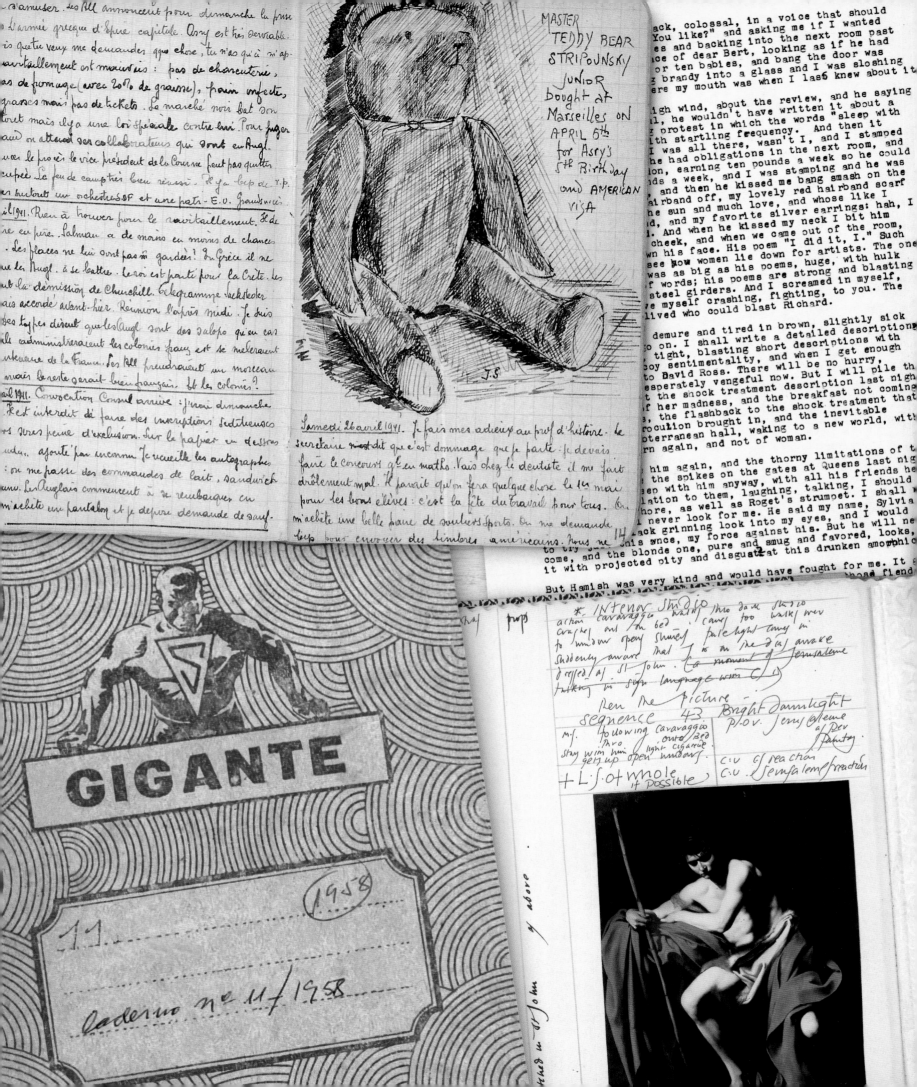

French handwritten journal (left page):

...s'amuser. Les BBC annoncent pour dimanche la prise
d'armée grecque d'Épire capitale. Asry est très désirable.
...s quatre veux me demander qqe chose, tu n'as qu'à m'ap-
...ravitaillement est mauvais : pas de charcuterie,
...as de fromage (avec 20% de graisse), pain infecte,
graisses mais pas de tickets. Le marché noir bat son
...lein mais il y a une loi spéciale contre lui. Pour juger
...qu'on attaqué ses collaborateurs qui sont en Angl.
...vant le procès le vice président de la Cour ne peut pas quitter
...cupée. Le feu de camp très bien réussi. Il y a beaucoup de r.p.
...es surtout en orchestres DF et une part. E.V. Grand succès.
...il 1941. Rien à trouver pour le ravitaillement. Il de...
...re en pire. Salman a de moins en moins de chances.
...Les places ne lui sont pas m gardées? En Grèce il ne
...que les Angl. à se battre. Le roi est parti pour la Crète. Les
...ub la démission de Churchill. Télégramme Jacksteder
...ais accordé avant-hier. Réunion l'après midi. Je suis
...des types disent que les Angl sont des Jalops qu'en cas
...ils administreraient les colonies pas est se mêleraient
...uences de la France. Les BBL prendraient un morceau
...mais le reste serait bien français. Et les colonies?
...il 1941. Convocation Consul arrive : j'irai dimanche
...C'est interdit de faire des inscriptions séditieuses
...vas sous peine d'exclusion. Sur le papier en dessous
...endu... ajouté par inconnu Je recueille les autographes
...on me passe des commandes de lait, sandwich
...inu. Les Anglais commencent à se rembarquer en
...m'achète un pantalon et je depuis demande de sauf-

Samedi 26 avril 1941. Je fais mes adieux au prof d'histoire. Le
secrétaire me dit que c'est dommage que je parte je devais
faire le concours gl en maths. Vais chez le dentiste il me fait
drôlement mal. Il paraît qu'on fera quelque chose le 1er mai
pour les bons élèves : c'est la fête du travail pour tous. On
m'achète une belle paire de souliers sports. On me demande
bcp pour envoyer des timbres américains. Nous ne... 14

Drawing label (center):

MASTER
TEDDY BEAR
STRIPOUNSKY
JUNIOR
bought at
Marseilles on
APRIL 6th
for Asry's
5th Birthday
and AMERICAN
VISA

Typed fragment (right page):

...ack, colossal, in a voice that should
...You like?" and asking me if I wanted
...es and backing into the next room past
...ce of dear Bert, looking as if he had
...or ten babies, and bang the door was
...g brandy into a glass and I was sloshing
...here my mouth was when I last knew about it
...igh wind, about the review, and he saying
...ll, he wouldn't have written it about a
...protest in which the words "sleep with
...ith startling frequency. And then it
...I was all there, wasn't I, and I stamped
...he had obligations in the next room, and
...ion, earning ten pounds a week so he could
...nds a week, and I was stamping and he was
...and then he kissed me bang smash on the
...airband off, my lovely red hairband scarf
...he sun and much love, and whose like I
...d, and my favorite silver earrings; hah, I
...I. And when he kissed my neck I bit him
...cheek, and when we came out of the room,
...own his face. His poem "I did it, I." Such
...see how women lie down for artists. The one
...was as big as his poems, huge, with hulk
...f words; his poems are strong and blasting
...steel girders. And I screamed in myself,
...e myself crashing, fighting, to you. The
...lived who could blast Richard.

...demure and tired in brown, slightly sick
...o on. I shall write a detailed description
...tight, blasting short descriptions with
...coy sentimentality, and when I get enough
...o David Ross. There will be no hurry.
...esperately vengeful now. But I will pile th
...t the shock treatment description last nigh
...f her madness, and the breakfast not coming
..., the flashback to the shock treatment that
...ocution brought in, and the inevitable
...terranean hall, waking to a new world, with
...n again, and not of woman.

...him again, and the thorny limitations of t
...the spikes on the gates at Queens last nig
...eep with him anyway, with all his friends he
...lation to them, laughing, talking, I should
...hore, as well as Roget's strumpet. I shall
...never look for me. He said my name, Sylvia
...ack grinning look into my eyes, and I would
...to try ...this... nce, my force against his. But he will ne
...come, and the blonde one, pure and smug and favored, looks,
...it with projected pity and disgust at this drunken amorphic
But Hamish was very kind and would have fought for me. It ...

GIGANTE magazine cover (lower left):

GIGANTE

1958

11

Quaderno n° 11/1958

Film/script notes (lower right):

* INTERIOR STUDIO this dark studio
action Caravaggio wakes camera too wildly ...
Crashes and on bed — camera too wildly in
to window open shutter pale light camera in
Suddenly aware that J is in the day awake
dressed as St John. (A moment of Jerusalem
talking in sign language when C.)

Run the picture —
Sequence 43. Bright Dawn light
M.S. following Caravaggio P.O.V. Jerusalem
thro onto Bed at Dev
Stay with him light cigarette Pantry
gets up open window
+ L.S. of whole C.U. of reaction
if possible C.U. of Jerusalem of reaction

7

1940–PRESENT

This period opened with widespread destruction and death in World War II. Many diaries bore witness to these terrible events, from the Holocaust in Nazi-occupied Europe to the dropping of the atomic bomb on Hiroshima in Japan. After the war, movements for social change took shape, and the drive for forms of liberation, from anticolonialism to the assertion of gay rights, became a central theme of personal writing. Meanwhile, authors such as the American poet Sylvia Plath explored disturbing themes of psychological dislocation with unprecedented frankness. In the last 30 years, the rapid pace of technological progress has changed the way in which many people record their personal views and experiences. It remains to be seen whether the instant sharing of material on social media will ultimately supplant the reflective private diary.

The Diary of a Young Girl

1942–1944 ▪ PEN AND INK ON PAPER ▪ TWO EXERCISE BOOKS, 215 LOOSE SHEETS ▪ DUTCH

ANNE FRANK: DIARIST

A small cloth-bound book, chosen as a birthday present by a 13-year-old Jewish girl in German-occupied Amsterdam in 1942, was the starting point for one of the world's most famous diaries. Anne Frank's first entries brim with the excitement of becoming a teenager, but her life was already unraveling as the Nazis intensified their grip on the Jewish population. Within weeks, Anne wrote that her sister had been called up for deportation and that her father planned to take the family into hiding.

On July 6, they made their way to the building on Prinsengracht where Otto Frank ran his business. For weeks he had been quietly furnishing an annex inside the building, but now haste was essential. Anne describes stuffing her diary into a satchel and walking through summer rain in layers of clothes: "No Jew in our situation would have dreamed of going out with a suitcase full of clothing." The Franks were joined by Hermann and Auguste van Pels and their son, Peter, 15, and later by Fritz

Pfeffer, a dentist. For the two years in hiding before they were discovered, Anne recorded the tensions of living with seven others, speaking in whispers, and barely moving during the day when workers were in the rooms below. Prosaic details of chores and studies sit alongside personal reflections on her maturing body and emotions and her hopes for the future. The teenager longed to be a writer but could not have foreseen that through her diary she would become famous and speak for the millions of Jews caught in the Holocaust for generations to come.

▲ **BIRTHDAY GIFT** Anne's red, white, and green checked notebook with a metal lock was a gift for her 13th birthday on June 12, 1942. The Franks were suffering under Nazi rule, but Anne's descriptions of her presents, party, and classmates are upbeat. Her diary is destined to be an intimate friend: "I hope I will be able to confide everything to you," she writes.

HOLOCAUST DIARIES

Hundreds of personal records, now published or kept in archives, represent a tiny proportion of the journals kept by Jews victim to the Holocaust. Published accounts include the diary of Petr Ginz, a Czechoslovak schoolboy who started an underground newspaper in the Theresienstadt ghetto at 14 and was gassed in Auschwitz two years later. Eighteen-year-old Renia Spiegel recorded life in Poland under Soviet and Nazi occupation; her diary was kept safe by a friend after she was found in hiding and shot. Joseph Stripounsky's notebooks, filled with maps, sketches, and descriptions of his family's flight from Nazi-occupied Belgium, and their year in hiding in France waiting for US visas, form part of an archive of some 200 diaries of survivors and victims in the US Holocaust Memorial Museum in Washington, DC.

➤ **Joseph drew his brother's** teddy bear just before the family emigrated to the US via Spain and Portugal

> In the summer of 1941 "Granny Hollander" fell very ill (she was staying with us by then), she had to have an operation and my birthday didn't mean much. It didn't in the summer of 1940 either, for the fighting in the Netherlands was just over then. Granny died this winter 1941–1942. And no one will ever know how much she is in my thoughts and how much I love her still. The celebration of this 1942 birthday was to make up for everything then, and Granny's little light shone over it.

THE DIARY OF ANNE FRANK, JUNE 20, 1942

Using a fountain pen, Anne switched between cursive handwriting and hand printing to suit the content of each entry

◄ **FAMILY AND FRIENDS** Early pages of the diary contain a mix of schoolgirl gossip and family memories. Photos of beach trips include one from 1939 with Anne's late grandmother sitting "sweetly and peacefully" in the background. Anne is consoled by the fact that her sister Margot, then 13, does not look "well developed" so has no right to look down on Anne at the same age.

In detail

During their two years in hiding, the families received news from a radio, accessed out of hours in the office below, and from trusted helpers who brought them supplies. Anne wrote about friends who were being transported to certain death, the drone of English bombers passing overhead, gunfire and shelling close by, and heart-stopping episodes when burglars broke in downstairs. "The perfectly round spot on which we're standing is still safe, but the clouds are moving in on us." Anne's diary was her salvation. In the original copy, her descriptions of dire meals and smuggled birthday treats sit alongside accounts of her studies, her awakening sexuality, and arguments with her mother. In her revised diary, she erased the more candid entries.

On August 1, 1944, the writing stops. Three days later, the Gestapo discovered the families and deported them to Westerbork and then Auschwitz. Margot and Anne were sent on to Bergen-Belsen where both died of typhus just a few weeks before the camps were liberated. Otto was the sole survivor from the annex.

> " When I write I can shake off all my cares. My sorrow disappears, my spirits are revived! "

THE DIARY OF ANNE FRANK, APRIL 5, 1944

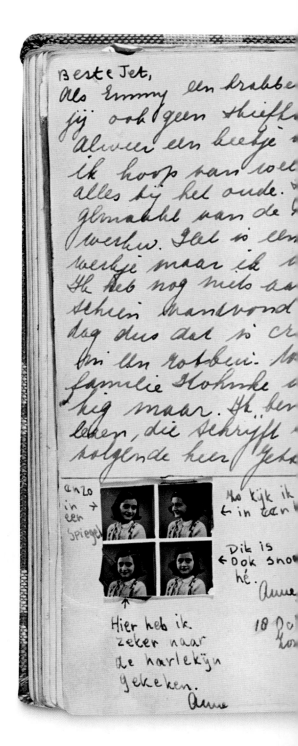

▲ **PROHIBITION AND PERSECUTION** The Nazi occupation of the Netherlands in May 1940 was followed by a raft of regulations: Jews were under curfew, forced to wear yellow stars, and forbidden to own businesses, travel on public transportation, or use stores, schools, and recreational facilities for non-Jews. Extradition to camps began in June 1942. In October, Anne wrote: "Our many Jewish friends and acquaintances are being taken away in droves."

▲ **SECRET SANCTUARY** Otto Frank created a hiding place in an annex in the tall building on Prinsengracht where he ran his business. A single door, later concealed by a bookcase, led to five rooms with beds, a stove, sink, and toilet. In November 1942, Anne wrote a guide to what she called their "Unique Facility for the Temporary Accommodation of Jews and Other Dispossessed Persons."

PREPARED FOR **PUBLICATION**

In March 1944, Anne was inspired by a radio broadcast by the Dutch arts and education minister Gerrit Bolkestein, exiled in London, urging citizens to keep records of life under occupation to be shared after the war. The teenager began to edit her diaries, altering names to preserve anonymity, making them ready to become a story called *Het Achterhuis* (*The Secret Annex*).

After Otto Frank returned from Auschwitz, helper Miep Gies handed him the notebooks and loose pages she had salvaged during the Franks' arrest; he was astounded by the emotional maturity of his daughter's writing. When he later published Anne's book, selecting entries from both versions of her diary, the choice of title was simple: *Het Achterhuis*. Published in English as *Anne Frank: The Diary of a Young Girl*, Anne's book is now in 70 languages and has sold more than 20 million copies.

➤ **The first edition** of *Het Achterhuis* (1947)

▼ **IMAGINARY CORRESPONDENCE** Many of the diary entries are addressed to real or imaginary friends—Jet, Marianne, and most often, Kitty. Anne describes learning French verbs and shorthand and reading extensively. Memories of skating segue into a screenplay with Anne ice dancing in a fur-trimmed dress. She has attached pictures of movie stars to her wall and captions her own photograph: "If I looked like this all the time, I might have a chance of getting to Hollywood."

Exploring the Inner Self

1944-1954 ■ INK, CRAYON, AND GOUACHE ON PAPER ■ 170 PAGES ■ MEXICAN

FRIDA KAHLO, ARTIST

The diary of Frida Kahlo (1907-1954) is a unique fusion of words and colorful images in which Kahlo explored her thoughts, fears, beliefs, and artistic themes. She kept the diary for the 10 years leading up to her early death at the age of 47.

Kahlo suffered continuous pain all her life, following a bus crash when she was at school. She had numerous operations and illnesses and expressed her suffering in startling images featuring amputated limbs or self-portraits in which her internal organs appear outside her body. Other recurring subjects in her diary are her fascination with ancient Mexican gods and personal relationships, notably with her husband, the charismatic Mexican artist Diego Rivera.

Kahlo worked rapidly, using colored inks, crayons, and gouache, and filled the small pages of her diary with dramatic and surprising images.

Many pages contain no words at all and are crammed with bizarre hybrids of humans and animals, Aztec gods, psychological symbols, and strange, unique forms. This imagery is very different from that of Kahlo's carefully detailed paintings. Working quickly made it easier for her to explore the depths of her consciousness. Some of the text is "automatic writing"—a way of writing without thinking that was believed to reveal the workings of the unconscious mind. It is often associated with Surrealism, but Kahlo did not regard herself as a Surrealist.

Kahlo seems to have used automatic writing and a fluid style of drawing to express her pain and anxieties and come to terms with herself. She did not intend to publish the diary. It was locked away for decades after her death, and even after it was discovered, only a few pages were exhibited. The diary was not published in full until 1995, when its vibrant imagery and creative self-exploration quickly made it a bestseller.

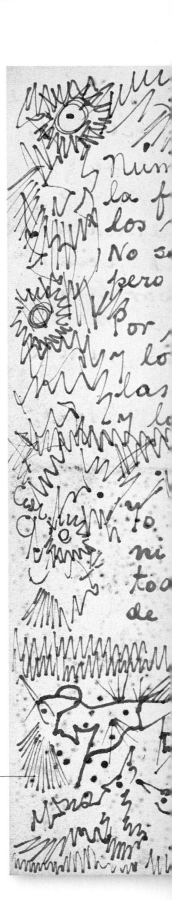

Squiggles show how quickly Kahlo drew

> " I've been sick for a year now. Seven operations on my spinal column. Doctor Farill saved me. He brought me back the joy of life. I am still in a wheelchair, and I don't know if I'll be able to walk again soon. I have a plaster corset even though it is a frightful nuisance, it helps my spine. I don't feel any pain. Only this ... bloody tiredness, and naturally, quite often despair. A despair which no words can describe. I'm still eager to live. I've started to paint again. "

THE DIARY OF FRIDA KAHLO

◀ **THE TWO FRIDAS** This double self-portrait was painted in 1939, just after Kahlo's divorce from Rivera. On the left, she is wearing traditional Mexican dress and her exposed heart is broken. On the right, she wears modern clothes and her heart is intact. In Kahlo's diary, she said the work referred to her imaginary childhood friend, but she later said it was inspired by her split with Rivera.

▼ **FREE ASSOCIATIONS** Each page of the diary is different. Here, Kahlo talks about colors and the free associations that they have for her. "I'll try out the pencils sharpened to the point of infinity," she begins. Magenta (*solferino*) recalls the "blood" of the prickly pear; yellow is linked to madness; dark green reminds her of leaves, sadness, and science; blue represents electricity and purity. "Nothing is black," she says, "Really nothing."

This esoteric verse moves from colors to a stark statement of despair

la economía, ui
de la palabra,
os azules son .
qué - también rojos,
nos de color.

úmeros redondos
rvios coloridos
ellas están hechas
undos son sonidos .

uisiera abrigar
menor esperanza,
mueve al compás
ue encierra la panza

Probaré los lápices tajados al
punto infinito que mira siem-
pre adelante:

El verde - luz tibia y buena
Solferino - azteca. TLAPALI vieja
Sangre de tuna, el más
vivo y antiguo
tierra color. de mole, de hoja que se va
locura enfermedad miedo
parte del sol y de la alegría
electricidad y pureza amor.
nada es negro - realmente nada
hojas. tristeza, ciencia, Alema-
nia entera es de este color

más locura y misterio
todos los fantasmas usan
trajes de este color, o cuando
menos ropa interior.

Color. de anuncios malos.
y de buenos negocios.
distancia. También
la ternura puede ser
de este azul..
sangre? Pues, quien sabe!

In detail

Many pages of Frida Kahlo's diary dwell on her personal life, Mexican history and traditions, and her interest in politics, especially socialism. Although these subjects from the private and the public spheres seem far apart, they were very closely linked for Kahlo. Her diary expresses her deep love for her husband, Diego Rivera, whose name appears again and again. A committed communist, Rivera shared many of his ideas with Kahlo, and the diary celebrates this link. It also pairs socialist beliefs with images drawn from Mexican history and traditional culture, which were dear to both Rivera and Kahlo. So one page of the diary bears the twin slogans, "Viva Stalin Viva Diego," while another places the names of leading communists such as Marx and Lenin opposite a bold image of an Aztec temple. By combining subjects like this, using her rapid brushstrokes and bold, round handwriting, Kahlo showed her great passion for her country, for Diego, and for her art.

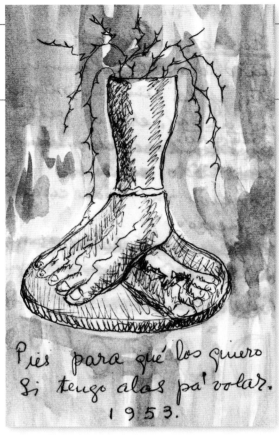

▲ **PORTRAYING PAIN** Of more than 30 operations Kahlo endured, one of the worst was having her right foot amputated after contracting gangrene. The diary shows Kahlo's remarkable fortitude in the face of her suffering. Beneath a drawing of her amputated foot, she writes, "Feet what do I need them for If I have wings to fly."

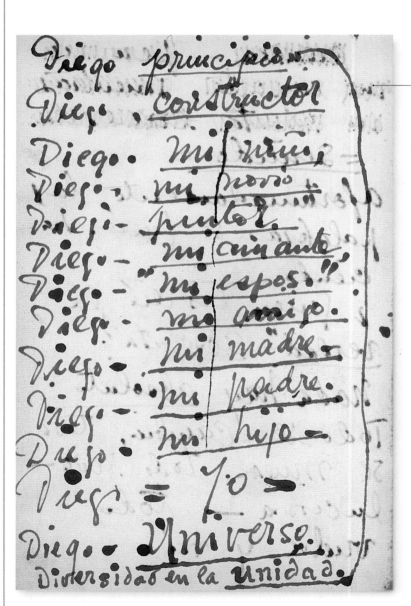

The writing on the next page shows through

MEXICANIDAD

In the mid-20th century, many artists and intellectuals became fascinated by the religion and traditions of ancient Mexico. This was known as *Mexicanidad* (Mexicanness). Before the Mexican Revolution of 1910–1920, the country had endured long periods under foreign rule, followed by much political instability and efforts at modernization. Traditional Mexican ways had been marginalized, so *Mexicanidad* was an attempt to reconnect with the country's native culture and establish a Mexican national identity. Artists such as Diego Rivera and Frida Kahlo celebrated and drew on Aztec art, Mexican textiles, folk dances, and local religious ideas.

▲ *Dance in Tehuantepec*, Diego Rivera, 1935

▲ **ENDURING PASSION** Kahlo and Rivera remained very close after their divorce in 1939, and they remarried in 1940. Many of Kahlo's diary entries reveal her passion for Rivera. Here, each line lists what he meant to her. Diego is her husband, lover, friend. She concludes: "Diego = me. Diego • Universe."

The title makes it clear that the dance is in honor of the life-giving sun

A strange hybrid of an Aztec dog and a human

" Anguish and pain, pleasure and death are no more than a process for existence. "

THE DIARY OF FRIDA KAHLO

◀ **DANCE TO THE SUN** In this full-page image, mythological creatures such as Aztec dogs dance with more enigmatic figures to celebrate the sun. The bright colors suggest both the warmth of the sun and a joyful, carnival atmosphere. Kahlo crowded the figures on to the page without any concern for conventional perspective or composition, emphasizing the spontaneity and exuberance of the dance.

Surviving Hiroshima

1945 ▪ TYPESCRIPT ▪ JAPANESE

MICHIHIKO HACHIYA: DOCTOR

The first entry in Michihiko Hachiya's diary is dated August 6, 1945, and reads, "The hour was early; the morning still, warm, and beautiful." It must have been just before 8:15 a.m., because that is when the crew of the US B-29 bomber flying 31,000 ft (9,400 m) above Hachiya, in the city of Hiroshima, released the atomic bomb. Hachiya recalls a strong flash of light, and then another. He finds himself in darkness and swirling dust, surrounded by rubble, and stark naked.

The diary covers the next 56 days and documents Hachiya's work as director of Hiroshima Communications Hospital in the aftermath of the blast. Having received serious burns to his body, he makes his way to the hospital to tend to himself as well as to the floods of other wounded and sick people. His diary notes that at first the doctors did not know what they were dealing with—diagnosing patients with vomiting and diarrhea as suffering from dysentery. As the days pass, more information reaches them, and they realize that they are facing radiation sickness. The diary also describes the ruins of Hiroshima: "For acres and acres, the city was like a desert

> " Gradually things around me came into focus. There were the shadowy forms of people, some of whom looked like walking ghosts. Others moved … like scarecrows, their arms held out from their bodies with forearms and hands dangling. These people puzzled me until I suddenly realized that they had been burned and were holding their arms out to prevent the painful friction of raw surfaces rubbing together. A naked woman carrying a naked baby came into view. I averted my gaze. Perhaps they had been in the bath. But then I saw a naked man, and it occurred to me that, like myself, some strange thing had deprived them of their clothes. "

HIROSHIMA DIARY, AUGUST 6, 1945

except for scattered piles of brick and roof tiles. I had to revise my meaning of the word destruction." He hears of looting and the black market that quickly emerges and how the news of Japan's surrender was greeted with horror by those around him.

Despite being less than 1 mile (2 km) from the epicenter of the blast, Hachiya lived until the age of 76, dying in 1980. In 1995, part of his hospital was turned into an atomic bomb museum, where his original diary was displayed.

In context

◀ **THE AFTERMATH** About 70 percent of Hiroshima's buildings were destroyed. "Hiroshima was no longer a city," Hachiya writes, "but a burnt-over prairie." He describes how everything was flattened as far as he could see and how close the distant mountains looked. "How small Hiroshima was," he notes, "with its houses gone."

▶ **HELPING THE SICK** At least 66,000 people were killed and around 69,000 more were injured in the explosion alone, including 90 percent of the city's doctors and nurses. Caring for casualties was made worse by the fact that the bomb detonated right above the Shima Hospital, located in the center of the city.

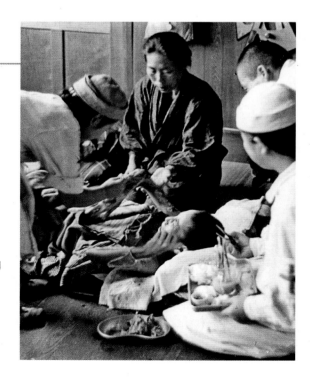

Moving instinctively, I tried to escape, but rubble and fallen tim-
ers barred the way. By picking my way cautiously I managed to reach the
roka and stepped down into my garden. A profound weakness overcame me,
so I stopped to regain my strength. To my surprise I discovered that I
was completely naked. How odd! Where were my drawers and undershirt?

What had happened?

All over the right side of my body I was cut and bleed
large splinter was protruding from a mangled wound in my t
something warm trickled into my mouth. My cheek was torn,
as I felt it gingerly, with the lower lip laid wide open.
neck was a sizable fragment of glass which I matter-of-
dislodged, and with the detachment of one stunned and
studied it and my blood-stained hand.

Where was my wife?

Suddenly thoroughly alarmed, I began to yell

Yaeko-san! Where are you?"

Blood began to spurt. Had my carotid arter
I bleed to death? Frightened and irrational, I

This typescript is the final edit of the English translation, complete with proofing marks

6 August 1945

The hour was early; the morning still, warm, and beautiful.
Shimmering leaves, reflecting sunlight from a cloudless sky, made a
pleasant contrast with shadows in my garden as I gazed absently through
wide flung doors opening to the south.

Clad in drawers and undershirt, I was sprawled on the living
room floor exhausted because I had just spent a sleepless night on duty
as an air warden in my hospital.

Suddenly, a strong flash of light startled me - and then another.
So well does one recall little things that I remember vividly how the light
chamber of a stone lantern in the garden became brilliantly lit and I
debated whether this light was caused by a magnesium flare or sparks
from a passing trolley.

Garden shadows disappeared. The view where a moment before all
had been so bright and sunny was now dark and hazy. Through swirling
dust I could barely discern a wooden column that had supported one
corner of my house. It was leaning crazily and the roof sagged
dangerously.

HIROSHIMA DIARY
THE JOURNAL OF A JAPANESE PHYSICIAN
AUGUST 6 - SEPTEMBER 30, 1945

MICHIHIKO HACHIYA, M.D.
TRANSLATED AND EDITED BY WARNER WELLS, M.D.

◄ THE A-BOMB Hachiya reworked his diary entries and titled them *Hiroshima no Genbaku Zatsuwa* (*Stories from the Hiroshima A-bombing*). They were first published in a Japanese medical journal in 1950. Under the supervision of American doctor Herner Wells, the English translation was published as *Hiroshima Diary* in 1955.

▲ EYEWITNESS ACCOUNT Hachiya wrote his journal like an academic: he recorded the events as they unfolded with little reference to his emotions. In the opening pages, his firsthand account of being injured by the blast is remarkably calm and rational: "All over the right side of my body I was cut and bleeding.... Embedded in my neck was a sizable fragment of glass which I matter-of-factly dislodged."

February 26 (con)

diamond" and he yelled back, colossal, in a voice that should
have come from a Pole, "You like?" and asking me if I wanted
brandy, and me yelling yes and backing into the next room past
the smug shining blub face of dear Bert, looking as if he had
delivered at least nine or ten babies, and bang the door was
shut and he was sloshing brandy into a glass and I was sloshing
it at the place xxx where my mouth was when I last knew about it.

We shouted as if in a high wind, about the review, and he saying
Dan knew I was beautiful, he wouldn't have written it about a
cripple, and my yelling protest in which the words "sleep with
the editor" occurred with startling frequency. And then it
came to the fact that I was all there, wasn't I, and I stamped
and screamed yes, and he had obligations in the next room, and
he was working in London, earning ten pounds a week so he could
later earn twelve pounds a week, and I was stamping and he was
stamping on the floor, and then he kissed me bang smash on the
mouth and ripped my hairband off, my lovely red hairband scarf
which has weathered the sun and much love, and whose like I
shall never again find, and my favorite silver earrings: hah, I
shall keep, he barked. And when he kissed my neck I bit him
long and hard on the cheek, and when we came out of the room,
blood was running down his face. His poem "I did it, I." Such
violence, and I can see how women lie down for artists. The one
man in the room who was as big as his poems, huge, with hulk
and dynamic chunks of words; his poems are strong and blasting
like a high wind in steel girders. And I screamed in myself,
thinking: oh, to give myself crashing, fighting, to you. The
one man since I've lived who could blast Richard.

And now I sit here, demure and tired in brown, slightly sick
at heart. I shall go on. I shall write a detailed descriptions
of shock treatment, tight, blasting short descriptions with
not one smudge of coy sentimentality, and when I get enough
I shall send them to David Ross. There will be no hurry,
because I am too desperately vengeful now. But I will pile them
up. I thought about the shock treatment description last night:
the deadly sleep of her madness, and the breakfast not coming,
the little details, the flashback to the shock treatment that
went wrong: electrocution brought in, and the inevitable
going down the subterranean hall, waking to a new world, with
no name, being born again, and not of woman.

I shall never see him again, and the thorny limitations of the
day crowd in like the spikes on the gates at Queens last night:
I could never sleep with him anyway, with all his friends here
and his close relation to them, laughing, talking, I should
be the world's whore, as well as Roget's strumpet. I shall never
see him, he will never look for me. He said my name, Sylvia,
and banged a black grinning look into my eyes, and I would like
to try just this once, my force against his. But he will never
come, and the blonde one, pure and smug and favored, looks, is
it with projected pity and disgust at this drunken amorphic slut.

But Hamish was very kind and would have fought for me. It gave
him a kind of glory to take me away from them, those fiends,
and I am worth fighting for, I had been nice, to him, he said.

A Troubled Genius

1950–1962 ▪ TYPESCRIPT AND MANUSCRIPT ▪ TWO BOXES OF LOOSE SHEETS AND NOTEBOOKS ▪ AMERICAN

SYLVIA PLATH: POET

Born in 1932, Sylvia Plath began a diary at the age of 11 when she was growing up in Massachusetts, US. By then, she had already suffered the loss of her father, a trauma that was to mark her for life. Her natural talent as a poet and a writer of short stories was evident from an early age, but so was her emotional instability. In 1953, while attending the elite Smith College, she was given electric shock treatment for depression and she later attempted suicide, taking an overdose of sleeping pills.

The early diaries reveal a young woman growing up as a typical American teenager, but acutely observant of the details of the world around her, intensely competitive in her literary ambitions, and given to extreme outbreaks of depression and rage. Awarded a scholarship to study at Cambridge University, in 1956, she met and married the British poet Ted Hughes. From 1957 to 1959, the couple

❝ So how do I express my hate for my mother? In my deepest emotions I think of her as an enemy: somebody who "killed" my father... I lay in my bed when I thought my mind was going blank forever and thought what a luxury it would be to kill her... But I was too nice for murder. I tried to murder myself; to keep from being an embarrassment to the ones I loved and from living myself in a mindless hell. How thoughtful: Do unto yourself as you would do to others. I'd kill her, so I killed myself. ❞

THE JOURNALS OF SYLVIA PLATH, DECEMBER 12, 1958

lived in the US, where Plath taught for a year at Smith College. Her diaries are full of love and admiration for "huge derrick-striding Ted." In March 1958, she wrote: "I married a real poet and my life is redeemed."

Seeking emotional honesty, Plath's diaries are often obsessed with her inner conflicts, which drove her into therapy. But her writing is also rich in details of her everyday life, including a good deal of housewifery: "Spent ten minutes at least tonight scrubbing my fingers to the bone over that damned black-faced pot I burned...." Her central concern, however, is always with her development as a poet: "How my voice must change to be heard."

◀ **FATEFUL ENCOUNTER** On February 26, 1956, while a student at Cambridge, Plath typed this diary entry describing the previous night's drunken party, the occasion of her first, violently sexual encounter with her future husband, Ted Hughes. She describes him tearing off her headband and earrings, while she "bit him long and hard on the cheek ... blood was running down his face."

In context

◀ **SELF-PORTRAIT** Sylvia Plath was an artist as well as a poet. She made this self-portrait in gouache in her teens, before her first suicide attempt in 1953. It suggests the complex and troubled self-questioning associated with the episodes of depression that plagued her short life.

▶ **POETIC COUPLE** Throughout their marriage, Ted Hughes was a far more successful poet than Sylvia Plath, publishing the prize-winning collections *Hawk in the Rain* (1957) and *Lupercal* (1960). Although the couple tried to be supportive of one another, Plath was competitive and inevitably experienced envy and frustration as she struggled to get her own work recognized.

Poetry and death

In late 1959, Hughes and Plath returned to the UK, living first in London and then at Tawton, in rural Devon. Plath gave birth to a daughter in 1960 and a son in 1962, suffering a traumatizing miscarriage between the two births. Meanwhile, partly under the influence of American poet Robert Lowell, she had begun making literature out of her deepest emotional conflicts. This "confessional" approach informed her novel *The Bell Jar*, which she completed in 1961.

While living in Devon in 1962, Plath found out that Hughes was having an affair. Isolated and distressed, she wrote her finest poetry, working in the early morning while her two young children slept. After returning to London, in February 1963, she committed suicide by putting her head in a gas oven. Only fragments have survived of the diaries that Plath kept in the last three years of her life, mainly covering the first half of 1962. One late journal was apparently lost, and another, covering the period just before her suicide, was destroyed by Hughes after her death.

> ➤ **LOVE AND AMBITION** Plath wrote this diary entry around midnight on March 2, 1958, when she and Hughes were living in Massachusetts. In a positive mood, she expresses marital love: "I need Ted to kiss & smell & sleep with & read by as I need bread & wine"—and her determined literary ambitions—"Goal set: June 1959: a novel & a book of poems."

POSTHUMOUS **RECOGNITION**

Plath published her first collection of poems, *The Colossus*, in 1960, but she did not win recognition as a major poet until five years later, with the posthumous publication of the collection *Ariel*. More than half of the poems in *Ariel*, including the celebrated "Lazarus" and "Daddy," had been written in an exceptional burst of creativity during the last months of her life. Like her only novel, *The Bell Jar* (1963), the poetry is largely autobiographical, drawing upon her deepest fears and emotional conflicts, her personal experience of motherhood, her troubled relationships with her parents and her husband, and her abiding obsession with death.

> ➤ **First edition** cover of Plath's second poetry collection, *Ariel*, published in 1965, two years after her death

ARIEL

Poems by Sylvia Plath

> 66 The black force grew imperceptibly. I felt panic-stricken … I had nothing to do with it, it controlled me. 'I can't help it,' I cried, or whispered, and then in three great bursts, the black thing hurtled itself out of me, one, two, three, dragging three shrieks after it: Oh, Oh, Oh …. 'Here he is!' I heard Ted say. It was over. I felt the great weight gone in a moment…. The afterbirth flew out into a pyrex bowl, which crimsoned with blood. It was whole. We had a son. I felt no surge of love. I wasn't sure I liked him. 99

THE JOURNALS OF SYLVIA PLATH, JANUARY 17, 1962

UPBEAT LETTER Writing from Massachusetts in summer 1959, Plath tells her sister-in-law, Olwyn Hughes, of literary success—she has sold two poems to *The New Yorker* and Hughes is proving to be "the great poet of our generation." Yet only 10 days earlier, Plath had written in her diary: "Everything has gone barren. I am part of the world's ash...."

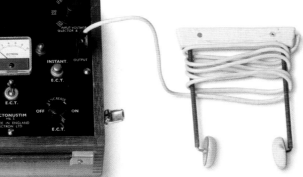

DUBIOUS TREATMENT
In 1953, Plath was given electroconvulsive therapy (ECT), which was intended to cure depression. Electrodes were attached to her head, sending an electric shock to her brain. Plath described her experience of this treatment in *The Bell Jar*, published shortly before her death in 1963.

66 It is as if **my life** were **magically run** by two electric currents: joyous positive and despairing negative.... 99

THE JOURNALS OF SYLVIA PLATH, JUNE 20, 1958

Life in a Favela

1955-1966 ■ PEN AND INK ON PAPER ■ 37 SURVIVING NOTEBOOKS ■ BRAZILIAN

CAROLINA MARIA DE JESUS: DIARIST

A vibrant and unique diarist, Carolina Maria de Jesus (c.1914-1977) went to school for only two years. Her disadvantaged upbringing eventually led her to a favela (slum) called Canindé next to a dump in São Paulo, Brazil. A single mother, who had been sacked from her job as a cleaner when she became pregnant, she built a shack from odds and ends and scraped a living by gathering bits of paper, bottles, and cans that she exchanged for coins. She even scavenged through garbage bins to find food for her three children. In 1958, a journalist covering a story in the favela heard Carolina yell at a group of men at a playground, "If you continue mistreating these children, I'm going to put all of your names in my book!" Intrigued, he asked to see her "book" and was shown notebooks filled with Carolina's writing, which he took to his editor.

The notebooks were a diary of life in the favela—not just Carolina's life but also those of her fellow *favelados*. She described their daily struggle to find food, cope with poverty and discrimination, and retain their sense of humanity. Carolina wrote: "a favela is the garbage dump of São Paulo, and I am just a piece of garbage." Far from pitying herself, however, Carolina had an impassioned outlook: "Brazil needs to be led by a person who has known hunger. Hunger is also a teacher. Who has gone hungry learns to think of the future and of the children." It was extraordinary that a woman from the slums could be such an articulate writer.

Part of the diaries was made into a book, *Quarto de Despejo: Diário de uma Favelada*, and published in 1960. It was published in English as *Child of the Dark: The Diary of Carolina Maria de Jesu*s two years later. Despite its enormous success, Carolina returned to live in the favela a few years on and later died in poverty.

▲ **FAVELAS** As a result of mass migration, shantytowns sprang up in cities such as Rio de Janeiro and São Paulo (above) in the second half of the 20th century. Often sprawling over the hills around the cities, they lacked basic sanitation, electricity, and health facilities. The rickety shacks were built from corrugated iron and old boards.

> ❝ ... whoever **is born** and can **put up with** this **life until death** must be ... **a hero.** ❞

CHILD OF THE DARK, JULY 28, 1958

▼ **THE NOTEBOOKS** Carolina wrote her diary in old notebooks she found at the dump. By the time she published her first book, she had filled around 20 such notebooks. This one describes what happened in December 1958, including finding some bags of rice in a warehouse and the birth of a stillborn child. On this page, Carolina finds a radio but has no electricity to make it work.

Señor Eduardo owned a shop where Carolina exchanged bottles and paper for coins or bread

▲ **JUNK ROOM** The literal translation of the title of Carolina's book is "Junk Room." It reproduces diaries that Carolina wrote at different times: in 1955, and from 1958 to 1960. It soon became one of the most successful books in Brazilian publishing history and was later sold in more than 40 countries.

The handwriting is remarkably neat and legible despite the tatty paper

> XMAS DAY. João came in saying he had a stomachache. I knew what it was for—he had eaten a rotten melon. Today they threw a truckload of melons near the river. I don't know why ... these senseless businessmen come to throw their rotten products here near the favela, for the children to see and eat. In my opinion, the merchants of São Paulo are playing with the people just like Caesar when he tortured the Christians. But the Caesars of today are worse than the Caesars of the past. The others were punished for their faith. And we, for our hunger! In that era, those who didn't want to die had to stop loving Christ. But we cannot stop loving eating.

***CHILD OF THE DARK*, DECEMBER 25, 1955**

The Bolivian Diary

1966–1967 ■ PEN AND INK ON PAPER ■ TWO NOTEBOOKS ■ ARGENTINE

ERNESTO "CHE" GUEVARA: REVOLUTIONARY

In November 1966, a Uruguayan special envoy of the OAS checked into a hotel in La Paz, the capital of Bolivia. In reality, it was Ernesto "Che" Guevara (1928–1967), the Argentine-born revolutionary who was one of the main leaders of the successful 1959 revolution in Cuba led by Fidel Castro. A leading member of the Cuban government, he had denounced injustice at the United Nations General Assembly and other international forums, and in 1965, he provided military support and training for rebel forces in the Congo. He had traveled to Bolivia incognito to support the Bolivian revolutionaries in their fight for liberation.

From the capital, he headed into the jungle to launch a guerrilla campaign against the country's government, which had come to power after a military coup. With him were around 60 fellow revolutionaries, mostly Bolivians and Cubans. On his way to Bolivia, Guevara had bought a diary, which he used to record the 11 months of his campaign. He wrote in his diary every day, reporting on the group's progress as they moved through the difficult terrain, trying to find food and

shelter, evade the government forces, set up ambushes, and, crucially, recruit the support they needed from the local people. This proved disappointing. Guevara noted, "Talking to these peasants is like talking to statues. They do not give us any help. Worse still, many of them are turning into informants."

The small group fought hard, carrying out two successful ambushes on military patrols and taking a town, but battles with the US-trained Bolivian Army gradually depleted their numbers. Throughout the hardships, illness, setbacks, and hunger, Guevara recorded what happened in his diary:

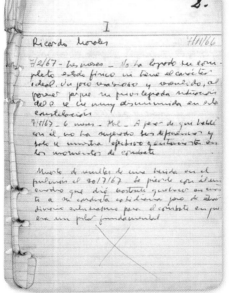

"I am now 39," he wrote in June 1967, "and I am relentlessly approaching the age when I must think about my future as a guerrilla. But for now, this is what I am." He made his final entry on October 7, 1967, the day before his capture by the Bolivian Army. He was executed without trial on October 9; the two notebooks in which he kept his diary were found in his backpack.

◄ **UNDER LOCK AND KEY** Guevara made his daily entries in a spiral-bound notebook, seen here, and a German diary (see opposite). The Bolivian Army confiscated both notebooks, but they later turned up in London. They were recovered by the Bolivian Ministry of Foreign Affairs and are now kept secure in a vault in the country's central bank.

THE **MOTORCYCLE DIARIES**

Brought up in a middle-class family, surrounded by books, Guevara was a prolific writer. He wanted to know more about Latin America, so he went on several trips, which he wrote about in diaries. His best-known trip, made in 1952 when he was a medical student, was around South America on a motorcycle with the biochemist Alberto Granado. "The enormity of our endeavor escaped us in those moments," wrote Guevara, "All we could see was the dust on the road ahead and ourselves on the bike, devouring kilometers in our flight north." During the nine-month, 5,000-mile (8,000-km) odyssey, Guevara was struck by the social injustice he encountered. "Wandering aimlessly through our 'Capital America' has changed me more than I thought," he wrote. This may have been the foundation of his radicalization. His diaries were published as *The Motorcycle Diaries* in 1993.

▶ **Che Guevara** with "The Mighty Two," his 500cc Norton motorcycle, which he used at the beginning of his trip, 1952

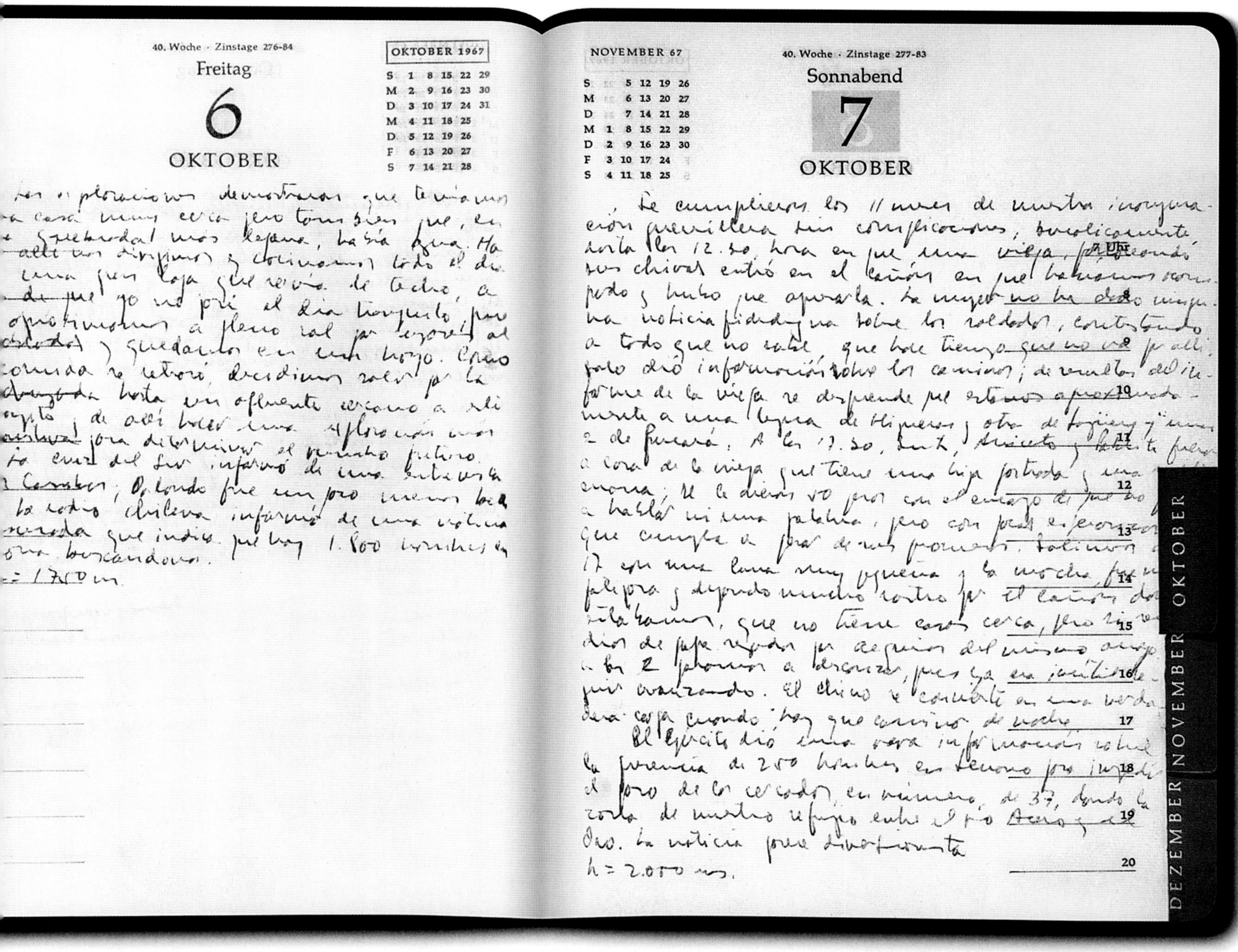
40. Woche · Zinstage 276-84
Freitag
6
OKTOBER
OKTOBER 1967
NOVEMBER 67
40. Woche · Zinstage 277-83
Sonnabend
7
OKTOBER
OKTOBER
NOVEMBER
DEZEMBER

▲ **FINAL THOUGHTS** The last entry in Guevara's diary records how the exhausted and sick guerrillas encounter an old woman herding goats. They ask her whether soldiers are in the area but are unable to get any reliable information. Scared that she will report them, they pay her some money to keep quiet. Guevara notes that he has little hope that she will hold her silence.

> The future belongs to the people, and gradually, or in one strike, they will take power, here and in every country. The terrible thing is the people need to be educated, and this they cannot do before taking power, only after. They can only learn at the cost of their own mistakes, which will be very serious and will cost many innocent lives.

CHE GUEVARA, *THE MOTORCYCLE DIARIES*

▲ **THE END OF THE REVOLUTION** A few hours after Guevara wrote the final entry in his diary, the revolutionaries were encircled by a superior force of Bolivian government soldiers, and Guevara was wounded and captured. He was taken to a school in the village of La Higuera, a few miles away, and was executed the following day by the CIA-backed soldiers.

A Maverick's Notes

C.1970–1994 ▪ INK AND COLLAGE ON PAPER ▪ MORE THAN 40 SKETCHBOOKS AND DIARIES ▪ BRITISH

DEREK JARMAN: MOVIE DIRECTOR

Derek Jarman was not only a movie director but also a poet, artist, set designer, gardener, and an outspoken gay rights activist. From the mid-1970s to 1993, he made 11 feature films, notably *Caravaggio* (1986), *Edward II* (1991), and *Blue* (1993), which were landmarks in what was later dubbed the "New Queer Cinema"—independent movies that celebrated gay culture. He was also one of the first people to make music videos, directing them for The Sex Pistols, The Smiths, and The Pet Shop Boys. On the political front, he rallied against the British government's Section 28 legislation, which essentially banned gay teachers from working in schools and intensified prejudice against gays.

In 1986, Jarman was diagnosed as HIV positive. Soon after, he bought a small fisherman's cottage on the beach at Dungeness, in southeast England, in the shadow of an enormous nuclear power station, and created a garden in the inhospitable shingle around the cottage. Throughout the time he lived there, he kept diaries and large, elaborate sketchbooks, in which words and images play an equally important role. "For as long as I knew him, there was always a sketchbook on the go," wrote his frequent collaborator, the actress Tilda Swinton. The sketchbooks were usually photograph albums that Jarman customized himself. As well as snippets of his ideas, drafts of dialogues and voice-overs, poetry, and drawings, he stuck in photographs, tickets, newspaper clippings, and interesting things that he found outside, such as colorful feathers or pressed flowers. The books provide a rich and fascinating insight into a prolific creative mind at work.

Jarman died from an HIV-related illness in 1994. Two volumes of his diaries, *Modern Nature* (1991) and *Smiling in Slow Motion* (2001), have been published, as well as excerpts from his sketchbooks.

Cafe Grans
Oranienstrasse
1000 Berlin 3

Baerwaldstr. 9
1000 Berlin 61

THE GARDEN AT **PROSPECT COTTAGE**

On January 1, 1989, Derek Jarman began the diary that became *Modern Nature*. It starts by describing the small fisherman's cottage on the headland at Dungeness that he had bought on a whim. It then records how he created a garden on the shingle beach, making a colorful, flowering oasis, punctuated by dramatic, sculptural pieces of driftwood. Having recently discovered that he was HIV positive, Jarman found refuge in nurturing life in his humble garden. He describes trying to make things grow in the seemingly barren terrain and the joys of coaxing life from the stony ground. Interwoven through this account are memories of his childhood and trips to London to film and edit, and to visit hospital, but the diary always returns to his garden—a source of inspiration and optimism with its constant promise of rebirth.

VINTAGE **JARMAN**

MODERN NATURE

▶ **The UK cover of** *Modern Nature,* showing Derek Jarman's shingle garden at Prospect Cottage, Dungeness

❝ Nothing that I have ever worked on has produced such problems as this life of Caravaggio. Everyone is excited by it and everyone is suspicious. My friends find two years of delays inexplicable, my lack of funds annoying. They feel I should get on and do something, why shipwreck myself in the chiaroscuro. Films about painters usually end up pleasing no one, a tug of war in which neither the artist or the filmmaker is victorious. ❞

SKETCHBOOK, DECEMBER 20, 1982

> ❝ The day of our death is sealed up.
> I do not wish to die … yet. ❞

MODERN NATURE, AUGUST 1, 1990

The voice-over begins with a list of the places in and around Italy to which Caravaggio fled after killing a man in a sword fight

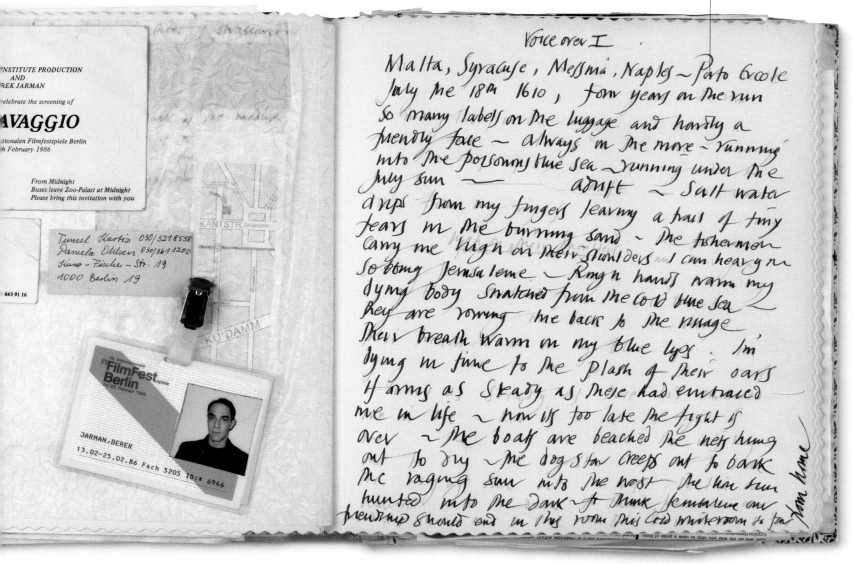

▲ **CARAVAGGIO** This page of the *Caravaggio* sketchbook shows the beginning of the final script of *Caravaggio*, which was read in voice-over. Opposite it are an invitation to a screening at the Berlin International Film Festival in 1986 and Jarman's press pass. Some of the sheets in the sketchbooks are of tissuelike paper, so text and part of a Berlin map show through from the previous page.

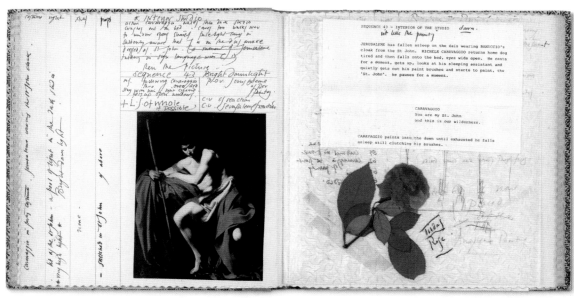

◄ **SOURCES OF INSPIRATION** These pages are from Jarman's *Caravaggio* sketchbook, which he began in 1985. As well as diary entries, it contains notes for the movie's shoots. These pages have directions for a scene in which characters pose for a painting of St. John the Baptist. The pressed flower is labeled "Tilda's Rose"—Tilda Swinton appeared in this movie.

Directory: 1940-Present

▼ THE WAR RECORDS OF MOLLY LAMB

CANADIAN (1942–1945)

Molly Bobak (1920–2014), née Molly Lamb, trained as a painter at the Vancouver School of Art. In 1942, she joined the Canadian Women's Army Corps, formed recently to provide support services to Canada's military forces, which were participating in World War II.

From November 1942 to June 1945, Lamb kept a sketch diary titled *W110278: The Personal War Records of Private Lamb, M.* It was presented in an imitation of a newspaper format, with satirical headlines, mock articles referring to Lamb in the third person, and amusing but sharply observed illustrations. The diary follows Lamb's stuttering progress from canteen and laundry duties to eventual officer status. Sent as a war artist to Europe in summer 1944, she continued the diary for another year, sympathetically documenting the lives of her fellow put-upon Canadian women in uniform, from drill and parades to cleaning and cooking. The sketch diary was first published in 1992 under the title *Double Duty* and was made available online in 2015.

AN ITALIAN WAR DIARY

BRITISH/ITALIAN (1943–1944)

The diary of Iris Origo (1902–1988) is celebrated as a moving portrait of the sufferings and heroism of civilians caught up in war. Origo, who was of Anglo-American parentage, married an Italian aristocrat and was living on an estate at Val d'Orcia in Tuscany when World War II began.

Already a published author, Origo briefly kept a diary from 1939 to 1940, but her main journal begins at the start of 1943, with Italy facing military disaster. She recorded the mixed attitudes of local people as the fascist dictatorship of Benito Mussolini collapsed into chaos and the country was fought over by Allied and German armies.

Origo's estate provided a haven for refugees from the war. Menaced from all sides, she kept her diaries hidden under the floorboards of her house. Eventually, as the fighting drew ever closer, she was forced into perilous flight, leading the evacuee children to safety. Written as a memoir, the 1943–1944 diaries were first published as *War in Val d'Orcia* in 1947.

THE CHEEVER JOURNALS

AMERICAN (1947–1982)

An eminent American author of short stories and novels, John Cheever (1912–1982) filled 29 notebooks with private diary entries over a period of 35 years. Into these copious journals, he poured the spiritual anguish of a deeply conflicted life, torn between Christian faith and "carnality," the desire for order and rampant alcoholism, a frustrated marriage, and homosexual longings.

Alongside repeated expressions of self-lacerating despair and loneliness, Cheever evokes the beauty of the natural world and records the mundane everyday details of his family life in the New York suburbs or small-town New England—the places that supplied the material for much of his fiction. The later diaries cover his eventually successful struggle with alcohol addiction and the public acceptance of his sexuality.

Extensive excerpts from Cheever's diaries were published in book form in 1990. They were greeted with dismay at their revelation of the despairing inner life of a largely upbeat public figure but also with admiration at writing that was judged to be as good as any of his fiction.

THE ORTON DIARIES

BRITISH (1966–1967)

Playwright Joe Orton (1933–1967) kept a diary for the last nine months of his life, from December 1966 until August 1967, when he was murdered by his partner Kenneth Halliwell. The success of Orton's subversive black farce *Loot* had recently made him a fashionable figure in the London of the Swinging Sixties, appearing on TV and being courted by the Beatles for a movie script.

The diary travels between the writer's public life as a media and theatrical figure, his bickering domesticity with Halliwell, his working-class family in Leicester, and vacations in North Africa. Everywhere Orton describes, with much comic detail, his uninhibited pursuit of sex.

Writing material that he intended "to be published long after my death," Orton set out to provoke shock and laughter, succeeding on both counts.

Private Molly Lamb's sketch diary, detailing her early army experiences

For instance, in one anecdote on attending his mother's funeral, he steals her false teeth to use as a theatrical prop. The strains of his relationship with Halliwell are outlined with painful clarity, although there is no direct anticipation of its tragic ending. The last entry is dated eight days before Orton's death. The diaries were published in 1986.

DANG'S DIARY

VIETNAMESE (1968-1970)

Dang Thuy Tram (1942-1970) was a young woman trained as a doctor in Hanoi, North Vietnam. By the time she began to keep a diary, in April 1968, she was serving as a battlefield surgeon with the North Vietnamese Army and communist guerrillas in Kuang Ngai province, South Vietnam, the scene of heavy fighting against US and South Vietnamese forces.

One of Dang's diaries fell into the hands of US special forces in December 1969. Another was found on her when she was killed in a firefight with American soldiers in June 1970. Preserved by an American intelligence officer, Fred Whitehurst, the diaries were first published in Vietnam in 2005, under the title *Last Night I Dreamed of Peace*. Vividly evoking the horrors of war, the journals are infused with her youthful idealism, loneliness, commitment to her patients, and devotion to the Communist cause.

▲ THE ANDY WARHOL DIARIES

AMERICAN (1976-1987)

American artist Andy Warhol (1928-1987) saw the elimination of the personal touch as an essential element in his creative projects, often using assistants to make the works that appeared under his name. His approach to writing followed the same principle. In 1975, he published a book of aphorisms and monologues, *The Philosophy of Andy Warhol (A to B and Back Again)*, which was actually written by his secretary and collaborator Pat Hackett based on phone conversations with the artist. From 1976, Warhol applied the same

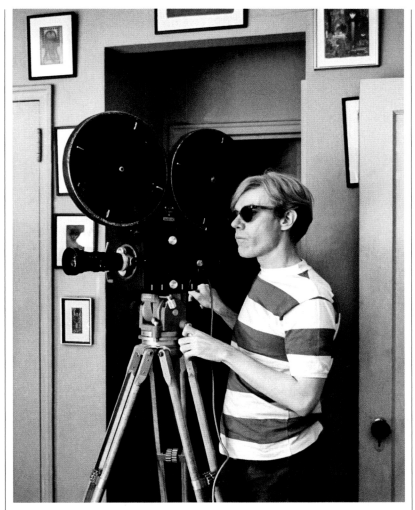

Andy Warhol filming, May 4, 1966

technique to keeping a daily record of his life. He telephoned Hackett every morning from Monday to Friday to give an account of the previous day—the Monday session covered the weekend—and she typed up the content of his phone calls.

One major purpose of the diary was to record Warhol's expenses for tax purposes, but it also became a receptacle for his acid comments on the celebrities with whom he relentlessly socialized, his commercial views on art, and his personal manias and hypochondria. A selection from the 20,000-page typescript was published as *The Andy Warhol Diaries* in 1989.

ALAN BENNETT'S DIARIES

BRITISH (1980 ONWARD)

A noted screenwriter, playwright, and actor, Alan Bennett (born 1934) began keeping a sporadic diary in the early

1970s. First published in the *London Review of Books*, a literary magazine with which Bennet is associated, from 1980 onward, the diaries have appeared in book form as part of the collections *Writing Home* (1994), *Untold Stories* (2005), and *Keeping On Keeping On* (2016). Initially writing longhand on loose-leaf notepaper, Bennett later revised and edited the entries for publication. The original manuscripts are held by the Bodleian Library in Oxford.

Wry, modest, observant, and humorous, Bennett's diaries cover subjects ranging from domestic life in his native Yorkshire to travels across the world connected with his busy working life. Personal problems, such as his struggle with cancer, are glossed over lightly. Bennett's left-wing political take on current events and social issues is trenchantly expressed, but his chief strength as a diarist lies in his sketches of local eccentrics and his dramatist's ear for precise turns of speech in the people he meets.

COBAIN'S JOURNALS

AMERICAN (1988-1994)

When Nirvana singer and guitarist Kurt Cobain committed suicide in 1994 at the age of 27, he left behind a collection of ring-bound notebooks scrawled with fragmentary accounts of his daily experiences; random reflections on music, politics, and society; first drafts of song lyrics; unsent letters; lists of favorite bands; sketches for album covers; and comic drawings. Mostly undated, but arranged in broadly chronological order, the notebooks were published in 2002 under the title *Journals*.

The journals begin with a letter written in 1988, before the release of Nirvana's first album. By their end, Cobain is struggling to cope with fame, compelled to live as "a reclusive Rock Star." Strikingly misspelled and erratically punctuated—"Yeah, punctuation I was stoned a lot when I was learning that stuff"—the texts express the thoughts of an earnest and troubled individual: imaginative, perceptive, and self-aware. Although plagued by ill-health and depression, Cobain voiced his generation's anger and wonder at the state of the world.

ZLATA'S DIARY

BOSNIAN CROATIAN (1991-1993)

In September 1991, Zlata Filipović (born 1980), a 10-year-old girl living in the Bosnian city of Sarajevo, was given a diary. She began recording her daily life as a middle-class child—playing tennis, listening to Madonna records, buying new skis. But in spring 1992, she found herself caught up in the Bosnian War, one of the complex conflicts that followed the collapse of Yugoslavia. During the war, Sarajevo was besieged and subjected to artillery bombardment.

The diary describes the breakdown of Zlata's world as schools closed, her friends fled the city, and the cellar of her family home became a refuge from shelling. Written in Croatian, entries from her diary were published locally, and she became a minor celebrity, visited by foreign correspondents covering the conflict. Her diary ends in March 1993, when she escaped with her family to Paris.

Index

Page numbers in **bold** refer to main entries.

Acknowledgments

DK would like to thank the following for their help with this book:
Rose Blackett-Ord for editorial assistance; Nandini D. Tripathy for proofreading; Helen Peters for the index; Anukriti Arora and Sampda Mago for design assistance; Sonia Charbonnier for creative technical support; Christopher Scanlon for additional photography; Senior DTP Designers Harish Aggarwal and Neeraj Bhatia; Jackets Editorial Coordinator: Priyanka Sharma; Managing Jackets Editor: Saloni Singh

The publisher would like to credit the following for the text extracts in the book.

The relevant page numbers appear in **bold** before the writers' names:

15 Merer, "The Logbook of Merer" in *Les Papyrus de la Mer Rouge I: Le "Journal de Merer", Annexe I*, Pierre Tallet, English translation by Colin Clement, Institut français d'archéologie orientale, 2019 (accessed at amers.hypotheses.org/536).

17 Pliny the Younger, *Letters*, translated by William Melmoth, revised by F.C.T. Bosanque and further revised by Charles E. Muntz, 2010 (accessed at cmuntz.hosted.uark.edu/texts/pliny-the-younger/pliny-on-vesuvius.html).

19 Ennin, *Ennin's Diary: The Record of a Pilgrimage to China in Search of the Law*, translated by Edwin O. Reischauer, Ronald Press, 1955.

21 Murasaki Shikibu, "The Diary of Murasaki Shikibu" in *Diaries of Court Ladies of Old Japan*, translated by Annie Shepley Omori and Kochi Doi, Houghton Mifflin, 1920.

23 Margery Kempe, *The Book of Margery Kempe*, translated and edited by B.A. Windeat t, Penguin Classics, 2000.

25 Luca Landucci, *A Florentine Diary from 1450 to 1516*, by Luca Landucci, translated by Alice de Rosen Jervis, J.M. Dent & Sons, 1927.

26 Leonardo da Vinci, *Leonardo da Vinci: Notebooks*, OUP World's Classics, 2008.

35 Antonio Pigafetta, *The First Voyage Around the World (1519-1522): An Account of Magellan's Expedition*, University of Toronto Press, 2007.

39 Yi Sun-shin, *Nanjung Ilji; the War Diary of Admiral Yi Sun-shin*, translated by Ha Tae-hung, Yonsei University Press, 1977.

41 Peter Hagendorf, "A Soldier's Life in the Thirty Years War" in *The Thirty Years War: A Documentary History*, translated and edited by Tryntje Helfferich, Hackett Publishing Company, 2009.

43 William Bradford, *Bradford's History "Of Plimoth Plantation."*, Wright & Potter, 1898.

45 Abel Janszoon Tasman, *Abel Janszoon Tasman's Journal of His Discovery of Van Diemens Land and New Zealand in 1642, with Documents Relating to His Exploration of Australia in 1644*, translated by J. de Hoop Scheffer and C. Stoffel, F. Muller, 1898.

46 Edward Barlow, *Barlow's Journal of his Life at Sea in King's Ships, East & West Indiamen & Other Merchantmen from 1659 to 1703, Vol. II*, Hurst & Blackett, 1934.

48, 51 Samuel Pepys, *The Diary of Samuel Pepys, Vol. 7: 1666*, University of California Press, 2000.

53 The Kangxi Emperor's scribes, *Kangzi qijuzhu* ("The Kangxi Era Imperial Diaries"), Zonghua Shuji, 1984, quoted in Michael G. Chang, "Historical Narratives of the Kangxi Emperor's Inaugural Visit to Suzhou, 1684", in *The Dynastic Centre and the Provinces: Agents and Interactions*, Brill, 2014.

55 Madame de Sévigné, *Madame de Sévigné: Selected Letters*, translated by Leonard Tancock, Penguin Classics, 1982.

57 Matsuo Bashō, "The Narrow Road to the Deep North" in *The Narrow Road to the Deep North and Other Travel Sketches*, translated by Nobuyuki Yuasa, Penguin Classics, 1966.

59 Duc de Saint-Simon, *Memoirs of the Duke of Saint-Simon on the Reign of Louis XIV and the Regency, Vol. II*, translated by Bayle St. John, Chatto & Windus, 1876.

64 Carl Linnaeus, *Lachesis Lapponica, or a Tour in Lapland, Vol. II*, translated by Charles Troilius, White, Cochrane & Co., 1811.

68 Ananda Ranga Pillai, *The Private Diary of Ananda Ranga Pillai, Vol. 2*, Asian Educational Services, 1985.

70 Elizabeth Sandwith Drinker, *The Diary of Elizabeth Drinker: The Life Cycle of an Eighteenth-Century Woman*, Northeastern University Press, 1994.

72 James Boswell, *London Journal 1962-1963*, Penguin Classics, 2010.

75 James Cook, *First Voyage Around the World*, Salzwasser Verlag, 2009.

80 Ahmad al-Salih, quoted in Rahilah Omar, *The History of Boné AD 1775-1795: The Diary of Sultan Ahmad as-Salleh Syamsuddin* (PhD thesis), University of Hull, 2003.

85 Johann Wolfgang von Goethe, *The Works of Johann Wolfgang von Goethe: Letters from Switzerland / Travels in Italy*, translated by A.J.W. Morrison, The Anthological Society, 1901.

86 Ralph Clark, *The Journal and Letters of Lt. Ralph Clark 1787-1792*, University of Sydney Library, 2003 (prepared from the print edition published by Australian Documents Library in association with the Library of Australian History, 1981; accessed at setis.library.usyd.edu.au/ozlit/pdf/clajour.pdf).

89 Alexander von Humboldt, quoted in Ramón Páez, *Travels and Adventures in South and Central America: First series: Life in the Llanos of Venezuela*, Charles Scribner, 1868.

96 Dorothy Wordsworth, *Dorothy Wordsworth: The Grasmere and Alfoxden Journals*, Oxford University Press, 2002.

99 Meriwether Lewis, *The Definitive Journals of Lewis & Clark: From Fort Mandan to Three Forks, Vol. 4*, University of Nebraska Press, 1987.

102 Anne Lister, *The Secret Diaries of Miss Anne Lister*, decoded and edited by Helena Whitbread, Virago, 1988.

105 Michael Shiner, "The Diary of Michael Shiner: Entries from 1831-1839", Naval History and Heritage Command (accessed at www.history.navy.mil/research/library/online-reading-room/title-list-alphabetically/d/diary-of-michael-shiner/1831-1839.html).

106 Rose de Freycinet, *A Woman of Courage: The Journal of Rose de Freycinet on Her Voyage Around the World, 1817-1820*, translated and edited by Marc Serge Rivière, National Library Australia, 1996.

111 Eugène Delacroix, *The Journal of Eugène Delacroix*, translated by Lucy Norton, Phaidon Press, 1951.

113 Sir Walter Scott, *The Journal of Sir Walter Scott: From the Original Manuscript at Abbotsford*, Harper & Brothers, 1890.

115 Charles Darwin, *The Beagle Record: Selections from the original pictorial records and written accounts of the voyage of H.M.S. Beagle*, Cambridge University Press, 1979.

119 Queen Victoria, "Queen Victoria's Journals" (Lord Esher's typescripts), Bodleian Libraries and Royal Archives with online publisher ProQuest (accessed at www.queenvictoriasjournals.org).

120 Søren Kierkegaard, *Kierkegaard's Journals and Notebooks, Vol. 1: Journals AA-DD*, Princeton University Press in cooperation with the Søren Kierkegaard Research Centre, 2007.

123 John Ruskin, *The Diaries of John Ruskin: 1848-1873*, Oxford University Press, 1958.

126 Charlotte Brontë, "Charlotte Brontë's Journal", British Library (accessed at https://www.bl.uk/collection-items/charlotte-brontes-journal).

128 Henry David Thoreau, *The Writings of Henry David Thoreau, Vol. 11: Journal*, Houghton Mifflin, 1906.

133 Robert and Clara Schumann, *The Marriage Diaries of Robert & Clara Schumann*, translated by Peter Oswald, Robson Books, 1994.

135 Leo Tolstoy, *The Diaries of Leo Tolstoy*, translated by C.J. Hogarth and A. Sirnis, J.M. Dent & Sons, 1917.

139 Henry Bates, *A Naturalist on the Amazons*, Macmillan, 1920.

142 The Goncourt brothers, *Pages from the Goncourt Journals*, translated and edited by Robert Baldick, Oxford University Press, 1962.

149 Mary Chesnut, *The Private Mary Chesnut: The Unpublished Civil War Diaries*, Oxford University Press, 1984.

150 John Muir, *John of the Mountains: The Unpublished Journals of John Muir*, University of Wisconsin Press, 1979.

153 Francis Kilvert, *Kilvert's Diary*, Vintage Books, 2013.

155 Vincent van Gogh, "712: To Theo van Gogh. Arles, on or about Thursday, 25 October 1888", translated by Imogen Forster and Sue Dyson, in *Vincent van Gogh - The Letters*, version January 2020, Amsterdam & The Hague: Van Gogh Museum & Huygens ING (accessed at http://vangoghletters.org/en/let712).

158, Antoni Gaudí, quoted in "Gaudí and his Concept of the House", Casa Vicens (accessed at casavicens.org/blog/gaudi-concept-house).

161 Beatrice Webb, "Beatrice Webb's typescript diary", LSE Digital Library (accessed at digital.library.lse.ac.uk/objects/lse:foj709hir/read/single#page/486/mode/2up).

162 Arthur Conan Doyle, *Dangerous Work: Diary of an Arctic Adventure*, The University of Chicago Press, 2012.

165 Beatrix Potter, *The Journal of Beatrix Potter from 1881 to 1897*, Frederick Warne, 1966.

168 Thomas Alva Edison, "The Thomas Edison Papers: Diaries and Journals", Rutgers, courtesy of Thomas Edison National Historical Park (accessed at edison.rutgers.edu/NamesSearch/SingleDoc php?DocId=MA001).

171 Jules Renard, *The Journal of Jules Renard*, translated and edited by Louise Bogan and Elizabeth Roget, Tin House Books, 2017.

172 Paul Gauguin, *Noa Noa: Voyage to Tahiti*, translated by Jonathan Griffin, Bruno Cassirer, 1961.

174 Alfred Dreyfus, *Five Years of My Life: The Diary of Captain Alfred Dreyfus*, Peebles Press International, 1977.

177 Isabelle Eberhardt, *In the Shadow of Islam*, translated by Sharon Bangert, Peter Owen Modern Classics, 2003.

186 Virginia Woolf, *The Diary of Virginia Woolf – Volume 1*: 1915–1919, Penguin Books, 1979.

189 Paul Klee, *The Diaries of Paul Klee 1898–1918*, University of California Press, 1964.

193 Käthe Kollwitz, *Die Tagebücher 1908–1943*, btb Verlag, 2012. Translated by Sofia Sheri (accessed at sophia.smith.edu/portfoliosssheri/2018/05/09/excerpt-from-the-diary-of-kathe-kollwitz/#more-90).

195, 197 Robert Falcon Scott, *Scott's Last Expedition, Vol. 1: Being the Journals of Captain R.F. Scott*, John Murray, 1 914.

201 Franz Kafka, *The Diaries of Franz Kafka*, translated by Joseph Kresh and Martin Greenberg, Penguin Modern Classics, 1972.

203 Carl Gustav Jung, *The Red Book: Liber Novus*, translated by Mark Kyburz, John Peck, and Sonu Shamdasani, W.W. Norton, 2009.

205 Louis Barthas, *Poilu: The World War I Notebooks of Corporal Louis Barthas, Barrelmaker: 1914–1918*, translated by Edward M. Strauss, Yale University Press, 2014.

207 Siegfried Sassoon, *Siegfried Sassoon Diaries, 1915–1918*, Faber & Faber, 1983.

210 Josep Pla, *The Grey Notebook*, translated by Peter R. Bush, New York Review Books Classics, 2013.

212 Howard Carter, "Howard Carter's excavation diaries", The Griffith Institute, University of Oxford (accessed at http://www.griffith.ox.ac.uk/discoveringTut/journals-and-diaries/season-1/journal.html#entry-of-25-11-1922).

214 Anaïs Nin, *Incest: From "A Journal of Love": The Unexpurgated Diary of Anaïs Nin, 1932–1934*, Harcourt, 1992.

217 George Orwell, *The Collected Non-Fiction: Essays, Articles, Diaries and Letters, 1903–1950*, Penguin, 2017.

219 Albert Camus, *Albert Camus, Notebooks 1935–1942*, translated by Philip Thody, Alfred A. Knopf, 1963.

225 Anne Frank, *The Diary of Anne Frank: The Critical Edition*, translated by Arnold J. Pomerans and B.M. Mooyaart-Doubleday, Doubleday, 1989.

228 Frida Kahlo, *The Diary of Frida Kahlo: An Intimate Self-Portrait*, translated by Sarah M. Lowe, Harry N. Abrams, 2005.

232 Michihiko Hachiya, *Hiroshima Diary: The Journal of a Japanese Physician, August 6–September 30, 1945: Fifty Years Later*, translated and edited by Warner Wells, M.D., The University of North Carolina Press, 1995.

235, 236 Sylvia Plath, *The Unabridged Journals of Sylvia Plath, 1950–1962*, Anchor Books, 2000.

239 Carolina Maria de Jesus, *Child of the Dark: The Diary of Carolina Maria de Jesus*, translated by David St. Clair, Dutton, 1962.

241 Ernesto "Che" Guevara, *The Motorcycle Diaries: A Journey Around South America*, translated by Ann Wright, Verso, 1995.

242 Derek Jarman, *Derek Jarman's Sketchbooks*, Stephen Farthing and Ed Webb-Ingall, Thames & Hudson, 2013

Yale University: Boswell Collection (cl, br). **74 Alamy:** Universal Art Archive (cla); The Natural History Museum (bl). **Princeton University Library:** Historic Maps Collection (br). **75 Getty:** Fine Art (bl). **National Library of Australia:** Digital Collections (t). **76 Bridgeman:** British Library Board (c). **77 Alamy:** Visual Arts Resource (bl). **Princeton University Library:** Historic Maps Collection (br). **State Library of Western Australia**: reproduced with the permission of the Library Board of Western Australia (tr). **78 Alamy:** Universal Art Archive (tl). **Scala:** Photo MNP (bl, br). **79 Alamy:** Vintage Archives (br). **Scala:** Photo MNP (tl, bl, tc). **80 Bridgeman:** British Library Board (br). **81 Bridgeman:** British Library Board(cl, cr). **82 Alamy:** Universal Art Archive (bl). **Getty:** Imagno (cla); DEA / A. Dagli Orti (br). **83 Bridgeman:** British Library Board (ca). **Matthias Naeschke:** Sebastian Naeschke (bl). **84 Alamy:** Universal Art Archive (tl). **Getty:** De Agostini (bl). **Scala:** bpk, Bildagentur fuer Kunst, Kultur und Geschichte, Berlin (br). **85 Klassik Stiftung Weimar:** Goethe und Schiller Archiv (cl). **Scala:** Congress of Deputies Library, Madrid / Album (br). **86 State Library of New South Wales. 87 State Library of New South Wales** (cr, bl, br). **88 akg-images** (bl). **Alamy:** Universal Art Archive (cla). **89 Scala:** Scala / bpk, Bildagentur fuer Kunst, Kultur und Geschichte, Berlin (l, r). **90 Scala:** Scala / bpk, Bildagentur fuer Kunst, Kultur und Geschichte, Berlin (bl). **Zentralbibliothek Zurich:** Entworfen von A. von Humbold, gezeichnet 1805 in Paris von Schönberger und Turpin, gestochen von Bouquet, die Schrift von L. Aubert, gedruckt von Langloi (bl). **91 Scala:** Scala / bpk, Bildagentur fuer Kunst, Kultur und Geschichte, Berlin. **92 Getty:** De Agostini (bl). **93 University of Michigan**: William L. Clements Library (tc). **94 Harvard University Herbaria** (cl). **INHA** (tl). **Mary Evans Picture Library:** Natural History Museum (bl). **Wikipedia:** Walden / Published 1854 in the United States by Ticknor and Field (tr). **95 British Library Board** (bl). **Library of Congress, Washington, D.C.**: Manuscript Division (tl**). 96 Bridgeman:** Felton Bequest (br); **Bridgeman** (bl). **Getty:** Culture Club (tl). 97 Bridgeman: Bridgeman (tr, cl). **98 Bridgeman:** Everett Collection (tl). **Missouri Historical Society, St Louis** (b). **99 Missouri Historical Society, St Louis. 100 Alamy:** Science History Images (br). **Bridgeman** (bl). **Cowan's Auctions LLC** (tr). **101 Missouri Historical Society, St Louis** (l, r). **102 Alamy:** Visual Arts Resource (cla). **West Yorkshire Archive Service Calderdale** (bl). **102-103 West Yorkshire Archive Service Calderdale** (tc). **103 Getty:** Fine Art Photographic (bc). **West Yorkshire Archive Service Calderdale** (cra). **104 Alamy:** Granger Historical Picture Archive (bl). **Library of Congress, Washington, D.C** (br). **105 Library of Congress, Washington, D.C.:** Manuscript Division (tl, tr). **SuperStock:** 4X5 Collection (bc). **106 Getty:** DEA Picture Library (br). **State Library of Western Australia**: reproduced with the permission of the Library Board of Western Australia (bl). **107 State Library of New South Wales** (l). **108 Getty:** Etienne Carjat (cla). **RMN:** RMN-Grand Palais (musée du Louvre) / Gérard Blot (bl). **109 RMN:** RMN-Grand Palais (musée du Louvre) / Michel Urtado (c). **110 RMN:** RMN-Grand Palais (musée du Louvre) / Gérard Blot (bl). **110-111 INHA** (c). **111 Getty:** Photo 12 (br). **RMN:** RMN-Grand Palais (musée du Louvre) / Hervé Lewandowski (cr). **112 Alamy:** Universal Art Archive (cla); Lebrecht Music & Arts (bl). **The University of Edinburgh** (br). **113 Scala:** © 2020. Photo The Morgan Library & Museum / Art (l, tr). **114 Alamy:** AF Fotografie (cla). **Bridgeman:** Historic England (bl). **114-115 Historic England Photo Library** (c). **116 Alamy:** The Natural History Museum (clb, crb). **117 Reproduced by kind permission of the Syndics of Cambridge University Library** (l). **Dorling Kindersley:** Natural History Museum, London / Dave King / Down House (cra). **118 Alamy:** Universal Art Archive (cla); Stephen Chung (cra); Universal Art Archive (bl). British Library Board (br). **119 The Royal Collection Trust © Her Majesty Queen Elizabeth II** (t). **120 Alamy:** Uber Bilder (cla); Vintage Archives (bl). **121 The Royal Library, Copenhagen** (t). **122 Alamy:** Universal Art Archive (bl). **Getty:** W. Jeffrey (cla). **The Ruskin: Library, Museum and Research Centre (**crb). **123 The Ruskin: Library, Museum and Research Centre. 124 Getty:** Heritage Images (bl). **Scala:** Photo The Morgan Library & Museum / Art Resource, NY (cr). **125 Getty:** DEA Picture Library (br). **Scala:** Photo The Morgan Library & Museum / Art Resource, NY (cl). **126 Alamy:** Vintage Archives (cla). **Bridgeman:** Bronte Parsonage Museum (bl, br). **127 Bridgeman:** Bronte Parsonage Museum (cl, cr). **128 Concord Museum** (br). **Library of Congress, Washington, D.C.** (cla).**The New York Public Library:** Detroit Publishing Company / The Miriam and Ira D. Wallach Division of Art, Prints and Photographs: Photography Collection (bl). **129 Scala:** Photo The Morgan Library & Museum / Art Resource, NY (tl); Photo The Morgan Library & Museum / Art Resource, NY (c). **130 Alamy:** The Natural History Museum (bl). Harvard University Herbaria. **131 Scala:** Photo The Morgan Library & Museum / Art Resource, NY (cl). **Wikipedia:** Walden / Published 1854 in the United States by Ticknor and Field (crb). **132 VAN HAM Kunstauktionen GmbH & Co. KG:** VAN HAM Fine Art Auctioneers / Saša Fuis (bl). **Manuscripts and Archives, Yale University Library:** Irving S. Gilmore Music Library (br). **133 Getty:** DEA / A. Dagli Orti / De Agostini (bl). Robert Schumann Haus, Zwickau: (t). **134 Getty Images:** adoc-photos (cla). **Scala:** Photo

Josse (br). **135 The State Museum Museum of L.N. Tolstoy. 136 The State Museum of L.N. Tolstoy. 137 Getty:** Heritage Images (bl). **SuperStock:** A. Burkatovski / Fine Art Images (tr). **The State Museum of L.N. Tolstoy** (br). **138 Alamy:** The Granger Collection (br); **AF Fotografie** (cla). **138-139 Mary Evans Picture Library:** Natural History Museum (cr). **140 Bridgeman:** Lux-in-Fine (cl). **140-141 Bibliothèque nationale de France, Paris. 141 Getty:** Imagno (br). **142 Bridgeman:** Patrice Cartier (cl). **143 Bibliothèque nationale de France, Paris. 144 Alamy:** The Artchives (bl). **145 The Metropolitan Museum of Art, New York** (t). **146 Archives nationales d'outre-mer** (tl). **Beinecke Rare Book and Manuscript Library, Yale University** (bl). **Getty:** David Nathan-Maister (tr). **Harvard University Herbaria** (bl). **147 Getty:** Heritage Images (tl). **University of the Pacific, University Libraries:** John Muir Papers, Holt-Atherton Special Collections / © 1984 Muir-Hanna Trust (bl). **148 Alamy:** The Granger Collection (br); Granger Historical Picture Archive (bl). **Getty:** Fotosearch / Stringer (tl). **149 Alamy:** World History Archive (tr). **South Caroliniana Library** (b). **150 Alamy**: AF Fotografie (cla). **University of the Pacific, University Libraries:** John Muir Papers, Holt-Atherton Special Collections / © 1984 Muir-Hanna Trust (bl). **150-151 University of the Pacific, University Libraries:** John Muir Papers, Holt-Atherton Special Collections / © 1984 Muir-Hanna Trust (t). **151 AF Fotografie** (br). **Alamy:** Pictorial Press Ltd (bl). **152 Bridgeman:** National Trust Photographic Library (bl). **Getty:** Hulton Archive (tl). **The Kilvert Society** (br). **153 Durham University Library Archives and Special Collections. 154 Alamy:** Historic Images (cr). **Getty:** Heritage Images (bl). **Courtesy National Gallery of Art, Washington** (tl). **155 Alamy:** Asar Studios (cl). **156 Getty:** Fine Art (tr, clb). **156-157 Getty:** Heritage Images (cb). **157 Alamy:** Peter Barritt (cra). **158 Getty:** Fine Art Images / Heritage Image (tl); Popperfoto / Paul Popper (bc). **159 Graphic Archive of the Barcelona School of Architecture, Universitat Politècnica de Caluny** (bl). **Institut Municipal Reus Cultura** (tl). **160 Getty:** Hulton Archive (tl). **London School of Economics & Political Science** (br). **161 Getty:** Culture Club (tr). **London School of Economics & Political Science** (bl, br). **162 Alamy:** Universal Art Archive (cla). **Conan Doyle Estate Ltd** (bl). **163 Alamy:** Universal Art Archive (bc). **Bridgeman:** British Library Board (tc). **Getty:** Universal History Archive (bl). **164 akg-images:** Science Source (bl). **Getty:** Hulton Archive (cla). **165 National Trust Images:** Image courtesy Frederick Warne & Co. Ltd / Penguin Books Ltd. **166 Alamy:** WorldPhotos (bl). **166-167 Scala:** © 2020. Photo The Morgan Library & Museum / Art (c). **167 Dorling Kindersley:** Image courtesy Frederick Warne & Co. Ltd / Penguin Books Ltd (br). Penguin Books Ltd: Image courtesy Frederick Warne & Co. Ltd / Penguin Books Ltd (tr). **168 Rutgers University:** Thomas A. Edison Papers: Courtesy of Thomas Edison National Historical Park. **169 Dorling Kindersley:** Science Museum, London / Dave King (tl). **Getty:** Hulton Archive (tl); Bettmann (br). **170 Alamy:** Chronicle (br). **Getty:** David Nathan-Maister (bl); adoc-photos (cla). **171 Bibliothèque nationale de France, Paris. 172 Alamy:** Vintage Archives (tl). **Getty:** Fine Art Images / Heritage Image (br). **173 Getty:** Fine Art Images / Heritage Image (br). **RMN:** ©RMN-Grand Palais (musée d'Orsay) / Hervé Lewandowsk (tl, tr); ©RMN-Grand Palais (musée d'Orsay) / Gérard Blot (bl). **174 Alamy:** Penrodas Collection (cla, br). **Getty:** David Nathan-Maister (bl). **175 Bibliothèque nationale de France, Paris** (tl, tr). **Getty:** David Nathan-Maister (bc). **176 Getty:** Apic (tl, bl); Art Media / Print Collector (br). **177 Archives nationales d'outre-mer. 178 Alamy:** Universal Art Archive (bl). **Dorling Kindersley:** The Science Museum, London / Clive Streeter (br). **Getty:** Print Collector (cla). **179 Bibliothèque nationale de France, Paris** (tl, tr, bc). **180 Beinecke Rare Book and Manuscript Library, Yale University** (b). **181 S. Fischer Verlag GmbH. 182 Griffith Institute, University of Oxford** (tl). **Harvard University Herbaria** (bl). **Scala:** Digital Image Museum Associates / LACMA / Art Resource NY (br). **UCL Special Collections** (bl). **182-183 Conservation Départementale des Musées de l'Aude:** Archives départementales de l'Aude + cote (t). **183 S. Fischer Verlag GmbH** (bl). **184 The New York Public Library:** Henry W. and Albert A. Berg Collection of English and American Literature, **The New York Public Library** / Literary Representative of the Estate of Virginia Woolf / The Society of Authors. **185 Bridgeman:** The Bloomsbury Workshop / Estate of Vanessa Bell / DACS 2020 (tr). **Getty:** Heritage Images (tl). **186 Getty:** H. F. Davis / Topical Press Agency (cl); Ralph Partridge (br). **187 The New York Public Library:** Henry W. and Albert A. Berg Collection of English and American Literature, The New York Public Library / Literary Representative of the Estate of Virginia Woolf / The Society of Authors (l). **Roland Smithies:** luped.com (cr). **188 Scala:** Digital Image Museum Associates / LACMA / Art Resource NY (bl). **Zentrum Paul Klee, Berne, image archive** (tl). **189 Zentrum Paul Klee, Berne, image archive** (t, bl). **190 Zentrum Paul Klee, Berne, image archive** (c, l). **191 akg-images** (br). **Zentrum Paul Klee, Berne, image archive** (t). **192 akg-images:** Erich Lessing (br). **Alamy:** Chronicle (tl). **Scala:** bpk, Bildagentur fuer Kunst, Kultur und

Geschichte, Berlin / Photo: Michael Herling / Aline Gwose (bl). **193 Akademie der Künste** (t). **akg-images** (bc). **194 Getty:** Hulton Archive (cla); Library of Congress (bl); Royal Geographical Society (br). **195 Bridgeman:** British Library Board (cl). **Dorling Kindersley:** American Museum of Natural History / Lynton Gardiner (cra). **196 Bridgeman:** British Library Board (cr). **Getty:** Universal Images Group (bl). **197 Bridgeman:** Christie's Images (tr); **Bridgeman** (cl). **Getty:** Bettmann (br). **198 Bridgeman** (c). **199 Alamy:** Uber Bilder (cla). **Getty:** Mondadori Portfolio (bl). **S. Fischer Verlag GmbH** (br). **200-201 The Bodleian Library, University of Oxford** (t). **200 Bridgeman:** Andrusier (bl). **201 Alamy:** INTERFOTO (cr). **Getty:** Three Lions (bl). **202 Dorling Kindersley:** W. W. Norton & Company (br). **Getty:** Bettmann (bl); Imagno (cla). **Library of Congress, Washington, D.C.** (fbl). **203 Dorling Kindersley:** W. W. Norton & Company. **204 Conservation Départementale des Musées de l'Aude:** Archives départementales de l'Aude + cote (tl). **Getty:** Leemage / Corbis (bl). **204-205 Conservation Départementale des Musées de l'Aude:** Archives départementales de l'Aude + cote (b). **205 Conservation Départementale des Musées de l'Aude:** Archives départementales de l'Aude + cote (tl, tr). **206 Alamy:** Historical Images Archive (bl); **AF Fotografie** (cla). **207 University of Cambridge:** University Library (tr, bl). **208 University of Cambridge:** University Library (b). **209 Alamy:** AF Fotografie (cra, br). **University of Cambridge:** University Library (bl). **210 Alamy:** Heritage Image Partnership Ltd (bl). **Fundació Josep Pla** (br); **Fundació Josep Pla:** col·l Josep Vergés (tl). **211 akg-images:** Album / Oronoz (crb). **Fundació Josep Pla:** col·l Josep Vergés (l). **212 Getty:** Apic (bl); Bettmann (cla). **213 Griffith Institute:** University of Oxford (tr, cr, l). **214 The Anais Nin Trust / The Anais Nin Foundation** (br). **Beinecke Rare Book and Manuscript Library, Yale University** (tl). **Getty:** API / Gamma-Raph (bl). **215 AF Fotografie** (br). **University of California, Los Angeles (UCLA):** Library Special Collections / Anais Nin Papers (l). **216 Alamy:** PictureLux / The Hollywood Archive (cla). **Getty:** Nat Farbman (bl); William Vandivert (br). **217 Alamy:** Granger Historical Picture Archive (br). **UCL Special Collections:** Reproduced by kind permission of Bill Hamilton as the Literary Executor of the Estate of the Late Sonia Brownell / © George Orwell, 1942 / A. M. Heath Literary Agents (l). **218 Alamy:** Penrodas Collection (tl). **Bridgeman** (bl). **Getty:** Sygma / Daniele Darolle (br). **219 Bridgeman:** Photo © Gusman (crb). **Dorling Kindersley:** Éditions Gallimard (l). 220 **Bridgeman:** British Library Board / Literary Representative of the Estate of Katherine Mansfield / The Society of Authors (bl). **221 Bibliothèque nationale de France, Paris** (tc). **222 Fundação Biblioteca Nacional, Brasil:** Permission from Vera Eunice Lima de Jesus (bl). **Mortimer Rare Book Room, Smith College Libraries (Massachusetts):** Faber & Faber Ltd / © Estate of Sylvia Plath (tr). **United States Holocaust Memorial Museum** (tl). **222-223 British Film**

Institute: © Derek Jarman Estate (bc). **223 Library and Archives Canada:** Molly Lamb Bobak and Bruno Bobak fonds (tl). **224 Alamy:** Heritage Image Partnership Ltd (bl). **Getty:** Anne Frank Fonds Basel (cla). **224-225 Getty:** Anne Frank Fonds Basel (bc). **225 United States Holocaust Memorial Museum** (tr). **226 akg-images:** ullstein bild (clb). **Alamy:** Granger Historical Picture Archive (cb). **227 Alamy:** AF Fotografie (tc). **Getty:** Anne Frank Fonds Basel (bc). **228 Getty:** Bettmann (cla). **Scala:** Photo Schalkwijk / Art Resource / © Banco de México Diego Rivera Frida Kahlo Museums Trust, Mexico, D.F. / © DACS 2020 (bl). **229 Scala:** Photo Schalkwijk / Art Resource / © Banco de México Diego Rivera Frida Kahlo Museums Trust, Mexico, D.F. / © DACS 2020 (clb, crb). **230 Scala:** Digital Image Museum Associates / LACMA / Art Resource NY / © Banco de México Diego Rivera Frida Kahlo Museums Trust, Mexico, D.F / © DACS 2020 (br); Photo Schalkwijk / Art Resource / © Banco de México Diego Rivera Frida Kahlo Museums Trust, Mexico, D.F. / © DACS 2020 (clb, tr). **231 Scala:** Photo Schalkwijk / Art Resource / © Banco de México Diego Rivera Frida Kahlo Museums Trust, Mexico, D.F / © DACS 2020 (cl). **232 Duke University Medical Center Archives** (tl). **Getty:** The Asahi Shimbun / Yasuo Tomishige (br); Universal History Archive / Universal Images Group (bl). **233 Alamy:** Vintage Archives (bl). **Duke University:** David M. Rubenstein Rare Book & Manuscript Library (cl, cr). **234 Mortimer Rare Book Room, Smith College Libraries (Massachusetts):** Faber & Faber Ltd / © Estate of Sylvia Plath. **235 Alamy:** Everett Collection Inc (cla). Estate of Robert Hittel: Faber & Faber Ltd / © Estate of Sylvia Plath (bl). Mortimer Rare Book Room, Smith College Libraries (Massachusetts): Black Star Publishing (br). **236 Faber & Faber Ltd:** © Estate of Sylvia Plath (bc). **236-237 Mortimer Rare Book Room, Smith College Libraries (Massachusetts):** Faber & Faber Ltd / © Estate of Sylvia Plath (tc). **237 Getty:** Science & Society Picture Library (br). John M. Olin Library / University of Washington, St. Louis, Missouri (tr). **238 Arquivo Nacional do Brasil** (tl). **Getty:** Gamma-Rapho / Bernhard Moosbrugger (bl). **239 AF Fotografie. Fundação Biblioteca Nacional, Brasil:** Permission from Vera Eunice Lima de Jesus (c). **240 Centro de Estudios Che Guevara:** Permission granted by Centro de Estudios Che Guevara (c). **Rex by Shutterstock:** Permission granted by Centro de Estudios Che Guevara (tl, br). **241 akg-images:** Permission granted by Centro de Estudios Che Guevara (br). **Centro de Estudios Che Guevara** (t). **242 Alamy:** Geraint Lewis (tl). **Penguin Books Ltd** (bc). **243 British Film Institute:** © Derek Jarman/The Keith Collins Will Trust 2020 (t, b). **244 Library and Archives Canada** (bl). **245 Getty:** Santi Visalli (tc). **End paper** iStock / Getty Images Plus / ranasu.

All other images © Dorling Kindersley
For further information see: www.dkimages.com

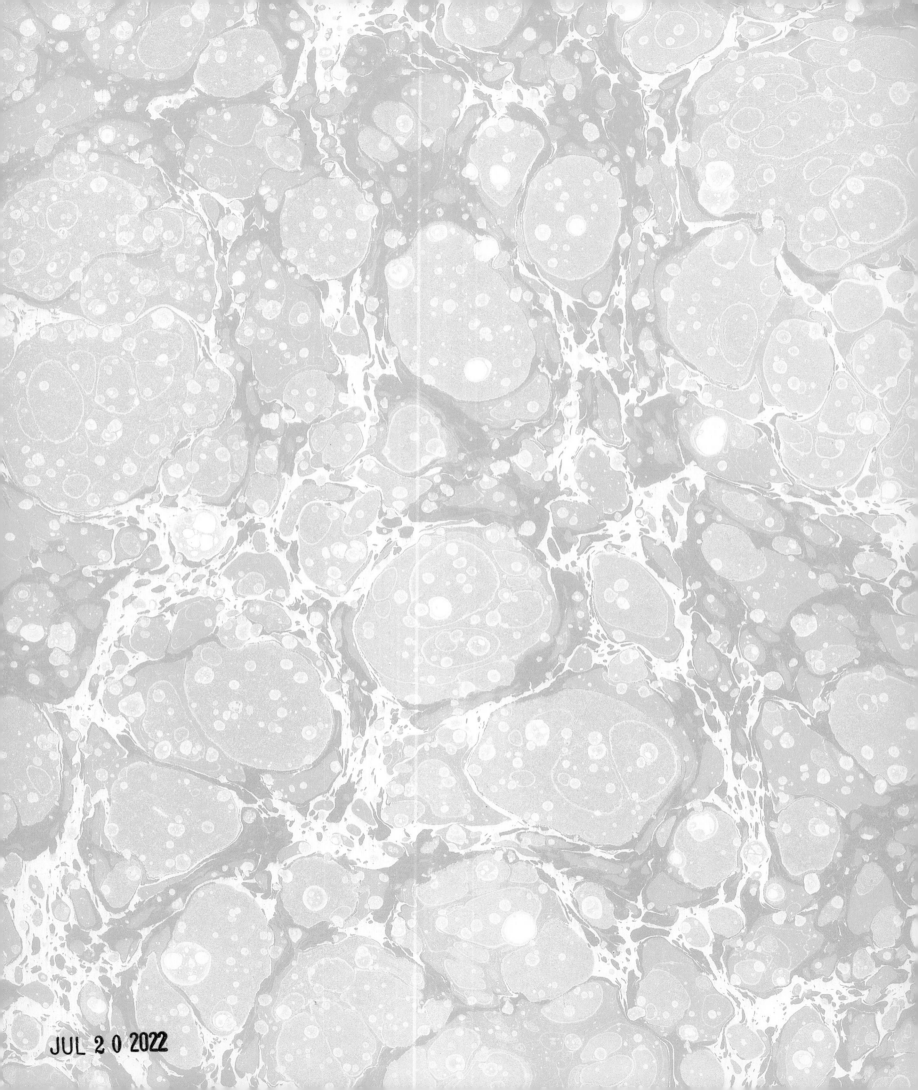